The ‘Uncertain’ Foundations of Post Keynesian Economics

This important new book introduces, analyses and takes forward Post-Keynesianism.

The author attempts to make a positive contribution to the development of Post Keynesian economics by refuting allegations of incoherence, detailing some of the salient implications of a transmutable conception of economic processes and then exploring what this means for how Post Keynesians conceptualise uncertainty. The book argues that the Post Keynesian distinctive view of time, understood as a non-deterministic open systems process, is a core and defining characteristic that is linked to its theoretical discussion of money and the principle of effective demand. It makes a vital contribution to the conceptualisation of uncertainty that is consistent with the methodological presuppositions of Post Keynesian economics. This permits a clarification of the relationship between other schools of thought such as Institutionalists, Sraffians and Austrians.

Covering areas such as the coherence of Post Keynesianism, the future of Post Keynesian economics and Keynesian methodological debates, this book is mandatory reading for all Post Keynesian scholars with a strong interest in economic methodology and the philosophical underpinnings of economics.

Stephen P. Dunn is a senior strategy advisor in the Department of Health for England and the Director of Provider Development, NHS East of England.

Routledge Frontiers of Political Economy

1 **Equilibrium Versus Understanding**
Towards the rehumanization of economics within social theory
Mark Addleson

2 **Evolution, Order and Complexity**
Edited by Elias L. Khalil and Kenneth E. Boulding

3 **Interactions in Political Economy**
Malvern after ten years
Edited by Steven Pressman

4 **The End of Economics**
Michael Perelman

5 **Probability in Economics**
Omar F. Hamouda and Robin Rowley

6 **Capital Controversy, Post Keynesian Economics and the History of Economics**
Essays in honour of Geoff Harcourt, volume one
Edited by Philip Arestis, Gabriel Palma and Malcolm Sawyer

7 **Markets, Unemployment and Economic Policy**
Essays in honour of Geoff Harcourt, volume two
Edited by Philip Arestis, Gabriel Palma and Malcolm Sawyer

8 **Social Economy**
The logic of capitalist development
Clark Everling

9 **New Keynesian Economics/Post Keynesian Alternatives**
Edited by Roy J. Rotheim

10 **The Representative Agent in Macroeconomics**
James E. Hartley

11 **Borderlands of Economics**
Essays in honour of Daniel R. Fusfeld
Edited by Nahid Aslanbeigui and Young Back Choi

12 **Value, Distribution and Capital**
Essays in honour of Pierangelo Garegnani
Edited by Gary Mongiovi and Fabio Petri

13 **The Economics of Science**
Methodology and epistemology as if economics really mattered
James R. Wible

14 **Competitiveness, Localised Learning and Regional Development**
Specialisation and prosperity in small open economies
Peter Maskell, Heikki Eskelinen, Ingjaldur Hannibalsson, Anders Malmberg and Eirik Vatne

15 **Labour Market Theory**
A constructive reassessment
Ben J. Fine

16 **Women and European Employment**
Jill Rubery, Mark Smith, Colette Fagan, Damian Grimshaw

17 **Explorations in Economic Methodology**
From Lakatos to empirical philosophy of science
Roger Backhouse

18 **Subjectivity in Political Economy**
Essays on wanting and choosing
David P. Le vine

19 **The Political Economy of Middle East Peace**
The impact of competing trade agendas
Edited by J.W. Wright, Jnr

20 **The Active Consumer**
Novelty and surprise in consumer choice
Edited by Marina Bianchi

21 **Subjectivism and Economic Analysis**
Essays in memory of Ludwig Lachmann
Edited by Roger Koppl and Gary Mongiovi

22 **Themes in Post-Keynesian Economics**
Essays in honour of Geoff Harcourt, volume three
Edited by Claudio Sardoni and Peter Kriesler

23 **The Dynamics of Technological Knowledge**
Cristiano Antonelli

24 **The Political Economy of Diet, Health and Food Policy**
Ben J. Fine

25 **The End of Finance**
Capital market inflation, financial derivatives and pension fund capitalism
Jan Toporowski

26 **Political Economy and the New Capitalism**
Edited by Jan Toporowski

27 **Growth Theory**
A philosophical perspective
Patricia Northover

28 **The Political Economy of the Small Firm**
Edited by Charlie Dannreuther

29 **Hahn and Economic Methodology**
Edited by Thomas Boylan and Paschal F O'Gorman

30 **Gender, Growth and Trade**
The miracle economies of the postwar years
David Kucera

31 **Normative Political Economy**
Subjective freedom, the market and the state
David Levine

32 **Economist with a Public Purpose**
Essays in honour of John Kenneth Galbraith
Edited by Michael Keaney

33 **Involuntary Unemployment**
The elusive quest for a theory
Michel De Vroey

34 **The Fundamental Institutions of Capitalism**
Ernesto Screpanti

35 **Transcending Transaction**
The search for self-generating markets
Alan Shipman

36 **Power in Business and the State**
An historical analysis of its concentration
Frank Bealey

37 **Editing Economics**
Essays in honour of Mark Perlman
Hank Lim, Ungsuh K. Park & Geoff Harcourt

38 **Money, Macroeconomics and Keynes**
Essays in honour of Victoria Chick, volume one
Philip Arestis, Meghnad Desai and Sheila Dow

39 **Methodology, Microeconomics and Keynes**
Essays in honour of Victoria Chick, volume two
Philip Arestis, Meghnad Desai and Sheila Dow

40 **Market Drive & Governance**
Reexamining the rules for economic and commercial contest
Ralf Boscheck

41 **The Value of Marx**
Political economy for contemporary capitalism
Alfredo Saad-Filho

42 **Issues in Positive Political Economy**
S Mansoob Murshed

43 **The Enigma of Globalisation**
A journey to a new stage of capitalism
Robert Went

44 **The Market**
Equilibrium, stability, mythology
S N Afriat

45 **The Political Economy of Rule Evasion and Policy Reform**
Jim Leitzel

46 **Unpaid Work and the Economy**
Edited by Antonella Picchio

47 **Distributional Justice**
Theory and measurement
Hilde Bojer

48 **Cognitive Developments in Economics**
Edited by Salvatore Rizzello

49 **Social Foundations of Markets, Money and Credit**
Costas Lapavitsas

50 **Rethinking Capitalist Development**
Essays on the economics of Josef Steindl
Edited by Tracy Mott and Nina Shapiro

51 **An Evolutionary Approach to Social Welfare**
Christian Sartorius

52 **Kalecki's Economics Today**
Edited by Zdzislaw L. Sadowski & Adam Szeworski

53 **Fiscal Policy from Reagan to Blair**
The left veers right
Ravi K. Roy & Arthur T. Denzau

54 **The Cognitive Mechanics of Economic Development and Institutional Change**
Bertin Martens

55 **Individualism and the Social Order**
The social element in liberal thought
Charles R. McCann Jnr.

56 **Affirmative Action in the United States and India**
A comparative perspective
Thomas E. Weisskopf

57 **Global Political Economy and the Wealth of Nations**
Performance, institutions, problems and policies
Edited by Phillip Anthony O'Hara

58 **Structural Economics**
Thijs ten Raa

59 **Macroeconomic Theory and Economic Policy**
Essays in honour of Jean-Paul Fitoussi
Edited by K. Vela Velupillai

60 **The Struggle Over Work**
The 'end of work' and employment alternatives in post-industrial societies
Shaun Wilson

61 **The Political Economy of Global Sporting Organisations**
John Forster and Nigel Pope

62 **The Flawed Foundations of General Equilibrium Theory**
Critical essays on economic theory
Frank Ackerman and Alejandro Nadal

63 **Uncertainty in Economic Theory**
Essays in honor of David Schmeidler's 65th birthday
Edited by Itzhak Gilboa

64 **The New Institutional Economics of Corruption**
Edited by Johann Graf Lambsdorff, Markus Taube and Matthias Schramm

65 **The Price Index and its Extension**
A chapter in economic measurement
S.N. Afriat

66 **Reduction, Rationality and Game Theory in Marxian Economics**
Bruce Philp

67 **Culture and Politics in Economic Development**
Volker Bornschier

68 Modern Applications of Austrian Thought
Edited by Jürgen G. Backhaus

69 Ordinary Choices
Individuals, incommensurability, and democracy
Robert Urquhart

70 The Labour Theory of Value
Peter C. Dooley

71 Capitalism
Victor D. Lippit

72 Macroeconomic Foundations of Macroeconomics
Alvaro Cencini

73 Marx for the 21st Century
Edited by Hiroshi Uchida

74 Growth and Development in the Global Political Economy
Social structures of accumulation and modes of regulation
Phillip Anthony O'Hara

75 The New Economy and Macroeconomic Stability
A neo-modern perspective drawing on the complexity approach and Keynesian economics
Teodoro Dario Togati

76 The Future of Social Security Policy
Women, work and a Citizens' Basic Income
Ailsa McKay

77 Clinton and Blair
The political economy of the third way
Flavio Romano

78 Marxian Reproduction Schema
Money and aggregate demand in a capitalist economy
A.B. Trigg

79 The Core Theory in Economics
Problems and solutions
Lester G. Telser

80 Economics, Ethics and the Market
Introduction and applications
Johan J. Graafland

81 Social Costs and Public Action in Modern Capitalism
Essays inspired by Karl William Kapp's Theory of Social Costs
Edited by Wolfram Elsner, Pietro Frigato and Paolo Ramazzotti

82 Globalization and the Myths of Free Trade
History, theory and empirical evidence
Edited by Anwar Shaikh

83 Equilibrium in Economics: Scope and Limits
Edited by Valeria Mosini

84 Globalization
State of the art and perspectives
Edited by Stefan A. Schirm

85 Neoliberalism
National and regional experiments with global ideas
Edited by Ravi K. Roy, Arthur T. Denzau and Thomas D. Willett

86 Post-Keynesian Macroeconomics Economics
Essays in honour of Ingrid Rima
Edited by Mathew Forstater, Gary Mongiovi and Steven Pressman

87 Consumer Capitalism
Anastasios S. Korkotsides

88 Remapping Gender in the New Global Order
Edited by Marjorie Griffin Cohen and Janine Brodie

89 Hayek and Natural Law
Eric Angner

90 Race and Economic Opportunity in the Twenty-First Century
Edited by Marlene Kim

91 Renaissance in Behavioural Economics
Harvey Leibenstein's impact on contemporary economic analysis
Edited by Roger Frantz

92 Human Ecology Economics
A new framework for global sustainability
Edited by Roy E. Allen

93 Imagining Economics Otherwise
Encounters with identity/difference
Nitasha Kaul

94 Reigniting the Labor Movement
Restoring means to ends in a democratic labor movement
Gerald Friedman

95 The Spatial Model of Politics
Norman Schofield

96 The Economics of American Judaism
Carmel Ullman Chiswick

97 Critical Political Economy
Christian Arnsperger

98 Culture and Economic Explanation
Economics in the US and Japan
Donald W. Katzner

99 Feminism, Economics and Utopia
Time travelling through paradigms
Karin Schönpflug

100 Risk in International Finance
Vikash Yadav

101 Economic Policy and Performance in Industrial Democracies
Party governments, central banks and the fiscal-monetary policy mix
Takayuki Sakamoto

102 Advances on Income Inequality and Concentration Measures
Edited by Gianni Betti and Achille Lemmi

103 Economic Representations
Academic and everyday
Edited by David F. Ruccio

104 Mathematical Economics and the Dynamics of Capitalism
Goodwin's legacy continued
Edited by Peter Flaschel and Michael Landesmann

105 The Keynesian Multiplier
Edited by Claude Gnos and Louis-Philippe Rochon

106 Money, Enterprise and Income Distribution
Towards a macroeconomic theory of capitalism
John Smithin

107 Fiscal Decentralization and Local Public Finance in Japan
Nobuki Mochida

108 The 'Uncertain' Foundations of Post-Keynesian Economics
Essays in exploration
Stephen P. Dunn

109 Karl Marx's Grundrisse
Foundations of the critique of political economy 150 years later
Edited by Marcello Musto

110 Economics and the Price Index
S.N. Afriat and Carlo Milana

111 Sublime Economy
On the intersection of art and economics
Edited by Jack Amariglio, Joseph W. Childers and Stephen E. Cullenberg

112 Popper, Hayek and the Open Society
Calvin Hayes

113 The Political Economy of Work
David Spencer

114 Institutional Economics
Bernard Chavance

115 Religion, Economics and Demography
The effects of religion on education, work, and the family
Evelyn L. Lehrer

116 Economics, Rational Choice and Normative Philosophy
Edited by Thomas A. Boylan and Ruvin Gekker

The 'Uncertain' Foundations of Post Keynesian Economics

Essays in exploration

Stephen P. Dunn

LONDON AND NEW YORK

Transferred to digital printing 2010
First published 2008
by Routledge
2 Park Square, Milton Park, Abingdon, Oxon OX14 4RN

Simultaneously published in the USA and Canada
by Routledge
270 Madison Avenue, New York, NY 10016

Routledge is an imprint of the Taylor & Francis Group, an informa business

Typeset in Times New Roman by Keyword Group Ltd

British Library Cataloguing in Publication Data
A Catalogue record for this book is available from the British Library

Library of Congress Cataloging in Publication Data
A catalog record has been requested for this book

ISBN10: 0-415-27864-3 (hbk)
ISBN10: 0-415-58879-0 (pbk)
ISBN10: 0-203-50236-1 (ebk)

ISBN13: 978-0-415-27864-5 (hbk)
ISBN13: 978-0-415-58879-9 (pbk)
ISBN13: 978-0-203-50236-5 (ebk)

For Lucy, Harry, Alexander and Catherine with love …

Summary

This book attempts to make a contribution to the conceptualisation of uncertainty that is consistent with the methodological presuppositions of Post Keynesian economics. It attempts to make a *positive* contribution to the development of Post Keynesian economics by refuting allegations of incoherence, detailing some of the salient implications of a transmutable conception of economic processes and exploring what this means for how Post Keynesians consider uncertainty. It is argued that the Post Keynesian distinctive view of time, understood as a non-deterministic, non-ergodic, open systems process, is a core and defining characteristic that is linked to its theoretical discussion of money and the principle of effective demand. This clarifies the relationship between other schools of thought such as Institutionalists, Sraffians and Austrians and a recognition of the limits to Keynes.

Biographical details

Dr Stephen P. Dunn, a 2003–4 Commonwealth Fund Harkness Fellow in Health Care Policy, is a senior strategy advisor in the Department of Health in England and the Director of Provider Development, NHS East of England, Cambridge. Previously he has been head of policy on the *Our Health, Our Care, Our Say* White Paper. He was a principal architect of the flagship NHS Foundation Trust policy and was primarily responsible for designing and implementing the financial regime under which Foundation Trusts operate. Dunn has been a policy advisor in the Strategy Unit in the Department of Health, providing policy advice directly to the Secretary of State for Health on a range of strategic issues including system management and regulation. He was also a principal contributor to the 20-year review and costing of health trends, led by Derek Wanless. The review underpinned the Chancellor's decision to nearly double UK health care expenditure between 2002/3 and 2007/8. He has served on several national committees on system management and regulation, resource allocation, incentives in the healthcare system and public performance ratings systems, and published numerous articles on Post Keynesian economics and the economics of the firm in leading international journals. In 2003–4 he was a Visiting Scholar at the Graduate School of Business at Stanford University and a Health Policy Researcher at the University of California, San Francisco. In 2000 Dunn received the prestigious K. William Kapp prize from one of Europe's largest economics associations. Dunn is a recognised international authority on J.K. Galbraith.

Contents

Preface

At the opening of the 1930s economic theory still rested on the assumption of a basically orderly and tranquil world. At their end it had come to terms with the restless anarchy and disorder of the world of fact. Partly this transformation was effected by the brutal force of events: by a slump without parallel and the unnerving spectacle of the rise of Nazism in a world cheated of the hope of peace. But partly it was the work of a mere handful of great theoreticians. One thing above all divided the new theory from the old: the discarding of the assumption (which had often been quite tacit) of universal perfect knowledge. What sense did it make to assume perfect knowledge in a world where every morning's newspaper was opened in fear and scanned with foreboding? But the ferment had been working in the world of theory from the beginning of the 1920s. Frank Knight's *Uncertainty and Profit* of 1921 puts entrepreneurship in the forefront of a treatise on value theory which largely sets forth the old orthodoxy. But perhaps its title was a portent. It was in Sweden that expectation was first taken seriously as a prime mover in the economic process. (Marshall, as always, was with the angels, but he did not blow this particular trumpet very loud.) Erik Lindahl and, more incisively and with one brilliant and epoch-marking stroke, Gunner Myrdal, developed the first 'economics of expectation'. Myrdal's essay, published in Sweden in 1931, in German in 1933, and in English only in 1939, would have served very well as the launching-pad for a theory of general output and employment, had the *General Theory* never been written. 1937 was the year of intensive Keynesian critical debate. In February Keynes himself declared in the *Quarterly Journal of Economics* that the *General Theory* was concerned with the consequences of our modes of coping with, or of concealing from our conscious selves, our ignorance of the future. Hugh Townshend, his intellectually most radical interpreter, simultaneously expressed the matter (in the *Economic Journal* for March) in terms, if anything, even more uncompromising. Uncertainty was the new strand placed gleamingly in the skein of economic ideas in the 1930s ... Until the 1930s, economics was the science of coping with basic scarcity. After the 1930s it was the account of how men cope with scarcity and uncertainty. This was by far the greatest of the achievements of the 1930s in economic theory.

(Shackle, 1967, pp. 5–7)[1]

The essays in this book are addressed to those that take history and uncertainty seriously. While much of what is contained within is addressed to my fellow Post Keynesians it will, I hope, be intelligible to all those who recognise that an unbridgeable gulf separates an unalterable past from an unknown, yet to be created, future. Sympathetic heterodox traditions should hopefully find much in here that resonates, given its stress on the essential open nature of historical time that many of them take as their starting point.[2]

The intellectual origins of the ideas advanced in this book stem from my long-held conviction that Post Keynesianism contains the essence of a new revolutionary approach to economics. As the ensuing pages will lay bare, under the intellectual influences of John Maynard Keynes, Joan Robinson, J.K. Galbraith, George Shackle and Paul Davidson I quickly came to the conclusion that the truly revolutionary contribution of Post Keynesian economics is to place uncertainty firmly at the centre of economic analysis. As will become apparent over the pages of this book, it is uncertainty that accords money its distinctive role. It is uncertainty in a credit-money production economy that underscores the importance of the principle of effective demand and the salience of history. It is the recognition of the centrality and importance of uncertainty that is, I believe, one of the most salient and distinctive contributions of Keynes and, more generally, Post Keynesianism. These conclusions, I should add, are ones that have not always been reached, even by those who assume the Post Keynesian mantle. In what follows there is a modest attempt to re-orientate Post Keynesian economics in a direction in which I believe it ultimately points – towards the explicit incorporation and study of uncertainty in economic analysis. While I am no doubt guilty, in what follows, of a perhaps over-zealous attempt to identify the core of Post Keynesian economics with a recognition of the salience of uncertainty, I plead forgiveness for this in light of the resistance of some Post Keynesians and other sympathetic economists to fully integrate the study of uncertainty into their conceptual and historical schemas.

Much of the material has been previously published and the links between the essays may not always be clear. Nevertheless, I believe that a coherent theme pervades the essays in this book: that Post Keynesianism should be defined in terms of its study of uncertainty, which also provides for coherence and should underpin its efforts to engage more constructively with other sympathetic approaches and articulate itself across a more comprehensive range of domains than has previously been attempted. As such it should be seen as a contribution to the development of a coherent and comprehensive Post Keynesian economics.

I should also apologise for what some might regard as a distracting degree of repetition. Although I have reworked the essays in bringing them together I have been encouraged to revise them in a way that would allow them to be read individually. Nevertheless, mindful of the committed reader, I have sought to signpost the duplication and highlight opportunities to advance quickly through the arguments.

Acknowledgements

The final task that remains to be discharged is the pleasant one of acknowledging those who have contributed to the development of the idea contained within this book. The conventional wisdom is that the life of a scholar is a solitary one. I can quite forthrightly dispel this myth. Without the time, patience and encouragement of several notable scholars the argument contained here would have been much impoverished. In this regard by far and away the greatest debt I have is towards my mentor and friend – Malcolm Sawyer. His unceasing help, advice, tolerance and encouragement in developing the ideas contained herein are warmly appreciated. Similarly, Paul Davidson, Geoff Hodgson, Tony Lawson and Fred Lee have all given their time, encouragement and wisdom beyond that which may be reasonably expected. I am proud to be able to class them all as close friends. Their intellectual and professional influence on me has been profound and, I believe, the awarding of the K. William Kapp prize in 2000 is as much a recognition of their larger contribution as of my smaller contribution.[3]

More broadly I should also like to thank Stacey Anderson, Philip Arestis, Roger Backhouse, David Bunting, Vicky Chick, Giuseppe Ciccarone, Peter Clarke, Maggie Coleman, Marco Crocco, Paul Davidson, David Dequech, Keith Derbyshire, Peter Dick, Ayesha Dost, Sheila Dow, Paul Downward, Lucy Dunn, Paul Dunne, Peter Earl, Vikku Entwistle, Erik Evenhouse, Giuseppe Fontana, Donald Franklin, Bill Gerrard, Keith Glaister, Mark Groom, Geoff Harcourt, David Harvie, John Hillard, Geoff Hodgson, Mike Hudson, Jeremy Hurst, Bill Jackson, Stefan Kesting, John King, Matthias Klaes, Thorbjoern Knudsen, Tony Lawson, Fred Lee, Paul Lewis, Hal Luft, Anne Mayhew, Andrew Mearman, Alex Milmow, Gary Mongiovi, Mike Oliver, Luigi Pasinetti, Steve Pressman, Barkley Rosser, Libby Roughhead, Jochen Runde, Warren Samuels, Malcolm Sawyer, Janet Scholes, Nina Shapiro, Mary Shearsmith, Lord Robert Skidelsky, Clive Smee, Courtney Smith, Peter Smith, John Smithin, Ron Stanfield, Engelbert Stockhammer, Jim Sturgeon, Pavlina Tcherneva, Ted Winslow and Nick York for their discussions, critical comments and other assistance in the development of the ideas contained therein. Notwithstanding all this help and encouragement I should point out however, that I am solely responsible for the views expressed herein!

The Commonwealth Fund, a New York City-based private independent foundation, also supported part of the research undertaken here. Especially I must thank Karen Davis and Robin Osborn who continue to be so supportive in all that I do. Nevertheless, the views presented here are those of the author and not necessarily those of the Commonwealth Fund, their directors, officers or staff.

A special thank you should also be extended to Simon Leary. As a friend and mentor he is largely responsible for encouraging me in the final push to publish the ideas contained in this book against the heavy demands of a Senior Policy Advisor in Government. For this I am most grateful.

Perhaps most importantly, I should thank my family. Both of my parents, Harry and Lynn, and my brother, Russell, have provided unyielding love and support over the years and if there were not a more deserving recipient I would have liked to dedicate this book to them. While they have nurtured and cherished me, Lucy, my wife and partner, has endured my relentless fascination with Post Keynesian Economics over several years in the belief that one day things might be different. It is to her that I dedicate this book in some small hope that it will repay the lost time together. Lucy's parents, Roger and Kate, also deserve a warm thank you for their kind and welcoming hospitality which greatly facilitated the writing of several parts of this manuscript.

Finally I would like to acknowledge my co-authors of Chapter two – Malcolm Sawyer and Philip Arestis – as well as the editors and publishers of the following journals and essay collections for their permission to reproduce here revised versions of material that appears in their pages:

'Prolegomena to a Post Keynesian Health Economics', *Review of Social Economy*, 2006, Autumn, Vol. 64, No. 3, pp. 273–192.

'Transforming Post Keynesian Economics: Critical Realism and the Post Keynesian Project' in P. Lewis (ed.), *Transforming Economics: Perspectives on the Critical Realist project*, 2004, London, Routledge.

'Keynes, Uncertainty and the Competitive Process' in W. Samuels (ed.), *Research in the History of Economic Thought and Methodology*, 2004, Elsevier, Vol. 22A, pp. 65–92.

'Keynes and transformation' in S. Mizuhara and J. Runde (eds), *The Philosophy of Keynes' Economics: Probability, Uncertainty and Convention*, 2003, London, Routledge.

'Nonergodicity' in J. King (ed.), *The Elgar Companion to Post Keynesian Economics*, 2003, Cheltenham, Edward Elgar.

'Towards a transmutable economics? A comment on Wynarczyk', *Economic Issues*, 2002, Vol. 7, No. 1, March, pp. 15–20.

'A Post Keynesian approach to the theory of the firm' in S.C. Dow and J. Hillard (eds), *Post Keynesian Econometrics and the Theory of the Firm: Beyond Keynes, Volume One*, 2001, Cheltenham, Edward Elgar.

'Bounded Rationality is not fundamental uncertainty: a Post Keynesian perspective', *Journal of Post Keynesian Economics*, 2001, Vol. 23, No. 4, pp. 567–587.

'Wither Post Keynesianism?', *Journal of Post Keynesian Economics*, 2000, Vol. 22, No. 3, pp. 343–364.

with Arestis, P. and Sawyer, M. 'On the coherence of Post Keynesian economics: a commentary on Walters and Young', *Scottish Journal of Political Economy*, 1999, Vol. 46, pp. 339–345.

with Arestis, P. and Sawyer, M., 'Post Keynesian economics and its critics', *Journal of Post Keynesian Economics*, 1999, Vol. 21, pp. 527–549.

Stephen P. Dunn
Suffolk
2007

NOTES

1 Scarcity in this context refers to the scarcity of entrepreneurial talent: 'I would say that we are not justified in treating the "under-employed" economy as exempt from scarcity. General output in conditions of heavy general unemployment is less than in the "fully" employed economy, and scarcity of goods for consumption must be more, not less, acute. What is scarce, and what causes the extra scarcity (the extra poverty) in the under-employed economy is *enterprise*. The willingness to embark resources in the production of specialised, techno-vulnerable goods is what we used, forty years ago, to call a *limitational factor*. It is a *sine qua non*' (Shackle, 1983–4, p. 245).

2 As both Hodgson (2001a) and Nash (2000) point out, the recognition of the salience of uncertainty for economics has a long history pre-dating Keynes. Not only did Frank Knight (1921) elevate uncertainty to the core of his treatise on entrepreneurship but, as Knight himself noted, the salience of uncertainty for economic analysis was discussed and noted by members of the German historical school and Cliffe Leslie throughout the nineteenth century, and is perhaps traceable back to Kant. Thus Shackle is, strictly speaking, mistaken to suggest that economic theory still rested on the assumption of 'a basically orderly and tranquil world'. As Hodgson (1988, 1993, 1999a, 2001a) has argued strongly, there is no 'tranquil world' in the writings of Friedrich List, Gustav Smoller, Werner Sombart, Cliffe Leslie, Thorstein Veblen, John Commons, Wesley Mitchell or Karl Polanyi. That is to say, paraphrasing Keynes, that the recognition of the salience of uncertainty could only live on furtively, below the surface, in the underworlds of the historical school or the older style Institutionalists. To ignore the historical school or the older style Institutionalists neglects many important precursors to Keynes and, as Hodgson (2001a) surmises, is perhaps the product of a narrow, insular, largely English, very Cambridge mentality that should now be transcended. Such considerations underpin the argument developed below that Post Keynesianism should seek an increased dialogue with other methodologically compatible schools of thought.

3 The prestigious K.William Kapp prize is awarded annually for the best article on a theme in accord with the European Association for Evolutionary Political Economy (EAEPE) theoretical perspectives. The 2000 Kapp prize was awarded for my article 'Wither Post Keynesianism?' which forms the basis of Chapter seven. EAEPE is one of the largest associations for economists in Europe.

1 Introduction

> *The Post Keynesian system dwells in historical time; it is designed to analyze the consequences that may be expected to follow a change taking place at a particular date in particular circumstances.*
>
> Joan Robinson (1977, p. 1327)

For many Post Keynesianism represents a loose association of ignorant and incoherent idiot savants who know what they are against but do not know what they are for. Unable to do the sophisticated maths and formalism employed by the mainstream Post Keynesians carp from the sidelines, engaging in ritualistic debunking, without seeking to make any positive contribution to the economic theory or the study of economic phenomena. The heart of the problem is that many Post Keynesian economists are the slaves of a cadre of defunct economists. And while earlier generations of Post Keynesian economists posed interesting questions, the interesting features of their work have now been internalised and superseded by recent advances in formal theory, reducing contemporary Post Keynesianism to the status of a degenerating research programme (cf. King, 2002).

The degeneracy of Post Keynesianism is exemplified, its critics argue, by its lack of coherence. What exactly is Post Keynesian economics? And does it have any discernable foundations? Does it have a consistent approach or a coherent contribution to make? Such questions pervade this book, which seeks to examine the foundational nexus between Post Keynesian economics and its conceptualisation of uncertainty. The purpose is to identify a coherent foundational core that can characterise a confident Post Keynesian economics. This should further contribute to the coherent evolution of the Post Keynesian research programme that overcomes recent criticism.

But before we proceed with the principal argument of this book – that Post Keynesiansim should be characterised through its approach to uncertainty and the principle of effective demand – we must introduce the reader to Post Keynesian economics and the debates that surround its claim to represent a distinctive school of thought. We begin by considering the genesis of Post Keynesianism, proceeding later in this book to examine in more detail its characteristics and methodological foundations. In doing so we introduce the reader to the three strands that Post Keynesianism has historically been associated with: the Keynesian, Kaleckian and Sraffian approaches.[1]

THE GENESIS OF POST KEYNESIANISM

John King (2002) has recently dated the origins of Post Keynesian economics with the publication of *The General Theory of Employment, Interest and Money* (Keynes, 1936). Nevertheless the term Post Keynesianism is a relatively new one that emerged in the early 1970s (Lee, 2000a,b). It has generally been viewed as synonymous with the vision and ideas of the heterodox Cambridge economists such as, among others, Kaldor and Robinson who formed the vanguard of the Keynesian revolution. These non-orthodox economists, while making several positive contributions in the development of alternative theories, were generally associated with a critique of orthodox economic theorising, with the unintended consequence that the sole unifying characteristic of Post Keynesianism was originally seen by the economics establishment as negative, i.e. in terms of its unified opposition to neoclassical economics (Hahn, 1982, 1989; Solow in Klamer, 1984; Dow, 1990a). However, since its inception Post Keynesian economics has always been conceived, by its practitioners at least, as a positive programme with the aim of developing theoretical structures that incorporate categories which reflect such generalised features of capitalist experience as money, effective demand, cost-plus pricing, stagnation and unemployment (see Lee, 2000a,b). Indeed, Eichner and Kregel (1975, p. 1294, italics added) by the mid-1970s felt confident enough to claim that a diverse set of ideas, broadly subsumed under the label Post Keynesianism, contained the '*potential* for becoming a *comprehensive, positive* alternative to the prevailing neoclassical paradigm'.

Since this modest start Post Keynesian economists have made far-reaching contributions to economic theory, the history of economic thought and the methodology of economics.[2] A number of review articles and volumes have been published on the subject of Post Keynesian economics (see for example Hamouda and Harcourt, 1988; Chick, 1995; Arestis, 1990, 1996a) and the *Journal of Post Keynesian Economics* has been established and continues to thrive (see Davidson and Weintraub, 1978; Galbraith, 1978; Davidson, 1998a). Recently, Post Keynesians have felt confident to proclaim that it represents a distinctive approach whose positive contribution has an impressive heritage reaching back to the classical economists (Arestis, 1990, 1996a; Chick, 1995; Arestis *et al.*, 1999a; see also Holt and Pressman, 2001). A history of Post Keynesian economics has now been written and a handbook compiled (see King, 2002, 2003).

However confusion in the mainstream over what constitutes a Post Keynesian approach to economics still persists (see for example the puzzlement expressed by neoclassical proponents such as Hahn, 1982, 1984, 1989; Solow in Klamer, 1984; Backhouse, 1988).[3] Even a leading Post Keynesian such as Dow (1990a, p. 346) acknowledged that there 'is a sense of confusion, even among post-Keynesians, as to what post-Keynesianism is'. What exactly is Post Keynesianism?

THE BROAD CHURCH

The reason for this confusion stems from the stormy marriage and fusion of three approaches that are viewed by many as competing for the attention of self-styled Post Keynesians. The first strand of Post Keynesianism concerns the economics of John Maynard Keynes. This strand attempts to build on Keynes' revolutionary insight that the operation of a monetary economy existing in historical time is radically different to an exchange economy (Davidson, 1972; Minsky, 1975; Chick, 1983; Moore, 1988; Henry and Wray, 1998). As the future is unknowable in advance of its creation, the future expectations and actions of economic agents will substantially affect the future path of any (monetary) economy (Davidson, 1981, 1993a). In this perspective it is money, and money-denominated contracts, that are pivotal institutions which allow the effects of an uncertain future to be mitigated (Davidson, 1972, 1994).

The second strand of Post Keynesianism is essentially Kaleckian. Drawing on a Marxist heritage, Kalecki (1954, 1968, 1971) and his followers (Sawyer, 1985b, 2000; Sardoni, 1987; Kriesler, 1987; Reynolds, 1987; Arestis, 1990; Lavoie, 1992; cf. Trigg, 1994) present a macroeconomic analysis of aggregate demand (and its composition) in terms of social classes and oligopolistic competition. As with Keynes (see Sawyer, 1982, 1985b for a comparison), investment demand is viewed as driving the level of economic activity (of which the endogeneity of money is a central tenet).

The third strand historically identified with Post Keynesianism is that of Sraffa and his followers (Hamouda and Harcourt, 1988; Arestis, 1990). The Sraffian (or neo-Ricardian) school is the most contentious approach to be incorporated under the Post Keynesian umbrella.[4] The Sraffian approach reasserts the classical emphasis on the production and use of surplus in the reproduction of the economic system. The salience of the Sraffian input–output framework is that it emphasises the production and distribution of a surplus in the context of interdependency. Moreover, it provides an important internal critique of neo-classical economics and of itself provides the opportunity to create a viable coherent alternative to neo-classical economics based on closed-system reasoning (we shall elaborate upon this in more detail below). This project has chosen as its focus the long-run analysis of income and employment aiming to link 'Keynes' theory of effective demand, set in the short run and in a monetary economy, to that of the classical authors, who were concerned with income distribution and accumulation in the long period' (Lavoie, 1992, p. 2; see also Garegnani, 1978, 1979). The Sraffian school has generally been linked to the other Post Keynesian strands by its aim to place Keynes' principle of effective demand in a long run setting (Kregel, 1973).[5]

A SHARED POINT OF DEPARTURE

There is an agreed research agenda that is shared by both the Keynesian and Kaleckian strands that reflects Davidson's (1982, pp. 9–18) characterisation of the Post Keynesian approach as underpinned by six key propositions:

1 The economy is a historical process.
2 In a world where uncertainty is undeniable, expectations have an unavoidable and significant effect on economic outcomes.
3 Economic and political institutions play a significant role in shaping economic events.
4 The distribution of income and power is relevant to the study of economic processes.
5 Real capital is non-malleable and embodies historical decisions and is conceptually distinct from financial capital.
6 Income effects are more dominant than substitution effects in creating and resolving economic problems.

This represents a unifying agenda which is acknowledged by those aligned with the Kaleckian wing (Reynolds, 1987; Sawyer, 1988a, 1989, 1991, 1995; Arestis, 1992, 1996a; Arestis and Sawyer, 1993; Downward, 1999, 2000). Moreover, the acceptance of this set of propositions also explains, to a degree, the different policy positions and analytical conclusions sometimes expressed by Post Keynesians. A focus on history, uncertainty and the socio-political and institutional context is likely to give rise to a diverse set of policy prescriptions, legal and socio-political arrangements, systems of industrial relations, fiscal systems, cultures, labour market institutions and so on across different countries over different epochs in time. Such an approach informs the discussion of the different, traditionally viewed as competing, Post Keynesian approaches to the pricing process discussed in chapter nine. An approach that deals with historical processes that are constantly in flux is unlikely to propose consistent and uniform policy prescriptions and/or reach similar theoretical conclusions. The heterogeneity and pluralism of Post Keynesian *analysis* is consistent with its commitment to realism and history (Dow, 1996a).

SRAFFIANS: THE UNCERTAIN ALLIANCE

Nevertheless, although there are common elements and characteristics across the Keynesian and Kaleckian strands it is their distinct differences that continue to fuel accusations of incoherence. Indeed the incoherence of Post Keynesian economics is one of the main criticisms levelled against it. This assertion is rejected throughout this book. A central proposition, maintained throughout, is that a coherent methodological vision that characterises Post Keynesianism can be discerned and can be expressed as a commitment to open systems theorising, i.e. taking historical processes and uncertainty seriously, which underpins the principle of effective demand, the Post Keynesians' recognition of the salience of a monetary economy and their analysis of the evolving industrial structure. It is this historical and evolutionary approach that provides for the uniting of Post Keynesians around a shared agenda.

Consistent with the shared vision noted in the previous section, all Post Keynesians concern themselves with the specific historical institutions, such as money, money-denominated contracts, national systems accounting, the institutions of the financial and labour markets, that inhabit historical transmutable economies.[6] The position adopted and developed here more explicitly is that history and uncertainty should be viewed as being at the heart of Post Keynesianism – which spells the ejection of the Sraffian order from the Post Keynesian church. The argument sustained here is that if, in delineating the Post Keynesian programme, some reference needs to be made to the Sraffians 'then the project seeking coherence may have to be abandoned' (Pratten, 1996a, p. 35). Rather than abandon this project, the argument here is that the programme should be further sustained and that Sraffians should no longer be automatically viewed as part of the core of the Post Keynesian programme.[7] Accordingly any attempt to extend the comprehensiveness of Post Keynesianism into previously neglected domains must be consistent with this methodological framework.

It is the desire to align their approach within pre-Keynes economics that is a principal reason why the Sraffian approach, as conventionally expressed, is incompatible with a Post Keynesian approach. Keynes drew a sharp distinction between classical economics, which was defined to include Ricardo, James Mill, Marx and J.S. Mill, and, confusingly for many, neo-classical economists such as Marshall, Edgeworth and Pigou. This distinction is based primarily on the rejection of an approach, which Keynes labelled classical economics, which eschewed a concern for uncertainty, or more specifically, as we shall argue, nonergodic open processes (cf. the opening Shackle quote in the preface). Keynes' system contained a revolutionary new analytical vision of the nature of capitalist economies (Shackle, 1972).[8] However, this did not mean that classical theory had the wrong focus, rather that the diagnosis of the maladies of capitalism would be fundamentally different. This is why Keynes called his theory *General* and emphasised the importance of money and its link to the principle of effective demand (cf. Hodgson, 2001a).

AN OUTLINE OF THE ARGUMENT

The objective of this book is to explore the potential contribution that Post Keynesian economics can make to the study of economic processes. In doing so we reaffirm Eichner and Kregel's (1975) proposition that Post Keynesian economics contains the potential to be a positive, coherent and comprehensive approach to the study of economic phenomena. The argument developed is that while Post Keynesianism, incorporating both the Keynesian and Kaleckian wings, can be considered coherent, it is still far from comprehensive and much foundational work is still to be done. In what follows we begin by making a *positive* contribution to the development of Post Keynesian economics by refuting allegations of incoherence and detailing some of the implications of this ontological vision more broadly.

The book is aimed at elaborating more fully the 'uncertain foundations' of Post Keynesian economics. In doing so we argue that the Post Keynesian distinctive view of time, understood as a non-deterministic, nonergodic, open systems process, is a core and defining characteristic which is indissolubly linked to its theoretical discussion of the principle of effective demand and recognition of the salience of the institution of money. What is more, we argue that the import of uncertainty can be used to underpin a wider set of dialogues with other traditions and approaches that will contribute to the evolution of the Post Keynesian research agenda.

Part I examines the nature of Post Keynesianism and considers whether it can be viewed as a coherent approach. Chapter 2 introduces the reader to the main allegations of incoherence levelled at Post Keynesian economics. This chapter focuses on the conventional criticisms of Post Keynesian economics where it is argued that Post Keynesian economics has not been established as an alternative to the neoclassical orthodoxy and that it lacks an agreed set of foundations and a distinctive methodology. The chapter considers eight themes: the lack of a central organizing theme and coherence in Post Keynesian economics; methodological issues; expectations, uncertainty, and time; market structure and the nature of prices; the analysis of money; economic policy; the relationship between the work of Michal Kalecki, Sraffa and the work of John Maynard Keynes; and Post Keynesian economics and neo-Ricardianism. This Chapter 2 also surveys expressed positions to determine and assess positivistically the nature of Post Keynesianism, i.e. to assess the coherence of Post Keynesian economics on its own terms, in other words on account of what Post Keynesians say Post Keynesianism is.

From this perspective we argue that coherence of Post Keynesian economics in terms of an overarching theme can be found in its emphasis on the role of effective demand in a monetary production economy, and that this serves to distinguish Post Keynesian economics from most other schools of thought. From this comes the broad policy agenda of Post Keynesian economics – policies and institutional arrangements supportive of high levels of aggregate demand in pursuit of the objective of full employment. Post Keynesians are institution builders; it is institutions that can provide stability, and, if designed correctly, stability near full employment.

Having laid the foundations for a more in-depth exploration of Post Keynesianism, we then proceed in Chapter 3 to focus specifically on the methodological discussion of self styled-Post Keynesians and argue that Post Keynesianism is also coherent at this level. We argue that a coherent methodological vision that characterises Post Keynesianism can be discerned and can be cogently summarised as representing a commitment to open-systems theorising.

What is more, we argue that this underpins Post Keynesians' their articulation of the principle of effective demand and radical discussion of time and uncertainty. Importantly, we argue that Sheila Dow's (1996a) and Tony Lawson's (1997a, 2003) methodological distinctions between open and closed systems are compatible, and underpin Paul Davidson's (1996) distinctive view of time which informs the distinction between immutable (ergodic) and transmutable (nonergodic) processes. That is to say that they should be thought of as complementary, and not competing, approaches. It is in this sense that it is argued that Post Keynesian economics tends towards coherence, with the role of aggregate demand in the context of a monetary production economy being a central feature (Arestis, 1996a).

Having argued that Post Keynesianism is coherent at the methodological level, Chapter 4 considers in more detail the relationship and possible gains from trade to be had with Critical Realism, associated with Tony Lawson (1997a, 2003), and the possible consequences for the Post Keynesian conceptualisation of uncertainty. We note that Critical Realism should be viewed as part of a more general philosophical project aimed at understanding the most general statements that can be made about science and social theory (Lawson, 2006a). In contrast, Post Keynesianism should be understood as *a* Critical Realist elaboration of the study of macroeconomics under uncertainty, of how society copes with scarcity and uncertainty. Although Post Keynesian economics is still relatively youthful and although many Post Keynesians have given penetrating accounts of the inconsistencies, fallacies and limitations generated by the mainstream project, they have not always been clear about the foundational source of these ills. This is where the under-labouring role of Critical Realism can help inform and clarify the development of Post Keynesian economics (cf. Lawson, 2004a). Critical Realism offers the prospect of strengthening its methodological foundation and evolving its conceptualisation of uncertainty. Similarly Post Keynesian economics offers a macroeconomic analysis that is consistent with the open systems approach of Critical Realism.

Part II considers the nature of uncertainty and its nexus to such an open systems approach. In Chapter 5 we explore Keynes' conception of uncertainty, which remains a major influence on Post Keynesian thinking. What is surprising is that although much has been written on Keynes' conceptualisation of uncertainty and how it evolved between the *Treatise on Probability* and the *General Theory*, little attention has been devoted to examining the ontological presuppositions that underlie Keynes' discussion of uncertainty. As this chapter makes clear, although Keynes' approach to uncertainty appears suggestive and consistent with an open systems approach he nevertheless does not seek to identify the generative mechanisms and interactions that give rise to uncertainty and sometimes seems to treat uncertainty as an a-historical *deus ex machina*. Such an approach, however, has clear limits and leaves the origins and emergence of uncertainty unaddressed. Shackle and Davidson, however, have understood this need and sought to highlight how the origins of uncertainty are to be found in the creative emergent processes associated with competition and capital accumulation.

In Chapter 6, therefore, we follow on from this discussion and consider the technical view of uncertainty expounded by Davidson and Shackle. We consider their view of 'fundamental' uncertainty, which has been influential in the Post Keynesian literature, and demonstrate how it can be marshalled to improve conceptual clarity. We argue, for example, that the salience of the concept of 'fundamental' uncertainty has often been ignored and/or conflated with bounded rationality by many economists including even some Post Keynesian economists.[9] Davidson's distinction between closed, immutable, ergodic processes and open, transmutable, nonergodic processes, however, provides for a technical definition of 'fundamental' uncertainty and historical time and facilitates the identification of the implicit nexus between the bounded rationality concept and the assumption of immutability. We conclude by noting that while bounded rationality is a key behavioural assumption that economists may wish to utilise, its analytic distinctiveness from the Post Keynesian view of creativity and time, which is embedded in its methodological approach, should be recognised.

Part III considers the future of Post Keynesian economics as a viable and vibrant research programme. Chapter 7 considers the future viability of Post Keynesianism in the context of the numerous commentators who have been keen to herald its demise. If the long-term vitality of the research programme is in question, then any attempt to develop and extend the comprehensiveness of the project might appear misguided and unwarranted. Building on the argument advanced in Part I, we argue that the source of this confusion relates primarily to its distinctive methodological underpinnings. Nevertheless, we acknowledge that Post Keynesianism must bear some of the responsibility for this state of affairs, which is rooted in the uncomfortable historical alliance with the Sraffians – which must now be abandoned. Although Post Keynesianism is not dying, it is at a crossroads. Serious choices must be made as to its future direction. Chapter 7 concludes by outlining some of the opportunities that present themselves to Post Keynesianism which will aid its continued development and prevent its demise. We argue that the distinctive view of uncertainty advanced by Post Keynesians is a potent heuristic and could underpin future dialogues with other approaches that appear to share a similar methodological approach. This allows us to identify a range of potential 'gains from trade' with these other traditions that could underpin the development of a vibrant Post Keynesian economics. Subsequent chapters then seek to elaborate further some of the claims made therein.

Chapter 8, for example, explores the relationship of Post Keynesianism and the Austrian school of thought. This chapter considers the claim that both Austrian and Post Keynesian economics share a similar axiomatic and, by implication, methodological base. It is argued that while both traditions appear to emphasise the nominal importance of money, creativity and uncertainty, if the Austrians (and others for that matter) are indeed committed to taking uncertainty seriously then they must abandon their *a priori* faith in the omnipotence of the market. Recognising this fact – which requires an analytical understanding of the distinction between closed, immutable, ergodic processes and open, transmutable, nonergodic processes – would encourage greater cross-fertilisation across the Post Keynesian and Austrian traditions.

In Chapter 9 we attempt to delineate a core of Post Keynesian pricing theory that is consistent with the open system approach outlined in the first part of the book. We argue that an explicit recognition of the open system nature of Post Keynesian economics would strengthen the proposition advanced that the doctrines of administered prices, normal cost prices and mark-up prices associated with the seminal contributions of Gardiner Means, Philip Andrews and Michal Kalecki respectively can be considered as constituting the core of Post Keynesian price theory. Similarly, this discussion develops and reinforces the argument made throughout that Institutionalists and the role of grounded theory have much to contribute to Post Keynesian microeconomics (Lee, 1998, 2002). Chapter 9 concludes by suggesting that Post Keynesian microeconomists need to begin to move beyond theories of pricing and consider the implications of its distinctive approach for the theory of the firm.

In Chapter 10 we consider the distinction between institutions such as markets, firms, and money and their connection to an environment that is uncertain and plagued by informational problems.[10] We argue that Post Keynesianism must move beyond their discipline's traditional confines and constructively engage the more recent and innovative approaches which have recently attempted to distinguish between a variety of microeconomic institutions such as firms and markets and their different coordinating roles. The failure of Post Keynesians to engage positively with alternative traditions, however, represents a missed opportunity. As outlined in Chapter 9, Post Keynesians articulate a multifaceted and institutionally rich view of pricing and advance a precise technical definition of uncertainty which could underpin the gains from trade to be had from an increased dialogue with those working at the more heterodox end of the theory of the firm.

In Chapter 11 we consider what a Post Keynesian approach to health economics might look like. We highlight the relevance of Post Keynesian themes such as the salience of history, uncertainty, distributional issues, and the importance of political and economic institutions for healthcare economics and health policy. A Post Keynesian approach has the potential to generate numerous insights that can inform the way in which economists and non-economists think about health and health care, informing and contributing to diverse areas such as methodology, microeconomics, industrial organisation and macroeconomics. Post Keynesian economics offers an interesting perspective on health economics and there is the opportunity for encouraging a dynamic, more plural and relevant health economics.

NOTES

1 The emphasis here is on the traditional conception of Post Keynesianism. Historically, the core of Post Keynesianism has been associated with Keynes, Kalecki and Sraffa. Post Keynesianism, however, has evolved beyond the narrow vision of its formative years, recognising the complementary contributions and influences of many Institutionalists and radicals. However, these linkages have been pursued in an *ad hoc* manner and have not been systematised in a coherent and satisfactory fashion. A key theme in what follows is that the contributions of Institutionalists can be integrated into

Post Keynesianism by virtue of their open systems historical approach, i.e. that the core of Post Keynesianism must be extended beyond that of Keynes and Kalecki while excluding Sraffa.

2 King (1996) has collated and documented the wide range of contributions that can be gathered under the heading of Post Keynesian economics and systematised it into a comprehensive annotated bibliography. King (2002) has also developed a comprehensive history. For a variety of reactions to this history see the *Journal of Post Keynesian Economics*, Spring 2005 issue. It should be noted here that this work can be viewed at one level as a refutation of many of the core contentions of King's (2002) thesis.

3 See for example the not untypical comments by Lucas, Solow and Blinder among others (see Klamer, 1984, for further details of the orthodox reaction to Post Keynesianism which ranges from disdain to ignorance):

'I am very unsympathetic to the school that calls itself post-Keynesian. First of all, I have never been able to understand it as a school of thought. I don't see an intellectual connection between Hyman Minsky, on the one hand, ... and someone like Alfred Eichner, on the other, except that they are all against the same thing, namely the mainstream, whatever that is. The other reason why I am not sympathetic is that I have never been able to piece together (I must confess that I have never tried that hard) a positive doctrine. It seems to be mostly a community which knows what is against but doesn't offer anything that could be described as a positive theory.' (Solow, quoted in Klamer, 1984, p. 137)

'Paul Davidson and Sidney Weintraub ... actually may have something valuable, but I'm not very well read on this ... their concept of uncertainty has never been formalised and mathematized, and there also isn't empirical evidence to go with it that I'm aware of.' (Blinder, quoted in Klamer, 1984, p. 161)

'Post Keynesian economists, well, I don't know whether to take them seriously [laughter]' (Lucas, quoted in Klamer, 1984, p. 35).

What is frequently, and perhaps conveniently, forgotten is that Leonard Rapping, who collaborated with Lucas (Lucas and Rapping, 1969, 1970), subsequently became a Post Keynesian economist (see the discussion with Rapping in Klamer, 1984).

4 As Sraffa 'was Ricardian without accepting Say's Law' (Hamouda and Harcourt, 1988, p. 216) we follow Sawyer (1989, p. 229) in adopting the term Sraffian 'since this term indicates the immediate origins of the approach in the work of Sraffa and avoids considerations of the relationship between this approach and the work of Ricardo'.

5 As we shall argue below, Sraffians who have decided to go down this closed system, long-period equilibrium road must be excluded from the core Post Keynesianism. However, it should be noted that the input–output approach need not be confined to a long-period (closed-system) framework (cf. Lee, 1998, Chapters 11 and 12). Indeed, there is an increasing recognition that there appears a choice as to whether Sraffians should and need adopt a short or a long-period approach (Dow, 1999). While it is clearly legitimate for Sraffians to adopt a long-period framework, those that do so must recognise that one of the unfortunate consequences of such a choice is that they must be excluded from the core of Post Keynesianism. It is becoming increasingly clear that, while many Sraffians have made contributions to the development of Post Keynesian economics which should not be ignored, those who continue to adopt the closed-system long period setting are unlikely to make any future contributions to the development of Post Keynesian economics.

6 See also the Institutionalist criticisms of the Sraffian long-period method (Clark, 1992).

7 This is far from settled. Over the course of writing this book I have been told by several close and eminent colleagues (a) not to abandon the Sraffians, (b) they have already been abandoned and the arguments I am making have already been assimilated, and (c) although there is much diversity in the various Post-Keynesian groups, they are reconcilable, provided Sraffian ideas are dropped. I take such conflicting assertions and views to mean that such matters have not been satisfactorily resolved and it is for such reasons that I consider such issues at length.

8 It should be emphasised that this vision was far from coherent and/or comprehensive. It is precisely for this reason that many interpretations of Keynes proliferate. Remnants of marginalism that are incommensurable with the study of uncertain, open systems pervade the *General Theory* (cf. Shackle, 1983–4). As Joan Robinson wryly remarked, they sometimes had trouble pointing out to Maynard what the fundamental theoretical revolution was! The purpose of Post Keynesian economics is to build on this vision.

9 For example, the Kaleckian Toporowski (1996, p. 171) has suggested that 'For Keynes, with whom Kalecki's work on capitalism is usually associated, the problem with capitalism is that the capitalists' rationality is limited by uncertainty and this makes their decisions subject to volatile shifts in their expectations (Keynes, 1936, Chapter 12; Keynes, 1937). This theory of the "bounded rationality" of capitalists is most developed in the work of George Shackle who, among Post Keynesian economists was the least influenced by Kalecki ... while those Post Keynesian economists who have been most influenced by Kalecki (e.g. Joan Robinson, G.C. Harcourt, Jan Kregel) have tended to be the least committed to "bounded rationality", many have tried to combine Keynes' insights into uncertainty with Kaleckian analysis.' This passage is revealing in three respects. Firstly, as we shall argue in Chapter 6 bounded rationality is quite distinct from the stress on fundamental uncertainty of Shackle and Davidson and should not be conflated. However, as we shall also document, Toporowski is not alone in committing this conflation. Secondly, we would strongly argue that Joan Robinson (1974, 1977, 1980, 1985) and Jan Kregel (1976, 1977, 1980, 1983), or even Geoff Harcourt (1981, 1992a; Harcourt and Kenyon, 1976), were anxious to incorporate the study of uncertainty into their analysis. Thirdly, and more broadly, as these citations attest, Kaleckians have been keen to incorporate uncertainty (wrongly referred to by Toporowski as bounded rationality) into their analytical schemas and this underscores the contention advanced in this book that Post Keynesian economics can be delineated by its distinct methodological vision.

10 As Kregel (1998a, p. 45) points out, 'the arguments of Keynes, Robinson, Richardson, and Coase all lead to the same result ... The real problem concerns the impact of imperfect information and the ways individuals respond to uncertainty over the future implication of currently available information, including prices'.

Part I

The uncertain foundations of Post Keynesian economics

2 The incoherence of Post Keynesian economics?

A characteristic of some post-Keynesian writers – no names no pack drill – is that their positive contributions are superior to their presentation and knowledge of the work of the people they are attacking and which they are attempting to supersede.

Geoff Harcourt (1985, p. 125)

INTRODUCTION

Since its inception, Post Keynesian economics has been constantly criticised by many for its incoherence (see Backhouse, 1988; Caldwell, 1989; Hahn, 1982, 1989; Solow in Klamer, 1984; Walters and Young, 1997). It is argued that the claim first made by Eichner and Kregel (1975) – that Post Keynesian economics can be established as a viable alternative to the neo-classical orthodoxy – has not been established. Contrary to the repeated claims of its proponents, Post Keynesian economics lacks an agreed set of common foundations. Constructive criticism is always welcomed for any body of thought, particularly an active one, evolving in the light of changing economic issues, circumstances and experience.

The purpose of this chapter is to dismiss many of conventional claims of incoherence made by critics of the Post Keynesian programme. We take as our focus the extensive set of criticisms advanced by Walters and Young (1997) and suggest that many of their claims are in fact incoherent, involving a considerable misunderstanding and misinterpretation of Post Keynesian economics. The argument developed in this chapter rejects Walters and Young's analysis, suggesting that they ignore a number of basic, important and critical contributions. In contrast, we argue here that Post Keynesian economics tends towards coherence, with the role of aggregate demand in the context of a monetary production economy being a central feature (Arestis, 1996a). This provides a foundation for the more detailed methodological discussion in later chapters.

The chapter proceeds by looking into eight themes which have historically been used to attack Post Keynesian economics. These are: the lack of a central organizing theme and coherence in Post Keynesian economics; methodological issues; expectations, uncertainty and time; market structure and the nature of prices; the Post Keynesian analysis of money; the Post Keynesian approach to economic policy; on the relationship between the work of Kalecki and the work of Keynes; and Post Keynesian economics and neo-Ricardianism.

THE LACK OF A CENTRAL ORGANISING THEME?

Walters and Young (1997, p. 334) charge that 'the frequently expressed idea that Post Keynesians are united by their opposition to neo-classical theory is insufficient to provide a view of what Post Keynesianism is or how it relates to other non-orthodox approaches'. This is setting up a straw-person in the sense that no-one would claim that opposition to X can establish what Z is. It has sometimes been remarked 'that the unifying feature of Post Keynesians is the dislike of neo-classical economics' (Sawyer, 1988a, p. 1). Since the mid-1990s, however, it has been acknowledged that 'Post Keynesian economics has passed through the important initial change of mounting a concerted critique of mainstream economics' (Arestis, 1996a, p. 111). Whilst one would agree with Walters and Young (1997, p. 334) that 'reciting opposition to orthodoxy does nothing to establish the nature or distinctiveness of Post Keynesianism as a separate school of thought', making such a statement in the context of a discussion of the coherence of Post Keynesianism seeks to imply that Post Keynesians recite opposition to neo-classical economics on a regular basis. A quick glance in, say, the *Journal of Post Keynesian Economics* or attendance at Post Keynesian conferences would soon reveal that little time is spent in reciting opposition to the orthodoxy.

In contrast to Walters and Young, we would argue that there are central themes in Post Keynesian economics that include a concern for history, uncertainty, distributional issues and the importance of political and economic institutions in determining the level of activity in an economy (see Davidson, 1982; Arestis, 1996a). But the major central theme is the key contribution of Keynes and Kalecki, namely that in a monetary production economy the level of economic activity is set by the level of effective demand, and that there is little reason to think that the level of effective demand will be consistent with full employment. The expansion of effective demand requires an extension of credit, and that generally involves the creation of money (Kregel, 1998b). Money is viewed as endogenously created within the private sector 'to meet the needs of trade'. Investment expenditure is seen to play a crucial role in the determination of the level of effective demand. It is precisely this key role for effective demand in a monetary production economy in the determination of the level of economic activity which is denied by neo-classical economics, monetarism in its various forms, new classical macroeconomics, Austrian economics and new Keynesianism (see Davidson, 1982–3, 1989c, 1999a). Moreover, the unemployment observed in advanced industrialised economies is taken as *prima facie* evidence for this point. Whilst Walters and Young mention these contributions later in the context of a discussion on fundamental uncertainty (1997, p. 343), they appear to forget about it in the rest of the paper.

Walters and Young (1997, p. 333) claim that 'there is no specific "unit of analysis" in Post Keynesian economics. Of course Post Keynesian economics rejects methodological individualism (see Chick, 1995; cf. Hodgson, 1986). A Post Keynesian response to the view that there has to be micro-economic foundations of macro-economics is that there has also to be macro-economic foundations of micro-economics. The work of Kalecki and Keynes makes it clear that Post Keynesian economics always had micro-economic foundations (albeit somewhat different ones). Post Keynesian analysis, along with some others, seeks to link individual, organisational and systemic behaviour. Individuals make their own decisions on what to buy, how much labour to supply etc., but do so in the context of sales efforts, the availability of credit, the level of aggregate demand, social norms etc., which implies 'no person is an island' rather than 'there is no such thing as society'.

The Post Keynesian perspective on these issues has been well summarised by Chick (1995). She argues that the relationship between individual preferences and decisions and the aggregate is complex. She goes on to explain that:

> (a) PKE [Post Keynesian economics] respects the need for well-developed theories of individual action. Nevertheless, two of the most important conclusions of Keynes, the paradox of thrift and the ineffectiveness of wage cuts to restore full employment, result from the operation of the fallacy of composition. The whole is sometimes less, sometimes more, than the sum of the parts. Individual actions have unintended macroeconomic consequences.
> (b) It follows that methodological individualism, which assumes that knowledge of atomistic behaviour is sufficient to construct macroeconomic outcomes, is rejected.
> (c) PKs reject atomism in favour of a conception of individual actions as socially conditioned or contingent. Thus
> (i) conventions play an important role;
> (ii) aggregation into groups with similar interests, constraints or conventions is both possible and for some purposes efficient.
> (d) Having accepted the validity of aggregation by interest groups, it is possible to analyze conflict between groups and its resolution. PKs consider this an important task (Chick, 1995, p. 26).

Walters and Young (1997, p. 334) argue that the approach which involves individual and social interactions at various levels 'does not, in itself, provide any distinctive theory of economic agency'. However, there is such a theory developed by Post Keynesians which can be described as the transformational conception of human agency. In this conception, 'Individuals *reproduce or transform* social structure which, at the moment of any individual act only can be treated as given ... human action in total is always reproductive/ transformational' (Lawson, 1994a, p. 520, italics added). Further, 'crucial economic decision-making, by definition, assures that the economic variables which impinge upon the decision-maker's environment are not ahistorical. Crucial decisions create a new future' (Davidson, 1989b, p. 153). There is an organicist (rather than an atomist) conception of that agency. For example, 'an organic view of the economic process takes a more complex view of human nature and of individual behaviour, seeing individuals as social beings' (Dow, 1991, p. 185).

Walters and Young (1997) claim that 'the desire for coherence within Post Keynesianism may ... be regarded as part of the attempt to mirror mainstream theory in order to rival its comprehensiveness' (p. 331). First, note that Post Keynesians would doubt the comprehensiveness in the applicability of the neo-classical theory (if that is identified with the mainstream). Walters and Young themselves note that Davidson (1991c), in particular, appears 'to regard neo-classical theory as a special case, assuming the neutrality of money and the validity of Say's law, of the more general Post Keynesian position' (p. 338). Keynes (1936) was entitled *The General Theory*, which can be read to signify that Keynes viewed his theory as a general one of which the full employment equilibrium was a special case. Second, there is a comprehensiveness of neo-classical economics in that it can be claimed to cover all areas of an economy and for all times and places. This is achieved by viewing all types of market as operating in essentially the same way, whereas Post Keynesian analysis would view financial, labour and product markets as operating in rather different ways. Third, we would not claim that Post Keynesian economics is comprehensive in its coverage: for example, Post Keynesianism has had little to say about production and employment relations, or technological change. There is a need to complement Post Keynesian analysis with a variety of others, and there are areas which either remain underdeveloped or need to be developed (see Chapter 7 for further details. Cf. Arestis, 1996a, p. 130).

METHODOLOGICAL ISSUES

All Post Keynesians recognise that it is necessary to theorize about what the world is like, which means to analyse the many factors that affect outcomes, rather than to make an abstract model that assumes away many specifics (Davidson, 1972, 1994; Dow, 1996a; Lawson, 1997a, 2003). Post Keynesians recognise that reflecting on how economics differs from other sciences – based on real world interactions, rather than abstract models – is essential to fashioning a successful social science (Dow, 1996a). Post Keynesians recognise the fact that the successes associated with the physical sciences are related to the fact that 'the natural sciences are not subject to underlying institutional or behavioural change' (Galbraith, 1970, p. 9). That is to say, in social science it difficult (i) to isolate the objects of analysis, and to (i) guarantee their constancy, so as to permit a deterministic or closed account of social phenomena.

Davidson's (1996) distinction between immutable and transmutable economic processes underscores this view of social processes. Immutability encompasses the ergodic and ordering axioms and embodies 'the presumption of a programmed stable, conservative system where the past, present and future reality are predetermined whether the system is stochastic or not' (Davidson, 1996, pp. 480–1).

Table 1 Conditions for closed theoretical systems

1. All relevant variables can be identified.
2. The boundaries of the system are definite and immutable; it follows that it is clear which variables are exogenous and which are endogenous; these categories are fixed.
3. Only the specified exogenous variables affect the system, and they do this in a known way.
4. Relations between the included variables are either knowable or random.
5. Economic agents (whether individuals or aggregates) are treated atomistically.
6. The nature of economic agents is treated as if constant.
7. The structure of the relationships between the components (variables, subsystems, agents) is treated as if it is either knowable or random.
8. The structural framework within which agents act is taken as given.

Source: Reproduced from Chick and Dow (2005, p. 367).

In immutable models history is predetermined and choice is neither genuine nor matters. Immutability refers to attempts to elaborate (real or imagined) universal event regularities and to develop theoretical structures of the general form 'whenever event (type) X, then event (type) Y'. Thus it closely parallels Lawson's (1997a, 2003) and Dow's (1996a) discussion of closed systems – defined in terms of the ability to isolate and guarantee the constancy of the objects of analysis – see Table 1. We explore this claim in more detail in Chapter 3.

In contrast, the broader notion of transmutability encompasses the stochastic discussion of nonergodicity within a creative and emergent conceptualisation of history in which choice is genuine, matters, and can make a difference in the long run – not least in affecting liquidity considerations and influencing the employment path of an economy over time (Davidson, 1993a). On this view of economic processes, sensible agents recognise that the environment in which they make decisions is characterised by the absence of programmed and predetermined processes and is creative, open, emergent and uncertain – see Table 2.

The implication of this view is that the methods of the physical sciences – which attempt to intervene, insulate and isolate some fixed or relatively stable causal mechanism through experimental methods of control – may obfuscate wider social reality. In other words, if social reality is complex, evolving and non-deterministic, then the employment of methods that are tailored to the study of immutable phenomena is likely to throw up fictitious and misleading accounts of human (individual and collective) behaviour (see Lawson, 2005b).

This transmutable conception of economic processes provides for a delineation between the Post Keynesian approach to modelling and theorising about economic processes and that of many Austrians, New Classicals, New Keynesian and New Institutionalist economists (see Table 3). It also underscores some of the methodological affinities between Post Keynesianism and the German historical school, the older institutionalists and Critical Realists, and provides for elaborations of the specific Post Keynesian view of expectations, uncertainty and time (see Lawson, 2004c, 2005c, 2006a,b).

Table 2 Conditions for open systems

Real-world systems

1. The system is not atomistic; therefore at least one of the following holds:
    a. outcomes of actions cannot be inferred from individual actions (because of interactions);
    b. agents and their interactions may change (for example, agents may learn).
2. Structure and agency are interdependent.
3. Boundaries around and within the social or economic system are mutable, for at least one of the following reasons:
    a. social structures may evolve;
    b. connections between structures may change;
    c. the structure–agent relation may change.
4. Identifiable social structures are embedded in larger structures; these may mutually interact, for the boundaries of a social system are in general partial or semi-permeable.

Implications for theoretical systems

5. There may be important omitted variables or relations and/or their effects on the system may be uncertain.
6. The classification into exogenous and endogenous variables may be neither fixed nor exhaustive.
7. Connections and/or boundaries between structures may be imperfectly known and/or may change.
8. There is imperfect knowledge of the relations between variables; relationships may not be stable.

Source: Reproduced from Chick and Dow (2005, p. 366).

Table 3 Conceptualisations of economic processes

A. Immutable reality (an ergodic system)

TYPE 1. In the short run, the future is known or at least knowable. Examples of theories using this postulate are:
(a) classical perfect certainty models
(b) actuarial certainty equivalents, such as rational expectations models
(c) New Classical models
(d) some New Keynesian theories.

TYPE 2. In the short run, the future is not completely known due to some limitation in human information processing and computing power. Examples of theories using this postulate are:
(a) bounded rationality theory
(b) Knight's theory of uncertainty
(c) Savage's expected utility theory
(d) some Austrian theories
(e) some New Keynesian models (e.g. coordination failure)
(f) chaos, sunspot and bubble theories.

B. Transmutable or creative reality (a nonergodic system)

Some aspects of the economic future will be created by human action today and/or in the future. Examples of theories using this postulate are:
(a) Keynes' *General Theory* and Post Keynesian monetary theory
(b) Post 1974 writings of Sir John Hicks
(c) G.L.S. Shackle's crucial experiment analysis
(d) Old Institutionalist theory.

Source: Reproduced from Davidson (1996, p. 485).

EXPECTATIONS, UNCERTAINTY AND TIME

Walters and Young (1997, pp. 330, 340) indicate that a number of authors such as Hamouda and Harcourt (1988), Arestis (1992), have claimed coherence within the *strands* identified as Post Keynesian. Walters and Young interpret this as coherence within *themes* such as price theory, fundamental uncertainty and endogenous money, whereas the above named authors' claims relate to the different strands or schools (e.g. Kaleckian, Keynesian, Institutionialist). Thus Walters and Young misunderstand the claim that is being made. Nevertheless, we discuss their contentions, and argue that their discussion is misleading in a number of respects. Each of these topics, especially fundamental uncertainty and endogenous money, is the subject of ongoing research and vigorous debate amongst Post Keynesians, and not everyone who accepts the label Post Keynesian ascribes to the same detailed analysis of, say, money or uncertainty; nor does it mean that all Post Keynesians place the same weight on, say, the significance of uncertainty.

Walters and Young appear to be concerned that a 'fundamental idea identified by Keynes – the influence of uncertainty on the behaviour of the principal agents in his system ... does not intersect with the perspective of Kalecki' (p. 343). A little later, their argument changes to 'it is clear that the Kaleckian view of the workings of the economic system cannot be modified by simply appending fundamental uncertainty, the origins of which arise out of this very different theoretical perspective' (p. 344).

It is clear that a significant part of Keynes' analysis concerned the 'dark forces of time and uncertainty', though this was given little attention in the Keynesian literature. However, a revival of interest has taken place in recent years within the Post Keynesian literature. It is also clear that 'Kalecki generally says little about expectations' (Walters and Young, 1997, p. 343, quoting from Sawyer, 1985b). The issue then arises whether there is a basic inconsistency between these approaches, which would appear to be the view of Walters and Young, but we argue that there is no essential inconsistency. Keynes' analysis draws on the distinction between risk and uncertainty. Under the former, which, following Paul Davidson, would now often be labelled the ergodic case, the decision maker is faced by the known probability distribution of outcomes which could flow from his or her actions: the probability distribution is fully known to the individual who can make optimizing calculations.

With uncertainty (nonergodicity), the future is unknown and the past and present provide only limited insights into the future. Precise optimizing calculations cannot be made because the required information is unavailable and cannot be made available because of pervasive uncertainty. As Coddington (1983) argued, one response to uncertainty is to say that nothing can be said about individual decision-making under these circumstances of pervasive uncertainty. Another response is 'the practical study of *procedures* employed by decision makers as bases for choices in situations of Keynesian uncertainty' (Earl and Kay, 1985, p. 47; see Dunn, 2000a,b, for further discussion). Sawyer (1985b) explored the (implicit) assumptions that Kalecki made on firms' expectations, and argued that he adopted what could now be labelled an 'adaptive expectations' approach: views of the future are heavily conditioned by present and past events. It can then be seen that Kalecki's analysis of price and investment decisions did not incorporate optimising behaviour under conditions of risk. In fact, he indicated that 'in view of the uncertainties faced in the process of price fixing it will not be assumed that the firm attempts to maximise its profits in any precise sort of manner' (Kalecki, 1971). It is rather that Kalecki modelled the main influences on firms' pricing and investment decisions in a way that is consistent with pervasive uncertainty.

Walters and Young (1997, p. 334) suggest that 'although the importance of time is often asserted, no particular view or theory of dynamics is developed as a characterisation of the Post Keynesian approach'. It is somewhat difficult to discern what is meant here, and it becomes very pertinent to ask: what is a theory of dynamics? Furthermore, the view of time in Post Keynesian economics is clear. Economic processes have to be analysed as taking place in historical time where past experience, as reflected in expectations, beliefs, institutions and so on, influences present perceptions and decisions which mould what happens in the future (where the future is not a re-run of the past). Consequently, analysis based on the use of logical time is of limited usefulness in the understanding of historical 'open-system' processes. Economic processes are path-dependent. As such, any outcome these processes produce, whether equilibrium or not, depends on the route followed. Post Keynesians model economic processes 'as a group of dynamic subsystems, so that economics is no longer the study of how scarce resources are allocated to infinite needs. Rather it is the study of how economic systems are able to expand their output over time by creating, producing, distributing and using the resulting social surplus' (Arestis, 1997, p. 41).

MARKET STRUCTURE AND THE NATURE OF PRICES

Walters and Young (1997) point to differences between Kalecki and Keynes over the formation of prices, and there are clearly differences as the former viewed price as a mark-up over average direct costs with the mark-up influenced by the degree of monopoly and average direct costs as approximately constant (with respect to output) over a wide range, whereas the latter viewed price equal to marginal cost, which rises with output. Surprisingly, Walters and Young do not inquire into the differences between the various treatments of mark-up pricing within and without the Post Keynesian literature (see Sawyer, 1992c and Chapter 9).

It is clearly of some significance to economic analysis to establish which approach to pricing is the most relevant (however relevance is judged), and indeed whether a single approach to pricing can adequately summarise a diverse reality. But the issue here relates to the interaction between the analysis of pricing adopted and the rest of the analysis. Walters and Young appear to believe that Keynes' analysis has to be accepted (or rejected) as a whole: they write that 'given that Keynes' view [on pricing] is rejected the key question is whether Post Keynesianism can simply take Kalecki (and other mark-up theorists) as the basis of their price theory and still retain the essential Keynesian insights regarding uncertainty and money' (Walters and Young, 1997, p. 341). If this means that Kalecki's approach to pricing is incompatible with the notions of uncertainty and liquidity preference, then this must be disagreed with. Kalecki and Keynes share the view that prices reflect costs (at a level of output determined by aggregate demand) and that price decisions have significant implications for real wages. In both cases, enterprises are surrounded by uncertainty and cannot calculate the 'optimal' price with precision. In both cases, the expansion of aggregate demand requires credit creation; liquidity preference considerations impact on the demand for and supply of money, but that is independent of any considerations as to how firms arrive at their pricing decisions.

In terms of the nature of prices, Walters and Young assert that 'many Post Keynesians ... seem to regard the *assumption* of competitive prices as inappropriate and equivalent to orthodox theory. It is this which seems to give rise to a preference for Kalecki's theory of monopoly power' (Walter and Young, 1997, p. 341 emphasis in original). No evidence is given for these statements. It is the case that many Post Keynesians would treat most prices as being set in imperfectly competitive settings (though accepting that some prices are set in atomistically competitive markets). It is also the case that orthodoxy involves the analysis of perfect competition, and if the assumption of competitive prices also means the analysis of perfect competition, then it would obviously be the case that the assumption of competitive prices draws on a piece of orthodox analysis. But most Post Keynesians would not see that as a reason by itself for dismissing competitive prices. Post Keynesians would also generally note that Keynes' analysis of competitive markets and prices diverged significantly from orthodoxy.

THE POST KEYNESIAN ANALYSIS OF MONEY

It should come as no surprise to anyone that there are differences of view on the analysis of money amongst Post Keynesian economists: articles by authors such as Arestis and Howells (1996), Cottrel (1994), Dow (1996b), Lavoie (1996a) and Pollin (1991) spell out these differences. However, the broad agreements should not be overlooked, especially when there is such a large gulf between the Post Keynesian approach and the orthodox one. The broad agreements would be that money is largely or wholly credit money, created within the private sector by banks. The non-bank public demand loans and, to the extent to which those loans are granted, money is created (and also money is destroyed by the repayment of loans). Increases in expenditure (whether representing a real increase or reflecting higher prices) have to be financed. In this process, the liquidity preference of the banking sector occupies central stage, as is demonstrated in Arestis and Howells (1996). The key role of money in the expansion of demand is clear from the following: 'the increase in output will result in an increased demand for money in circulation, and this will call for a rise in credits from the central bank. Should the bank respond to it by raising the rate of interest to a level at which total investment would decline by the amount equal to the additional investment caused by the new invention, no increase in investment would ensue, and the economic situation will not improve. Therefore the precondition for the upswing is that the rate of interest should not increase too much in response to an increased demand for credit' (Kalecki, 1990, p. 191).

It is of course true that 'Kalecki was generally little concerned with the detail of financial sectors or the nature of money *per se*' (Sawyer, 1985b). Nevertheless, we would argue that Kalecki's analysis can be enriched by further consideration of the financial sector and of the nature of money, noting that Kalecki was analysing a financial system which was rather rudimentary as compared with the current financial systems (see Davidson, 1994). The writings of both Arestis (1996b) and Sawyer (1996) on Kalecki's analysis of financial and monetary matters reveal that even with the rather limited attention Kalecki paid to these phenomena, his analysis is very much within the general outline put forward here.

This conclusion is reinforced when recent Post Keynesian developments in financial and monetary theory are considered. These are essentially an application to the financial sector of the theory of large firms setting the price of financial services as a mark-up over cost; the key input or cost is the price at which funds are available from the central bank. This is basically Kaleckian, not because endogenous money is a more reasonable hypothesis for a modern developed economy, but because it is constructed to answer the questions raised by Kalecki. We conceive of the recent monetary theory as having four strands. First, the focus on the link between planned increases in expenditure, the demand for and supply of loans, and the relationship between loan creation and money. Second, there is a pricing theory in terms of the relationship between central bank discount rate, rate of interest on loans and other rates. Third, there is the general view that loans create deposits and reserves, rather than reserves and deposits creating loans (as in the traditional credit multiplier story). Fourth, there are flow considerations (demand, supply of new loans) but there are also stock considerations. Money only remains in existence if there is a demand for that stock of money. Liquidity preference considerations (including in a significant sense, that of the banking sector as argued above) can influence both the demand for a money stock and the banks' portfolio position.

ECONOMIC POLICY

In terms of economic policy, Walters and Young (1997, p. 339) state 'it might be argued that a unified agenda could be built around an agreed set of policies'. They then claim that 'despite various attempts to construct a particular set of distinctive policies all that Post Keynesianism seems to be associated with in the policy arena is incomes policy'. This statement is misleading in terms of both the association of Post Keynesianism with incomes policy and the implied absence of policies that can be associated with Post Keynesianism. Whilst a few leading American Post Keynesians (notably Sidney Weintraub) did advocate a tax-based incomes policy, we would not see incomes policy as specifically Post Keynesian either in terms of most (or all) Post Keynesians advocating incomes policy or being exclusive to Post Keynesians (and clearly the advocacy of incomes policy in the 1960s and 1970s extended far beyond Post Keynesians). The only sense in which we would see incomes policy as being a part of Post Keynesian economic policy arises from the rejection by Post Keynesians of the monetarist inflation story whereby increases in the stock of money *cause* inflation, and the Post Keynesian view that inflation arises from the real side of the economy with the increases in the stock of money being caused by the inflationary process. The control of inflation requires something more than control of the stock of money (even assuming that such control were possible).

Arestis (1992, 1996a) considers Post Keynesian economic policies and, although reference is made to incomes policy, such a policy is criticized and rejected. But there is a clear and positive Post Keynesian economic analysis which argues that the capitalist system based on free market principles is inherently cyclical and unstable. Left to itself the market economy would not achieve, let alone maintain, the full use of existing resources, neither would it promote the equitable distribution of income and wealth. There is, thus, a potential role for economic policies. Economic policies, however, cannot be generalised to all situations and experiences. Concrete situations, historical experiences and sociological characteristics are of considerable importance for specific policy proposals.

Given this general principle, we would suggest that there is a widely shared and distinctive set of Post Keynesian economic policies, which stem from the agreement that high levels of employment require (as a necessary but not a sufficient condition) high levels of aggregate demand, and that in a decentralized market economy there are no automatic mechanisms which ensure those high levels of aggregate demand. Post Keynesians differ over the ways in which a high level of aggregate demand can be secured and over the constraints on the implementation and operation of such policies. For example, some would view fiscal deficits as the route whereas others would see such deficits as no longer possible under the constraints imposed by globalised financial markets. Some would focus on ways of stimulating investment (see the papers in Arestis and Sawyer, 1997a), whilst others would pay attention to the reform of institutional arrangements, both those governing the international financial system (for example, Davidson, 1992–3), and those more closely related to the European Union (Arestis, 1997; Arestis and Sawyer, 1997b). These proposals are not obviously incompatible, and reflect different perceptions of the constraints on economic policy.

ON KALECKI AND KEYNES AGAIN

In the course of their attacks on Post Keynesian economics, Walters and Young (1997) make assertions on the work of Kalecki and Keynes, a number of which can be found to be incorrect or misleading (or at most idiosyncratic interpretations of Kalecki and Keynes which would not be accepted by Post Keynesian scholars). Issue is taken in particular with the following statements:

> Keynes' story is one in which the aggregate consequences of rational individual behaviour in the face of uncertainty are not automatically made self consistent. The analysis is focused on the behaviour of individuals and deliberately abstracts from institutional detail and market rigidities; it is *deliberately* not 'realistic' (p. 343).

> Keynes' view of prices was to *assume* the functioning of competitive markets in order to illustrate the maladjustment of the system as a result of other key factors, in particular, the role of money in an uncertain environment (p. 340).

A competitive market is an institution as much as a monopolistic industry, and in that sense Keynes did not abstract from institutional detail. The purpose of Keynes' (1936) analysis was, however, to demonstrate that, as a matter of logic, a less than full employment equilibrium could exist in a purely competitive economy with freely flexible wages and prices and individual self-interested decision makers. In both Chapter 19 of *The General Theory* and even more explicitly in his 1939 *Economic Journal* response to Dunlop (1938) and Tarshis (1938), Keynes rejected the idea that his analysis of underemployment equilibrium required imperfect competition, administered prices and/or rigid wages.[1] Keynes (1936, p. 245) explicitly specified that the principle of effective demand that underpinned *The General Theory* is compatible with any level and degree of competition. He did not assume the functioning of competitive markets.

In Chapters 17–19 of his *General Theory,* Keynes argued that the fact of uncertainty would mean that even in competitive economy with perfectly flexible money wages and prices there would be no automatic market mechanism that would restore the full employment level of effective demand. Assumptions regarding the nature of competition, oligopoly and monopoly are not intrinsic to the Post Keynesian theory of unemployment in a monetary economy – this was Keynes' point. As we shall argue below in more detail, it is the existence of money and uncertainty that generates a low level of effective demand and thus 'involuntary' unemployment, not the nature of competition or scale economies (Davidson, 1985b; Chick, 1983, 1992; Dutt, 1992; Sawyer, 1992a,b; Shapiro, 1997; Kregel, 1998a). The conclusion that perfect competition would not exhibit unemployment pertains to a neoclassical world of perfect foresight in which Say's law is operable.

This is why Post Keynesians argue that it is a pre-Keynes view to argue that 'involuntary' unemployment is only possible under oligopolistic or imperfect competition.[2] Indeed, such a conclusion is consistent with Kalecki's own approach and initial formulation of the principle of effective demand (Kalecki, 1934) which assumed 'free competition'.[3] If we are to concern ourselves with the nature of employment in a decentralised *monetary economy* evolving in *historical time* under conditions of pervasive *uncertainty*, then, as Davidson (1985b) and others have argued, the industrial structure is *irrelevant* to a theory of unemployment.

What is more, it is for such reasons that Keynes in *The General Theory* modifies the conventional view of competition to incorporate the reality of uncertainty. Although *The General Theory* appears to exhibit many of the characteristics of perfect competition it nevertheless entails a significant departure from it. As Chick (1992, p. 149) notes, in the General Theory 'the small firm is demand-constrained and cannot sell an indefinitely large amount' and, moreover, 'the established theory of perfect competition imposes the assumption of perfect foresight. By contrast, in *The General Theory*, producers are uncertain of the demand they face'. She further argues that 'once the question of uncertainty is addressed, the *General Theory* is compatible with any or all market structures'. In a similar vein, Dutt (1992) argues that 'Keynes believed that his analysis of unemployment equilibrium did not require any form of market imperfection, but that his theory departed in some obvious way from the neo-classical assumption of perfect competition' (specifically, Keynes did not assume perfect knowledge, nor that firms could sell as much as they wished at the prevailing price).

However, to embrace money and uncertainty is to embrace historical time and dynamic change. And one of the most significant institutional and historical developments over the last century has been the undoubted growth of the large corporation (Galbraith, 1991). The rise of the megacorp means that the basic Keynesian vision requires further elaboration if it is to function as a contemporary guide to research, analysis and policy-making. That is to say, the significance of oligopolistic competition for (macroeconomic) analysis, as Sawyer (1992a,b) notes, may lie in other areas.[4]

Walters and Young (1997, p. 341) insist that 'it is not the adoption of the assumption of imperfect competition which causes problems with regard to the compatibility of Keynesian and Kaleckian views. Rather it is the particular formulation of firms' imperfectly competitive behaviour in Kalecki which is at odds with Keynes' explanation for effective demand failure. Once monopolistic firms' behaviour becomes pivotal this obscures the insight that markets of a variety of forms may deliver inappropriate signals for reasons arising out of the role of money'. We find some difficulty in disentangling what is being said here. Making monopolistic firms' behaviour pivotal may obscure the insight, but that does not necessarily mean that there is incompatibility: to emphasise point X may obscure point Y but it does not make X and Y incompatible. What is meant by making firms' behaviour pivotal? If it is to mean that in the absence of monopolistic pricing (i.e. some form of competitive pricing, however defined) there would be full employment according to the Kaleckian analysis, then that would fly in the face of Kalecki's own work. As noted above, in his initial formulation of the principle of effective demand Kalecki (1934) assumed 'free competition'. His approach to pricing based on the degree of monopoly was developed from his observations on pricing behaviour and cost conditions, and was intended as a relevant analysis of pricing with the implications for income distribution being clearly derived.

Walters and Young (1997, p. 342) further suggest that 'the underlying theories of competition in Kalecki and the classicals are quite different. In particular, it may be argued that this is due, in part, to the neo-classical influence on Kalecki's analysis of oligopolistic firms'. Although, in Kalecki (1940), he derived a supply curve under imperfect competition that could be deemed neo-classical, in that it assumed profit maximisation by 'black box' firms with full information, his papers both before and after that date do not show any neo-classical influence. Walters and Young also overlook the profound influence of classical economists, including Marx, on Kalecki, which was surely much greater than any neo-classical influence. The sense in which Kalecki's approach may be seen as neo-classical is that it would view higher concentration leading to a higher degree of monopoly leading to a higher mark-up of price over cost, which is, of course, similar to the thesis found in the structure–conduct–performance approach. Whilst that approach did at one time attain the status of orthodoxy, it embodies a quite different view of the determinants of profits and profit share as compared with the neo-classical emphasis on marginal productivity, and hence one should not regard the structure–conduct–performance approach as neo-classical (see Sawyer, 1985a). In Kalecki, profits share is influenced by the degree of monopoly, and the volume of profits by investment expenditure, whereas in the neo-classical approach marginal productivity considerations are paramount (see Sawyer, 1990, for more details).

Indeed, Kalecki's approach to pricing based on the degree of monopoly was developed from his observations on pricing behaviour and cost conditions, and was intended as a relevant analysis of pricing with the implications for income distribution being clearly derived. Conditions of oligopolistic competition will generate different levels and patterns of investment and savings, with obvious consequences for the distribution of income, level of growth and aggregate demand that may call for a reassessment of the nexus between the individual and industrial society.[5] While these and other considerations relating to the existence of oligopolistic market structures can be further elaborated, it may be noted that if macroeconomics requires a microeconomic foundation then oligopolistic competition may be an appropriate theoretical building block. As Galbraith (1973b, p. 342) has remarked, the emergence of the large corporation fundamentally changes the analysis of the nature of modern economies:

> [While Keynes] was right to the extent that economics is concerned with the production of goods and the prevention of depressions ... [h]e did not see that, with economic development, power would pass from the consumer to the producer. And, not seeing this, he did not see the increasing divergence between producer or planning purpose and the purpose of the public. And he did not see that – since power to pursue the planning purpose is unequally distributed – development would be unequal. And therewith the distribution of income. Nor did he see that the pursuit of such purpose would threaten the environment and victimise the consumer. And he did not see that the power which allows producer purpose to diverge from public purpose would ensure that inflation would not yield to a simple reversal of the policies that he urged for unemployment and depression. Nor did he foresee the problems of planning co-ordination, national and international.

The dominance of the large corporation has been a generalised feature of advanced capitalist economies since the late nineteenth and early twentieth century and thus provides a supportive realist foundation for contemporary Post Keynesian economics (Sawyer, 1992a,b; Galbraith, 1967, 1973b; Arestis *et al.*, 1999a).

POST KEYNESIAN ECONOMICS AND THE SRAFFIANS

As noted in Chapter 1, the stress on uncertainty and history made by followers of Keynes and Kalecki sits uncomfortably with the Sraffian use of long-period analysis (where there would be an equalisation of the rates of profit and full capacity utilisation in the long period). As Henry (1984–85, p. 220; see also Clark, 1987–88, 1992; cf. Mongiovi, 2000) notes, 'Equilibrium solutions require knowledge of future information which cannot be distilled for decisions to be made today. Hence there is no reason why equilibrium, or even a tendency towards it, should be expected'. Or as Joan Robinson (1974, p. 48; see also Robinson, 1985) argues, '[a]s soon as ... uncertainty ... is admitted, equilibrium drops out of the argument and history takes its place'. The assumption that there are persistent forces which drive the economy towards a normal or long-period position sits rather uncomfortably with the Post Keynesian proposition that the world is characterised by uncertainties, nominal contracts and path dependency (Davidson, 1993a). Stemming from this basic difference a number of aspects of the relationship between Post Keynesian and Sraffian economics can be highlighted.

The first concerns the relationship between the Kaleckian approach and the Sraffian one. Walters and Young (1997) argue that 'if Kalecki's mark-up theory is to be placed within a Sraffian or classical setting then we are entitled to enquire for what gain. The two are quite different ways of considering the evolution of market prices and are designed to illuminate different issues and answer different questions' (p. 342). We can agree that the Kaleckian and the Sraffian analysis as they were initially developed were designed for different purposes, and, drawing on a 'horses for courses' perspective, both can be utilised depending upon circumstance. The potential gain from some synthesis would clearly be a richer and more general analysis: how far a synthesis can be achieved is still a matter of debate. We are fully aware that it is a matter of some dispute between some Kaleckian authors and Sraffian ones on the characterisation of the long period, namely whether it has to be characterised by full capacity utilisation and an equalised rate of profit.

Another aspect concerns the way in which the long-period analysis is regarded. If the long period is regarded as a position which will be eventually attained and which is independent of the path of the economy, then long-period analysis could not be reconciled with the Post Keynesian perspective. As Roncaglia (1995, p. 17) notes, 'the interpretation of Sraffa's output as 'long period centers of gravitation'... is therefore an obstacle to the integration of Sraffian and Keynesian analyses, and should be abandoned'. However, if long period is viewed as a position which will never be attained, though being one towards which the economy would be tending at any particular time, there can be a degree of compatibility between the

Sraffian and the Post Keynesian where different analyses are seen as relevant for different issues and different questions. As Harcourt and Spajic (1997, p. 25) point out, 'Kalecki and Joan Robinson and their followers, and Paul Davidson and his (though the *theories* differ considerably), argue that the long-period method is a non-starter for *descriptive* analysis'. But the long-period method may still be useful for other types of analysis.

CONCLUDING COMMENTS

The purpose of this chapter has been to argue that the coherence of Post Keynesian economics in terms of an overarching theme comes from the role of effective demand in a monetary production economy, and this serves to distinguish Post Keynesian economics from most other schools of thought. We have also argued that the broad policy agenda of Post Keynesian economics would be policies and institutional arrangements supportive of high levels of aggregate demand in pursuit of the objective of full employment. Post Keynesians are institution builders; it is institutions which can provide stability and, if designed correctly, stability near full employment. Consequently, we would agree that there are three major strands in Post Keynesian economics, derived from Kalecki, Keynes and the Institutionalists. We have suggested that the unifying agenda of these strands is the role of effective demand in a monetary production economy where institutional characteristics are paramount. The three themes which Walters and Young identify have indeed played a large role in Post Keynesian economics, and while there are differences of view on these three themes, these differences are relatively minor as compared with the similarities of view, and with differences between Post Keynesian and orthodox economists on these themes. Over the course of the next two chapters we highlight the embeddedness of these themes, and in particular the centrality of the principle of effective demand in its distinctive ontological and methodological approach.

NOTES

1 Dunlop (1938) and Tarshis (1938) had argued that the purely competitive model was not empirically justified and that it was monopolistic and administered pricing and wage fixities that were the basis of Keynes' unemployment equilibrium.
2 See, for example, Dennison and Galbraith's (1938) diagnosis of the causes of the great depression and Galbraith's later repudiation of this pre-Keynesian view (Galbraith, 1981, pp. 63–6; Galbraith, 1998).
3 This underpins the contention of some that Kalecki (1934) discovered the principle of effective demand before Keynes (1936). My own reading of the early Kalecki is that his articulation of the Principle of Effective Demand still relies on imperfections – as opposed to the fact and nature of uncertainty as in Keynes – but, in contrast to some of his later writings, focuses on imperfect labour markets rather than imperfect product markets (as embodied in his notion of the degree of competition). It is for such reasons that I believe the salience of Kalecki lies in other areas.

4 Sawyer (1992b) notes that oligopolistic competition has three particular ramifications for macroeconomic analysis. First, as Weitzman's (1982) analysis demonstrates, it is impossible to sign the real wage employment relationship; it can be positive or negative, as 'firms can operate subject to increasing or decreasing returns and the mark-up of price over (marginal or average) costs can vary with the level of output' (Sawyer, 1992b, p. 84). Secondly, each firm faces a downward-sloping demand curve for its product (which is positioned in relation to the general level of aggregate demand) and, consistent with a profit-maximising assumption, firms make pricing and output (and hence employment) decisions. Here prices are endogenous and thus any constancy of price can be rationalised at the level of the individual firm so as to make imperfectionist price rigidity arguments irrelevant. Thirdly, as firms have a limited degree of control over prices, there is no need to invoke a fictional auctioneer to describe the adjustment process whereby firms meet the market demand. Moreover, trading will not take place at disequilibrium situations if prices are endogenous (see Chapter 6 for a further elaboration of this argument).

5 See, for example, Galbraith (1958, 1967, 1970, 1973a,b; cf. Canterbery, 1984) and Baran and Sweezy (1966).

3 Towards a methodological foundation

Practical economists, who believe themselves to be quite exempt from any methodological influences, are usually the slave of some defunct methodologist.

Kevin Hoover (1995, p. 733)[1]

I feel quite strongly that the way one defines Post Keynesianism is methodological, and that's why I've always thought it was important to be quite explicit about methodology.

Sheila Dow (in King, 1995, p. 154)

INTRODUCTION

In the last chapter we discussed and rebutted many of the criticisms levelled against Post Keynesianism. In this chapter we provide a more detailed assessment of the methodological foundations of Post Keynesian economics. This is especially warranted since Hodgson (2001a, pp. 230–1) remarks that 'in the early years, Post Keynesianism lacked any developed methodological foundations ... [However], not only was Post Keynesianism originally founded on weak and undeveloped methodological foundations, but also, by the close of the century, 'Post Keynesian' economics had still failed to provide itself with an agreed and sufficient set of common core principles around which dissidents could gather. This omission might well prove fatal.'

Here we reject this prognosis.[2] We argue that what characterises Post Keynesianism is its distinctive ontological and methodological orientation. A coherent methodological vision that characterises Post Keynesianism can be discerned and can be summarised as representing a commitment to nonergodic, open-systems theorising, i.e. *taking uncertainty seriously*. Moreover, we argue that the unifying principles of the salience of money, uncertainty-mitigating institutions and the principle of effective demand are embedded in this ontological view. In the next section we discuss in outline the nature of Post Keynesianism, examining its genesis and outlining its common themes and delineation, and then proceed by documenting the claim that Post Keynesianism is committed to theorising about open systems which is characterised by a stress on agency, transformation, organic interdependence and explanation. This also allows for further clarification of the relationship with the Sraffians.

POST KEYNESIANISM AT A GENERAL LEVEL

Many specific attempts at defining Post Keynesianism (such as those of Hamouda and Harcourt, 1988; Lawson, 1994a; Lee, 1998, 2000b; King, 2003) generally begin by examining the theories and approaches of those who explicitly accept the label, i.e. Post Keynesianism is what Post Keynesians say it is. In this vein Lawson (1994a) suggests that a consideration of those contributions in which the Post Keynesian label is invoked reveals at a general level five nominal features. Firstly, there is a rejection or perceived deficiency with 'orthodox economics', however constituted (see Arestis, 1996a; Dow, 1991, Hodgson, 1989; Lavoie, 1992; Sawyer, 1988a). Indeed, this was a key feature of its formative years (see Davidson, 1993b, pp. 434–5, and Arestis, 1996a; cf. Solow in Klamer, 1984; Hahn, 1982, 1989) and a reason it has attracted a degree of criticism as to whether it represents a progressive alternative approach (Chick, 1995).

Secondly, there is a significant emphasis on the methodological distinctiveness of the Post Keynesian approach (see, for example, Lawson, 1994a; Chick, 1995; Dow, 1996a). There is a desire to provide a clear understanding of actually existing *real* economies, the 'economics of the real world' to paraphrase Davidson's (1972) seminal work on the economics of Keynes. Generally this entails highlighting the (perceived) inadequacies of mainstream economics and (specifically) locating them in their methodology (e.g. see Robinson, 1974, 1980; Davidson, 1996; Dow, 1996a, 1997b; Lawson, 1994c, 1997a). This concern seems to reinforce the belief among the mainstream that Post Keynesian economics is concerned with negative critique, especially when leading orthodox economists view methodology as a distraction (see Hahn, 1992a,b; Backhouse, 1992; King, 1992; Lawson, 1992, 1994c, 2004c, 2005b, 2006c; Hoover, 1995).

Thirdly, certain (general) themes do continually appear, such as a concern for history, uncertainty, distributional issues, the role of effective demand and the importance of political and economic institutions in determining the level of activity in an economy (Davidson, 1981; Sawyer, 1988a; Arestis, 1996a). A common point of departure is Joan Robinson's (1956) intended aim of completing a 'generalisation of *The General Theory*'. This entails an adherence to the *principle of effective demand* in the analysis of contemporary economies and links the economics of Keynes to the economics of Kalecki (who independently discovered this principle). This involves the rejection of 'Say's Law' – that supply creates its own demand – in both the short and the long run and suggests that the main economic problem is not the scarcity of resources but the scarcity of demand (see also below). Moreover, the excess capacity observed in many advanced industrialised economies, stylised as high levels of unemployment, is taken as *prima facie* evidence for this point.

Fourthly, Post Keynesians believe that in some sense the (diverse) array of *theories* collected under the label are *potentially* complementary and thus can ultimately be presented as a viable *alternative* to the conventional wisdom (Lavoie, 1992; Arestis, 1996a; cf. Hamouda and Harcourt, 1988). Indeed, Eichner and Kregel (1975) explicitly acknowledged this possibility. Eichner wished to present Post Keynesian theory as an integral whole, just as comprehensive and coherent as the neoclassical approach. Lavoie (1992, p. 1) re-affirms this commitment when he asserts his belief that 'post-Keynesian economics can be presented within a framework that is just as coherent as the neoclassical framework, and that as a consequence it can offer a viable alternative to those that are disenchanted with orthodox economics.'

The fifth element of Post Keynesianism generally is the linkage of its approach to the traditions rooted in the economic writings of Keynes, Kalecki and some classical economists (Davidson, 1996; Sawyer, 1988a; Arestis, 1996a). However, although there are common elements and characteristics across these traditions, it is their distinct differences that fuel accusations of incoherence and undermine its aim to present itself as a viable positive alternative to neoclassical economics (Hamouda and Harcourt, 1988; Backhouse, 1988; Walters and Young, 1997, 1999a). Indeed, the incoherence of Post Keynesian economics is one of the main criticisms levelled against it (Chick, 1995).

Such an approach to defining Post Keynesianism amounts to a positive delineation and description of what constitutes Post Keynesianism, i.e. a description of 'what is' rather than a more normative 'what ought to be'.[3] In the next section we consider the Post Keynesian approach. This allows us in the next chapter to highlight the methodological embeddedness of the Principle of Effective Demand and thus define Post Keynesian economics more normatively.

POST KEYNESIAN METHODOLOGY

It is typically forgotten that the now seminal attempt to assess the coherence of Post Keynesianism by Hamouda and Harcourt (1988) considered the different *theoretical* propositions of the different strands and only made a limited attempt, in a brief conclusion, at evaluating whether the pursuit of coherence was warranted. Moreover, while they concluded that such *theoretical* coherence was unlikely, they did suggest, in a frequently overlooked concluding footnote, that what united Post Keynesians was a particular world view *and method* (Hamouda and Harcourt, 1988, p. 232; see also Pratten, 1996a,b; cf. Lawson, 1997b).[4] So it is of interest that Walters and Young (1997, p. 334) suggested that self-styled Post Keynesians espouse 'significantly *different* and *mutually incompatible* methodological strategies'. This in itself represents a significant extension of the (critical) appraisals of coherence of Post Keynesian economics, which had previously focused upon theory rather than methodology.

Walters and Young start from the premise that Post Keynesian methodology is what leading Post Keynesian methodologists say it is. They contrast the Critical

Realism expounded by Lawson (1989a, 1994a) with the Babylonian method of Dow (1985) and the generalising approach of Davidson (1991c).[5] In doing so, Walters and Young ignore a series of important methodological contributions of these authors and present a misleading caricature of Post Keynesian methodology. A separate, more extended treatment of Post Keynesian methodology which gives more consideration to the relationship between Davidson and the other methodological approaches is clearly warranted, given Walters and Young's (1999a, pp. 346–7) further assessment that:

> The assertion of consistency between the different methodological traditions is unconvincing. First, although not discussed in depth, the contention that an important wing of post-Keynesianism has a generalising tendency, which is inconsistent with other methodological approaches is not seriously disputed. The axiomatic approach employed by Davidson's strand of post-Keynesianism would appear to be at odds with Critical Realists' dismissal of axiomatic theories on the basis of their deductivism (Lawson, 1997a). This is not ameliorated by the claim that any such approach is 'not general in terms of history'. In a similar vein the attempt to combine Critical Realism with Babylonianism by means of their shared open-system presumption fails to address some important differences. In our view the main one is the claimed ability of Critical Realism to 'fix' the underlying causal mechanisms in a world contrasted with Babylonianism's acceptance of the irreducible complexity of social reality.

We shall briefly outline these methodologies and, contra Walters and Young (1997, 1999a,), highlight the common themes that are discernible in each of these contributions.

Critical Realism argues for a conception of *objective* reality that is open, structured, and governed by causal mechanisms (Lawson, 1997a, 2003). It advances a distinct, layered ontology that comprises three levels: the *empirical* domain of experience and impression, the *actual* domain of events, and the *deep* or *real* domain of structure, powers, tendencies and generative mechanisms. These domains are viewed as distinct and out of phase with each other. Critical Realists argue that intransitivity occurs at the level of structure and not at the level of observed event regularities and thus that the aim of science is to identify and explain (retroduce) the structures and mechanisms that characterise the *real* domain (Lawson, 1995b, 1996b, 1997a, 1999b, 2003). The objective is to move beyond surface phenomena and develop abstractions that are appropriate and concerned with real social structures (and not artificial constructs) and essential (although not necessarily the most general). The social structures are not in any sense fixed or immutable but are reproduced or transformed through the intentions and actions of (economic) agents (Lawson, 1996a). Critical Realists argue that mainstream economics, in applying a closed-system ontology to the study of open processes, results in inconsistencies at the levels of method, social theory and methodology (Lawson, 1987, 1997a, 2003, 2005c).

Lawson (1989b, 1994a, 1997a, 2003, 2006c) contends that mainstream economics is best distinguished by its (generally implicit) deductivist, closed-system method. A closed system is one in which a relatively strict regularity of events occurs. Where events are not regularly of events conjoined the system can be said to be open. In Critical Realism, event regularities are shown mostly to occur in conditions where an intrinsically stable mechanism is insulated from the effects of countervailing mechanisms. Where this occurs, a regularity is often produced, correlating the mechanism's 'triggering conditions' and its 'effects'. Such a closure is the aim of natural scientific experiments. Outside closure conditions, any event is likely to be the product of a changing mix of (emergent) mechanisms, so that actual events are rarely well correlated with each other. The latter sets of conditions are referred to as open systems.[6]

Critical Realists argue that, apart from astronomy, the majority of strict event regularities identified by science have been generated under the conditions of experimental control. Experimental control is an attempt to intervene, insulate and isolate some fixed or relatively stable causal mechanism (Siakantaris, 2000). One can 'define a "closed system" simply as one in which a constant conjunction of events obtains; i.e. in which an event of type *a* is invariably accompanied by an event of type *b*' (Bhaskar, 1978, p. 70).[7] According to this perspective the purpose of (economic) science is to elaborate (real or purely imagined) universal event regularities and to develop theoretical explanations of the (general) form 'whenever event (type) X then event (type) Y'. This approach, applied to economics, assumes that closed systems, and the event regularities that typify them, characterise the social realm. Two forms of closure, the intrinsic and extrinsic forms, are central to this scientific approach and permit a determinate and atomistic explanation of event regularities (Lawson, 1989b, 1997a). The intrinsic condition of closure refers to the constant immutability of the structures of the phenomena under study and can loosely be summarised as suggesting that a cause, always and everywhere, results in the same effect. The extrinsic condition requires that the phenomena in question can be isolated from, and made orthogonal to (un-correlated with), external influences, and refers to the fact that an effect has the same cause. When linked together, these two closure conditions permit a definitive and exhaustive explanation of event regularities over time and space. An additional criterion of additiveness is also identified which is invoked so as to permit the elaboration of event regularities at the aggregate level (Bhaskar, 1978, pp. 75–7; Lawson, 1997a, pp. 80–1). This principle, which is closely bound up with the notion of atomicity, suggests that complex systems can be combined, decomposed and analysed in terms of their component parts.[8] Taken together, these closure conditions underpin the scientific approach which aims at a deductive and determinate account of phenomena at the level of events.[9] This entails the presumption that exact functional relationships can be postulated and the corresponding correlations between variables can be uncovered. 'Accordingly, the isolation of these empirical regularities in the social world defines theoretical work, whereas formal axiomatic reasoning defines theoretical work' (Downward, 1999, p. 15).

The absence of any such conditions of closure represents a *sufficient* condition for the identification of open systems – *defined in terms of the absence of strict event regularities* (Bhaskar, 1978, pp. 69–79). Critical Realists argue, in sharp contrast to mainstream economists, that the social world cannot be subject to experimental closure as the conditions for closure do not apply, because the phenomena under consideration are transmutable, i.e. economic agents possess the capacity for creative, crucial substantive choice (Lawson, 1998b). As a result, even while (event) regularities in the social realm are not ruled out, where they do arise they do so because of the unceasing interaction between the reflexive choices of human agents and the social structures and institutions that underpin them. This implies that such stylised facts will be partial and multifaceted and neither predictable nor universal (see Lawson, 1989a). As Lawson (1997a, p. 219) points out, 'given the dependence of social mechanisms upon inherently transformative human agency, where human beings chose their courses of action (and so could have always acted otherwise), strict constancy seems a quite unlikely eventuality'. While Critical Realists argue that there appears, *a posteriori*, clear limits on the possibility of bringing about closure in the social realm and concomitantly permitting the subsequent identification of causal relationships, the inescapable hermeneutic moment in the social sciences provides an alternative and compensatory route which facilitates the identification of underpinning causal mechanisms and fundamentally changes the nature of economic enquiry (see Lawson, 1997a, pp. 199–226). As Lawson (1997a, p. 35) notes, 'the impossibility of engineering, and the absence of spontaneously occurring, closed social systems, necessitates a reliance upon non-predictive, purely explanatory, criteria of theory development and assessment in the social sciences'.

Walters and Young (1997, 1999b), however, suggest Critical Realism is internally deficient, unnecessary, incompatible with and potentially destructive to Post Keynesianism. They argue that while the Critical Realist approach lends itself to a powerful critique of predictive econometrics (Lawson, 1989b, 1997a, 1999b; Runde, 1998), it 'cannot solve the problems of distinguishing between theories on the basis of their realism' (Walters and Young, 1999b, p. 105). Walters and Young argue that the 'weak epistemological basis' of Critical Realism furnishes Post Keynesianism with an inadequate set of methodological guidelines to assess Post Keynesian research: how does one know that one has uncovered the relevant causal mechanism? According to Walters and Young, Critical Realism can only be understood as a means of expressing or interpreting theory rather than evaluating theory.[10] However, it is clear that Walters and Young have not read Lawson (1997a) or the earlier contributions upon which much of the argument is based. Lawson devotes nearly half of the book to precisely such epistemological issues. Lawson (1997a, Chapter 15) suggests that one appraises theories on the basis of their relative explanatory power, as measured by their ability to account for interesting partial event regularities, i.e. stylised facts, referred to as contrastive *demi-regs* (see for example Arestis *et al*., 1994; see also the contributions and discussion in Downward, 2003).[11] Proponents of Critical Realism, however, argue that it is the task of individual sciences to assess and investigate the specific social structures, totalities and processes that emerge and warrant further examination. Inasmuch as Post Keynesianism represents a distinct Critical Realist approach it seeks, as we shall see below, to investigate the specific institutional structures that generate different levels of employment across different epochs, cultures and continents. Walters and Young's critique ultimately serves to highlight areas of potential confusion and the need for further elaboration, and it further underscores the inherent problems of fallible, open-systems theorising and the process of describing the changing social structures that are embedded within them (see also McKenna and Zannoni, 1999). The criticisms that Walters and Young make relate to the ontology of the social system and not the *method* of Critical Realism.[12]

Walters and Young next consider the Babylonian approach of Sheila Dow (1985, 1990b, 1996a, 1997a). Babylonianism starts from the premise that reality is complex, transmutable and organically linked. This clearly casts doubt on the usefulness of general *theoretical* structures in illuminating such reality. Two main claims are made against Babylonianism *vis-à-vis* the methodological coherence of Post Keynesianism. Firstly, the central tenets of Babylonianism, pluralism and holism, are seen as diametrically opposed to notions of consistency and coherence. Such a confusion, however, stems from Walters and Young's failure to consider to what the pluralism espoused by Babylonians refers (Dow, 1999). Pluralism may relate to ontology, epistemology and method. Dow (1997a, p. 89) argues that Post Keynesian methodology is 'grounded in an appropriate ontological and epistemological position, i.e. that reality and knowledge of it are understood as open-systems'. The methodological pluralism advocated by Dow (1997a, p. 97) is an 'exercise in open-system meta-methodology'. Babylonians argue that it is because of the complexities – i.e. organic interdependencies – and openness of the social system, the ontological position, that theoretical pluralism, i.e. the plurality of different means of investigation, is inevitable and is to be welcomed (Dow, 1990b).[13] This clearly parallels the argument of Critical Realism that, given that social structures are reproduced and transformed by human agency, *pluralism of theory* is likely and perhaps desirable (Lawson, 1994a, pp. 525–6; Dow, 1997c). While this is akin to a 'horses for courses' argument it does not and need not mean 'anything goes' (Dow, 1996a, 1997a, 2001; cf. Lawson, 1997b). Indeed a key argument running throughout the first half of this thesis is that Sraffian 'does not go' with Post Keynesian economics defined as an open-systems approach!

Walters and Young (1999a, p. 347) perceive a second point of tension between the organic complexity associated with Babylonianism and the Critical Realist desire to identify the 'deep' causal structures that underpin reality. Such 'deep' causal structures are not fixed, however; rather they are continually reproduced and transformed through human action. Any enduring causal structure is contingent upon human agency, which is itself suffused in organic complexity (which is distinct from atomistic complexity) and emergence. The organicism espoused by Babylonians places clear limits on the likelihood that the structures under investigation can be isolated from other potential influences and can be 'closed' and thus that a deductive, determinate account of the phenomena is warranted (see Dow, 1996a; Lawson, 1997a; Rotheim, 1999; Mearman, 2002a; Chick and Dow, 2005).

Perhaps the most obvious area of potential tension is that Critical Realism has frequently been interpreted as dualistic, an approach which Babylonianism eschews (Dow, 1985, 1990b). Lawson (1997a), however, devotes a significant proportion of time upon such epistemological issues, outlining the distinction between *dualities*, which refers to how structures and actions presuppose each other, and a 'dualistic' philosophy which attempts at scientific classification on the basis of two mutually exclusive categories with fixed meanings. As Dow argues (1997c, pp. 530–1) Critical Realism itself 'has suffered from misunderstandings from a dualist perspective which have suggested, for example, that it is objectivist, deterministic, claims truth, rejects abstraction, rejects empirical work and so on. What is made clear ... is that Critical Realism falls into none of these categories'. It has been for such reasons that Dow (1985, 1996a), when examining the methodological advances made since the first edition of her seminal book on 'the methodology of macroeconomic thought', felt compelled to include a new section on Critical Realism, in which *she stressed its compatibility with Babylonianism.* Clearly there are some semantic differences between Babylonianism and Critical Realism but these are to be found in their different origins and should not be interpreted as substantive differences. As Dow (1999) makes clear, the Babylonian method is broadly consistent with Critical Realism.

Notwithstanding the fact that Babylonianism and Critical Realism may be compatible, what about the 'encompassing' or 'generalising' methodological tradition of Post Keynesianism associated with Paul Davidson? Davidson (1994) suggests that the content of the Keynesian revolution consisted in the rejection of three axioms of the classical system: (i) the axiom of an ergodic economic environment; (ii) the axiom of the long-run neutrality of money; and (iii) the axiom of gross substitution across all commodities and factor inputs.[14] He argues that because it was based on fewer (less restrictive) axioms, Post Keynesian theory is a more general theory, which encompasses classical theory as a special case.[15]

This may be incompatible with the other methodological traditions, primarily for two reasons (see also Lewis and Runde, 1999). Firstly the invocation of an 'axiomatic approach', appears, at face value, to suggest a Cartesian or logical positivist mode of reasoning which seems to run counter to the strictures of Babylonianism and Critical Realism. Secondly, the Babylonian method explicitly emphasises the problems that surround *general theories*. However, while Davidson espouses an ontology based on the rejection of the ergodic axiom and the championing of agency and uncertainty, it is far from clear that this constitutes a fully defined methodology. Choosing between theories and approaches on the basis of fewer, less restrictive assumptions does not constitute a specific methodological approach *per se*. Clearly, however, the seeming acceptance of *a priori* axiomatic deductive reasoning can be taken to *imply* an orthodox methodological orientation which is clearly questioned by both Critical Realism and Babylonianism. Yet this ignores Davidson's (1999b) acknowledged rhetorical strategy of 'engagement with the mainstream' and the paradigmatic shift in vision that his approach necessitates.

The rejection of the ergodic axiom by Davidson is founded upon both hermeneutics *and* scientific realism which ultimately divests the 'axiom' concept of the theoretical status typically accorded to it. For it should be recalled that axioms, according to Hahn (1985, p. 5) at least, refer to incontrovertible statements of event regularities that are so widely agreed upon as to make additional justification unnecessary (see also Lawson, 1997a, Chapter 8). Davidson (1982–3, 1988, 1996) rejects the idea that the acceptance of the ergodic axiom is an incontrovertible proposition, beyond dispute. He challenges this assumption, in a manner not too dissimilar to Lawson (1997a), on empirical grounds, the fact that most macroeconomic time series are non-stationary – a sufficient but not a necessary condition for the existence of nonergodic processes – and upon a hermeneutic recognition that humans possess the capacity for real, crucial choices, i.e. the fact that they could have acted differently (also a sufficient condition for the existence of nonergodic processes, see below). Thus in discarding the ergodic axiom Post Keynesians reject the presupposition of the immutability of economic phenomena over time and thus acknowledge the importance and salience of history in economic analysis.[16]

In any case, both Critical Realism and Babylonianism share this generalising, rhetorical twist (see Lawson, 1999a; Dow, 1999, p. 22; Davidson, 1999b). For example, Lawson has suggested that although Post Keynesians 'join with Critical Realism in accepting its *a posteriori* assessment that the world is open and structured, it does not follow (as some have supposed) that Post Keynesians ought thereby not to engage at all in formalistic methods such as econometrics. The possibility of successes with the latter requires local closures. But closures themselves have been shown to presuppose, and indeed to be a special configuration of, an open and structured system, that is a special case of the sort of system that does widely obtain' (Lawson, 1999a, p. 7). Any situation in which an event regularity occurs is a closed system. All other situations can be described as open. Mostly, systems are open in this sense; a closure is a very special limiting case. This is just another way of saying, as Davidson (1988, p. 163, italics added) points out, that 'In the real world, some economic processes may be ergodic, *at least for short sub-periods* of calendar time, while others are not'. Post Keynesians accept that to deny the possibility of ergodic, constant conjunctions of events in the social realm would be anti-scientific. Indeed, the activities of insurance companies would appear to provide *prima facie* evidence that it might be both reasonable and profitable to assume that certain processes might approximate closed, ergodic systems. Post Keynesians, however, argue that such local closures are 'few and far between' and that when they do arise they are generally uninteresting compared to the salience of the uninsurable competitive process and their unintended macroeconomic consequences. To restrict oneself to the study of ergodic, closed systems clearly places severe limits on the domain of validity of economic analysis and thus prohibits the elucidation of interesting real-world causal processes.[17] It is this sense in which Post Keynesianism is more general, in the sense of having greater relevance by incorporating the study of *both* ergodic and nonergodic processes.[18] That is to say, the anti-deterministic ontological view embraced by Post Keynesians is less limiting than an overly narrow, closed system view (cf. Bhaskar, 1978; Lawson, 1997a, 2003).

There appears, however, to be some unease surrounding Davidson's approach-specific view of time, conducted in terms of the ergodic/nonergodic distinction, and Critical Realism. For instance, Critical Realists such as Runde (1993) and Downward and Mearman (1999) submit that Davidson's analysis is entirely conducted at the level of events and contravenes the tenets of the methodological approaches of both Critical Realism and Babylonianism. They suggest that ergodicity and nonergodicity are philosophical duals expressed at the level of events and thus do not necessarily share a realist ontology. A passage commenting on Davidson (1993b) by Runde (1993, p. 384) is illuminating in this respect:

> Davidson's official position thus consists of an epistemological dichotomy between knowledge and uncertainty and a corresponding ontological opposition between ergodic and nonergodic processes. The basic presupposition appears to be an ontology of what Bhaskar calls empirical realism. In terms of this doctrine, the basic objects of the real world are the objects of actual or possible experience and the aim of science is to isolate and identify empirical realities. Where such regularities obtain, where the world is ergodic in Davidson's terminology, 'scientific knowledge' is possible. Otherwise, in 'nonergodic situations' it is possible only to have (historical) knowledge of past and/or current events ... The main difference between Davidson and the orthodoxy, if I am right, is that he is far less inclined to assume that economic events are governed by ergodic processes.

Runde argues that although the world is open, it is characterised by reasonably enduring social structures and tendencies. Runde reiterates the fact that Critical Realism advances a distinct, layered ontology in which the phenomena identified at the empirical and actual level emerge from the causal mechanisms operating at deeper levels. This, at first sight, might appear to be at odds with the ergodic/nonergodic approach of Davidson (1993b), who has attacked the notion that there are 'natural' and immutable laws governing economic behaviour. However, the deeper mechanisms and social structures identified by Critical Realists are themselves transmutable and conditioned by human agency (Lawson, 1997a). They are in no sense 'natural'.

Such an argument is fallacious and perhaps more inspired by a perception of Davidson as engaging in aggressive, argumentative posturing than any fundamental methodological issues. It ignores a fundamental aspect of Davidson's discussion of nonergodicity: the role of crucial decision-making (Davidson, 1982–3, 1988, 1996). Crucial decision-making is a *sufficient* condition for the existence of nonergodic and open processes (cf. Davidson, 1996; Lawson, 1997a; Runde, 1997b) and is the deep causal mechanism that generates the statistical property (demi-reg) of nonergodicity that emerges in the empirical and the actual domains.[19] As Lawson (1997a, 2003) notes, real choice presupposes openness. And *it is real choice that creates uncertainty* (the argument contained in Chapter 6). To quote Arestis: '[t]he essence of *uncertainty* in Post Keynesian economic theory is grounded in a nonergodic, non-deterministic world understood as an open-system' (Arestis, 1996a, p. 117).

Moreover, as we shall elaborate further below, Davidson (1996) suggests that decision-making in situations where information gathered from the past provides an insufficient basis in which to assess future outcomes is, in a real and meaningful sense, creative. 'Crucial economic decision-making, by definition, assures that the economic variables which impinge upon the decision-maker's environment are not ahistorical. Crucial decisions create a new future' (Davidson, 1989b, p. 153). In those situations where a decision cannot be undone, where the economic landscape is forever changed and the circumstances of the decision cannot be repeated, then the decision is crucial. Crucial decisions, according to Davidson, refer to those non-routine situations that take place in historical open time, i.e. under circumstances in which re-contracting is expensive (unlike in Arrow–Debreu type constructions).

Similarly, Runde (1993) is wrong to suggest that Davidson neglects social structures – a key tenet of the Babylonian and Critical Realist approaches. Davidson accepts the role of social structures and human institutions which 'involve established laws, customs, practices and mechanisms to govern behaviour and develop socially acceptable outcomes ... [they are] 'rules of the game' (Davidson, 1989a, p. 107; cf. Robinson, 1962a, 1978). Davidson argues that social conventions, institutions and structures are a creative response to an uncertain future which can be intentionally changed by human action although often resulting in unintended consequences. However, Davidson, as a monetary theorist, chooses to focus on how money-denominated contracts represent an *enduring* institutional response that mitigates the impact of an open, uncertain future and its implications. In his seminal contribution to Post Keynesian monetary theory, Davidson (1972) clearly highlights that the unintended effect of a system of production and distribution, which relies on such contracts, is that no automatic tendency to generate full employment is assured (see also the next section). Having identified the unintended consequences of such social structures, Davidson (1989a, p. 107; see also 1985a) argues that if high levels of unemployment are unacceptable then 'civilised humans must strive to develop relevant, new human institutions compatible with their history and their culture' which permit aggregate demand to be expanded so to increase employment. Indeed Davidson, Dow and Lawson all recognise the importance of social structures, which are emancipatory and predicated upon real substantive choice (see also Galbraith, 1973b).

This commitment to open-system theorising is the methodological glue that binds Post Keynesians together. Post Keynesians argue that the mainstream economics is characterised by its methodology of ergodic, closed-system reasoning which ultimately prohibits a substantive role for money and its associated institutions, historical time and the nature of choice under uncertainty (Robinson, 1974, 1977; 1980; Chick, 1995; Dow, 1996a, 1997a; Davidson, 1996; Lawson, 1997a). Moreover, four common (organically linked) elements can be identified in these approaches. They are: (i) a transformational conception of human agency which presupposes openness where choice is genuine, emergent and matters;[20] (ii) an organicist conception of social reality with its concomitant rejection of atomism and methodological individualism; which (iii) prevents (full) closure and the elaboration of a deterministic (ergodic) account of (maximising) economic phenomena[21]; and hence (iv) the aim of economic science is then explanation and not prediction.[22] Post Keynesians aim to provide *causal explanations* of a concrete economic phenomenon which are couched in terms of abstract, but nevertheless descriptively adequate statements of the phenomenon concerned, as opposed to other approaches that by their own admission represent fictitious idealisations (Hicks, 1979; Shackle, 1979a; Davidson, 1980; Dow, 1996a; Lawson, 1997a, 2003; Runde, 1997a; Mearman, 2002b). As this stresses a consistent and coherent methodological approach this claim deserves to be substantiated by direct reference to the works of those apparently in conflict. A brief review highlights evidence for this view:[23]

(i) On a transformational conception of human agency:

> Individuals reproduce or transform social structure which, at the moment of any individual act only can be treated as given ... human action in total is always reproductive/transformational (Lawson, 1994a, p. 520, italics added).
>
> [T]he *imperative of action* requires that agents somehow construct hypotheses on which to *base that action* in spite of a lack of knowledge (Dow, 1990b, p. 149, italics added).
>
> Entrepreneurship, which is one facet of human creativity, by its very nature involves cruciality (Davidson, 1996, p. 499).
>
> Keynes ... developed a logically consistent alternative model of an entrepreneurial economy where decision-makers recognise that the external reality in which they operate is in some, but not necessarily all economic dimensions, uncertain (i.e. nonergodic) and therefore *transmutable or creative* (Davidson, 1996, p. 482, italics added).

(ii) On an organicist conception of that agency:

> Structure and human agency, in sum, each presuppose, although neither can be reduced to, identified with, or explained completely in terms of, the other (Lawson, 1994a, p. 520).
>
> An organic view of the economic process takes a more complex view of human nature and of individual behaviour, seeing individuals as social beings (Dow, 1991, p. 185).
>
> Nonergodic situations and monetary theory are, in the real world, *inextricably linked*, for it is 'problems of the real world in which our previous expectations are liable to disappointment and expectations concerning the future affect what we do today. It is when we have made this transition [to a nonergodic world of economic events] that the peculiar properties of *money as a link*

between the present and the future must enter our calculation' (Keynes, 1936, 293–4). Money matters only in a world without ergodic processes (Davidson 1982–3, p. 190, Davidson's parenthesis, italics added).

(iii) On their commitment to open systems theorising:

> I have argued ... that the world is open in the sense that universal constant conjunctions of events are a rare event even in natural sciences and more so in the social realm (Lawson, 1995a, p. 26).
>
> Now if choice is real any agent could always have done otherwise, each agent could have acted differently that he or she in fact did ... Choice ... presupposes that the world is open and actual events need not have been (Lawson, 1994a, p. 517).
>
> The Babylonian mode of thought is another attempt to theorise about a complex reality, but one which does not aim at a complete, closed theoretical structure (Dow, 1990b, p. 146)[24].
>
> If, therefore, the economic system is open, in the sense that neither agents nor the model builder has absolute and complete information, then there will always be unobservable economic variables which can impinge on expectations and, through the latter, on output, employment and prices (Davidson, 1989b, p. 155).

(iv) On the view that the aim of (Post Keynesian) economics is explanation and not prediction:

> To the extent that a realist/open-system view is held then the conclusion would seem to follow that [economic] science is possible but must, in general be explanatory rather than predictive (Lawson, 1989b, p. 257).
>
> [T]he goal of economics is primarily to *identify* the structures governing, the conditions surrounding, facilitating as well as being transformed through, some human activities of interest. *Social explanation* entails providing an understanding of certain practises and activities of interest, that is, identifying and understanding the unacknowledged conditions of these practises, their unconscious motivations, the tacit skills drawn upon, as well as unintended consequences (Lawson, 1994a, p. 520, italics added).
>
> [The] choice of methodology by post-Keynesians reflects a realist approach to economics, where realism means a *concern to understand* causal processes (Dow, 1991, p. 186, italics added; see also Dow, 1990b, pp. 146–7).
>
> The primary goal of science is to explain (Davidson, 1993b, p. 431).
>
> For Post Keynesians following the trails blazed by Keynes and Shackle, therefore, the task of economic analysis is to study the human institutional relations which provided stability to the economic structure in the past,

> and then continue to foster the development of economic institutions which will hopefully maintain stability at desired levels as the economy evolves over the future (Davidson, 1989b, p. 149).

Thus, ignoring some of the questions of presentation and rhetoric, basic methodological themes can be identified and outlined. While some further clarification and debate may still be needed, a fundamental methodological vision that characterises Post Keynesian economists can be discerned – *a commitment to open-system theorising*, an approach which exhibits, at core, a stress on emergent agency, transformation, organic interdependence and explanation.[25] Thus while, as Lawson (1999a, p. 13) points out, such 'discussion and debate over connections and limitations are still at an early stage', it is suggested that there is a high degree of coherence that can be found at the methodological level. The next chapter considers the link between the open-system method that Post Keynesians embraced and their adherence to the principle of effective demand – which together accounts for the distinctiveness of the Post Keynesian approach.[26]

THE IMPLICATIONS FOR THE SRAFFIANS

Clearly, however, the inclusion of the Sraffian school under this definition of the Post Keynesian umbrella is highly contentious given its closed-system methodology which underpins its equilibrium approach (Hodgson, 1989, pp. 97–100; Lawson, 1994a, p. 506, footnote 6; Pratten, 1996a, b). The uneasy accord with the Sraffians must be ended, given that they openly adopt many of the precepts of a closed-system modelling strategy.[27] As Pratten (1996a, p. 35; see also 1996b) has argued, Sraffian 'economics, to the extent that it takes closure for granted as a natural and useful starting point for analysis, retains an underlying commitment to deductivism and so is difficult to reconcile with Post-Keynesianism'. Similarly, Downward (2000) also argues that the Sraffian system is not consistent with an open-systems ontology, specifically because of its closure assumptions. Indeed, such a diagnosis underpins the argument developed here that it is the inclusion of the Sraffian strand and the use of Post Keynesianism as a portmanteau concept, so as to provide strength in numbers, that has generated much confusion and fuelled derisory accusations of incoherence.

This conclusion is perhaps less controversial than it might first appear. There has been a growing recognition that Sraffians are (methodologically) incompatible with other traditions that are typically viewed as part of the core of the Post Keynesian programme within Post Keynesians (Hodgson, 1989; Arestis, 1996a; Holt, 1996; Pratten, 1996b). Dow (1999) offers a somewhat different perspective to that presented here, arguing that the Sraffian perspective can be considered as part of a political economy tradition which *itself* can be characterised by its open-systems method. She suggests that 'political economy can be characterised as adopting an open-system approach, each school of thought within political economy can be distinguished by its distinctive vision of reality' (Dow, 1999, p. 22). Dow (1999, p. 22, note 8) recognises that such a characterisation of political economy is far from uncontroversial, given that, for example, Sraffian economics as currently expressed could not be categorised as an open-system approach. However, she submits that Sraffian economics could be 'brought back' under the political economy label if it is 'expressed rather as a partial system, it need not be excluded; the generalising strategy of open-system theorising can include partial analyses of systems as if closed.'[28] We would agree with this statement: that if Sraffian economics is expressed as a partial system it could indeed be brought back under the open-system umbrella.[29]

However, this should not imply that the political economy label should be viewed as synonymous with the open-systems method. It would seem to ignore the historiography of the Sraffian approach to suggest that they can *only* be considered part of the political economy tradition if they embrace an open-system approach to theorising. This is surely a rational reconstruction of the term political economy that even Sraffians would reject. Radical political economy is typically defined by the questions it asks and not its method *per se*. It is associated with several different paradigmatic modes of economic analysis that take as a common focus issues such as the importance and role of the distribution of income, the dynamic nature of capitalist accumulation and the production and distribution *of an economic surplus*.[30] Sraffians and Post Keynesians accept this focus and openly embrace the classical political economy tradition (Pasinetti, 1974, 1977; Sawyer, 1989). This explains why Lavoie (1992, p. 2), for example, indicates that 'several streams of non-orthodox economics can be regrouped under the same umbrella, notably the Post Keynesians, the neo-Ricardians, the (Marxist) Radicals and the Institutionalists, ... call[ing] the common elements of these four approaches the post-classical research programme'. So it would seem somewhat misguided to define political economy in terms of open-system theorising.

As such we would argue that while Post Keynesianism should be defined and described in terms of its open-systems approach (which underpins its recognition of the importance of the principle of effective demand – the argument of the next chapter), the temptation to do the same with political economy should be resisted as it obscures their fundamental points of departure and insight. Post Keynesians are interested in the rich set of philosophical and moral questions that form part of the heuristic core of the political economy tradition. However, their answers are likely to differ from other political economy approaches, given their focus upon the salient institutions of money and their nexus to uncertain open processes.

CONCLUDING COMMENTS

It is erroneous to conclude that Post Keynesianism is methodologically incoherent; it is in this area that Post Keynesianism's coherence can be found. There exists a fundamental methodological vision shared by all Post Keynesians who argue that history, time and money matter. Post Keynesians are *committed to open-system theorising* which is characterised by its stress on *agency, transformation, organic interdependence* and *explanation*. As we shall see in the next chapter, Post Keynesians reject the closed, ergodic approach which ultimately renders the concept of choice vacuous and hinders the development of 'serious monetary theory'. Post Keynesian monetary theory is founded on the recognition that the world is, in a fundamental sense, open and that this underscores the recognition of the salience of money-denominated contracts and their nexus to the principle of effective demand. Moreover, this rejection of the assumption of governing immutable processes distinguishes Post Keynesians not only from orthodox neoclassical theory, but also from other schools of thought which, implicitly or explicitly, invoke such closed-system methods and argue for a predetermined (immutable) path.[31] Nevertheless, this all begs the question: is Post Keynesianism anything more than a philosophical position? The response developed in the next chapter is that the principle of effective demand is embedded within this methodological view and underpins the distinctiveness of Post Keynesian economics as an open-systems approach.

NOTES

1 I am sure the fact that Hoover is paraphrasing Keynes (1936) needs no elaboration.
2 Chick (1995) lists five main criticisms against Post Keynesianism. Post Keynesianism, it is argued, is (i) incoherent, (ii) not scientific, (iii) not modern (i.e. mathematical), (iv) not theory, (v) not economics. Chick rejects these criticisms by suggesting: (i) Post Keynesian economics is defined by a coherent methodology and not a Lakatosian hardcore of principles (indeed this is the argument here); (ii) orthodox analysis is based on the Cartesian or logical positivist mode of thought and this type of logic is designed for the closed system. Post Keynesians, Chick argues, utilise other forms of logic designed for open systems; (iii) Post Keynesians use mathematics, although its use occurs where necessary and not as a matter of course; (iv) this criticism relates to the fact that it rejects the axioms of profit and/or utility maximisation and the idea of 'fundamental forces'. This relates to the Post Keynesian analysis of open systems; (v) the fact that Post Keynesianism draws on a wide array of disciplines does not mean it is not economics. An organic approach necessarily implies that analysis cannot be conveniently demarcated. It should be apparent that the rejection of these criticisms is linked to the common methodological outlook developed throughout.
3 It should be noted that the suggestion that Hamouda and Harcourt, Lawson and Lee espouse a positive delineation of Post Keynesian economics is not meant to impart the pejorative association of a widely discredited methodology. Rather it is meant to draw attention to the fact that many Post Keynesians, when trying to outline the tenets of their approach, either (a) highlight the recurrent and dominant themes of self-confessed Post Keynesians or (b) provide a definition of Post Keynesian economics which is marshalled to then delineate its core.
4 By his own admission, Harcourt is 'not very interested in methodology' (Harcourt and King, 1995, p. 54). Lawson (1997b, p. 3) has suggested Harcourt's methodological approach is 'rather lax' and 'that the most compelling translation of [Harcourt's] "horses for courses" [approach to theory] in the scientific context pertains to the (usual) situation where the accepted goal is to illuminate (reveal/explain/understand) some feature of reality, and takes the form of the directive that where given methods, techniques or procedures are to be employed, the objects chosen for analysis are of such a nature that the methods appear capable of illuminating them; or where definite aspects of reality

are to be illuminated, the methods and procedures followed be fashioned to insights available concerning the nature of such material'. Comim (1999) provides an alternative interpretation and defence of Harcourt's method.

5 The references are Walters and Young's. As I'm sure Davidson, Dow and Lawson would attest, they are not particularly representative of their work. Walters and Young prefer Dow (1985) to the more recent, revised and expanded version completed to encompass the subsequent methodological debate (Dow, 1996a). Davidson (1991c) is a first-year introductory volume and is less comprehensive than the more advanced *Post Keynesian Macroeconomic Theory* (Davidson, 1994). Moreover, focusing upon Lawson (1989a, 1994a) ignores the wide range of contributions that he has made that came to feature in Lawson (1997a). Walters and Young miss basic contributions and scandalously ignore the chronology and evolution of Post Keynesian thought.

6 For a detailed definition and elaboration of the precepts of open systems ontology and theorising and its nexus to Post Keynesianism, see Mearman (2002a).

7 Mearman (2006), Chick and Dow (2005) and Hodgson (2006, Chapters 5, 6 and 7) question to quite a technical degree the definition of open systems used by Lawson. Chick and Dow (2005) provide a useful assessment of the nature of open-system theorising and the conceptualisation of open-system thinking. Nevertheless, as Chick and Dow (2005, p. 378) conclude, although there is a need to clarify meanings, the 'difference between our understanding of open and closed systems and that of the critical realists seems to stem primarily from different use of language, different starting-points and different emphases'. As they acknowledge, the gulf that separates mainstream economists and more heterodox approaches stems from an underlying difference in mode of thought (see also Bigo 2006, p. 512). This mode of thought, we would posit, is in essence a stress on agency, transformation, organic independence and explanation, i.e. the broad conclusion argued for here holds at a general level, notwithstanding the active discussion that is currently underway in the literature.

8 Indeed, this methodological tenet implicitly underpins the methodological individualism espoused by many mainstream theorists. This should not be conflated with the Austrians here who adopt a distinct subjectivist variant of methodological individualism (see Hodgson, 1988; Dow, 1996a). Indeed, one might distinguish between the Austrians and the neoclassical approach in terms of acceptance or recognition of the additiveness closure condition. Such a suggestion underscores the argument sometimes made by Post Keynesians that Austrians need to outline more precisely their distinctiveness from the mainstream and the nature and meaning of their discussion of uncertainty (see Chapter 8 below).

9 See Chick and Dow (2005) for a useful clarification of the nature and meaning of open systems and the implications for theory development.

10 They also assert that such an approach lends itself to 'simplistic' realism which justifies its approach in terms of surface phenomena.

11 Lawson (1989a, 1997a) has chosen to change the terminology in order to convey a more precise delineation of the alternative method envisaged in Kaldor's (1972, 1985) original formulation. As he argues, 'although previously I have adopted the terminology of *stylised facts* myself, I now consider this strategically unwise. For I take it that use of the term *stylised* in this context means something like "to cause to conform to a style of expression often extreme in character rather than the appearance of nature" (*Webster's Third New International Dictionary*). In other words, a supposed "stylised fact" is intended to express a partial regularity reformulated as a strict one, in the form of a law. Kaldor, of course, saw this as a matter of mere presentation ... and always emphasised the role of such "facts" as suggestive of a phenomenon in need of an explanation. Increasingly, however, we can see mainstream deductivist modellers attempting to legitimise their "whenever this then that" formalisations as stylised facts interpreted as Kaldorian. In other words, the terminology, or rather its lineage, is being used to attempt to justify some fictitious set of idealisations, with the aim, in turn, of

facilitating nothing more than model tractability, or some such. It is in order to avoid further encouraging this trend that I have preferred the terminology of demi-regs' (Lawson, 1997a, p. 208).

12 To quote Tony Lawson (1994a, p. 526) on this: 'Critical Realism *per se* does not license any particular substantive claim. Of course where Critical Realism is accepted, the aim, will be to discriminate between competing accounts on the basis of explanatory power and the like (see Lawson, 1989a). However, the extent to which this is possible will be severely dependent upon, amongst other things, the context of analysis. But more generally, all theory is fallible; it is historically specific and potentially transformable. It is, then not surprising, and it is perfectly desirable, that competing accounts are sought – even if the aim must be continually to seek to determine, and then provisionally at least to maintain, those accounts that provide the adequate (explanatory powerful) expressions of the relevant aspect(s) of reality.' Lawson (1998a), in an essay in Paul Davidson's *Festschrift*, provides an interesting attempt at 'operationalising' the line and manner of investigation suggested by Critical Realism.

13 This is distinct from the orthodox approach to complexity theory, which typically considers the import of complexity at the epistemological level.

14 It could be argued that this lack of gross substitutability suggests common ground for Kalecki and even for Sraffa's fixed coefficient models. Differences with the latter two schools of thought occur only to the extent that Sraffians use closed-system reasoning and thus reject both nonergodicity (they argue for persistent centres of gravity) and a role for non-neutral money (which all Post Keynesians accept). See, for example, Lawson (1994a) and Pratten (1996a, 1996b), who argue at length that Sraffians utilise a closed-system approach and thus should not be considered as part of the Post Keynesian core. Downward (2000; see also Downward *et al.*, 1996; Downward, *et al*, 1996) presents a realist appraisal of Post Keynesian price theory in this manner, in sharp contrast to Walters and Young (1999b, p. 105), who somewhat schizophrenically argue, that using open-system reasoning to delineate the nominal features of Post Keynesianism 'would narrow the range of insights and diminish the early pluralism'. On the one hand Walters and Young argue that the pluralism of Post Keynesianism undermines its coherence, and on the other argue that its diversity is to be welcomed. Clearly the coherence of argument is an anathema to Walters and Young.

15 Davidson (1996, p. 494) provides evidence for this assertion by suggesting that in 'the preface to the German-language edition of *The General Theory*, Keynes stated that he had called "his theory a general theory ... [because] it is based on fewer restrictive assumptions [weniger enge Voraussetzungen stutz] than orthodox theory" (cf. Schefold, 1980, p. 175). In other words, theories that require fewer axioms are more general.'

16 *The General Theory* is in essence a theory of a monetary economy. In earlier drafts of *The General Theory* Keynes sought to explicitly distinguish between monetary economics and real-exchange economies (Keynes, 1973b, p. 409).

17 As Potts (2000, p. 47; cf. Mearman, 2002a) notes, 'all reference to technological changes, entrepreneurial processes, imagination, creativity, uncertainty and suchlike is excluded from the domain of analysis. Such phenomena only exist with respect to an open system, and in so far as they are regarded as important explanatory factors, the closed system format becomes the subject of critique.'

18 Process, as used throughout this thesis, refers to more than just a sequence of events: '*process* denotes here the genesis, reproduction and decline of some structure, mechanism or thing, the formation, reformation and decay of some entity *in time*. Clearly, if society is intrinsically dynamic, social science must be alert, and its methods tailored, to this condition' (Lawson, 1997a, p. 34, italics added).

19 Nonergodicity is thus a *necessary* but not a *sufficient* condition for the existence of an open-system process. For example, chaotic models are deterministic immutable reality closed-system models (Davidson, 1996). However, deterministic complexity

models can generate nonergodic time paths, which place severe limits on the ability of agents to successfully predict the future (Rosser, 1998). Since immutable closed-system models generate nonergodic time paths nonergodicity is not a sufficient condition for the existence of an open-system. But all open systems are nonergodic (by definition) and therefore nonergodicity represents a necessary condition for the existence of transmutable processes. Davidson (1996), however, has recognised this and expanded his discussion beyond the purely stochastic associations of the ergodic axiom, noting that in classical non-stochastic, deterministic models, the *ordering* axiom plays the same role as the ergodic axiom in stochastic models – making calendar time meaningless or at least unimportant. Davidson subsumes the rejection of both the ordering and ergodic axioms under the rubric of transmutability, which is synonymous with Lawson's characterisation of open systems. See Chapter 6 for a further elaboration of this argument.

20 As Mearman (2002b, pp. 574–5) points out, '[t]he existence of real agency is one identifying mark of an open system because, therein, real agency is allowed because the system has no predetermined outcomes'.

21 As Potts (2000, p. 48) somewhat idiosyncratically puts it: 'In an open system it is not the relative quantities of ingredients that is the underlying dynamic, but the way they are put together. And if this is to be sensibly interpreted, then the complete set of connections cannot be meaningfully defined *a priori*'.

22 As Caldwell (1989, p. 58) has pointed out: 'Post Keynesians value explanation in economics more than they do predictions'.

23 We have chosen to restrict the citations to pre-1997 contributions to highlight the fact, referred to above in note 5, that Walters and Young missed several basic contributions.

24 Dow (1996a, pp. 13–14) defines a closed system as one whose boundaries and component variables are known, whose interactions are knowable and determinate, where deductive logic is appropriate, and where behaviour is independent.

25 Potts (2000, p. 47) suggests that we may analytically describe 'a system [as] "closed" when we can exhaustively define everything in the set of things that exist, and then permit nothing else to enter'. This accords with the discussion above. Nevertheless, while Potts (2000) offers the prospect of refining the contrast between closed (immutable, ergodic) and open (transmutable, nonergodic) systems in terms of the distinction between integral and non-integral space, it is perhaps too early to import this analytical treatment into a defence of the Post Keynesian approach. While Potts (2000) offers an original synthetic approach to heterodoxy in his rush to identify an all-encompassing method he carelessly embraces closed-system attempts to theorise about cognitive and heuristic structures and their links to hierarchical structures, which we would reject (cf. Dunn, 1999, 2001a; see also 2002). We do not pursue the linkages as such further here.

26 It should be noted that while the distinction between open and closed systems is largely identified with Critical Realism, the use of the term does not entail an unqualified acceptance of the Critical Realist perspective. Rather it is intended to highlight a concern for the serious study of 'fundamental' uncertainty as it bears down upon economic agents.

27 Indeed, the 'Questions for Kaleckians' debate initiated by Steedman (1992) and the Kaleckian responses by Sawyer (1992d) and Steindl (1993), among others, can be made intelligible from this perspective. Kaleckians, aware of the importance of uncertainty and open-system processes, make little use of closed-system equilibrium analysis, especially at the macroeconomic level (see Sawyer, 1992d, p. 153).

28 As Joan Robinson (1962a, p. 78) observes: 'The concept of equilibrium, of course is an indispensable tool of analysis. Even Marx makes use of the case of simple reproduction to clear the ground for his analysis of accumulation in terms of saving and investment; simple reproduction, where the stock of all capital goods is being kept intact, has a great deal in common with Pigou's "through-going stationary state".

But to use the equilibrium concept one has to keep it in its place, and its place is strictly in the preliminary stages of analytical argument, not in the framing of hypotheses to be tested against the facts, for we know perfectly well that we shall not find facts in a state of equilibrium'.

29 For example, Arestis (1996a) recanted his earlier (Arestis, 1990) inclusion of the Sraffians under the Post Keynesian label. However, in his discussion of production, prices and pricing he suggests that the 'post-Keynesian production model is an input–output model that is characterised by the assumption that inputs can be used only in fixed proportions with each other in production' (Arestis, 1996a, p. 121; cf. Lee, 1985, 1998). Moreover, he acknowledges that while Leontief (1951) framed it in both theoretical and empirical terms it 'can be related to Sraffa's (1960) fixed-coefficient model and Pasinetti's (1981) input–output model, both of which highlight issues of distribution and growth' (Arestis, 1996a, p. 121). In parenthesis it is worth highlighting the fact that the Sraffian system does not presume fixed production coefficients. Rather, Sraffa assumed given output and thus production coefficients might (will) change as output changes (cf. Lee, 1998, and his discussion of production theory and costs).

30 Sawyer (1989, p. 3) appends the prefix 'radical' onto such a delineation and definition of political economy in order to distinguish it from the constitutional political economy approach of Buchanan (1987) which augments the orthodox approach by evaluating different 'rules of the game' which are typically taken as given.

31 The rejection of the ergodic axiom makes the concept of the long run as 'an asymptotic end of a process of learning' meaningless in terms of description of some real-world situations. Kalecki also rejects the long-run construction and so shares this foundation with all Post Keynesians (see Chapter 6 below).

4 Delineating Post Keynesian economics

To stress the basis of all economic activity in more or less uncertain expectations is precisely to emphasize the openness and incompleteness of economic theorizing and explanation.

Alan Coddington (1976, p. 1263)

The ability to define what may happen in the future and to choose among alternatives lies at the heart of contemporary societies.

Peter L. Bernstein (1996, p. 2)

INTRODUCTION

In the last chapter we argued that Post Keynesianism exhibits a coherent methodological vision, which can be summarised as a commitment to a nonergodic, open-systems mode of theorising that enables economists to take uncertainty seriously. That is to say, Post Keynesians adopt a similar non-deterministic view of social process that is largely congruent with the Critical Realist distinction between closed-and open-system theorising.

This, however, raises a further set of important and urgent questions that need to be addressed if Post Keynesians are to continue to make progress in their quest to develop an alternative approach to economics. Firstly, is Post Keynesian economics anything more than a philosophical position? Is it just an inferior version of, or forerunner to, Critical Realism that has since been superseded by the systematic elaboration of Lawson (1997a)? Are there some substantive assessments shared by all Post Keynesians, but not necessarily held by those who adopt a Critical Realist perspective? Similarly, if Critical Realism connects competing heterodox traditions, then what distinguishes them?

This chapter assesses how, if at all, Critical Realism can assist the continued development of the Post Keynesian project. We elaborate the claim that it is only possible to do full justice to Post Keynesian insights about money, unemployment, effective demand, and political and economic institutions, e.g. nominal wage contracts, within an open-systems framework like that outlined by Critical Realism. We argue that the unifying recognition of the salience of money, radical uncertainty, institutions and the principle of effective demand is embedded in this ontological view. A greater understanding of Critical Realism and its open-systems methodology would further allow Post Keynesians to develop their ideas about money, contracts, conventions, effective demand and so on. These insights can then be built on by integrating insights from other heterodox traditions that adopt a view of social processes as transmutable and open – the argument of Chapter 7.

The structure of this chapter is as follows. Over the next two sections we consider the relationship between Critical Realism and Post Keynesianism, noting their accord at an ontological level, i.e. that both Critical Realism and Post Keynesianism are committed to an open-systems mode of theorising. The reader familiar with the argument of previous chapters is encouraged to skip these sections as by now they will be seen to rehearse familiar arguments. The latter part of this chapter highlights how the central themes of monetary accumulation under conditions of uncertainty and their relationship to the principle of effective demand are linked to the open-systems ontology that Post Keynesians espouse – and accounts for its distinctiveness. We also indicate the further import of Critical Realism to Post Keynesianism, arguing that it can be marshalled to further inform theorising about uncertainty itself.

CRITICAL REALISM

Critical Realism is a philosophical approach to economics that has been systematised in the 1980s and 1990s. It seeks to provide insights at a higher level of abstraction than substantive theory. It under-labours for social science and accordingly should not be conceived as a substitute for substantive scientific enquiry. One of the principal contributions that Critical Realism has sought to make is to identify the essence of mainstream economics (Lawson, 2006a). Many critics of mainstream economics, including some Post Keynesians, isolate and focus upon its substantive claims that are expressed through its theories of rationality and equilibrium. In sharp contrast, Critical Realists such as Lawson (1997a, pp. 69–107) contend that mainstream economics is best understood and delineated in terms of its, generally implicit, deductivist, closed-system method. According to this perspective mainstream economics seeks to elaborate (real or purely imagined) universal event regularities and to develop theoretical explanations of the (general) form 'whenever event (type) X, then event (type) Y'. This approach, applied to economics, assumes that closed systems, and the event regularities that typify them, characterise the social realm.

As noted above, Critical Realists argue that apart from astronomy, the majority of strict event regularities identified by science have been generated under the conditions of experimental control.[1] Critical Realists argue, in sharp contrast to mainstream economists, that the social world is not closed because the phenomena under consideration are transmutable, i.e. economic agents possess the capacity for creative, crucial substantive choice. As Lawson (1997a, p. 219) points out, 'given the dependence of social mechanisms upon inherently transformative human agency, where human beings chose their courses of action (and so could have always acted otherwise), strict constancy seems a quite unlikely eventuality'. As a result, even while (event) regularities in the social realm are not ruled out, where they do so arise they do so because of the unceasing interaction between the reflexive choices of human agents and the social structures and institutions that underpin them. This implies that such occurrences will be partial and multi-faceted and neither predictable nor universal. Moreover, mainstream economics, by applying a closed-system ontology to the study of open processes, results in inconsistencies at the level of method, social theory and methodology (Lawson, 1997a, pp. 5–14, 36–42).

In response to the widespread (explanatory) failures of deductivism, Critical Realism argues that the most philosophically tenable conception of *objective* reality is one that is open, structured, and governed by causal mechanisms (Lawson, 1997a, pp. 43–65). Critical Realism proposes a reorientation of social enquiry to questions of ontology. It advances a distinct, layered ontology that comprises three levels: the *empirical* domain of experience and impression, the *actual* domain of events, and the *deep* or *real* domain of structure, powers, tendencies and generative mechanisms. These domains are viewed as distinct and out of phase with each other and unlikely to give rise to strict event regularities. Critical Realists argue that intransitivity occurs at the level of structure and not at the level of observed event regularities, and thus that the aim of science is to identify and explain (retroduce) the structures and mechanisms that characterise the *real* domain (Lawson, 1997a, pp. 24–6). This moves beyond the essentially flat ontology exhausted by events and experiences postulated by the deductivist approach.

However, although Critical Realists maintain that, *a posteriori*, there appear to be clear limits on the possibility of bringing about closure in the social realm, the inescapable hermeneutic moment in the social sciences provides an alternative and compensatory route which facilitates the identification of underpinning causal mechanisms and fundamentally changes the nature of economic enquiry (see Lawson, 1997a, pp. 199–226). From this perspective the objective of social inquiry is to move beyond surface phenomena and develop abstractions that are appropriate and concerned with real social structures (and not artificial constructs). These social structures are not in any sense fixed or immutable but emerge and are reproduced or transformed through the intentions and actions of (economic) agents. As Lawson (1997a, p. 35) notes, 'the impossibility of engineering, and the absence of spontaneously occurring, closed social systems, necessitates a reliance upon non-predictive, purely explanatory, criteria of theory development and assessment in the social sciences'.

OPEN SYSTEMS AND TRANSMUTABILITY

As noted above, there are many connections between the methodology of Post Keynesian economics and Critical Realism. Post Keynesians incorporate many of the insights that can be gleaned from the realist perspective into their account of the processes of the social realm. Both Critical Realism and Post Keynesian economics view social positions, rules and relations as those that are created at any point in time through the shared and mimetically derived actions of agents. Social structure and human agency are recursively related, that is to say, each is both a condition for, and a consequence of, the other (Lawson, 1997a, pp. 160–73). Post Keynesians typically employ a methodology that sometimes explicitly, or implicitly, approximates a realist understanding of science, nature and society.

The Critical Realist focus on methodology and associated distinction between open and closed systems is broadly similar to the Post Keynesian distinction between immutable (ergodic) systems and transmutable (nonergodic) systems. Post Keynesians, following Davidson (1982–3, 1988, 1996), argue that mainstream models are underpinned by the hypothesis of ergodicity. Ergodicity refers to the property by which the time and space averages, that originate and are computed from any data generating process, either coincide for a series of infinite observations or converge as the number of observations increases (with a probability of one) for a finite number. That is to say, averages from past realisations collapse on the objective probability distribution that governs current and future outcomes. Under the ergodic hypothesis the passage of time does not affect the joint probability laws governing processes, so that history and time ultimately do not matter.

The distinction made by Post Keynesians between ergodic and nonergodic processes corresponds closely to the Critical Realist distinction between closed and open systems. Assuming that observable events can be exhaustively described by some invariant conditional probability distribution is tantamount to saying that the process under consideration (a) can be subject to experimental control and (b) exhibits strict event regularities. The principal distinction is, however, that the regularities under consideration are expressed in probabilistic terms, i.e. they are stochastic event regularities. Stochastic process theory, in other words, is just one more (probabilistic) expression of orthodox economics' commitment to deductivism (Lawson, 1997a, pp. 17, 69, 76).

Like Critical Realists, Post Keynesians oppose the characterisation of the social world as closed and the dogmatic adherence to a formalistic and deductivist closed-system approach to modelling in the face of compelling evidence that social scientists have failed to find significant event regularities in the social realm. Following Keynes (1973c, p. 289), both Post Keynesians and Critical Realists recognise that 'the economic environment is not homogenous over time'. Both Post Keynesians and Critical Realists accept that economics is a moral science, that economics deals with introspection, values, motives, expectations and psychological uncertainties:

> One has to be constantly on guard against treating the material as constant and homogenous. It is as though the fall of the apple to the ground depended on the apple's motives, on whether it is worth falling to the ground, the whether the ground wanted the apple to fall, and on mistaken calculations on the part of the apple as to how far it was from the centre of the earth. (Keynes, 1973c, p. 300).

Consistent with this, and also with Critical Realism, Post Keynesians seek to go beneath purely stochastic considerations, identifying the underlying causal mechanisms and emergent properties and structures that generate nonergodic time series. In a much-neglected aspect of his discussion of nonergodicity, Davidson (1982–3, p. 192) emphasises the link to Shackle's concept of creative, crucial decision-making, arguing that the existence of crucial decision-making represents a sufficient condition for the existence of nonergodic processes. Where creative human agency is present, simply processing information from the past is likely to provide insufficient information about the course of future events to guide current activity.

In linking nonergodicity to Shackle's concept of crucial decision-making, Davidson advocates a broader, creative view of agency than that contained within mainstream models of human behaviour. Accordingly, he has expanded the concept of ergodicity to incorporate non-stochastic processes (Davidson, 1991a). Deterministic models of decision-making which are elaborated in logical time require Savage's ordering axiom – the presumption, at least in principle, that agents can make a transitive ordering over all possible outcomes. This involves a pre-programmed future and invokes a substantive rationality that is inconsistent with the creativity which Post Keynesians impute *a posteriori* to agents. Post Keynesians recognise that it is impossible to form a transitive ordering over a yet-to-be created future in which circumstances inconceivable at the point of origination emerge.

Subsequently, and in response to the numerous meanings that could be imputed to nonergodicity, as well as to encompass developments in complexity and chaos theory, Davidson (1996) has reformulated his discussion in terms of a distinction between immutable and transmutable economic processes. Immutability encompasses the ergodic and ordering axioms and embodies 'the presumption of a programmed stable, conservative system where the past, present and future reality are predetermined whether the system is stochastic or not' (Davidson, 1996, pp. 480–1). In models which assume that socio-economic reality is immutable, history is predetermined and choice is neither genuine nor matters. Under such a reformulation immutability refers to attempts to elaborate (real or imagined) universal event regularities and to develop theoretical structures of the general form 'whenever event (type) X, then event (type) Y'. Thus the Post Keynesian conceptualisation of time closely parallels Lawson's discussion of closed systems. In contrast, the broader notion of transmutability advanced by Post Keynesians encompasses the stochastic discussion of nonergodicity within a creative and emergent conceptualisation of history in which choice is genuine, matters, and can make a difference in the long run – not least in affecting liquidity considerations and influencing the employment path of an economy over time. As Arestis (1996a, p. 117) observes: '[t]he essence of *uncertainty* in Post Keynesian economic theory is grounded in a nonergodic, non-deterministic world understood as an open-system.' All Post Keynesians share this vision and this paves the way for the recognition that the fact that the socio-economic world is open can be used by Post Keynesians to underpin their claims to coherence, especially at the methodological level.

In summary, the commitment to transmutable open-system theorising is the methodological glue that binds Post Keynesians and Critical Realists together. Post Keynesians argue that mainstream economics is characterised by a methodology of ergodic, closed-system reasoning which ultimately prohibits a substantive role for money and its associated institutions, historical time and the nature of choice under uncertainty.[2] Post Keynesians argue that economic agents are social embedded agents who, either individually or collectively, can make a difference in the long run. This means that outcomes are neither predetermined nor preordained and that economic science must value explanation above prediction. Like Critical Realists, Post Keynesians aim to provide *causal explanations* of concrete economic phenomena which are couched in terms of abstract, but nevertheless descriptively adequate, statements of the objects of investigation, as opposed to other approaches that by their own admission represent fictitious idealisations (Hicks, 1979; Shackle, 1979a; Davidson, 1980; cf. Lawson, 1997a; Lee, 2002). While some further clarification and debate may still be needed, a fundamental methodological outlook that characterises Post Keynesian economists can be discerned – *a commitment to open-system theorising*, an approach which exhibits, at core, a stress on agency, transformation, organic interdependence and explanation (see the previous chapter).

Thus, while, as Lawson (1999a, p. 13) points out, such 'discussion and debate over connections and limitations are still at an early stage', it is suggested that Post Keynesian coherence and synergies with Critical Realism can be identified at the methodological level. However, although we can accept that Post Keynesianism and Critical Realism may share similar ontological perspectives and that this can underpin claims of methodological coherence, the question arises: what (if anything) actually distinguishes Post Keynesianism and Critical Realism? As Lawson (1999a, p. 9) has asked, is Post Keynesianism 'ultimately anything more than a philosophical position?'

POST KEYNESIAN ECONOMICS: AN OPEN-SYSTEMS APPROACH

Although Critical Realism is ontologically bold, it is epistemologically cautious. The 'primary aim of the project of Critical Realism in economics in particular is to bring ontological considerations (back) into the economics picture and to indicate real possibilities in the social realm, [although] it cannot determine *a priori* which possibilities are to be actualised in any local context' (Lawson, 1999a, p. 7; see also Lawson, 2006a,b, 2007b). The project systematised as Critical Realism does not in itself seek to uncover or investigate the specific structures and emergent processes that warrant scientific investigation. Proponents of Critical Realism argue instead that it is the task of the individual sciences to assess and investigate the specific social structures, totalities and processes that emerge and warrant further examination. Nevertheless, it is unlikely that a definitive Critical Realist account would emerge in these individual sciences. Given that the world is dynamic and open it is unsurprising that social scientists utilising a Critical Realist framework compose different explanatory accounts of certain phenomena. Moreover, even if a dominant explanation does emerge, on account of its ability to render intelligible the relevant phenomenon, it does not follow that such a rationalisation is conclusive. All knowledge is provisional, fallible and possibly transient. Science is itself a social enquiry and the conclusions of science are not in any sense fixed or immutable but emerge and are reproduced, or transformed, through the actions of scientists.

According to the general Critical Realist perspective, the objective of economics is to understand and explain the institutions, conventions and social processes by which human agents *reproduce* and *transform* society. A Post Keynesian economics informed by Critical Realism 'attempts to identify those structures, mechanisms, and so on, that allow us to think about questions of employment, output, growth, inflation, and distribution, and from which we can retroduce scientific statements about observable outcomes to explanations in terms of the causal mechanisms that facilitated or produced these outcomes' (Rotheim, 1999, p. 80). Inasmuch as Post Keynesianism can represent a distinct realist approach, it seeks to investigate the specific institutional structures that generate different levels of employment across different periods in history and across different countries and regions.[3] From this perspective Post Keynesian economics should be viewed as a specific mode of enquiry into developed capitalist economies which agues that they are best understood through their financial institutions and the money–credit nexus.

At the centre of this methodological core is the principle of effective demand (cf. Dow and Earl, 1984). This principle is embedded in the rejection of the *a priori* assumption that the economic world can be characterised as ergodic or as a closed system. The Post Keynesian explanation of the level of (un)employment is based on the principle of effective demand; it is not based upon wage rigidity, adaptive expectations, bounded rationality, money illusion, market structure, or any other imperfection that one chooses to identify (see Davidson, 1982–3, 1985b, 1994; Sawyer, 1995).

The principle of effective demand embodies the recognition that certain structures and institutions, such as the wage bargain and the civil law of contracts, may have emerged as a sensible response to mitigate the impact of an uncertain future. As Arrow and Hahn (1971, pp. 356–7) have argued: 'the terms in which contracts are made matter. In particular, if money is the good in terms of which contracts are made, then the prices of goods in terms of money are of special significance. *This is not the case if we consider an economy without a past or a future* [i.e. in a closed theoretical system] ... If a serious monetary theory comes to be written, the fact that contracts are made in terms of money will be of considerable importance.' Closed theoretical models such as general equilibrium constructions, however, entail an economy where money is merely a neutral numeraire which does not impinge on real production and consumption decisions.

In contrast, an open-systems approach to economic theorising provides a foundation for 'serious monetary theory' by emphasising the need for contracts made in terms of non-neutral money. In the absence of conditions of ergodicity or closure, i.e. the absence of strict event regularities, stochastic or otherwise, agents are truly uncertain as to the future. Such a perspective recognises the fact that production takes place through historical time and that in contemporary capitalism money-denominated contracts facilitate the efficient organisation of time-consuming production (and exchange) activities by providing some assurances to the contracting parties as to the delivery of future commitments (Davidson, 1988, p. 333). Similarly, such contracts provide information as to the likely relationship between the current and future costs and commitments and allow agents to plan in the context of an uncertain future. Moreover, liquid assets such as money help people deal with uncertainty by providing them with the ability to respond to unforeseen contingencies and discharge contractual commitments when they arise.

Post Keynesians recognise the importance of specific entrepreneurial institutions – particularly the civil law of contracts – and the use of money in mitigating the impact of uncertainty and allowing agents and organisations to plan for the future (Davidson, 1972; Rotheim, 1999). This implicitly suggests an overlap with the (older) Institutionalists (see Dunn, 2000a), but draws attention to the Post Keynesian interest in the *specific* institutions that generate different levels of employment within different periods in history (cf. Arestis and Eichner, 1988). Classical theory, which requires neutral money and re-contracting without penalty in order to maintain a closed theoretical schema, is clearly incompatible with Post Keynesian economics.

In an uncertain, open world, if society organises its production and trading relationships via the use of nominal contracts then we have what Keynes referred to as an entrepreneurial system, where money is used to settle all obligations that arise in production and exchange agreements (Davidson, 1972, 1994; Rotheim, 1999). Goods trade for money and money for goods but goods do not trade for goods. In order for money and other non-producible 'resting places for saving' to exist, and for involuntary unemployment to emerge, the elasticity of substitution between non-producibles, i.e. money, and the products of industry must be approximately zero.[4] In the absence of constant conjunctions of events, i.e. in an open system, the future appears uncertain and agents, as expectations about the future become more cautious, will defer or abandon planned purchases of goods and services and choose to hold liquid asserts that will enable them to preserve their (crucial) decisions till another day. As the demand for goods and services falls, then so does the (derived) demand for labour, resulting in an increase in (involuntary) unemployment. Concomitantly, as the demand for liquid assets, such as money, increases, then so does its price level. However, as liquid assets are non-producible, then, as the price rises, unemployed workers cannot voluntarily re-employ themselves by producing liquid assets. Moreover, as liquid assets are non-substitutable, the rising price will not induce a spill-over of demand towards reproducible assets and thus will not effect an expansion in employment in such goods-producing industries (Davidson, 1972, 1974).

It is the recognition of the salience of uncertainty and of historical time as it bears upon the decision to act which, in conjunction with the essential properties of money, that of zero elasticity of both production and substitution, represents a necessary and sufficient condition for the emergence of unemployment. As the future becomes more uncertain, individual agents deciding to hold non-reproducible, non-substitutable liquid assets, i.e. money, are then able to defer entering into contractual commitments with other agents and are saved to make a decision another day. However, while such decisions to hold money are sensible from an individual perspective, they do not necessarily make sense from the point of view of the whole economy. Unemployment develops as the demand for liquidity expands in response to an increase in dispersed 'fundamental' uncertainty. As Hahn (1977, pp. 31, 39) stated, an unemployment equilibrium can occur as long as there are 'resting places for saving other than reproducible money... if we study an economy which is not a barter economy... then any non-reproducible asset allows for a choice between employment-inducing and non-employment-inducing demand.'

It is this recognition of the substantive role for money in a credit production economy, in which goods buy money and money buys goods but goods do not buy goods, that undermines the *a priori* demonstration of the effectiveness of the market in coordinating economic activity. Davidson (1996, p. 20) notes correctly that Arrow and Hahn (1971, p. 361) have demonstrated that 'all general (full employment) equilibrium existence proofs are jeopardized in a world with fixed money contracts over time; no general equilibrium may exist. A nonergodic setting provides the analytical basis for the use of fixed money contracts and therefore provides for the possibility of the existence of long-period unemployment equilibrium – and the possibility of the non-existence of a general (i.e. full employment) equilibrium in the absence of deliberate government policy to assure there is never a lack of aggregate effective demand.' It is for these reasons that Post Keynesians develop theoretical structures that highlight how political and economic institutions can act as a channel for effective demand and influence the amount of activity in an economy, and why they explicitly consider the distributional *and normative* implications of their analysis (Arestis and Sawyer, 1998, 1999).

It is the openness or transmutability of the socio-economic world, i.e. set in historical time and displaying radical uncertainty, which, in conjunction with the essential properties of money, has underpinned Post Keynesian explanations of unemployment, distinguishing it from other open-systems approaches. Post Keynesian economists have developed theoretical frameworks that highlight how political and economic institutions act as a conduit for effective demand, determining the level of activity in an economy, yielding the possibility of involuntary unemployment (Robinson, 1962a; Davidson, 1994). The fact that the solution to such problems, as Keynes (1931) noted, 'lies outside the operations of individuals' relates to identification of the importance of the fallacy of composition (which is committed when a conclusion is drawn about a whole based on the features of its constituents when, in fact, no justification is provided for the inference) and its nexus to a monetary economy existing in historical time.[5] As Davidson notes:

> In a nonergodic [open] system plagued by persistent long-period underemployment equilibrium, society can intelligently control and improve the performance of the economy by developing governmental policies to influence, directly or indirectly, entrepreneurial animal spirits sufficiently to offset agents' excessive aggregate demand for liquidity. Keynes' suggestion (1936, pp. 377–9) that policies be designed to assure that there is never a lack of effective demand does not require a prescient government. All that is necessary is the development of institutions that act as a balance-wheel by providing a guiding influence (a) in stimulating effective demand whenever the private sector displays a propensity to produce a lack of effective demand and (b) in reducing demand whenever over full employment conditions prevails.
>
> (Davidson, 1996, p. 21)

A Post Keynesian economics informed by Critical Realism recognises the associated problems with fine-tuning and hydraulic Keynesianism and the importance and influence (sometimes positive, sometimes negative) of government activism and regulation upon entrepreneurial confidence and expectations. While it is clear that neither governments *nor individuals* are omniscient or omnipotent, it is possible to draw attention to the causal mechanisms and social structures that underpin the ability of governments to pump-prime effective demand and repay and sustain loans and finance deficits above and beyond the level that we might think prudent from an individual point of view.[6] That is to say, Post Keynesian economists have highlighted the fact that a government differs from individual agents in many important dimensions, not least in terms of: its democratic accountability; its relative longevity; the fact that it can borrow at rates substantially below those at which individuals can; and its legal authority to levy taxes, print money and enforce contractual (debt) obligations. It is these mechanisms and structures, which are embedded in social conventions and practices, that underpin the identification of the significance of the principle of effective demand.

Moreover, such caution in policy-making recognises that knowledge of the economy is provisional, fallible and historically contingent and is grounded in a retroductive methodology. Nevertheless it does not undermine the *a posteriori* conclusion that a monetary production economy passing through real time is unlikely to generate a high and stable level of employment, and thus there is *prima facie* evidence that as mass unemployment develops, there develops a role for what Arestis and Sawyer (1998, p. 187) refer to as 'coarse' tuning whereby 'over the medium term the government seeks to ensure an adequate level of aggregate demand through the usual channels of the balance between taxation and government expenditure and ... through the balance between savings and investment.'

UNCERTAINTY AS AN EMERGENT PROCESS

Nevertheless, while the ontological distinction between closed and open systems is broadly similar to the distinction between immutable and transmutable processes, it is clear that the Post Keynesian discussion of uncertainty can be further extended with reference to the Critical Realist method. As discussed above, Post Keynesians have been keen to follow Keynes and integrate the fact that individuals cannot know the future into their economic analysis.[7] However Keynes' and much Post Keynesian discussion, while suggestive of a transformative conception of the economic process, does not seek to identify the generative mechanisms and interactions that give rise to uncertainty and reverberate through the state of long-term expectations. Occasionally Post Keynesians appear to employ and treat uncertainty as an ahistorical *deus ex machina* in order to drive a stake into institutional stability – see, for example, the discussion of Keynes in the next chapter. Such an approach, however, leaves the origins and emergence of the salience of uncertainty unaddressed. Why is the future uncertain? Is it just that we simply cannot know the future? Or are there reasons why our knowledge about the future is limited? And how can uncertainty increase over time? How and why do economic agents become more uncertain? By employing the Critical Realist method and considering history, we come to view uncertainty both as a product of human agency and as having a causal and irreducible impact upon human agency. This is also the argument of Shackle and Davidson. That creative crucial decision-making by economic agents injects emergent and essential novelty into the competitive process and creates uncertainty as to the recoverability of investments for other economic agents.

The Critical Realist method argues for the importance of the concept of emergence for scientific enquiry. Emergence may be defined 'as a relationship between two features or aspects such that one arises out of another and yet, while perhaps being capable of reacting back on it, remains causally and taxonomically irreducible to it' (Lawson, 1997a, p. 63). The argument developed is that uncertainty itself should be viewed as a dynamic emergent process of interaction between pre-existing social structures, such as money and accounting practices, and human agency. What is more, the reality of uncertainty is reproduced and transformed in significance over time.[8] The existence and presence of uncertainty, as it influences and is influenced by economic action, is embedded in the inherited practices of the present and reproduced and transformed in its contemporary significance over time.

The widespread recognition and usage of forward-looking epistemological concepts such as risk and uncertainty is a comparatively recent phenomenon, bound up with the many advances promulgated through the Renaissance. Indeed, historical study suggests it is only comparatively recently that the notions and reality of risk and uncertainty have emerged into everyday discourse and become themselves objects of scientific (real) inquiry:

> The revolutionary idea that defines the boundary between modern times and the past is the mastery of risk: the notion that the future is more than a whim

of the gods and that men and women are not passive before nature. Until human beings discovered a way across that boundary, the future was a mirror of the past or the murky domain of oracles and soothsayers who held a monopoly over knowledge of anticipated events.

(Bernstein, 1996, p. 1).

Except for some marginal instances in the Middle Ages, there was no concept of risk or uncertainty nor any need for such concepts. Bernstein (1996) and Giddens (2003) date the emergence of the notion of risk to the 16th and 17th centuries. They argue that Western explorers first used it as they journeyed off into the unknown in search of new continents, cultures and experiences in the pursuit of riches and wealth:

> The profit on an investment in goods that must be shipped over long distances before they reach their market depends on more than just the weather. It also depends on informed judgements about consumer needs, pricing levels, and fashions at the time of the cargo's arrival, to say nothing of the cost of financing the goods until they are delivered, sold and paid for. As a result forecasting – long denigrated as a waste of time at best and a sin at worst – became an absolute necessity in the course of the seventeenth century for adventuresome entrepreneurs who were willing to take the risk of shaping the future according to their own design.
>
> (Bernstein, 1996, p. 95)

The phrase 'risk' seems to have entered the English language 'through Spanish or Portuguese, where it was used to refer to sailing into uncharted waters. Originally, in other words, it had an orientation to space. Later, it became transferred to time, as used in banking and investment, to mean calculation of the probable consequences of investment decisions for borrowers and lenders. It subsequently came to refer to a wide range of other situations of uncertainty' (Giddens, 2003, pp. 21–22)[9].

A series of factors – money, the desire for accumulation and exploration, the development of rules and routines, such as double-entry book-keeping, and new institutions, such as the Joint Stock Corporation – combined to underpin the emergence of uncertainty and risk as salient social categories and business concepts (Bernstein, 1996). That is to say, the forward-looking nature of monetary accumulation combined with new accountancy practices and new organisational models to characterise the emergence of capitalism, and gave rise to the increasingly widespread usage of future-oriented concepts such as risk and uncertainty, simultaneously underscoring their reality. The emergence of such epistemological concepts reflects the embryonic reality of uncertainty. As Weber (1930, p. 76) pointed out, the chief characteristic of the modern capitalist economy is that it 'is rationalised on the basis of rigorous calculation, directed with foresight and caution towards the economic success which is sought in sharp contrast to the hand-to-mouth existence of the peasant, and to the privileged traditionalism of the guild craftsman and of the adventurers' capitalism, orientated to the exploitation of political opportunities and irrational speculation'.

Uncertainty in modern industrial societies refers to situations which we have very little historical experience for confronting. The emergence of uncertainty as a salient scientific category within contemporary society reflects emergent novelty that is propelled forward through the dynamics of accumulation and finds a conduit via social structures and conventions, such as the invention of double-entry book-keeping. As Schumpeter (1943, p. 132) argues, 'the function of entrepreneurs is to reform or revolutionise the pattern of production by exploiting an invention or, more generally, an untried technological possibility for producing a new commodity or producing an old one in a new way, by opening up a new source of supply of materials or a new outlet for products, by reorganising an industry and so on'.

Uncertainty thus finds its salience and genesis in the creative, emergent processes associated with competition and capital accumulation. As Schumpeter (1943, p. 83) recognised, '[t]he fundamental impulse that sets and keeps the capitalist engine in motion comes from the new consumers' goods, the new methods of production or transportation, the new markets, the new forms of industrial organisation that capitalist enterprise creates'. It is such nascent novelty, which occurs as a result of the creative actions of some agents, that generates radical uncertainty for others, especially around the decision to invest.

This was the point made by Cliffe Leslie – one of the leading figures in the English historical school, but now forgotten. Leslie recognised that variety, disruption and uncertainty were themselves embedded in the incessant pursuit of avarice:

> The desire for wealth, or of its representative – money – instead of enabling the economist to foretell values and prices, destroys the power of prediction that formerly existed, because it is the mainspring of industrial and commercial activity and progress, of infinite variety and incessant alteration in the structure and operations of the economic world.
>
> (Leslie, 1888, p. 223)

The evolving reality of uncertainty is closely intertwined with the social structures and conventions that underscore the calculation of profit and loss and rise and concomitant accounting processes and practices which fuel the pursuit of avarice and the creatively destructive competitive process.[10] And whereas some structures and conventions pertain to particular macroeconomic contexts, others are more localised, such as the particular positions and associated practices, rules and relations generated and found within particular *microeconomic* institutions and processes. That is to say, the microfoundations of the reality of uncertainty are organically linked to its macroeconomic expression. Uncertainty emerges from localised social contexts to generate an irreducible macroeconomic climate that bears down on economic agents, themselves operating in localised social contexts. Uncertainty emerges as the outcome of the very impact of agents' transformative actions upon the world. Of course the individual elements generating uncertainty are multi-layered and cross-cutting, but it is clear that we can identify specific social structures – such as double-entry book-keeping and new organisational forms and financial institutions – that fuel the incessant drive to introduce new, novel product innovations and technological revolutions, which generate and promulgate uncertainty.

CONCLUDING COMMENTS

In summary, Critical Realism can be viewed as part of a more general philosophical project aimed at understanding the most general statements that can be made about science and social theory. Post Keynesianism can be understood as a Critical Realist elaboration of the study of macroeconomics under uncertainty, of how society copes with scarcity and uncertainty. Nevertheless, while representing different traditions and approaches with different aims and objectives, both Post Keynesians and Critical Realists are united in the belief that, *a posteriori*, the search for sharp empirical regularities in economics is misplaced, and both identify the reason for this in their understanding of the distinctiveness of human choice. Both wish to refute the repeated claims of the mainstream that, whatever the defects of their programme, there is no alternative to their project.

Post Keynesian economics is still quite young, and while many Post Keynesians have given penetrating accounts of the inconsistencies, fallacies and limitations generated by the mainstream project, they have not always been clear about the foundational source of these ills. This is where the under-labouring role of Critical Realism can help inform and clarify the development of a retroductive macroeconomics. The codification of the realist approach embodied in Tony Lawson's (1997a) *Economics and Reality* represents a potential catalyst for the Post Keynesian project to achieve a similar foundational breakthrough. There exists a fundamental methodological vision shared by all Post Keynesians who argue that history, time and money matter. Post Keynesians are *committed to open-system theorising*, which is characterised by its stress on *agency, transformation, organic interdependence and explanation*. Critical Realism offers the prospect of developing an alternative methodological foundation for such a project. Post Keynesian economics offers the prospect of developing a macroeconomic and microeconomic framework that is consistent with this vision.

What is more, the Critical Realism critique of the generally implicit, deductivist, closed-system method of the mainstream is particularly instructive in explaining the obfuscation of the reality of uncertainty within orthodox economics. The orthodox method of closed-system reasoning misrepresents uncertainty by conceptualising it as a subjective probability embedded within a closed-system conceptualisation of the economic process. That is to say, the method of mainstream modellers precludes the recognition and incorporation of the salience of radical uncertainty into their theoretical schemas, despite the widespread evidence of the absence of strict event regularities within the social realm.

Post Keynesians reject the closed, ergodic approach of mainstream modellers as it ultimately renders the concept of choice vacuous and hinders the development of 'serious monetary theory'. In contrast, Post Keynesian monetary theory is founded on the recognition that the world is, in a fundamental sense, open, and that this underscores the recognition of the salience of money-denominated contracts and their nexus to the principle of effective demand. Moreover, this rejection of the ergodic axiom distinguishes Post Keynesians, not only from orthodox neoclassical theory, but also from other schools of thought, which, implicitly or explicitly, invoke such closed-system methods and argue for a predetermined (ergodic) path, denying the reality of uncertainty.

Nevertheless, Post Keynesian economics should not be thought of as *the* Critical Realist account of the macroeconomics of credit production monetary economies. Nonetheless it is the strongest and most substantive articulation of the theoretical implications of assuming that the economic environment is not homogenous over time. In the absence of sharp empirical regularities characterising the social realm, decisions about the future will be fuelled with uncertainty. Post Keynesian economics recognises this fact in elaborating the principle of effective demand.

NOTES

1 Mearman (2006) questions this claim, suggesting that the the solar system is not closed according to the closure conditions identified by critical realism. See Bigo (2006) for a discussion and refutation of the arguments raised by Mearnman from a Critical Realist perspective.

2 We shall discuss this assertion in greater detail below.

3 To quote Tony Lawson (1994a, p. 526) on this: 'Critical Realism *per se* does not license any particular substantive claim. Of course where Critical Realism is accepted, the aim, will be to discriminate between competing accounts on the basis of explanatory power and the like. However, the extent to which this is possible will be severely dependent upon, amongst other things, the context of analysis. But more generally, all theory is fallible; it is historically specific and potentially transformable. It is, then not surprising, and it is perfectly desirable, that competing accounts are sought – even if the aim must be continually to seek to determine, and then provisionally at least to maintain, those accounts that provide the adequate (explanatory powerful) expressions of the relevant aspect(s) of reality.'

4 The low elasticity of production is an essential feature of liquid assets that enables it to preserve its 'moneyness'. As Davidson points out (1972, p. 232; see also Keynes, 1936, p. 237), 'a low elasticity of productivity of money is essential if an increase in the demand for money as a store of value is not to destroy the purchasing power or exchange value of that store of value'.

5 See also Lawson (1997a, pp. 277–81), who highlights the relationship of policy to emancipatory goals.

6 See Arestis and Sawyer, 1997a, 1998, for a more detailed elaboration of a set of 'Keynesian policies for the new millennium'.

7 Indeed, the General Theory can be viewed as the exemplification of this recognition. As Coddington (1983, p. 53, emphasis added) has pointed out, 'it is not the fact of uncertainty that is important for Keynes' argument, *but rather how individuals are supposed to respond to the fact of uncertainty*'. The essence of the General Theory is that 'our desire to hold money as a store of wealth is a barometer of the degree of our distrust of our own calculations and conventions concerning the future' (Keynes, 1973c, p. 116).

8 As Critical Realists point out, human activity appears to depend on networks of social structures, which are pre-existing in the sense that they are the product of the creative actions of agents, made in the past. Everyday activities in Western societies, such as speaking, writing, reading and withdrawing monies from automated tiller machines, are dependent on pre-existing social structures which constrain and enable action. And as they pre-exist any individual act they can be viewed as autonomous and potential objects of enquiry. Such structures impinge on current actions as an objective reality that is ontologically distinct from and irreducible to individual subjective beliefs and actions. Notions of uncertainty, as it pertains to action, can thus be conceived as emerging from social structures such as money and a range of profit and loss accounting procedures.

9 Giddens is seemingly conflating risk and uncertainty and would benefit from the precise technical discussion contained in Chapter 6 below.

10 As Giddens (2003, p. 24) has observed, '[m]odern capitalism embeds itself into the future by calculating future profit and loss, and therefore risk [and uncertainty], as a continuous process. This wasn't possible until the invention of double entry bookkeeping in the fifteenth century in Europe, which made it possible to track in a precise way how money can be invested to make more money.'

Part II

The nature of uncertainty

5 Uncertainty, transformation and Keynes

Keynes brought time back into economic theory.... The descent into time has brought economic theory also into touch with history.

Joan Robinson (1962a, pp. 73–4)

INTRODUCTION

John Maynard Keynes was clearly challenging the Benthamite calculus that underpins much of orthodoxy. The decision to invest suggests a decision which broaches an uncertain future. And as the future is uncertain it must presumably be imagined prior to decision and action. It is such chains of reasoning that have led many Post Keynesians to stress that Keynes' contribution endorsed the view that social reality was transmutable and underpinned his wider theoretical schema. However, there have been no attempts to reflect at length on the extent to which Keynes' conceptualisation of uncertainty is embedded in his ontological vision. This chapter addresses this gap and helps clarify the types of considerations that are involved in theorising about processes that are transmutable. We reflect on aspects of Keynes' social, literary and economic contributions and consider whether Keynes espoused a view of uncertainty and action that is transmutable, and the extent to which it was embedded in a creative view of the competitive process developed above.

The purpose of this chapter is to attempt to make sense of Keynes' discussion in order to inform the elaboration of an alternative conception of the economic process to the closed-system, immutable ontology that pervades much economic theorising, and to indicate the types of ontological considerations that are involved in theorising about open systems. The assessment is provocative, but the intention is to encourage further reflection and debate on the nature on the ontology underlying Keynes' vision and how it needs to be developed if Post Keynesians are to develop a better understanding of what it means to engage in open-system theorising. In doing so we will broach a series of substantive issues pertaining to how the nexus between uncertainty and the historical evolution of capitalism should be conceptualised in future research.

The outline of the chapter is as follows. In the next section we briefly consider the philosophy of practice and action embedded in Keynes' *Treatise on Probability*.

We then consider the link between Keynes' discussion of uncertainty and the notion of animal spirits and enterprise elaborated in the *General Theory* and after. We then proceed to assess Keynes' view of the competitive process. This discussion is then further illuminated with reference to his musings on the social system and the processes of capitalism suggested by the *General Theory*. We conclude by noting that aspects of Keynes' discussion of uncertainty are ahistorical and need to be further augmented by a philosophy of emergence and transmutability. That is to say, by methodologically grounding the many insights that Keynes generates we would significantly clarify opaque aspects of his discussion and provide a more secure foundation for further development.

'A GUIDE TO CONDUCT': THE *TREATISE ON PROBABILITY*

The renewed interest in the *Treatise on Probability* (Keynes, 1921) has raised three principal issues. Firstly, what is the ontological and epistemological nature of Keynes' theory of probability and action under uncertainty? What is the nature of the continuity, if any, between the discussion contained in the *Treatise* and in the *General Theory*? And what does this mean for a theory of behaviour under conditions of 'fundamental' uncertainty? For present purposes we do not propose a detailed exegesis on such matters, as comprehensive discussions are to be found elsewhere (see Bateman, 1987, 1996; Carabelli, 1988; Davis, 1994; Dequech, 1997c, 1999a; Meeks, 1991; O'Donnell, 1989; Runde, 1990, 1994).[1] However, we will briefly encroach onto aspects of this debate as it pertains to our assessment of the nature of Keynes' discussion of the transmutability of the entrepreneurial process.

It is possible to view the *Treatise* as an attempt to extend the domain of rational judgement and action to the study of uncertainty.[2] Keynes (1921, p. 9) seeks to challenge and move beyond frequency theories of probability and 'to emphasise the existence of a *logical relation between two sets of propositions* in cases where it is not possible to argue demonstratively from one to the other'. That is to say, Keynes considers the nature of acting in instances when one is unable to assign probability ratios to future events, namely under conditions of uncertainty.[3]

According to Keynes, any conclusion or proposition a is related to a given premise or such available evidence h via a probability relation, which can be written as $a|h$. This probability relation can be thought of as the 'objective' degree of belief that it is rational to hold in any judgement given current knowledge. Keynes then introduces the notion that the weight of argument refers to the amount of available relevant evidence. The weight of argument relates to the confidence that one has in the evidence pertaining to any probability relation. Nevertheless, as Runde (1990) notes, Keynes employs several different definitions of 'weight' in the *Treatise*, using it to refer either to the absolute amount, or the degree of completeness, of the relevant evidence, or to the balance between knowledge and ignorance. Thus additional information that reveals either the incompleteness of the existing relevant evidence, or one's relative ignorance, may in fact reduce the probability; but new information always increases the evidential 'weight' (Keynes, 1921, p. 77). The discovery of additional evidence h_1 augments the weight of argument and gives rise to a new probability relation $a|hh_1$. However, there is no unique monotonic relationship between the weight of argument and the degree of belief held in any proposition. The accretion of new knowledge or evidence may or may not alter the probability relation. It does not entail that the previous argument is wrong; it merely yields a new judgement (see Lawson, 1985; Runde, 1990; Gerrard, 1992a,b). As such, probability relations need not correspond to numerical values or be directly comparable, and this extends the province of probability to the study of rational decision-making under uncertainty.[4]

For Keynes, deciding on a course of action meant judging the means to deliver ends, where '[j]udgement of means took place in the "twilight of Probability". Rational action was constrained by two further principles, the "weight of argument" and the doctrine of "least risk" … [P]robability might be the "guide of life"; but the guide had to make his way through the fog of uncertainty' (Skidelsky, 1992, p. 409). The central argument of the *Treatise* is that the perceptions of probability, 'weight' and 'moral risk', roughly, the magnitude of the expected loss (or 'badness') that might eventuate under averse conditions, depend upon the exercise of judgement. *Ceteris paribus*, 'a high weight and the absence of risk increase *pro tanto* the desirability of the action to which they refer' (Keynes, 1921, p. 348).

What is clear from this discussion is that Keynes' concern with the nature of acting is ahistorical and primarily philosophical.[5] That is to say, the *Treatise* does not provide many clues as to the nature of the social ontology within which the decision-maker is embedded.[6] As O'Donnell (1989) makes plain, while Keynes' view of the physical world in the *Treatise* is deterministic, his treatment of the social realm is more ambiguous. Keynes does not tell us, in the *Treatise*, 'how stable he thought social, as opposed to natural structures were' (Skidelsky, 1992, p. 61). In the *Treatise* Keynes does not explicitly challenge the notion of immutability of the cosmos. 'Keynes' theory is both optimistic about the power of human reason and pessimistic about its ability to penetrate the secrets of the universe. We have only limited insight into the "nature of reality"' (Skidelsky, 1992, p. 61). Keynes leaves the conceptual door ajar: '[w]hether there is a map in heaven, there is none on earth' (Skidelsky, 1992, p. 61).[7]

Keynes' discussion primarily considers the rational grounds for acting in the absence of numerical probabilities rather than the psychological nature of acting or the emergent novelty, creativity or reproducibility associated with action and imagination.[8] But, '[h]aving opted for the supremacy of reason, [one] rejects what conflicts with reason … [one cuts oneself off] from the most ascendant and superb of human faculties. Imagination, the source of novelty, the basis of mens' claims, if they have one, to be makers and not mere executants of history, is exempted' (Shackle, 1979b, p. 44). Keynes does not consider the emergent historical processes that shape and contextualise the decision to act.[9] Moreover, notions such as evidential completeness or relative ignorance appear to place clear bounds on knowledge. But if knowledge, especially economic knowledge, is embedded in an unending, emergent, creative process existing in historical time, then in what sense does it have meaning to talk about the completeness of economic knowledge, or to make evaluations of the balance between knowledge and ignorance with respect to the evolution of rationality, especially as decisions constantly have to be made at discrete points in time?[10]

For the Keynes of the *Treatise* the guidelines for action in an uncertain world can be deduced from logic on the basis of available evidence. The conceptualisation of action is epistemic and ahistorical. The *Treatise* displays little evidence that institutions, time and history are important for Keynes' philosophy of practice.[11] It is an appeal to reason, not observation.[12] For the Keynes of the *Treatise* the question of how to act is approached from an ethical and philosophical perspective; he does not consider the origins of action, nor does he offer considerations of how his philosophical treatment may find conduits for expression in the realm of practical affairs. For this we must turn to his economic writings.

UNCERTAINTY AND ANIMAL SPIRITS

Many commentators have claimed that the revolutionary essence of the *General Theory* is the role accorded to uncertainty. This, though, is misleading. Coddington (1983, p. 53, emphasis added) has cogently summarised the role of uncertainty in the *General Theory*: 'it is not the fact of uncertainty that is important for Keynes' argument, *but rather how individuals are supposed to respond to the fact of uncertainty*.'[13] In developing this aspect of his argument, Keynes begins by noting the salience of the passing of time:

> All production is for the purpose of ultimately satisfying a consumer. Time usually elapses, however – and sometimes much time – between the incurring of costs by the producer (with the consumer in view) and the purchase of the output by the ultimate consumer. Meanwhile the entrepreneur (including both the producer and the investor in this description) has to form the best expectations he can as to what the consumers will be prepared to pay when he is ready to supply them (directly or indirectly) after the elapse of what may be a lengthy period; and he has no choice but to be guided by these expectations, if he is to produce at all by processes which occupy time.
>
> (Keynes, 1936, p. 46)

Keynes divides these expectations, upon which business decisions depend, into two groups: long- and short-term expectations. Short-term expectations refer to the expected revenue associated with a production run against the current capital stock, whereas long-term expectations refer to 'what the entrepreneur can hope to earn in the shape of future returns if he purchases (or, perhaps, manufactures) "finished" output as an addition to his capital equipment' (Keynes, 1936, p. 47). Accordingly, the volume of current and future investment depends upon the state of these forward-looking long-term expectations as they impinge on the psychological propensities to act:

> It would be foolish, in forming our expectations, to attach great weight to matters which are very uncertain.* It is reasonable, therefore, to be guided to a considerable degree by the facts about which we feel somewhat confident, even though they may be less decisively relevant to the issue than other facts about which our knowledge is vague and scanty. For this reason the facts of the existing situation enter, in a sense disproportionately, into the formation of our long-term expectations; our usual practice being to take the existing situation and to project it into the future, modified only to the extent that we have more or less definite reasons for expecting a change.
>
> (Keynes, 1936, p. 148)

Thus the decision to invest depends upon the 'most probable forecast' that can be made and the 'confidence' in the forecasts of the future (cf. the discussion regarding 'Uncertainty as an emergent process' in the previous chapter). It is such business confidence that is pivotal to enterprise:

> The outstanding fact is the extreme precariousness of the basis of knowledge on which our estimates of prospective yield have to be made. Our knowledge of the factors which will govern the yield of an investment some years hence is usually very slight and often negligible. If we speak frankly, we have to admit that our basis of knowledge for estimating the yield ten years hence of a railway, a copper mine, a textile factory, the goodwill of a patent medicine, an Atlantic liner, a building in the City of London amounts to little and sometimes to nothing; or even five years hence.
>
> (Keynes, 1936, pp. 149–50)[14]

Nevertheless, a salient and oft-ignored aspect of this discussion is that Keynes embeds the state of long-term expectations within the evolution of the institutions of capitalism, such as the emergence of the joint-stock corporation and rise of the stock market:

> In former times, when enterprises were mainly owned by those who undertook them or by their friends and associates, investment depended on a sufficient supply of individuals of sanguine temperament and constructive impulses who embarked on business as a way of life, not really relying on a precise calculation of prospective profit. The affair was partly a lottery, though with the ultimate result largely governed by whether the abilities and character of the managers were above or below the average. Some would fail and some would succeed. But even after the event no one would know whether the average results in terms of the sums invested had exceeded, equalled or fallen short of the prevailing rate of interest; though, if we exclude the exploitation of natural resources and monopolies, it is

> probable that the actual average results of investments, even during periods of progress and prosperity, have disappointed the hopes which prompted them … If human nature felt no temptation to take a chance, no satisfaction (profit apart) in constructing a factory, a railway, a mine or a farm, there might not be much investment merely as a result of cold calculation. Decisions to invest in private business of the old fashioned type were, however, decisions largely irrevocable, not only for the community as a whole, but also for the individual. With the separation between ownership and management which prevails to-day and with the development of organised investment markets, a new factor of great importance has entered in, which sometimes facilitates investment but sometimes adds greatly to the instability of the system.
>
> (Keynes, 1936, pp. 150–1)

Such passages are instructive in several respects. Firstly, the view of the entrepreneur, being based upon 'sanguine temperament' and 'constructive impulses', appears to emphasise the creative and transmutable potential embedded within the competitive process. Secondly, the recognition of the emergence of the stock exchange appears to embed the discussion of uncertainty into a historical process. Thirdly, such institutional developments fundamentally change the nature of the investment process, so that 'certain classes of investment are governed by the average expectation of those who deal on the Stock Exchange as revealed in the price of shares, rather than by the genuine expectations of the professional entrepreneur' (Keynes, 1936, p. 151). Nevertheless, the competitive processes within which they are engaged is 'partly a lottery', a metaphor that is suggestive of situations of risk, and partly dependent on the genetic endowments of the entrepreneurs. Thus one could quite plausibly interpret this passage as being implicitly underpinned by an immutable, ergodic conception of the competitive processes of capitalism.

Moving on, Keynes argues that a uniquely correct market valuation (of future prospective yields) cannot be calculated because current knowledge does not provide a sufficient foundation for a precise mathematical expectation:

> We are assuming, in effect, that the existing market valuation, however arrived at, is uniquely *correct* in relation to our existing knowledge of the facts which will influence the yield of the investment, and that it will only change in proportion to changes in this knowledge; though, *philosophically speaking*, it cannot be uniquely correct, since our existing knowledge does not provide a sufficient basis for a calculated mathematical expectation.
>
> (Keynes, 1936, p. 152, emphasis added)

This passage seemingly suggests a strong conception of the economic process as transmutable. *Even if* agents had the ability to collect and successfully process all the information relating to past and current outcomes, such (market) information does not, and could not, provide the evidential basis for forecasting future outcomes. In such a world the past provides a limited guide as to the course of future events, economic agents are unable to discover the future and are truly uncertain, e.g. there presently *does not exist information* that will enable them to discover the uniquely correct market valuation. Nevertheless, the subsequent passages at times appear to directly contradict such a strong view.

Keynes (1936, p. 153) proceeds to link the problems of uncertainty to the decision to invest, noting that it is the 'precariousness [of this market valuation] which creates no small part of our contemporary problem of securing sufficient investment'. He then goes on to consider the factors that accentuate this precariousness, such as the 'gradual increase in the proportion of the equity in the community's aggregate capital investment which is owned by persons who do not manage and have no special knowledge of the circumstances, either actual or prospective, of the business in question, [so that] the element of real knowledge in the valuation of investments by those who own them or contemplate purchasing them has seriously declined', which gives rise to a 'conventional valuation which is established as the outcome of the mass psychology of a large number of ignorant individuals' (Keynes, 1936, pp. 153–4).[15,16]

Nevertheless, there is 'one feature in particular which deserves our attention' – the role of experts. Keynes (1936, p. 154) suggests that '[i]t might have been supposed that competition between expert professionals, possessing judgement and knowledge beyond that of the average private investor, would correct the vagaries of the ignorant individual left to himself'. From a perspective that recognises the transmutability of the economic process we would expect to find the subsequent passages, which elaborate on why this does not 'correct the vagaries of the ignorant individual left to himself', to allude to notions of novelty, emergence, imagination or the nature of economic time, i.e. a consideration of the fact that while experts may be able to correctly discern and interpret the information contained in the past (and the present) they cannot mirror this into the future. That is to say, from a perspective which embraces transmutability, all individual agents, *including expert professionals*, are ignorant of the available courses of action or of the extent of future states of the world because of the irreversible and open-ended nature of time, because the future has yet to be created, and not merely because of limitations in the processing abilities of economic agents. A conception of the economic process which *a posteriori* recognises its transmutability means that the future cannot be known prior to its *creation*, regardless of the processing powers we impute to agents – it is for this reason that a uniquely correct valuation cannot be arrived at.

According to Keynes, however, one of the reasons why a uniquely correct valuation cannot be made is not that the future cannot be known in advance of its creation, but that experts are forced to follow the short-termism of the herd – social convention dictates it:

> It is an inevitable result of an investment market organised along the lines described. For it is not sensible to pay 25 for an investment of which you believe the prospective yield to justify a value of 30, if you also believe that the market will value it at 20 three months hence. Thus the professional investor is forced to concern himself with the anticipation of impending changes … Professional investment may be likened to those newspaper

> competitions in which the competitors have to pick out the six prettiest faces from a hundred photographs, the prize being awarded to the competitor whose choice most nearly corresponds to the average preferences of the competitors as a whole; so that each competitor has to pick, not those faces which he himself finds prettiest, but those which he thinks likeliest to catch the fancy of the other competitors, all of whom are looking at the problem from the same point of view. It is not a case of choosing those which, to the best of one's judgement, are really the prettiest, nor even those which average opinion genuinely thinks the prettiest. We have reached the third degree where we devote our intelligences to anticipating what average opinion expects the average opinion to be.
>
> (Keynes, 1936, pp. 155–6)[17]

The nature of the stock market decrees that the professional expert investor is forced to follow the general market valuation rather than anything based upon fundamentals or 'intrinsic values' because the short-termism and ignorance of the stock market swamp reason.[18] To draw on Keynes' metaphor, it is not that is not possible to define beauty, rather the nature of the contest is such that beauty is defined by social conventions rather than by an objective assessment.[19] Indeed, there is nothing in Keynes' discussion that precludes the professional investor from forming a correct judgement:

> If the reader interjects that there must surely be large profits to be gained from the other players in the long run by a skilled individual who, unperturbed by the prevailing pastime, continues to purchase investments on the best genuine long-term expectations he can frame, he must be answered, first of all, that there are, indeed, such serious-minded individuals and that it makes a vast difference to an investment market whether or not they predominate in their influence over the game-players. But we must also add that there are several factors which jeopardise the predominance of such individuals in modern investment markets. Investment based on genuine long-term expectation is so difficult to-day as to be scarcely practicable.
>
> (Keynes, 1936, pp. 156–7)

For Keynes, the process of investment is a 'game' (see Skidelsky, 1992, p. 323).[20] The problem is that institutions and social conventions conspire against reason. If the professional investor is 'successful, that will only confirm the general belief in his rashness; and if in the short term he is unsuccessful, which is very likely, he will not receive much mercy. Worldly wisdom teaches that it is better for reputation to fail conventionally than to succeed unconventionally' (Keynes, 1936, p. 158). It is precisely for such reasons that Keynes normatively notes that '[t]he social object of *skilled* investment *should* be to *defeat the dark forces of time and ignorance* which envelop our future' (Keynes, 1936, p. 155, emphasis added). The fact that it is possible to defeat the 'dark forces of time and ignorance' is suggestive that perhaps ultimately a correct valuation is possible, i.e. that an immutable conception of economic processes hides behind the distorting irrationality of stock market investment. From a genuinely transmutable perspective, however, it would be impossible to defeat the 'dark forces of time and ignorance' – however much time the professional investor is faced with (cf. Davidson, 1998b). And hence Keynes appears inconsistent on such matters.

Keynes' discussion clearly centres on the unintended consequences of the institutional shift being observed in capitalism.[21] The rise of the joint stock company and its associated institutions has given rise to a cadre of dilettante investors who are able to alter their investment portfolios quickly and without appreciable cost, nor with consideration of the consequences of their actions upon the wider community. Consequently Keynes argues that if one were married to one's decisions, as in earlier times (see the quotation above), there would not be a market to follow, and one would be compelled to consider a longer time horizon for the prospective yield, rather than focusing on short-term yields and price movements:

> The spectacle of modern investment markets has sometimes moved me towards the conclusion that to make the purchase of an investment permanent and indissoluble, like marriage, except by reason of death or other grave cause, might be a useful remedy for our contemporary evils. For this would force the investor to direct his mind to the long-term prospects and to those only.
>
> (Keynes, 1936, p. 160)[22]

Nevertheless, the answer, though, is not to return to earlier, more primitive times, which is somewhat prescient given this was before marriage came to resemble the stock market; rather, Keynes (1936, p. 378) urged a 'comprehensive socialisation of investment' which could usher in a more rational approach to investment.[23] However, as we shall elaborate further in the next section, Keynes' (1936, pp. 376–9) advocacy of a socialisation of investment was aimed at offsetting the shrinking investment opportunities in an 'old' economy, which runs counter to the view that the essence of entrepreneurship is the creation of new investment opportunities.

Notwithstanding the instabilities generated by the febrile atmosphere of the stock exchange, however, there are further instabilities to be recognised: the fact that it is a 'characteristic of human nature that a large proportion of our positive activities depend on spontaneous optimism rather than on a mathematical expectation, whether moral or hedonistic or economic. Most, probably, of our decisions to do something positive, the full consequences of which will be drawn out over many days to come, can only be taken as a result of animal spirits – of a spontaneous urge to action rather than inaction, and not as the outcome of a weighted average of quantitative benefits multiplied by quantitative probabilities' (Keynes, 1936, p. 161). That is to say, given the uncertainties surrounding the future, investment is very much a matter of animal spirits (for a discussion see Koppl, 1991; Marchionatti, 1998). This again appears suggestive of a conception of the economic process which assumes transmutability, especially as this discussion seemingly encompasses the professional investor. Nevertheless, the causal sequence in Keynes is clear: it is because of the uncertain nature of the future that economic agents rely on their animal spirits, or fall back on convention. Moreover, the emergence of the stock exchange accentuates the precarious nature of such investment decisions. This is quite distinct from a creative view of the economic process. That is to say, we might have expected Keynes to argue that because of the animal spirits and novelty-inducing actions of agents (especially those concerned with investment), uncertainty for other agents emerges.

Fluctuations, in *The General Theory*, originate in business psychology and find their conduit in monetary circulation.[24] But although '[m]oney in its significant attributes is, above all, a subtle device for linking the present to the future; and we cannot even begin to discuss the effect of changing expectations on current activities except in monetary terms' (Keynes, 1936, p. 294), the focus is on the *reaction* to unforeseen events, rather than how the process of accumulation generates uncertainty. Even though Keynes links the notion of animal spirits to the plunge into the abyss of the unknown, he does not make the link with the emergent process of origination and fecundity which is fuelled by the competitive process.[25]

What is more, while the notion of animal spirits is perhaps the closest that Keynes comes to a stress on the creative and emergent nature of the competitive process, as a metaphor it is misleading, at best unflattering, at worst contemptuous, reducing the propensity to invest to animalistic and basic impulses and seemingly eschewing creativity and imagination. Moreover, the notion of animal spirits raises pertinent questions about the continuity with Keynes' discussion in the *Treatise on Probability*, which attempts to sketch out a theory of *rational* decision-making under situations when non-numerical probabilities cannot be assigned. That is to say, the notion of animal spirits points to what we may call the 'non-rational' interpretative thesis associated with Shackle (1967) and Winslow (1986a,b), among others.

In summary, the whole focus on expectations is as a *reaction* to new events, to new circumstances, to 'shifting and unreliable evidence' (Keynes, 1936, p. 315).[26] Keynes' whole emphasis is quite distinct from one that suggests that expectations provide the raw imagination to create a new future. Expectations in Keynes refer to the response to circumstance rather than the creation of circumstance.[27] Arguably, both are important and should be part of the same general story (see Davidson, 1996). Moreover, the precariousness of expectations is founded on the 'uncontrollable and disobedient psychology of the business world' (Keynes, 1936, p. 317). This results in the associated suggestion that if this psychology could be tamed, then the associated problems of a collapse in business confidence could be overcome. Indeed, this is the more general argument of *The General Theory*, which deserves further consideration.

TRANSFORMATION AND *THE GENERAL THEORY*

Let us take stock of the argument thus far. It is clear from the discussion above that Keynes' discussion of uncertainty, as it impinges upon expectations, does not appear to find its origins in the creative dynamics of the economic process. That is to say, uncertainty does not have its origins in the novelty-inducing actions of economic agents.[28] But it should not be inferred from this discussion that one is necessarily arguing that Keynes was a theorist who assumed the future was immutable. Throughout *The General Theory*, and elsewhere, Keynes makes many pregnant suggestions as to the transmutability of the economic realm.[29] Indeed, in *The General Theory* Keynes develops a structured and differentiated social ontology. One can identify three different levels of transformation in *The General Theory*, focusing on the actions and influence of individuals, institutions and governments. The *General Theory* is a treatise devoted to changing the philosophies of governments and hence the institutional structures of the economy, especially as it impinges on the 'free' actions of individuals within the economy.

Keynes clearly rejects immutable, natural-law philosophy and embraces a view that agents, and groups of agents, can alter the rules of the game. For instance, Keynes warns us that although we oscillate around 'an intermediate position' below full employment and above that which would 'endanger life', we 'must not conclude that the mean position thus determined by "natural" tendencies, namely, by those tendencies which are likely to persist, failing measures expressly designed to correct them, is, therefore, established by laws of necessity … [It] is a fact of observation concerning the world as it is or has been, and *not a necessary principle which cannot be changed*' (Keynes, 1936, p. 254, emphasis added).[30] This clearly provides for an open, transformative view of the economic system.[31]

Indeed, Keynes (1936, p. 65) recognises the power of the individual, noting that a 'decision to consume or not to consume truly lies within the power of the individual; so does a decision to invest or not to invest. The amounts of aggregate income and of aggregate savings are the *results* of the free choice of individuals'. This is suggestive of a transmutable conceptualisation of the economic system, and especially the decision to invest. What is more, the organic link between individual choices and collective outcomes is apparent. That is to say that free choices made by individuals over, say, consumption are heavily constrained by the decisions of others which serve to determine that individual's income. Similarly, Keynes recognises the role of decentralised entrepreneurship:

> The advantages of efficiency of the decentralisation of decisions and of individual responsibility is even greater, perhaps, than the nineteenth century supposed; and the reaction against the appeal to self-interest may have gone too far. But, above all, individualism, if it can be purged of its defects and its abuses, is the best safeguard of personal liberty in the sense that, compared to any other system, it greatly widens the field for the exercise of personal choice. It is also the best safeguard of the variety of life, which emerges precisely from this extended field of personal choice, and the loss of which is the greatest of all the losses of the homogenous or totalitarian states. For this variety preserves the traditions which embody the most secure and successful choices of former generations; it colours the present with the diversification of its fancy; and, being the handmaid of experiment as well as of tradition and of fancy it is the most powerful instrument to better the future.
>
> (Keynes, 1936, p. 380)

Nevertheless, while this points to a transformative conception of choice there is a failure to explore how the emergent novelty associated with enterprise might generate uncertainty for other investors. There is failure to link the transformative actions of agents to the emergence of uncertainty in the minds of other agents.

Equally, when re-stating *The General Theory*, Keynes (1936, p. 252) notes the psychological propensities which 'limit the instability resulting from rapid changes in the prospective yields of capital assets due to sharp fluctuations in business psychology or to epoch-making inventions'. This allusion to epoch-making inventions suggests that Keynes does espouse a view which embodies the transmutability of the economic process.[32] Moreover, in his response to Tinbergen, Keynes (1973c, pp. 285–9), questioning the method of econometrics, asked: 'What place is left for expectation and the state of confidence relating to the future? What place is allowed for non-numerical factors, such as inventions, politics, labour troubles, wars, earthquakes, financial crises?', saliently arguing that 'the economic environment is not homogenous over time'.[33] Nevertheless, such creative acts are not linked up to a discussion and recognition of the nexus to the emergence and salience of uncertainty historically. There is a failure to link such allusions and insinuations to the creative and imaginative impulse associated with enterprise and the emergence of the salience of uncertainty throughout *The General Theory* and after.[34]

Moreover, such comments should be considered alongside Keynes' (1936, pp. 372–84) identification of the propensity of capitalism to stagnate due to the exhaustion of investment opportunities and a rising propensity to save (which embody the concomitant implication that there are notional limits to human demands). According to Keynes, in wealthy communities the propensity to invest is weaker, reflecting a lower propensity to consume and a capital richness. Keynes' (1936, p. 31) logic leads him to a stagnationist *obiter dictum*: 'not only is the marginal propensity to consume weaker in a wealthy community, but, owing to its accumulation of capital being already larger, the opportunities for further investment are less attractive unless the rate of interest falls at a sufficiently rapid rate'. But this seemingly points to the satiation of wants and capital, and not the manufacture of wants and the pervasive and invasive thrust of creatively destructive capital accumulation and the uncertainties that this generates. For Keynes, the entrepreneurial function is linked to the stagnating vices of the accumulating elite.[35] He fails to link the explosive energy of capitalism to the long-run 'pathological vices' of accumulation existing in historical time.

All in all, Keynes' discussion in *The General Theory* (and subsequent defence) is a short-run snapshot of a dynamic long-run process. This is clear from Keynes' employment of the shifting equilibrium model outlined in the *General Theory* (see Kregel, 1976). Keynes appears to treat uncertainty as an epistemological and/or as a reactive, psychological phenomenon, rather than viewing it also as a product of the processes of accumulation. As Schumpeter (1954, p. 1175) observed of *The General Theory*, but has now been forgotten, '[t]hose who look for the essence of capitalism in the phenomena that attend the incessant recreation of this apparatus and the incessant revolution that goes on within it must therefore be excused if they hold that Keynes' theory abstracts from the essence of the capitalist process'. But is it the case that elsewhere Keynes 'abstracts from the essence of the capitalist process'?

UNCERTAINTY AND THE ECONOMIC PROCESS

Keynes was not ahistorical. He recognised several institutional shifts, in *The General Theory* and elsewhere, that had occurred since Victorian times, such as 'the eclipse of the independent entrepreneur, maximising his profits, by the joint-stock company, mainly interested in the general stability of trade; the organisation of the labour market by trade unions; the increasingly dominant role of the banking system in determining monetary conditions; and growing state responsibility for investment through the rise of the public corporation' (Skidelsky, 1992, p. 229). Moreover, in the 1925 lectures 'Am I a Liberal?' and 'The Economic Transition in England', Keynes, drawing on Commons, attempted to develop a non-Marxist conceptualisation of the economic process circumscribed by three distinct epochs: the ages of scarcity, abundance and stabilisation.[36] The age of scarcity referred to pre-capitalist modes of governance and coercion, including communitarian, feudal and medieval power structures. The age of abundance was associated with the dawn of capitalism and the early success of an individualistic liberal economic order. The third age of stabilisation is characterised by:

> a diminution of individual liberty, enforced in part by governmental sanctions, but mainly by economic sanctions through concerted action, whether secret, semi-open, or arbitrational, of associations, corporations, unions, and other collective movements of manufacturers, merchants, labourers, farmers, and bankers … The transition from economic anarchy to a regime which deliberately aims at controlling and directing economic forces in the interests of social justice and social stability, will present enormous difficulties both technical and political.
>
> (Keynes, 1931, pp. 303–5)

However, the Keynes/Commons framework fails to provide a historical appreciation of the fact that widespread acknowledgement of the importance of risk and uncertainty and its nexus to accumulation is a comparatively recent phenomenon (cf. the argument developed in Chapter 4 above). There is no recognition of the link between the forward-looking nature of monetary accumulation that characterises the emergence of capitalism, and the rise and increasingly widespread usage of future-oriented concepts such as risk and uncertainty.[37] There is no attempt to link the emergence of uncertainty with the 'age of stabilisation', e.g. to the fact that many of the institutions of the 'age of stabilisation' may have emerged to mitigate the impact of an uncertain future.[38] But as we argued in the last chapter concepts such as risk and uncertainty are the product of social relations and are embedded in emergent structures and institutions.[39]

Moreover, Keynes contemplates an age when enormous technical and political difficulties are overcome such that the economic problem is largely solved.

In his essay 'Economic possibilities for our grandchildren', Keynes (1930c) ponders a future where people will be freed from the pathologies of money-making. Even Keynes' (mature) views on the relationship between saving and the macroeconomic position were embedded in a static (and even stagnating) conception of the nature of the economic process. Keynes 'came to see [saving] as excessive in relation to the investment opportunity available in an "old" economy like Britain's' (Skidelsky, 1992, p. 274). Keynes judged the economic problem to be largely solved with the near exhaustion of profitable ventures upon which enterprise could embark, i.e. a view of enterprise as decreasingly important and valuable. Arguably, this points to a view of enterprise which lays stress on the discovery of profitable opportunities rather than the creation of them (cf. the argument in Chapters 9 and 10 below).

Keynes' historical vision succeeds in playing down the creative and destructive nature of the competitive process and diminishes the impact of the '"new consumers" goods, the new methods of production or transportation, the new markets, the new forms of industrial organisation that capitalist enterprise creates' (Schumpeter, 1943, p. 83). As Plumptre (1983, p. 153) has commented, critically reflecting first-hand on Keynes' 'Economic possibilities for our grandchildren': 'society is not likely to run out of new wants as long as consumption is conspicuous and competitive'. Or, to put it another way, Keynes does not consider how firms engage in the creation of new wants and desires and attempt to mitigate uncertainties so as to preserve accumulation and to enable themselves to reproduce (cf. Galbraith, 1967; Dunn, 2001b,c). The creative manner of the competitive process and its nexus to uncertainty lies dormant in Keynes, and is perhaps symptomatic of the fact that he 'was less interested in processes than in outcomes' (Skidelsky, 1992, p. 274).

TRANSFORMATION AND THE ENTREPRENEUR

Keynes does on occasion, however, elsewhere allude to the creativity and change induced by the entrepreneur. In his essay 'The end of laissez faire', Keynes (1931, p. 291) argues that '[m]any of the greatest economic evils of our time are the fruits of risk, uncertainty, and ignorance'. Keynes' discussion is suggestive of a creative view of the economic process: '[i]t is because particular individuals, fortunate in situation or in abilities, are able to take advantage of uncertainty and ignorance, and also because for the same reason big business is often a lottery, that great inequalities of wealth come about; and these same factors are also the cause of unemployment of labour, or the disappointment of reasonable business expectations, and of the impairment of efficiency and production' (Keynes, 1931, p. 291).

This discussion appears to link the discussion of uncertainty to capitalism's incessant drive to introduce product innovations and technological revolutions. Moreover, such an interpretation links well with Keynes' (1931, pp. 276, 282–3) rejection of simplistic market-based selection-of-the-fittest arguments. If the future cannot be known in advance of its creation then the market (or governments for that matter) cannot select and learn the optimal rules and routines that characterise the environments because *they are not yet there to be discovered.* However, a moment's reflection reveals that such an interpretation is contentious. To describe the economic process as approximating a lottery is suggestive of a world of (ergodic) risk. Similarly, individuals 'take advantage of uncertainty' rather than create it. In Keynes uncertainty exists independently of the process of competition. Uncertainty is not transformed in its significance over time as new products, new methods of organisation, new governments and new institutional structures are originated within the process of competition and history.

Likewise, in his review of H.G. Wells' *The World of William Clissold*, Keynes (1931, pp. 315–20) recognised the 'creative force and constructive will' of the elite, arguing that the force for change came from men of knowledge and power – the business tycoons and the scientists. For Keynes it is the 'profiteer' who injects life into capitalism. Investment is an uncertain vocation: 'It is enterprise which builds and improves the world's possessions … [and] the engine which drives enterprise is … profit' (Keynes, 1930b, p. 132). Such creativity, however, was most important in the earlier individualistic 'age of abundance'. By the time of the 'age of stabilisation' all the profitable opportunities were nearing exhaustion; the entrepreneurial class had become degenerative, not least due to the corrupting pursuit of avarice.

For instance, in his essay 'Am I a Liberal?' Keynes (1931, p. 327) argued that the transmission of wealth and power via the hereditary principle underscores the decadence and decay of individualistic capitalism. As Skidelsky (1992, p. 259) documents, Keynes, unlike Marshall, 'had little respect for the business vocation …. Keynes ranked business life so low partly because he considered that the material goods produced by entrepreneurs has less ethical value than the intellectual and aesthetic goods produced by dons and artists, [and] partly because he despised the 'love of money' as a motive for action'. In sharp contrast to, say, Schumpeter, Shackle, Marshall, or even Marx, Keynes seems to regard the entrepreneur as a necessary evil and far from heroic: 'What chiefly impressed Keynes about British businessmen was their stupidity and laziness. He was a firm believer in the three-generation cycle: the man of energy and imagination creates the business; the son coasts along; the grandson goes bankrupt' (Skidelsky, 1992, p. 259).[40] And while Keynes talks about the 'spirit of enterprise', this is not equal to a recognition of the change – and uncertainty – inducing activities of enterprise.

Overall, Keynes' vision of the capitalist process is 'one lurching forward by fits and starts, while opportunities for exceptional profit cause, briefly, the gambling spirit to swamp the counsels of prudence' (Skidelsky, 1992, p. 335). Indeed, it is significant, although from our perspective unsurprising, that Keynes (quoted in Skidelsky, 1992, p. 267) argued that the 'necessity of profit as a spur to effort … was greatly exaggerated'. Keynes' theoretical discussion stands in sharp contrast to that of Knight (1921) who, while also identified with introducing the distinction between risk and uncertainty in economics, defended profit as a reward for risk-taking and uncertainty-bearing, and linked it up to the historical process of accumulation.[41] What Keynes 'underestimated was humanity's ingenuity in inventing ways to keep capital scarce' (Skidelsky, 1992, p. 609). Keynes seeks to play down a heroic conceptualisation of the entrepreneurial function. His elitist orientation led Keynes to regard entrepreneurs as a necessary evil who could contribute, not to civilisation, but to the possibility of civilisation.

CONCLUDING COMMENTS

In considering Keynes' conception of uncertainty and its role in the process of accumulation, it is clear that for Keynes the exigency of emergent creativity does not give rise to the uncertainties that pertain to the process of competition. This should not be surprising, as his conception of uncertainty across his social, literary and economic writings is primarily philosophical and ahistorical.[42] The failure to link creativity and novelty to uncertainty results in a usurpation of the antecedence and origins of uncertainty and its nexus to the process of accumulation.[43]

Keynes' whole discussion, while suggestive of a transmutable conception of the economic process, does not seek to emphasise the emergent creativity associated with the process of accumulation that gives rise to uncertainty and reverberates through the state of long-term expectations. In *The General Theory* and after, uncertainty is an ahistorical *deus ex machina* that drives a stake into institutional stability. Such an approach, however, leaves the origins and emergence of the salience of uncertainty unaddressed. Why is the future uncertain? Is it just that we simply cannot know the future? Or are there reasons why our knowledge about the future is limited?

Both Shackle and Davidson have recognised the salience of such questions and responded by noting that the origins of uncertainty are to be found in the creative, emergent processes associated with competition and capital accumulation. While it is not presented as such, Davidson's (1991a, 1996) discussion of nonergodicity or transmutability, which is consistent with Lawson's discussion of open systems, offers the prospect of further refining discussion. At a superficial level, Davidson's elaboration of nonergodicity parallels Keynes' *deus ex machina* treatment. However, as we shall elaborate in the next chapter, a much neglected aspect of Davidson's discussion is the role accorded to creative, crucial decision-making. Crucial decisions represent a *sufficient* (but not a necessary) condition for the existence of nonergodic processes and pave the way for developing a transmutable conception of the competitive process that integrates key insights from Shackle, Schumpeter *and Keynes*.

This must thus be viewed as a development of Keynes' largely *deus ex machina* treatment of uncertainty. While Keynes recognises that avarice and accumulation are the driving force of capitalism, this is not the same as locating the origins of uncertainty in the process of competition – a point that Schumpeter makes but never fully explores, perhaps reflecting intellectual rivalries and jealousies. Nevertheless, as we have seen, Keynes leaves the theoretical door slightly ajar, paving the way for the development of an economics that recognises the transmutable nature of the economic process. We begin this task in the next chapter.

NOTES

* 'By "very uncertain" I do not mean the same thing as "very improbable". *Cf.* My Treatise on Probability, chap. 6 on "The Weight of Arguments".' (Keynes, 1936, p. 148, note 1)

1 While it is safe to argue that uncertainty is a continuous strand in Keynes' thinking, it is far from clear that its theoretical status and relationship with his economics is unchanging. Thus, for the purposes of exposition, the discussions contained in the *Treatise*, the *General Theory*, and beyond, will be considered on their own terms, and no attempt to link them will be made. Treating the debates in this way strengthens the present argument and avoids entering an already overcrowded playing field.

2 Notwithstanding the fact that much of the *Treatise* deals with abstract issues of probability theory rather than an elaboration of the nature of human action.

3 Although it is important to note, as Lawson (1985, p. 913) has lamented, that '[u]nfortunately Keynes nowhere explicitly defines uncertainty in the *Treatise on Probability*'.

4 Lawson (1985, p. 911) notes that '[p]robability in this (inductive) framework is not, therefore, a property of the actual physical world but a property of the way in which we think about the world … If we interpret this probability relation as a degree of belief then clearly it is seen to be subjective in the sense that the information h may vary from person to person (and possibly also in the sense that individuals may differ in their reasoning powers). It is not, however, subjective in the sense that the probability bestowed upon a proposition a given the evidence h is subject to a human caprice. Rather the probability in a conclusion a given the evidence h is objective or fixed and corresponds to the degree of belief it is *rational* for a person to hold in the hypothesis given the information available.'

5 Following Hodgson (2001a, p. 50), 'the term "ahistorical" applies to any concept or theory that is claimed to pertain to *all* possible socio-economic systems'. It is abundantly clear from Keynes' discussion in the *Treatise* that his framework is applicable to all possible socio-economic systems. Keynes' (1921, pp. 272–5) distinction between the rational and the true is particularly illustrative in this regard.

6 Although Keynes' discussion, as with all decision theory, is philosophical in orientation, his approach need not preclude the processes of history. That is, the processes of history can provide the evidential basis upon which decisions are made. However, Keynes in the *Treatise* does not tell us whether the passage of time and decisions of agents affect the laws governing processes, i.e. whether human history ultimately matters.

7 Cf. Knight (1921, p. 198), who has suggested that it 'is *conceivable* that all changes might take place in accordance with known laws'.

8 Cf. Shackle (1979b, p. 48): 'Beginning I use here as the term for a taking-place in which some element, aspect or character is *ex nihilo*. No knowledge of antecedents, however complete and exact, would make possible a foreknowledge of that aspect of character.'

9 According to Keynes (1921, p. 356), '[t]he importance of probability can only be derived from the judgement that it is *rational* to be guided by it in action; and a practical dependence on it can only be justified by a judgement that in action we *ought* to act to take some account of it. It is for this reason that probability is to use the "guide of life", since to us, as Locke says, "in the greatest part of our concernment, God has afforded only the Twilight, as I may so say, of Probability, suitable, I presume, to that state of Mediocrity and Probationership He has been pleased to place us in here".'

10 With respect to the theory of value, Shackle (1972, p. 446) argues that: 'It shows men as acting rationally, whereas to be human is to be denied the necessary condition of rationality, complete relevant knowledge.'

11 Cf. Knight's (1921) famous treatise on entrepreneurship, which exhibits many similarities with Keynes' more philosophical treatment: 'The business man himself not merely forms the best estimate he can of the outcome of his actions, but he is likely also to estimate the probability that his estimate is correct. The "degree" of certainty or of confidence felt in this conclusion after it is reached cannot be ignored, for it is of the greatest

practical significance. The action which follows upon an opinion depends as much upon the amount of confidence in that opinion as it does the favourableness of the opinion itself (Knight, 1921, pp. 226–7)'.

12 Cf. Skidelsky (1992, p. 423), who argues that Keynes 'accepted the conventions of economics, especially the convention of rationality'. But, as Shackle (1972, p. xviii) has pointed out, 'there is a fundamental conflict between the appeal to rationality and the consideration of the consequences of time as it imprisons us in actuality, the theoretician is confronted with a stark choice. He can reject rationality or time'. Moreover, there is a sense in which Keynes (1933, pp. 448–9) recognised this later in life, as exemplified by his remarks in his essay 'My Early Beliefs' where he argued: 'I still suffer incurably from attributing an unreal rationality to other people's feelings and behaviour (and doubtless to my own, too). There is one small but extraordinarily silly manifestation of this absurd idea of what is "normal", namely the impulse to *protest* – to write a letter to *The Times*, call a meeting in the Guildhall, subscribe to some fund when my presuppositions as to what is "normal" are not fulfilled. I behave as if there really existed some authority or standard to which I can successfully appeal if I shout loud enough – perhaps it is some hereditary vestige of a belief in the efficacy of prayer … Our [early Bloomsbury's] comments on life and affairs were bright and amusing, but brittle … because there was no solid diagnosis of human nature underlying them.' Such passages are suggestive of the adoption of a transmutable perspective of 'life and affairs' as it appears to reject the notion of some invariant standard or authority against which action should be compared, and rationality adjudged. Nevertheless, there is a failure to link such a view of human action to the emergence of uncertainty and the nexus with accumulation. For a variety of perspectives on Keynes' approach to rationality see Bateman (1996), Meeks (1991), O'Donnell (1989) and Winslow (1993).

13 Coddington's (1983, pp. 53–4) reasoning is thus: 'if there is great uncertainty surrounding investment decisions, and producers respond to this by making, so far as is possible, the same investment decisions this period as last period (since, after all, the results of previous decisions are the one thing they do know something about), this would not result in private sector investment's being wayward and unruly; indeed, it might result in greater stability than would result from sophisticated calculations based on epistemologically privileged beliefs or an uncanny degree of foresight. Thus, the fact of uncertainty does not of itself establish the conclusion concerning the wayward and unruly behaviour of particular macroeconomics variables. Indeed, it is not evident that this argument helps to establish Keynes' conclusion rather than the opposite conclusion … For what is required within Keynes' scheme is not the uncertainty, as such, surrounding private sector investment decisions; it is the wayward and unruly behaviour of the aggregates resulting from the decisions taken in the face of this uncertainty. Indeed, Keynes' system requires private sector investment to display this unruliness in two quite distinct senses: first, when compared with private sector *consumer* expenditure (this is required in order for Keynes' model to work); and, second, when compared with *public* sector investment expenditure (this is required in order for Keynes' policies to work).'

14 But if the world is uncertain, then the world is uncertain, and it could be said that we have no basis for estimating the yield of a railway tomorrow: after all ten years hence is only the culmination of 3650 tomorrows. Do we find it more difficult to forecast what will happen in ten years relative to what will happen tomorrow because of complexity – that is, there are more things that could happen over 10 years than tomorrow – or because of change, and more things can change in 10 years? Indeed, it is for such reasons that many have tried to link Keynes' discussion to change and creativity or complexity (cf. Dequech, 1999a; Marchionatti, 1998).

15 Keynes claims that 'the vast majority of those who are concerned with the buying and selling of securities know almost nothing whatever about what they are doing. They do not possess even the rudiments of what is required for a valid judgement, and are the

prey of hopes and fears easily aroused by transient events and as easily dispelled. This is one of the odd characteristics of the capitalist system under which we live, which, when we are dealing with the real world, is not to be overlooked … [Hence] it may often profit the wisest to anticipate mob psychology rather than the real trend of events, and to ape unreason proleptically' (Keynes, 1930b, p. 323).

16 What is interesting is that here Keynes seems to assume that stock market valuations matter for real investment decisions, which is far from uncontentious. For example, Tobin's q, which reflects stock market valuation, has not been successful in investment equations.

17 A much overlooked aspect of this passage is the overlap and possible origins of the 'beauty contest' metaphor in Keynes' (1921, pp. 27–9) prior discussion in the *Treatise* of the salience of an actual competition run by the *Daily Express* for the logical theory of probability.

18 As Skidelsky (1992, p. 525) has highlighted: 'In the 1920s Keynes saw himself as a scientific gambler. He speculated on currencies and commodities. His aim was to play the cycle. This was the height of his "barometric" enthusiasm … when he believed it was possible, by forecasting short-term rhythms, to beat the market. The gambling instinct was never quite extinguished'. Keynes' whole philosophy of investment was governed by the principle of purchasing stock which he reasoned was under-priced 'relative to its intrinsic worth'. Indeed, it is quite clear from the following exegetical passages that Keynes held an 'intrinsic values' approach to investment at some point after 1924, which suggests that the discussion in the *General Theory* was an elaboration of Keynes' own investment philosophy: 'One is doing a fundamentally sound thing, that is to say, backing intrinsic values, enormously in excess of the market price, which at some utterly unpredictable date will in due course bring the ship home (Keynes, 1973a, p. 77)'.

'I preferred one investment about which I had sufficient information to form a judgement to ten securities about which I know little or nothing (Keynes, 1973a, p. 81)'.

'There are very few investors, I should say, who eschew the attempt to snatch capital profits at an early date more than I do. I lay myself open to criticism because I am generally trying to look a long way ahead and am prepared to ignore immediate fluctuations, if I am satisfied that the assets and the earning power are there. My purpose is to buy securities where I am satisfied as to assets and ultimate earning power and where the market price seems cheap in relation to these. If I succeed in this, I shall simultaneously have achieved safety-first and capital profits. All stocks and shares go up and down so violently that a safety-first policy is practically certain, if it is successful, to result in capital profits. For when the safety, excellence and cheapness of a share is generally realised, its price is bound to go up.... I am quite incapable of having adequate knowledge of more than a very limited range of investments. Time and opportunity do not allow more. Therefore, as the investible sums increase, the size of the unit must increase. I am in favour of having as large a unit as market conditions will allow and, apart from a small group of securities, this generally means a smaller unit than would be made necessary by the size of the investible fund'.

'As good examples of speculative attempts at capital profits I should instance South American shares and oil companies within the area of hostilities. I should not deny for a moment that such investments may result in capital profits. My objection is that I have no information on which to reach a good judgement, and the risks are clearly enormous. To suppose that safety-first consists in having a small gamble in a large number of different directions of the above kind, as compared with a substantial stake in a company where's [sic] one information is adequate, strikes me as a travesty of investment policy (Keynes, 1973a, p. 82)'.

'It is vastly easier to find 130 satisfactory investments than to find 325; particularly if you are largely depending on the repertory of one man … I myself follow fairly closely, or think I have some knowledge, of upwards of perhaps 200 investments;

and whilst, say, 50 others (at the outside) may be followed closely by other members of the Finance Committee, I should say that the Provincial holds 50 to 100 securities about which none of the Board know much. Now out of the 200 which one tries to follow more or less, there are probably less than 50 in all classes about which, at any given time, one feels really enthusiastic. I am convinced that the good results shown by King's are mainly due to the large proportion of its assets held in the less than 50 favourite securities. To carry one's eggs in a great number of baskets, without having time or opportunity to discover how many have holes in the bottom, is the surest way of increasing risk and loss (Keynes, 1973a, p. 99)'.

'One can put the distinction like this: By credit cycling I mean buying and selling according as you think shares cheap in relation to money. By my alternative I mean acting according as you think them cheap in relation to other shares, with particular reference to the possibilities of large relative appreciation; – which means buying them on their intrinsic value when, for one reason or another, they are unfashionable or appear very vulnerable on a short view. One may be, and no doubt is, inclined to be too slow to sell one's pets after they have had most of their rise. But looking back I don't blame myself much on this score; – it would have been easy to lose a great deal more by selling them too soon (Keynes, 1973a, p. 101)'.

'As time goes on I get more and more convinced that the right method in investment is to put fairly large sums into enterprises which one thinks one knows something about and in the management of which one thoroughly believes. It is a mistake to think that one limits one's risks by spreading too much between enterprises about which one knows little and has no reason for special confidence. Obviously this principle ought not to be carried too far. The real limitation, however, on its application in practice is in my experience the small number of enterprises about which at any given time one feels in this way. One's knowledge and experience are definitely limited and there are seldom more than two or three enterprises at any given time in which I personally feel myself entitled to put *full* confidence (Keynes, 1973a, p. 57)'.

Nevertheless, the whole notion of fundamentals or intrinsic values is suggestive of an immutable conception of economic processes (see Davidson, 1998b).

19 For an extended reflection on Keynes' views on 'beauty', see O'Donnell (1995).

20 Indeed, gambling and gaming metaphors pervade the *General Theory*. But such metaphors are clearly suggestive of situations of risk and not radical uncertainty. Arguably, this points to Keynes' belief that it is institutions and convention that conspire against rationality, and not imagination and creativity which undermine it.

21 Cf. Skidelsky (1992, p. 556), who has suggested that 'Keynes contention, in chapter 12, is that the uncertainty attaching to expectations of the future yield of investment have given birth to a particular institution through which most of investment is channelled in a capitalist society – the stock market'.

22 Keynes (1936, p. 161) continues to note that the 'only radical cure for the crises of confidence which afflict the economic life of the modern world would be to allow the individual no choice between consuming his income and ordering the production of the specific capital-asset which, even though it be on precarious evidence, impresses him as the most promising investment available to him. It might be that, at times when he was more than usually assailed by doubts concerning the future, he would turn in his perplexity towards more consumption and less new investment. But that would avoid the disastrous, cumulative and far-reaching repercussions of its being open to him, when thus assailed by doubts, to spend his income neither on the one nor on the other.'

23 Many have interpreted this as an argument for nationalisation. Clearly this is not what Keynes had in mind. Rather it was that more rational institutions for allocating capital could, and should, be devised so as to reconcile public and private interest. But this need not entail public provision nor 'exclude all manner of compromises and of devices by which public authority will co-operate with private initiative … it is not the

ownership of the instruments of production which it is important for the State to assume. If the State is able to determine the aggregate amount of resources devoted to augmenting the instruments and the basic rate of reward to those who own them, it will have accomplished all that is necessary' (Keynes, 1936, p. 378).

24 Accordingly, it is business psychology which should be the focus of investigation for the study of economic vacillations and this leads one to Keynes' study of Freud and the dismal disdain of money-making and enterprise (see Winslow, 1986a,b, 1989, 1990, 1992).

25 Indeed, Keynes tends to make scant reference to the creativity of the entrepreneur, preferring to reserve it for the more aesthetic, higher pursuits. In 'My Early Beliefs' Keynes (1933, pp. 436–7) argues as still 'nearer the truth than any other that I know' his previous convictions that 'nothing mattered except states of mind' and that 'the appropriate subjects of passionate contemplation and communion were a beloved person, beauty and truth, and one's prime objects in life were love, the creation and enjoyment of aesthetic experience and the pursuit of knowledge'. Indeed this forms the foundation of the contrast, in 'Economic Possibilities for Our Grandchildren', between capitalism and the ideal republic. Here he anticipates a future when we shall be 'free… to return to some of the most sure and certain principles of religion and traditional virtue – that avarice is a vice, that the exaction of usury is a misdemeanour, and the love of money is detestable, that those walk most truly in the paths of virtue and sane wisdom who take least thought for the morrow. We shall once more value ends above means and prefer the good to the useful. We shall honour those who can teach us how to pluck the hour and the day virtuously and well, the delightful people who are capable of taking direct enjoyment in things, the lilies of the field who toil not, neither do they spin' (Keynes, 1931, pp. 330–31).

26 But, as Schumpeter (1936, p. 793) pointed out, '[a]n expectation acquires explanatory value only if we are made to understand why people expect what they expect. Otherwise expectation is a mere *deus ex machina* that conceals problems instead of solving them'.

27 We may consider Keynes' correspondence with Townshend, his most intellectually radical interpreter according to Shackle (1967), on 7th December 1938. Keynes (1979, p. 294) noted that '[t]o avoid being in the position of Buridan's ass, we fall back, therefore, and necessarily do so, on motives of another kind, which are not "rational" in the sense of being concerned with the evaluation of consequences, but are decided by habit, instinct, preference, desire, will etc.' But it should be remembered that Buridan's ass relates to the problem of decision-making such that when faced with deciding between two equidistant and equally desirable bales of hay the ass starved to death owing to the absence of grounds for preferring to go to one bale of hay than another. However, from a transmutable perspective the bales of hay were *pre-existing* and the allusion is clearly one of scholastic philosophy rather than one of considering the consequences of imagination and of practical action.

28 Compare, for example, Cliffe Leslie (1988, p. 223) who recognised that variety, disruption and uncertainty were themselves embedded in the corrupting pursuit of avarice.

29 There are also many other equally pregnant immutable metaphors in the *General Theory*. Keynes (see for example 1936, pp. 9, 50), in several places, appears to characterise the economic system and process as 'a machine'. One should also consult Skidelsky (1992, p. 406), who argues that the zeitgeist was very much that 'society was a machine whose working could be improved by deliberative action, with unintended side-effects being equally amenable to correction and control, much as a mechanic fine-tunes an engine'. Equally, as noted above (see note 20), gambling metaphors pervade the *General Theory* (see for example Keynes, 1936, pp. 150–1, 155–6, 159, 381), and especially Chapter 12, which is illuminating in terms of the present

discussion as they relate ostensibly to situations that approximate ergodic risk. Does it really matter what metaphors Keynes uses to think about the economy? Clearly it does! Metaphors shape the way we frame problems, understand solutions and act. Changing the metaphors provides us with the freedom to act differently. Indeed, the employment of such metaphors can be viewed as encouraging the hydraulic view of the economic process that came to exemplify the Keynesianism of the 1960s (cf. Coddington, 1983).

30 Cf. Keynes (1973c, p 300; referred to by Skidelsky, 1992, p. 540), who in a letter to Harrod, 16th July 1938, noted: 'I also want to emphasise strongly the point about economics being a moral science. I mentioned before that it deals with introspection and with values. I might have added that it deals with motives, expectations, psychological uncertainties. One has to be constantly on guard against treating the material as constant and homogenous. It is as though the fall of the apple to the ground depended on the apple's motives, on whether it is worth falling to the ground, on whether the ground wanted the apple to fall, and on mistaken calculations on the part of the apple as to how far it was from the centre of the earth'. While in one sense this captures the thinking, acting, transforming subject, the emphasis pertains to whether the apple wanted to do something and how it evaluated a course of action, rather than capturing the creativity associated with decision and agency.

31 The same can also be said of Keynes' (1936, p. 243) discussion against the natural rate of interest.

32 Skidelsky (1992, p. 326) holds that 'Keynes followed both Schumpeter and Robertson in holding that innovations come in waves; but he had no real theory of profit'.

33 This points to a clarification of a detail left ambiguous in the *Treatise on Probability*, that social structures are not immutable through time. See also note 32.

34 One should consider Keynes' 1937 *Quarterly Journal of Economics* article, which provides perhaps the most compelling evidence of a radical conceptualisation of uncertainty: 'By 'uncertain' knowledge, let me explain, I do not mean merely to distinguish what is known for certain from what is only probable. The game of roulette is not subject, in this sense, to uncertainty; nor is the prospect of a Victory bond being drawn. Or, again, the expectation of life is only slightly uncertain. Even the weather is only moderately uncertain. The sense in which I am using the term is that in which the prospect of a European war is uncertain, or the price of copper and the rate of interest twenty years hence, or the obsolescence of a new invention, or the position of private wealth owners in the social system in 1970. About these matters there is no scientific basis on which to form any calculable probability whatever. We simply do not know. Nevertheless, the necessity for action and for decision compels us as practical men to do our best to overlook this awkward fact and to behave exactly as we should if we had behind us a good Benthamite calculation of a series of prospective advantages and disadvantages, each multiplied by its appropriate probability, waiting to be summed (Keynes, 1973c, p. 113)'.

But what is clear from such passages is that the whole tone of Keynes' *QJE* article is reactive and does not use concepts such as creativity, imagination and novelty. That is to say, the emphasis does not allude to the creative and change-inducing role of entrepreneurs and firms who 'reform or revolutionize the pattern of production by exploiting an invention or, more generally, an untried technological possibility for producing a new commodity or producing an old one in a new way, by opening up a new source of supply of materials or a new outlet for products, by reorganizing an industry and so on' (Schumpeter, 1943, p. 132). Rather, the *QJE* article is best interpreted as an attempt to establish reasonable grounds for belief under conditions of uncertainty such that, in addition to ordinary logic and empirical analysis, knowledge is also composed of conventions and intuition (Davis, 1994).

35 And although the rentier would disappear, the entrepreneur would still have a role, it would not be linked to the novelty-inducing creativity of the entrepreneur;

rather, 'enterprise and skill' is associated with the 'estimation of prospective yields about which opinions could differ' (Keynes, 1936, p. 221).

36 Commons (1934, pp. 773–88), in his *Institutional Economics*, outlined three 'economic stages', namely: 'a period of Scarcity preceding the 'industrial revolution', the latter beginning in the Eighteenth Century … a period of Abundance with its alternations of oversupply and undersupply for a hundred years or more … and a period of Stabilization, beginning with the concerted movements of capitalists and labourers in the Nineteenth Century (Commons, 1934, p. 773)'.

37 Notwithstanding Gidden's (2003) idiosyncratic conceptualisation of risk, his comments in his Reith lectures are apposite: 'Risk is the mobilising dynamic of a society bent on change, that wants to determine its own future rather than leaving it to religion, tradition, or the vagaries of nature. Modern capitalism differs from all previous forms of economic system in terms of its attitudes towards the future … Modern capitalism embeds itself into the future by calculating future profit and loss, and therefore risk, as a continuous process. This wasn't possible until the invention of double entry bookkeeping in the 15th Century in Europe, which made it possible to track in a precise way how money can be invested to make more money.'

38 At a superficial level Galbraith's (1977) *The Age of Uncertainty* appears to fill this void. However, Galbraith's contention is that the great certainties of the Victorian age have given way to social upheaval and the uncertainties associated with a delicate ideological stand-off between Communism and Capitalism, rather than elaborating on the increasing preoccupation with the uncertainties of accumulation. Nevertheless, Galbraith's (1967) *The New Industrial State* can be viewed as an attempt to theorise on the rise and emergence of the large corporate enterprise as a means to mitigate the uncertainties that pertain to investment and accumulation (see also Dunn, 2001c).

39 As Giddens (2003, pp. 21–22) notes, 'Apart from some marginal contexts, in the Middle Ages there was no concept of risk. Nor … was there in most other traditional cultures. The idea of risk appears to have taken hold in the sixteenth and seventeenth centuries, and was first coined by Western explorers as they set off on their voyages across the world. The word 'risk' seems to have come into English through Spanish or Portuguese, where it was used to refer to sailing into uncharted waters. Originally, in other words, it had an orientation to space. Later, it became transferred to time, as used in banking and investment – to mean calculation of the probable consequences of investment decisions for borrowers and lenders. It subsequently came to refer to a wide range of other situations of uncertainty.'

40 This should be no surprise to students of Keynes. He was statist and elitist, embracing the ascendance to power of the new class of Platonic Guardians (Skidelsky, 1992, p. 224). Prior to the twentieth century, nineteenth-century economists argued for a liberal political system to underwrite economic prosperity. Keynes in effect reversed this and sought to sustain economic prosperity and safeguard the liberal political system. Keynes 'welcomed the "aggregation of production" as tending to stabilise the economy; he accepted uncritically the view that captains of industry were constrained, by the size of their undertakings, to serve the public interest; and he assumed, without further argument, that an interconnected elite of business managers, bankers, civil servants, economists and scientists, all trained at Oxford and Cambridge and imbued with a public service ethic, would come to run these organs of state, whether private or public, and make them hum to the same tune. He wanted to decentralise and devolve only down to the level of Top People' (Skidelsky, 1992, p. 228).

41 For Keynes (1930a, p. 111), profit is defined as 'the difference between the costs of production of the current output and its actual sales proceeds'. This clearly does not preclude a conceptualisation of profits as a reward for risk-taking, or stepping into an uncertain future, but nevertheless, the difference of emphasis is palpable.

42 In Keynes' (1930b) 'amateur' economic history in the *Treatise on Money* what is striking is the absence of 'any explicit reference to uncertainty' (Skidelsky, 1992, p. 335).

43 As Hodgson (2001a, p. 3) has pointed out, '[i]f history matters – at least in the sense of social development being path dependent – then our analyses must explore the particularities of the past. While we may retain general principles or guidelines, detailed analyses of particular events, structures and circumstances are required.'

6 Fundamental uncertainty is not bounded rationality

The analytical consequences of accepting the fact of uncertainty remain, on the whole, unexplored.

Tony Lawson (1985, p. 909)

At the bottom of the uncertainty problem in economics is the forward-looking character of the economic process.

Frank Knight (1921, p. 237)

INTRODUCTION

The distinctive view of time, understood as a non-deterministic, uncertain, open-systems process, is a core and defining characteristic of Post Keynesian economics. As we noted above in Chapter 4, the recognition of the salience of uncertainty is inextricably linked to the theoretical identification of the role and nature of money and its nexus to accumulation and the principle of effective demand. Nevertheless while it is increasingly acknowledged that the concept of uncertainty emphasised by Post Keynesians means something more than probabilistic mathematical risk, the economics literature is far from clear what this 'something more' means. As Davidson (1988, p. 159) points out, many economists continue to dismiss 'fundamental' uncertainty as an 'ill-defined notion which simply muddies the water of scientific investigation' – a concept that is anti-theoretical and ultimately results in nihilism. Indeed, one could argue that a lack of precision on this matter has informed some of the dismissive accusations of degenerative incoherence which, as we have noted throughout, have been levelled against Post Keynesian economics and its adherents' interpretation of Keynes. Accordingly, many Post Keynesians have recognised the need to clarify the differing conceptual foundations of risk and 'fundamental' uncertainty in different theories, but have done little to clarify aspects of the resulting confusion (see, for example, Rosser, 1999, pp. 182, 185; also 2000, 2001).

In this chapter we aim to consider in more detail the Post Keynesian approach to uncertainty and the implications for theorising of adopting an open-systems view of economic processes. Drawing on Paul Davidson's (1982–3, 1988, 1989c, 1991a, 1994, 1996) seminal contribution, we argue that 'fundamental' uncertainty is conceptually distinct from the notions 'behavioural' uncertainty and bounded rationality and argue, more importantly, that this needs to be recognised.[1] Davidson delineated situations of risk and 'fundamental' uncertainty respectively in terms of the statistical concepts of ergodic and nonergodic processes, a language that is familiar to economists, in order to promote a wider appreciation of the salience of this distinction. As noted in Chapter 4 above, he has broadened this definition by distinguishing between governing, immutable, closed-system processes and a transmutable open-system conception of economic action (Davidson, 1996, 1999b). Unfortunately the salience of this conceptual distinction is not always recognised, even by those who profess an open-systems approach.

In what follows we argue that the Post Keynesian concept of 'fundamental' uncertainty is conceptually distinct from the 'behavioural' uncertainty to which proponents of the bounded rationality approach to the study of economic decision-making refer. Bounded rationality refers to behaviour that is '*intendedly* rational but only *limitedly* so' (Simon, 1961, p. xxiv). It is used to 'designate rational choice that takes into account the cognitive limitations of the decision-maker – limitations of both knowledge and computational capacity' (Simon, 1987b, p. 266). Bounded rationality, however, relates to the *behavioural characteristics* of agents, whereas 'fundamental' uncertainty relates to the essential unknowability of the future, to creative human agency and to the unique nature of unfolding time. Nevertheless, the importance of this distinction is not generally recognised by economists. In a world in which the present and the future are truly open and transmutable, no matter how much rationality we impute to agents, the course of outcomes remains unpredictable. If the world, including the future, is immutable and closed, then, unless arbitrary and ad-hoc constraints are imposed, agents following rules or satisficing procedures can come to be substantively successful.

As we shall see, confusion exists because of the similar implications of 'fundamental' uncertainty and bounded rationality. Both approaches seemingly imply a conception of choice that is meaningful, genuine and realistic, i.e. choice matters, can make a difference to outcomes, and corresponds to the generalised features of experience. Both approaches seemingly imply a rejection of the maximisation hypothesis (Rosser, 2001). This has led to 'fundamental' uncertainty being subsumed in and conflated with the concept of bounded rationality. The consequence is that this distinction has not been appreciated, with the result that the richness and distinctness of concepts such as 'fundamental' uncertainty are much diminished.

In what follows we focus principally on Simon's discussion of bounded rationality, not least because his conceptualisation appears at first sight more radical than the numerous reformulations evident in the literature. We begin by outlining some of the similarities between the concepts of bounded rationality and 'fundamental' uncertainty that underscore this conflation. We then proceed to highlight the conflation of bounded rationality and 'fundamental' uncertainty, paying particular attention to those who seemingly observe this distinction, e.g. some Post Keynesians themselves. In the subsequent sections we further consider the idea of the immutability and transmutability of social processes and their nexus to notions of bounded rationality and fundamental uncertainty. We demonstrate how the concept of bounded rationality has typically been linked to, and embedded within, an underlying conception of social process as immutable and potentially subject to closure, and that ultimately, in the long run, bounded rationality collapses into the substantive rationality of pre-programmed choices. We conclude by suggesting that the study of the distinction between decision-making under complexity and uncertainty is far from inessential and that the distinctiveness of the Post Keynesian contribution should be recognised in analyses.

BOUNDED RATIONALITY AND 'FUNDAMENTAL' UNCERTAINTY COMPARED

'Fundamental' uncertainty and the concept of bounded rationality, as advanced by Herbert Simon (1957, 1959, 1976), appear to hold quite similar implications. Simon (1987a, p. 222, emphasis added) argues that the 'term "bounded rationality" has been proposed to denote the *whole range of limitations* on human knowledge and human computation that *prevent* economic actors in the real world from behaving in ways that approximate the predictions of classical and neoclassical theory: including the absence of a complete and consistent utility function for ordering all possible choices, inability to generate more than a small fraction of the potentially relevant alternatives, and inability to foresee the consequences of choosing the alternatives'. Similarly, the notion of fundamental uncertainty has been advanced as a direct challenge to the predictions of classical and neoclassical theory and the inability to form rational expectations and/or form a complete transitive ordering over all possible alternative future outcomes (Davidson, 1996).

In those situations in which either bounded rationality or 'fundamental' uncertainty is present, decisions *have* to be made; the past, either because it cannot be fully comprehended or because it may substantially differ from a yet-to-be originated future, can only provide a limited guide to future events. Maximisation or optimisation is simply not possible in the short run if the world is either complex or open and 'fundamentally' uncertain (Rosser, 2000, 2001).[2] The implications should be immediately apparent: both under fundamental uncertainty and bounded rationality decisions are taken in light of the constraints of the past but are not determined by it (Garner, 1982).

Much of the confusion evident in the literature exists because of these similar implications. Both approaches seemingly imply a conception of choice that is meaningful, genuine and realistic, i.e. choice matters, can make a difference to outcomes, and corresponds to the generalised features of experience. This has led to the creative view of economic agency that underpins the Post Keynesian view of fundamental uncertainty being subsumed in, and conflated with, the concept of bounded rationality. The consequence is that the import of this distinction has not always been appreciated, with the result that the richness and distinctness of concepts such as fundamental uncertainty are much diminished.

The fact that there is so much muddled thinking on such matters is not, however, surprising considering the numerous interpretations, (re)formulations and fusions of the (sometimes interrelated) concepts of bounded rationality, 'behavioural' uncertainty and complexity that abound in the literature (for a survey, see Conlisk, 1996). Many fail to realise that the Post Keynesian view of fundamental uncertainty offers a radically different view of the nature of the informational problems that confront agents. Simon defined bounded rationality as 'rational choice that takes into account the cognitive limitations of the decision-maker – *limitations* of both knowledge and computational capacity' (Simon, 1987b, p. 266, italics added) and conceived it as a direct challenge to the strong notions of rationality associated with neoclassical economics (Sent, 1997). Others, such as Sargent (1993), however, have attempted to reformulate the concept and use it to strengthen and shore up neoclassical economics. Similarly, the growth in interest in nonlinear, dynamic, chaotic, complex systems (see Rosser, 1998, 2000) has further modified (and muddied) the notions of complexity and bounded rationality, which quite markedly differs from Simon's original intentions.[3]

Notwithstanding all the refinements, extensions and revisionism associated with the bounded rationality concept, certain recurrent themes can be discerned. All of the various formulations of the bounded rationality concept relate it to the behavioural characteristics of agents and use it to refer to the limitations in the processing abilities of agents that prevent them from discerning the 'closed'-system laws and dynamics, stochastic or otherwise, that govern future outcomes. In sharp contrast we argue below, building on the methodological discussion advanced above in Chapter 3, that 'fundamental' uncertainty and the Babylonian view of complexity relate to the essential unknowability of the future, to the nature of unfolding time. The salience of this distinction is not generally recognised by economists. If the social world is amenable to closure and governed by immutable processes, then it is only by imposing arbitrarily constraints on the problem-solving abilities of agents that one can prevent them from becoming procedurally successful and converging upon the optimising mode of behaviour that is implicit in overarching laws. The assumption of bounded rationality is tantamount to saying economic laws exist and that they govern economic outcomes, but that economic agents have problems in discerning and exploiting this fact (in the short run at least). However, as we shall argue below, in a world in which the present and the future are truly open and transmutable, no matter how much rationality we impute to agents, the course of outcomes remains unpredictable because it has yet to be originated, not because it has yet to be discovered.

BOUNDED RATIONALITY AND 'FUNDAMENTAL' UNCERTAINTY CONFLATED

Because of the many similarities between decision-making in complex situations or under conditions of uncertainty many economists have conflated the concepts. Many economists have thus argued that 'the bounded rationality hypothesis of Herbert Simon accords well with George Shackle's views [on fundamental uncertainty]' (Ford, 1993, p. 692). Indeed, Simon (1972, p. 170), for example, has suggested that the distinction between deterministic complexity and uncertainty is inessential.[4] He notes that 'uncertainty about the consequences that would follow from each alternative, incomplete information about the set of alternatives, and complexity preventing the necessary computations from being carried out … tend to merge: … uncertainty, whatever its source, is the same' (Simon, 1972, pp. 169–70).[5] Radner (1970, p. 457) has similarly conflated problems of creativity and imagination with issues of computation and adopted the assumption of bounded rationality, given that substantive rationality 'requires that economic agents possess capabilities of imagination and calculation that exceed reality by many orders of magnitude'. Clearly, if the environment is complex, yet closed and deterministic, and decision-makers are limited in their information-handling capacities, then it may be unlikely that agents will have, or be able to process, all the information they require to make a globally optimal decision (Simon, 1972; Rosser, 1999, 2001).

Surprisingly Loasby (1989, pp. 140–54), an influential economist who generally recognises the difference between bounded rationality and uncertainty, sometimes exhibits a degree of fuzziness. He has previously suggested, in a manner reminiscent of Simon above, that there are two major causes of the 'unavoidable ignorance of both analyst and decision-maker … One is the extent of the complexity of the phenomena around them … The other is the very limited human ability to cope with such analysis' (Loasby, 1976, p. 2). Moreover, he goes on to suggest that the 'impossibility of foreseeing future knowledge *and* the impossibility of making full use of present knowledge are both facts of human life. What Simon has labelled "bounded rationality" is part of the human condition' (Loasby, 1976, pp. 2–3, italics added).[6] However, as we will argue below, the 'impossibility of foreseeing future knowledge' also arises in contemplation of a transmutable environment *even if* agents could make 'full use of present knowledge'. Ultimately it is not computational constraints that underscore the 'impossibility of foreseeing future knowledge' but rather the emergent novelty and indeterminate creativity of agents. In a nonergodic environment the processing capacities of agents will affect the *nature* of choice but not the *fact* of choice. An emphasis on choice under uncertainty need not be tied to any (behavioural) conception of the processing abilities of agents and is analytically distinct.

However, these pronouncements are not rare and permeate other followers of Shackle who attacked any notion of any determinacy in the cosmos, stochastic or otherwise, (which typically underlies models of bounded rationality or complexity).

For instance, Earl (1996b, italics added) has castigated Shackle (1972) for his 'extraordinarily narrow examination of the relationship between uncertainty and business decision-making compared with what would have been perfectly possible had Shackle made use of literature published in the preceding fifteen years. Shackle neglects the work of the Carnegie school (Simon, 1957; Cyert and March, 1963) on the use of rule-based procedures for coping with *uncertainty and complexity*.' He has noted that while 'Shackle writes as if unaware of Simon's 'satisficing' concept, he appears just as inclined as Simon (1959) to challenge the notion of optimisation' (Earl, 1993, p. 250). Moreover, although Earl (1989, 1993, 1996b) is replete with allusions to Shacklean creativity he seemingly fuses uncertainty together with complexity. Shackle rejects optimisation because of the fact of creative crucial choice, not the fact of complexity and/or limitations in the computational capacities of agents. Shackle neglects the Carnegie school because it does not accord with his view of time (cf. Shackle, 1959). Rule-based procedures may indeed be followed by those confronting either complexity or uncertainty (Garner, 1982; Downward, 1999, Chapter 7); however, this does not mean that one should combine them together and use them interchangeably. As we shall see, the nature by which rules based procedures will change over time differs depending on our assumption as to whether there are overarching immutable laws determining economic outcomes. This conceptual distinction is recognised by Shackle, who chooses to focus upon the philosophical aspects of time rather than the behavioural aspects of complexity and its underlying nexus to immutability (see Davidson, 1989b).[7]

Some Post Keynesians are also guilty of occasional conceptual fuzziness and of combining and conflating the two concepts. Harcourt, for instance, notes that Simon's 'contribution to economics is to change the economic person into a sort of Woody Allen, *satisficing* in an environment characterised by *uncertainty*, and a great deal of ignorance and anxiety' (Harcourt, 1992b, p. 195, italics added; cf. Harcourt, 1981). Similarly, Lavoie conflates and combines the two concepts. He has remarked that 'all situations of uncertainty require procedural rationality … and decisions made on the basis of procedural rationality would be by definition related to situations of uncertainty' (Lavoie, 1992, p. 54). Furthermore, he has asserted that two approaches to decision-making are ultimately inseparable, that 'the concepts of uncertainty and bounded or procedural rationality become intertwined' (Lavoie, 1992, p. 54). Strictly speaking, however, the problems of complexity are conceptually distinct from the situations of novelty and creativity and the resultant uncertainty that this leads to.

Others have also suggested that Keynes' views on rationality and uncertainty represent a variant of the bounded rationality story. Lawson (1985, p. 918), for instance, has cautiously concluded that 'the notion of rational behaviour … which I believe emerges from Keynes … is possibly similar to Simon's notion of "bounded rationality"'. Similarly, Gerrard (1992b, p. 11) has suggested that 'Keynes' methodology is more akin to that of the behavioural approach to economics associated primarily with the work of Herbert Simon'. Likewise, Minsky (1996, p. 360) has noted that 'With the acceptance of bounded rationality, the new classical economics has moved toward an essential analytical aspect of Keynes'.

He continues by noting that 'By accepting that agents need to learn the model of the economy they use in decision making and that the complexity of economic processes and the time consuming nature of learning means that agents are never sure of the validity of the models that they use, the new classical economists have moved towards Keynes' views about uncertainty in *A Treatise in Probability*' (Minsky, 1996, p. 358). Lawson, Gerrard and Minsky are not, however, alone in conflating bounded rationality with Keynes' discussion of uncertainty. Lavoie also has interpreted Keynes in terms of the bounded rationality concept. He has remarked that the 'environment in which bounded rationality can be put to use is quite different from the one warranted by substantive rationality. There is no need to know the probability distribution of all possible future events. True uncertainty, of the Knight/Keynes/Shackle variety, can be entertained.... In fact, it is shown by O'Donnell (1989) that, in both his major works on probability and economics, Keynes attempted to demonstrate that true uncertainty necessarily led to the adoption of a different kind of rationality, which we now call procedural rationality' (Lavoie, 1992, p. 12).

However, a close reading of O'Donnell reveals the fact that he doesn't claim that Keynes' distinctive approach to rationality (espoused in the *Treatise on Probability*) is synonymous with bounded rationality. O'Donnell (1989, p. 29) laments the fact that Keynes' distinctive approach has been neglected by people like Simon 'despite some obvious affinities'. However he notes subsequently that 'Keynes thus offers a notion of "bounded rationality", *although one conceptually different* from that informing Simon's work (1972, 1976)' (O'Donnell, 1989, p. 43, italics added). This obviously begs several further questions such as how does Keynes' notion of rationality differ from Simon's and the nature of continuity in Keynes' thought from the *Treatise* to the *General Theory* and so on (cf. Dequech, 1997b,c). However, for present purposes the key point to note is that Lawson, Gerrard, Minsky and Lavoie all subscribe to the thesis that the notion of rationality espoused by Keynes and Post Keynesians is essentially the same as Simon's. Thus *they* conflate (or appear to) uncertainty and bounded rationality – whether Keynes does or does not is a separate issue (for a discussion see the previous chapter).[8]

It is perhaps because of the similarities in the conclusions reached using these concepts that they are typically integrated and fused together in a theoretically confusing manner with the result that the salience and distinctiveness of *both* approaches are not recognised. Since both bounded rationality and 'fundamental' uncertainty imply that in certain areas of decision-making agents are unable to make optimising choices whose pay-offs are expected in the future, it is easy to conflate the concept of lack of information under bounded rationality with an analysis of decision-making under uncertainty. Bounded rationality, however, relates principally to the *epistemological* problems that confront agents. It implies that decisions (including the deferring of choice) need to be made. If the environment cannot be fully understood and its implications fully computed then decisions have to be taken; it is for this reason that agents engage in satisficing behaviour.[9] Maximisation, of utility or profit or whatever, is simply not possible in the short run.[10] Choice and decision for Simon is identified with the *informational processing abilities* of agents and, the shortfall with respect to deterministic omniscience. Agents cannot study the data and, in light of the structure of the problem, make the substantively rational decision that is embodied in the closed deterministic equations that characterise the system (Rosser, 1999).

In sharp contrast, we would argue that in an uncertain environment, where the past presents a limited and narrow guide to a future that has yet to be created, crucial decisions can and have to be made (Davidson, 1982–3, 1988, 1991, 1996; cf. Hargreaves Heap, 1986–7). In this view, however, agents are truly uncertain in that there are no deterministic laws or equations to discover. The ontology of the system is open and problems of acting cannot be reduced solely to problems of epistemology (Lawson, 1997a, 2003, 2005c, 2006c). It is thus perhaps timely that we return to the distinction between ergodic and nonergodic processes made by Paul Davidson, which will allow us to elaborate the reasons for this conflation and highlight the salience of the distinction between bounded rationality and complexity and 'fundamental' uncertainty.[11]

CLOSED 'IMMUTABLE' PROCESSES

Ergodic theory has been explicitly developed in the theory of stochastic processes, although the term was borrowed from statistical mechanics (Parry, 1987).[12] Samuelson (1969) has argued that economics' claim to be scientific rests on the acceptance of the 'ergodic hypothesis'. Given Samuelson's stature within the economics profession, it is not unreasonable to suggest that the conventional wisdom concerning 'economic knowledge about the future relationship among observable economic variables is defined in terms of the probability distribution functions and statistical averages generated by ergodic processes' (Davidson, 1988, p. 331). Davidson has concluded that the implication of this is that the inverse of knowledge, *un*knowledge, i.e. (fundamental) uncertainty, must be expounded in terms of the ergodic theory.

All stochastic processes yield time-series data (realisations) that allow the construction of averages such as the mean or standard deviation. These averages constitute our empirical knowledge about past and current real-world relationships. Time averages are calculated from time-series data, i.e. observations that relate to a period of calendar time, whereas space averages are computed from cross-sectional data, i.e. observations that relate to a given point in time across realisations. Davidson (1988) notes that we are dealing with an ergodic *stochastic* process if (a) for infinite realisations the time and space averages coincide, or (b) for finite realisations the time and space averages converge (with a probability of one) as the number of observations increases.[13]

This means that space or time averages calculated from past realisations collapse onto the objective probability distribution that describes all possible (past, present and future) realisations and that these time and space averages form reliable estimates of (and govern) both current and future events (Davidson, 1988, p. 331).[14] That is to say, the system or process can be isolated and its constancy guaranteed to permit predictions of the form 'if *x* then *z*% probability that outcome *y* will occur', i.e. in statistical terms the system can be considered closed and the future can be predicted with some degree of confidence. Or, to put it another way, *the past reveals the future* – the past represents a sample from the future. However, while the concept of ergodicity is generally understood to relate to stochastic processes, in a wider sense it implies, as Davidson (1996, pp. 480–1) points out, 'the presumption of a programmed system where the past, present, and future reality are predetermined whether the system is stochastic or not'.[15] An ergodic system is a stochastic description of a closed immutable system.

If the world confronted by decision-makers is a closed and ergodic system, then to ascribe any salience to history is fallacious. '*The future is merely the statistical reflection of the past*. Economic activities are timeless and immutable' (Davidson, 1994, p. 90). If relationships between economic variables are ergodic, then time in any substantive sense is unimportant.[16] Indeed Samuelson's (1969) stated aim in introducing the ergodic hypothesis was to remove a concern for path dependence and history and to place economics firmly in the scientific realm. However, the presumption of an immutable system in which history is predetermined, stochastically or otherwise, as Shackle (1972) has repeatedly pointed out, makes a mockery out of any notion of choice regarding the future. If the economic world is immutable and ahistoric then, in the long run, outcomes are pre-programmed and independent of the decisions made by economic agents.[17] Choice is neither genuine nor matters. It cannot make a difference in the long run.[18] As Lawson (1997a, p. 9) notes: 'in the formal "models" found in the mainstream journals and books, human choice is ultimately denied … Instead, individuals are represented in such a way that, relative to their situations, there is almost always but one preferred or rational course of action and this is always followed … [H]uman doings as modelled, could not have been otherwise'. Consequently any attempt to assign any uniqueness and importance to human agency and history is fallacious. The implication of this is that there can be no ignorance (in the long run at least – see below) as to the (probable) future outcomes of any system or process that permits closure as long as one is willing to allocate resources so as to ascertain knowledge regarding the processes (stochastic or not) that govern the system. Ignorance can ultimately yield to omniscience. Maximisation is theoretically possible in the long run. It is to this that we now turn.

CLOSED 'IMMUTABLE' PROCESSES AND BOUNDED RATIONALITY

The reason for this near-universal acceptance of the importance of the concept of bounded rationality among economists relates to the conclusion reached by Loasby (1976) and Davidson (1977) that there is no need for money, or any other salient institutions for that matter, in general equilibrium models. Even probabilistic versions of general equilibrium theory, which allow informational problems of a stylised and restricted kind, provide no reason for the institution of money given the existence of a competitive general equilibrium price vector. The conclusion drawn, perhaps wrongly, is that, because the probabilistic version of general equilibrium theory, which cannot describe institutions such as money (and firms), relies heavily on the assumption that agents are unboundedly rational, *ergo* any model that attempts to explain them must relax this assumption.[19] It is at this point that bounded rationality enters into the economists' theorising (cf. Sargent, 1993; Sent, 1997).

The assumption of bounded rationality to many seems a reasonable assumption that accords with human experience and appears consistent with a stress on the importance of uncertainty. Bounded rationality describes situations whereby agents are unable to provide for an exhaustive list of (future) states of the world and possible courses of action that relate to the problem at hand because of limitations in their computational (and linguistic) ability. According to proponents of bounded rationality, individuals making decisions in a complex world do not possess the computational skills necessary to process all of the relevant information available to them – it is for this reason that they satisfice and follow rules of thumb because they do not possess 'the wits to maximise' (Simon, 1957). However, while bounded rationality proponents discard the strong assumption, retained by rational expectation and general equilibrium theorists, that there are no bounds to agents' computational (or linguistic) capacities, they implicitly retain the assumption that the governing objective conditions that describe economic processes are ergodic and deterministic. The conventional approach to bounded rationality is conducted implicitly in terms of ergodic theory, or more specifically under the assumption of a governing immutable environment (see Table 3 on p. 20 above).

To suggest that the concept of bounded rationality is generally linked to ergodic, immutable processes is not unreasonable. As Loasby (1989, p. 143) has remarked, the writings of Herbert Simon, the progenitor of the concept of bounded rationality, 'sometimes give the impression that we do live in a fully defined [immutable] system, if we only had the wit to understand it.'[20] This is clearly suggestive of an ergodic (immutable) world in which the future is *potentially* knowable in the sense that the realisations of the past are a *reliable* guide to future events and these may, if resources are allocated to their understanding, form the basis for decision-making in the long run. The future already exists – it is embedded in the past.

The assumption of bounded rationality means that agents are unable to engage in maximising behaviour in the short run. Agents may be unable to form rational expectations about the future that are efficient, unbiased and without persistent errors *in the short run* because of their limitations in ability, i.e. as a result of constraints in agents' computing power. Agents are prevented from using existing market data to obtain short-run reliable knowledge regarding the future nature of all economic variables. However, over time, as the ergodic nature of the environment is more fully understood, i.e. as the potential for surprise diminishes as one learns about the objective probability distributions that describe the ergodic environment, or in a broader sense as one learns about the immutable laws that govern reality,[21] then expectations about the future, in the Marshallian long run – defined as the asymptotic end state of a process of learning – will facilitate more efficient decisions to be made about the future.[22] As Cyert and Simon note, 'As uncertainty gives way to certainty and as knowledge increases, the behavioural rules change and move closer to those derived by *a priori* reasoning' (Cyert and Simon, 1983, p. 105).

However, this need not imply that decision-making becomes inevitably more complex. If the environment is one in which the potential for systematic error is diminishing, i.e. as the nature of the ergodic process becomes more fully understood, then it is also likely to be one in which behaviour becomes increasingly routine. As Davidson (1996) points out, routine, repetitious activities are the hallmark of ergodic environments.[23] In the long run, activities become increasingly routine – everything is done the way it was yesterday. The assumption of bounded rationality cannot mean in any substantive sense that systematic mistakes will continue to be made *in the long run* if based on an ergodic conception of economic processes.

In the presence of a lack of full information and an inability to process all the available information, agents would not know what a maximising decision would be – in the short run. Whilst agents can judge whether the existing outcome is satisfactory, they are precluded in the short term from knowing whether it is a maximising one. However, as further information is acquired and as processing capacities are modified and advanced, agents may learn that an outcome which was previously judged as satisfactory can be improved upon. This epistemological feedback loop underpins the rational dimension to the concept which is so cherished – in Simon's (1957, 1959) nomenclature, the aspiration level adjusts to new information gleaned, resulting in an improved behavioural response to a complex environment. *Ex ante* maximisation ultimately replaces satisficing, resulting in the concept of decision being emptied of all its substantive content in the long run. Boundedly rational (satisficing) decisions, ultimately, are neither crucial nor novel.[24] The limitations of knowledge or computation can ultimately be overcome, otherwise the contrastive notion of rationality, which it is intimately bound up with, must be abandoned as a chimera.

What is the mechanism that assures that the learning process occurs? Consistent with the conventional wisdom some form of market-based Darwinian natural selection is invoked to suggest that those decision rules and routines that persist are in some sense optimal (cf. Friedman, 1953). In this ergodic Darwinian world agents 'learn' from their short-run mistakes and make provision for them so that their subjective assessment of the environment reveals (converges on) the objective ergodic environment (Davidson, 1996, p. 486). Those that do not learn the relevant routines and/or probability functions that govern the immutable process will fall foul of the market process.[25] Hodgson (1993, Chapter 13; see also 1994) points out that appeals by economists to simplistic 'evolutionary' arguments in extolling the virtues of the competitive process are common. Hodgson demonstrates, however, that the view that evolutionary processes lead generally in the direction of optimality and efficiency is in fact erroneous. We address such considerations in more detail in the Chapter 8.

HUMAN AGENCY

According to Post Keynesians, the world inhabited by economic agents is a world in which history *need not* be governed by stochastic processes or immutable laws (cf. Shackle, 1972). This conceptual discussion reflects an ontological distinction between ('certain') closed immutable systems and ('uncertain') open transmutable systems. Models based on an ontologically closed view of the world, such as rational expectations models (both New Classical and New Keynesian), make knowledge (epistemological) claims regarding the informational sets that agents are assumed to possess in order to obtain their short-run policy implications. Models that suggest that the future is not completely known but can be learned, i.e. that agents are subject to bounded rationality, invoke epistemological 'uncertainty'. They are not, however, founded on an ontologically open system view of uncertainty and organic complexity (Dow, 1996a). [26]

Following Davidson, Post Keynesians define 'fundamental' uncertainty about the future course of events in terms of 'the absence of governing ergodic processes'. Davidson has labelled this situation *nonergodic*.[27] In nonergodic environments *even if* agents have the ability to collect and successfully process all the information relating to past and current outcomes, this existing (market) information does not, and cannot, provide reliable data for forecasting future outcomes and learning about the future (Davidson, 1996, p. 482). There are no governing social and economics laws to discover or learn, because in a very real sense the future is open and not predetermined. As Davidson (1991a, p. 133) remarks:

> If, however, true uncertainty conditions prevail [i.e. nonergodicity] in certain decision making areas, then at least some economic processes are such that expectations based on past probability distribution functions can differ persistently from the time averages that will be generated as the future unfolds and becomes historical fact. In these circumstances, sensible economic agents will not rely on available market information regarding relative frequencies, for the future is not statistically calculable from past data and is truly uncertain.

In an 'open' nonergodic world *sensible* agents will recognise that the future is one that can significantly differ from past experience and present expectations.[28] In a nonergodic world, where statistical distributions of the past provide a limited guide to the course of future events, agents are truly uncertain as there currently *does not exist information* that will enable them to discover the future (cf. Hargreaves Heap, 1986–7). Decisions *have* to be made, including the maintenance of convention, and choice is *genuine*. As Robinson (1980, p. 219) pointed out, '"Today" is influenced, but not completely bound by the past. Any action or decision taken today is either the result of blind habit and convention or it is directed towards its future, which cannot yet be fully known'. As a result, agents, through their decisions and actions, invent or create the future within evolving and pre-existing conventions and institutions (Dequech, 1999b). Agents recognise that the environment in which they make decisions is in some dimensions characterised by the absence of governing ergodic processes, i.e. it is uncertain, and thus transmutable or creative.[29] This *creative economic reality* involves an uncertain future which *can be enduringly transformed* by the purposeful and intentional actions of individuals, groups such as unions and cartels and/or governments, '*often in ways not completely foreseeable by the creators of change*' (Davidson, 1996, p. 482, italics added; see also Shackle, 1955; Lawson, 1997a).

CREATIVE CRUCIAL DECISIONS

Decision-making in situations where information gathered from the past provides an insufficient basis in which to assess future outcomes is of necessity *creative and open* (Lawson, 1997a, 2003). In those situations where a decision cannot be undone, where the economic landscape is forever changed, when the circumstances of the decision are non-repeatable, then the decision is crucial (Shackle, 1955). Crucial decisions refer to those non-routine situations that take place in historical time, circumstances in which re-contracting is expensive (unlike in Arrow–Debreu type constructions).[30] 'Crucial' decisions made today, that turn out to be regretted tomorrow, cannot be remade without significant cost. In these (crucial) situations decision-making agents are tied to *the choices they make*. The future does not wait 'for its contents to be discovered, but for that content to be *originated*' (Shackle, 1980, quoted in Davidson 1982–3, p. 192). The non-routine, non-repeatable nature of such crucial choices does not mean, however, that such choices are rare. Davidson (1996, pp. 500–1) notes that:

> Crucial choices are more common than one might expect; where there are transactions costs: no decision is fully reversible … Because of the substantial transactions costs involved in investment, production, and (at least) big ticket consumption decisions, in these areas, agents are necessarily married to their choices; decisions in these areas are normally crucial and once an action is made, the possible future path is changed. In such a transmutable world, he who hesitates regarding choices in these areas and decides to remain liquid is saved to make a crucial decision another day.

Crucial choices refer to irreversible decisions that involve large sunk costs and contractual commitments. They relate to all areas of social and economic decision-making that involve large transaction costs *including* consumption decisions. They refer to the fact that one is locked in the decisions made at a certain point in time and can relate to any social, political or economic decision that commits substantial resources, e.g. they can pertain to decisions to go to war, to invest, to produce, to redistribute resource, to make (material) consumption decisions, i.e. any decision that cannot easily be undone. Once a course of action is decided upon and taken, the possible future course of events is irrevocably changed.

The concept of crucial decision-making is a portmanteau concept. Through the processes of investment and entrepreneurship creative crucial decision-making generates emergent novelty, i.e. the new products, new production processes, new organisational forms that capitalist enterprise promulgates. This creates uncertainty for other entrepreneurs or investors. Likewise, the decision to wait until another day saves one from committing resources. And in period of great potential change, e.g. on the eve of a great war, or in a time of rapid industrial and technological change, the herd-like decisions to wait and see accumulate and create uncertainty in the minds of entrepreneurs, such that animal spirits may be dimmed and a vicious cycle of cumulative causation ensues, in which both entrepreneurs and investors seek to postpone crucial decision-making. Such a perspective underscores the Post Keynesian focus on liquidity, on the ability to discharge contractual commitments. The deferring of large-scale expenditures allows agents to remain liquid and make a crucial decision another day.

As the discussion above intimates, the creativeness associated with crucial decision-making is inextricably linked to the notion of transmutability of the cosmos. The existence of crucial decisions represents a sufficient condition for the existence of non-deterministic, nonergodic, transmutable processes. Accordingly the decision not to spend one's income on today's products of industry, e.g. the decision to remain liquid, implies that income earners have a choice between 'employment-inducing demand and non-employment inducing demand' (Hahn, 1977, p. 39). In other words, in a world of crucial decisions and fundamental uncertainty, both investors and entrepreneurs can hold assets such as money which are non-substitutable and non-producible. And it is through the holding of such assets that Say's Law becomes untenable and an involuntary unemployment equilibrium can exist, even in the long run.[31] Agents possess the capacity to effect real change and determine historical outcomes in a manner that is not pre-ordained by the system dynamics. This principle of transmutability underlies and binds the concepts of cruciality and fundamental uncertainty. Combined with the essential properties of money – that of a zero elasticity of production and substitutability – such transmutability, which occasionally yields to widespread uncertainty, conspires to explain the existence of involuntary employment and underpins the principle of effective demand (see Chapter 4 above).

If crucial decision-making means that systems and processes are fundamentally 'open', then future states of the world cannot be fully specified because they are *yet to be created* – because economic agents possess the power to create a new future. This is suggestive of the fact that future states of the world cannot be anticipated. What has occurred in the past and the present need not occur again in the future. Individual agents are ignorant of the available courses of action or of the extent of future states of the world because of the irreversible and open-ended nature of time, because the future is transmutable, and not because of limitations in the processing abilities of economic agents. Agents are architects of the future. If processes and outcomes are truly transmutable or open, the future cannot be known prior to its *creation*, regardless of the processing powers we impute to agents. Time differs from complexity in an essential manner. We can never know *ex ante* history's direction, and thus no matter how much information and computational capacity a decision-maker has we can never *ex ante* predict with certainty the future. Agents, and groups of agents, make their own history. But the history created is one that was not necessarily intended (Shackle, 1972).

This discussion suggests an important clarification to how we understand and conceptualise decision-making. We may accept that it may be reasonable to assume an unchanging (ergodic) economic reality in situations of routine, repeatable decision-making (indeed, this is a key aspect of 'learning by doing' and bounded rationality approaches). In some situations it might be reasonable to assume an unchanging economic (immutable) reality and that the future will mirror the past and the current situation.[32] Indeed, the success of insurance companies provides evidence of this fact. Moreover, those expenditures that are directly related to current income (and employment) and do not involve substantial transaction costs, such as routine consumption decisions, appear to approximate closed ergodic processes and thus it may not be unreasonable to characterise decision-making in such contexts in behavioural, i.e. satisficing, terms (Earl, 1983, 1986).[33]

However, relying on the past may be an inappropriate and quite rigid approach to theorising in dealing with surprise and change, i.e. under conditions of transmutable nonergodicity, even in the long run.[34] Satisficing does not make sense in this context because the optimising benchmark against which the shortfall is to be compared is vacuous. Uncertainty resulting from situating decision-making into a flow of historical time, constructed as a sequence of unique events, cannot lead to *ex ante* maximisation even in the long run (Shackle, 1972). We can never know the end or conclusion to which our decisions will actually take us and we have nothing to compare it against. In an ergodic world *ex ante* decisions about the future made by boundedly rational agents may be mistaken *vis-à-vis* omniscient parties, but only in the short run. As noted above, those agents that continue to make mistakes *vis-à-vis* omniscient parties in the long run will be weeded out by some form of Darwinian competitive market process, i.e. there can be no mistakes in the long run.

The concepts of novelty and creativity, however, undermine the notion of rational maximisation *even in the long run*.[35] Although agents may strive for certain objectives when making decisions, such as profit maximisation, if the outcome is unsatisfactory in the sense that their expectations are disappointed and unfulfilled, it does not logically follow that the initial decision was wrong. Considering agents' informational set at the time when the initial decision was made, one cannot *a priori* or *a posteriori* say whether the decision is wrong, or how the world would have been different if another decision had been made. One might be disappointed, in terms of history, *after* it has been created, but one cannot be mistaken *vis-à-vis* any omniscient parties because there are no omniscient parties in an open and transmutable nonergodic world to judge decisions. As Robinson (1962a, p. 75) has pointed out, 'In history, every event has its consequence, and the question, What would have happened if that event had not occurred? is only idle speculation; in theory there is one position of equilibrium the system will arrive at, no matter where it starts'. Similarly, Shackle (1972, pp. 245–6) notes that:

> Rational choice, choice which can demonstrate its own attainment of maximum objectively possible advantage, must be fully informed choice ... The paradox of rationality is that it must concern itself with choosing amongst things fully known; but in the world of time, only this is fully known which is already beyond the reach of choice, having already become actual and thus knowable. Rational choice, it seems, must be confined to timeless matters.

One cannot make a maximising decision, i.e. one that is demonstrably superior, in an open transmutable world, i.e. in history (see Shackle, 1972, pp. 84, 229–30). 'How can choice be based on foreknowledge of what that choice is called on to create?' (Shackle, 1979b, p. 58). If the actual consequences of choice in the present depend on the unknown – and indeed, unknowable – future crucial decisions of others, economic agents can never be certain that they have adopted the best means to the achievement of their ends. One does not know what the maximising alternative is; rather, one can only observe the hypothesis that the decision chosen was expected to be the maximising decision. In what sense can the superiority of choice be asserted or demonstrated? In an uncertain world the notion of maximising is bereft of substantive content – it is vacuous. Choice under uncertainty, however, acquires substantive meaning, is genuine and *does matter in the long run*.

Moreover, it should be apparent that the definition of the long run as an 'asymptotic end state of a process of learning' requires revision in a world in which emergent novelty usurps the process of learning. It would perhaps be more precise, given a transmutable conception of economic processes, to jettison the notion of a long run, i.e. as an 'end of an adjustment process' construct, as a misleading guide to the study of open-ended processes. However, there is a sense in which the long run can be redefined *a la* Kalecki (1968, p. 263) as 'a slowly changing component of a chain of short period situations; it has no independent entity' and thus linked to a transmutable conception of economic process.[36] Indeed, as Keynes (1982, pp. 62–4, quoted in Skidelsky, 2000, p. 33) put it, 'Life and history are made up of short runs'. That is to say, the long run can only be defined in relation to the passing of actual historical time as specified by the analyst after consideration of the process being investigated. Under this conception, the long run is nothing but the historical accumulation of successive short runs. Choice under uncertainty, however, acquires substantive meaning, is genuine and *does matter in the long run*.[37]

CONCLUDING COMMENTS

In this chapter we have drawn out the differences between the concept of bounded rationality and a technically defined concept of 'fundamental' uncertainty. Uncertainty and complexity are not synonymous. Bounded rationality might appear to be a more realistic characterisation of choice, especially as it seemingly switches the focus towards the actual procedures used in decision-making. However, such a methodological approach necessitates an implicit theoretical trade-off. Bounded rationality directs attention to the shortfall with respect to omniscience and the incremental efforts to move towards it, and away from the problems of time. *Bounded rationality refers to a specific view of behaviour. Fundamental uncertainty refers to a specific view of time and choice.* Economists forget this at their peril. We would suggest that the 'impossibility of foreseeing future knowledge' arises in contemplation of a environment that is transmutable *even if* agents could make 'full use of present knowledge'. In an environment that is transmutable and 'open' the processing capacities of agents will affect the *nature* of choice but not the *fact* of choice. An emphasis on choice under uncertainty and a stress on the dynamic evolutionary nature of the competitive process is not, therefore, tied to any (behavioural) conception of the processing abilities of agents.

In an immutable world, in the long run, boundedly rational agents would, or at least have the potential to, learn all the relevant future intertemporal contingencies and incorporate them into maximising behaviour so as to obviate the need for crucial creative decision-making in the (very) long run. In a 'closed' ergodic world agents who are boundedly rational can learn all the relevant future intertemporal contingencies through time. The past provides a guide to the future – albeit a complex one! Conversely, processes that are open and transmutable mean that all future states of the world cannot be anticipated because they are yet to be created.

The distinction between bounded rationality and 'fundamental' uncertainty suggests that one need not make any claims about the rationality of agents *vis-à-vis* their ability to process information in rejecting the axiom of maximisation.[38] In nonergodic transmutable environments there is a fundamental asymmetry between the past and the future. Agents cannot learn all the relevant future intertemporal contingencies through time – the past does not provide a guide to the future in any substantive manner. Agents can learn, however, that the past does not provide a reliable guide to the future course of events, and thus recognise that they will have to invent, but cannot determine, the future by their actions within evolving and existing organisations and institutions. It is this conclusion, that the future is substantially different from the past, that time and history matter, which has generally been conflated with the behavioural assumption of bounded rationality. The result has been that the salience of this concept, not least the recognition of the fact that the future can never be known in advance of its creation, which has often been overlooked by economists.

NOTES

1 It could be argued that in addition to 'behavioural' and 'fundamental uncertainty', which we discuss in this chapter, we have omitted to discuss a third type of uncertainty which we shall label 'Richardsonian' uncertainty after G.B. Richardson (1959, 1960). Richardsonian uncertainty refers to the impossibility of forming rational expectations under conditions of perfect competition where actors remain independent in their choices. The incentive to invest requires, in part, either that there are limits to the competitive supply or that the profit opportunity is not known to anyone else except the investor. However, the conclusion that 'firms have no basis for expectation formation and investment decision, even if consumer preferences are known and stable' (Earl, 1983, p. 28) requires that a full set of Arrow–Debreu (futures) markets exists. One could argue that futures markets do not work effectively as bounded rationality precludes the successful global calculations that underpin the effective operation of futures markets (Hodgson, 1988, pp. 189–90). Alternatively, futures markets cannot exist at all in the case of not-yet-invented commodities which do not exist because they have not yet been created, a consideration that, as we shall see, characterises transmutable nonergodic environments. As Hodgson (1988, p. 190) notes, 'Richardson's argument depends implicitly upon the assumption that [fundamental] uncertainty is present, or that rationality is bounded, or both'. It is for these reasons that we do not refer to 'Richardsonian' uncertainty in the main text as it is subsumed under the concepts of either 'behavioural' or 'fundamental' uncertainty or both.

2 This discussion is also suggestive that both 'fundamental' uncertainty and bounded rationality imply that the competitive processes may be evolutionary in character (cf. Hodgson, 1993, 1994).

3 Horgan (1997, pp. 303–4), for example, records that it is possible to discern as many as forty-five different definitions of complexity. Rosser (1998, p. 289) has suggested that 'a dynamical system can be defined as "complex" if it is non-linear and can be characterised by possessing at least one of the following features: (a) discontinuities in state variables over time, (b) sensitive dependence on initial conditions, or (c) aperiodic ("erratic") fluctuation patterns. Most importantly the feature occurring above must arise endogenously from within the dynamical system itself rather than being the result of an exogenous influence such as a series of random shocks as in New Classical real business cycle models.'

4 Rosser (1999), writing in the *Journal of Economic Perspectives*, surveys developments in complexity theory. Rosser (1998, 1999; see also Hayek, 1967; Leijonhufvud, 1993) notes that deterministic complexity models impute *epistemological* problems to agents on account of computational limitations. Omnipotent parties are not confronted with epistemological problems, however. As Davidson (1991a, 1996) has pointed out, deterministic models of decision-making (stochastic or otherwise) are conducted in logical time and require Savage's ordering axiom for decision-making, i.e. the presumption, at least in principle, that each agent can make a transitive ordering of all possible alternative outcomes. Of course, if the system is too complex for the agent to have complete information, they can only transitively order those outcomes they have information about. However, unless *ad hoc* and arbitrary epistemological bounds are placed upon agents, they can in principle learn and discover the ontology that governs the system. See also footnotes 15 and 27.

5 One can find many instances of this conflation in Simon. For example, with Richard Cyert he has suggested that 'Since "uncertainty" is a time-honored word in economics, let us gather all of these imperfections and limits upon rationality – incomplete knowledge, inadequate means of calculation – under the umbrella of "uncertainty"' (Cyert and Simon, 1983, p. 104).

6 Likewise, Kay (1984, p. 78; cf. Earl, 1984), a former student of Loasby, who is also keen to distinguish between bounded rationality and uncertainty, notes that

'Problems arising from bounded rationality generally involve the associated issue of coping with uncertainty'. Similarly, he has remarked that the 'optimising component was criticised by Simon (1957, 1976) who suggested that many decision-making situations were characterised by genuine (by implication, Knightian or Keynesian) uncertainty, and such individuals frequently satisficed rather than maximised in such circumstances' (Kay, 1989, p. 192). Kay, while trying hard to observe the distinction, ultimately ends up combining the two concepts!

7 Instead of recognising the fact that Shackle recognised the analytical division between bounded rationality and fundamental uncertainty, Earl (1996b) berates him for his 'armchair theorist' approach and lack of (surface) 'realism'.

8 See, for example, O'Donnell and Davidson's exchange during the 1989 Keynes seminar in Canterbury (O'Donnell, 1991; cf. Dequech, 1997b,c).

9 Simon (1959, p. 263) notes that 'Models of satisficing behaviour are richer than models of maximising behaviour, because they treat not only of equilibrium but of the method of reaching it as well. Psychological studies of the formation and change of aspiration levels support propositions of the following kinds. (a) When performance falls short of the level of aspiration, search behaviour (particularly search for new alternatives of action) is induced. (b) At the same time, the level of aspiration begins to adjust itself downward until goals reach levels that are practically attainable. (c) If the two mechanisms just listed operate too slowly to adapt aspirations to performance, emotional behaviour – apathy or aggression, for example – will replace rational adaptive behaviour.'

10 As Loasby (1967, pp. 174–5) points out: 'Optimisation – or, more probably, sub-optimisation – may be possible in some situations; but it is difficult to see how a firm can be a thoroughgoing conscious optimiser without a great deal more information than it commonly possesses.... It is because optimisation is unworkable that satisficing takes its place. The practical alternative is usually sub-optimisation.'

11 As noted in Part I Lawson's (1997a) distinction between open and closed systems is broadly similar to Davidson's distinction between immutable (ergodic) systems and transmutable (nonergodic) systems. Both approaches can be marshalled to elaborate the distinction between bounded rationality and 'fundamental' uncertainty. Davidson's technical discussion offers a more developed assessment of the analytical consequences of the distinction. Until the consequences of accepting this distinction are properly understood it is perhaps not worth abandoning or subsuming Davidson's distinction into the broader critical realist framework just yet.

12 Petersen (1983, p. 43) notes that 'the two major sources of ergodic theory are mathematical physics (especially statistical mechanics and Hamiltonian dynamics) and the theory of stationary stochastic processes'.

13 Petersen (1983, p. 3) comments that the 'basic question of ergodic theory is the convergence of these [time and space] averages ... If the time mean of every measurable function coincides almost everywhere ... with its space mean, the system ... is called ergodic.'

14 One must be careful not to conflate the concepts of stationarity and ergodicity. A stochastic process is stationary if the estimates of time averages do not vary with the period under observation. Since some stationary stochastic processes are nonergodic, i.e. limit cycles, non-stationarity is not necessary for nonergodicity. But since all non-stationary processes are nonergodic non-stationarity is a sufficient condition.

15 Davidson (1991b, p. 178) has explicitly expanded the concept of nonergodicity to incorporate situations that are not defined with respect to stochastic processes. As noted in note 4 above, the ordering axiom plays the same role in deterministic models as the ergodic axiom in stochastic models.

16 Expanding on this, Davidson (1988, p. 332) refers to 'Billingsley (1978, p. 1) [who] states, if "the laws governing ... change remain fixed as time passes [then] ergodic

theory is a key to understanding these fluctuations"'. Whenever the 'passage of time does not affect the set of joint probability laws governing experimentation' (outcomes), then the assumption of ergodicity permits regularities to be perceived from what might at first sight be patternless fluctuations (Billingsley, 1978, p. 2, see also pp. 60–5). This pattern of regularities can then be reliably projected into the future.'

17 Ergodic theory, as Samuelson (1969, p. 184) points out, implies that if 'the state redivided income each morning, by night the rich would also be sleeping in their beds and the poor under the bridges.'

18 It also undermines the notion that mainstream economics, founded as it is on the ergodic axiom, is the science of choice and thus leads to inconsistencies at the level of social theory (see Lawson, 1997a).

19 Simon (1959, p. 254) has revealingly commented that 'Economists have been relatively uninterested in descriptive microeconomics – understanding the behaviour of individual economic agents – except as this is necessary to provide a foundation for macroeconomics. The normative microeconomist "obviously" doesn't need a theory of human behaviour: he wants to know how people ought to behave, not how they do behave. On the other hand, the macroeconomist's lack of concern with individual behaviour stems from different considerations. First, he assumes that the economic actor is rational, and hence he makes strong predictions about human behaviour without performing the hard work of observing people. Second, he often assumes competition, which carries with it the implication that only the rational survive. Thus, the classical economic theory of markets with perfect competition and rational agents is deductive theory that requires almost no contact with empirical data once its assumptions are accepted.'

20 Loasby (1989, p. 146) provides further support for this assertion when he asserts that 'Simon's own analysis no doubt helps buttress his belief in our ability to solve problems at least as fast as they are created; but although he recognises the practical importance of the varying speeds with which different interactions take effect, nevertheless, for one who prefers process to equilibrium as an organising principle, he seems to have very little sense of the significance of time in human affairs. Compare his writings with those of Marshall, Shackle, or the later Hicks, and one is immediately conscious of a great difference in attitude and style.' As noted above, time or history has no substantive role in an immutable world (in the sense alluded to above).

21 As Davidson (1996, p. 486) notes typically, in bounded rationality models 'agents form subjective expectations (usually, but not necessarily in the form of Bayesian subjective probabilities). In the short-run, subjective probabilities need not coincide with the presumed immutable objective probabilities. Today's decision-makers, therefore, can make short-run errors regarding the uncertain (i.e. probabilistic risky) future. Agents "learn" from these short-run mistakes so that subjective probabilities or decision weights tend to converge onto an accurate description of the programmed external reality.'

22 Many parallels could be drawn here with Day's (1967) discussion of the convergence of satisficing to marginalism given a stable (ergodic) environment which agents can learn about in the light of outcomes and feedback from the environment and subsequently revise their decision rules. Proponents of Simon's approach presumably would counter this argument by suggesting that bounded rationality refers to 'computational capacity' and not to the learning process. However, the 'rational' aspect to the concept of bounded rationality is suggestive that decision makers will attempt, especially if they find themselves making persistent mistakes, to revise their decision rules and devise more successful ones that, given the environment is stable (ergodic), will converge on omniscience in the long run (as defined above). To deny this would deny the 'rational' aspect of bounded rationality, which is highly coveted.

23 One should distinguish between routines that are embedded in pre-programmed deterministic models and conventions that emerge as a response and strategy for coping with the uncertainty (cf. Dequech, 1999a,b). The concept of convention implied in the latter is contingent upon the agency of individuals and not closed-system dynamics as posited by bounded rationality type approaches.

24 As Shackle (1972, p. 426) notes, 'The most dramatic and spectacular secret of success is novelty, and novelty is that which an infallible algorithm must, by definition, exclude'. This also has concomitant implications for theories of competition, bargaining, games, models of dynamic learning etc. (see also Loasby, 1989).

25 Davidson (1996, p. 486) notes that 'Those agents whose subjective probabilities do not converge on the objective probabilities will make persistent systematic forecasting errors. The market embodies some form of a Darwinian process of natural selection that weeds out the persistent error-makers who make inefficient choices until, in the long-run, only agents who do not make systematic errors remain.'

26 Likewise, Davidson (1996, p. 492; see also 1989c, 1993b) has suggested that Austrian theorists deal with 'epistemological uncertainty and a programmed external reality'. Whether or not this is an accurate description of Austrian theorists is irrelevant; rather, these comments suggest that Austrians would further benefit from a precise technical delineation of their concept of uncertainty. We return to this theme in Chapter 8.

27 Sawyer (1988b; see also Petersen, 1983; Parry, 1987) draws our attention to the fact that there are various possible meanings associated with the distinction between ergodic and nonergodic processes. Typically, the concept of an ergodic process is associated with the notion of 'a Markov process, where the probability of the system moving from one state (say S_i) to another (say S_j) in one period is interdependent of the time period considered and of the previous history of the system. Let us label that probability P_{ij}. The system is then considered to be ergodic if the transition probabilities are such that the system can effectively be in a stochastic equilibrium. There are several ways in which a system could be said to be nonergodic, if by that we merely mean that the system is not ergodic (whereas the technical definition would be a Markov process which did not have the property of being ergodic)' (Sawyer, 1988b, pp. 99–100). There are a number of ways in which it could be maintained that the system is not ergodic: 'First, it is conceivable that an individual is uncertain (i.e. does not know and cannot estimate the relevant P_{ij}'s), yet the process itself could be ergodic … The second possibility is the probabilities change over time and/or are not independent of previous events (i.e. it is not a Markov process). This may involve uncertainty (if the change of probabilities cannot be accurately forecast) and history matters. Thirdly, the system may be non-ergodic in the technical sense of not being capable of generating a stochastic equilibrium outcome, which indicates that to say a system is ergodic involves assumptions on the relationship between transition probabilities … previous transition probabilities would still hold, and in that way the probability of future outcomes, given the current situation, can be estimated … The fourth way is for the system to evolve in a deterministic manner but with movements between different states, i.e. the P_{ij}s take a value of 0 or 1. A self-perpetuating trade cycle could fall into that category. For example, suppose the economic cycle follows a sine curve pattern. Its previous movements are a good guide to future movements, and from its current position and rate of change its position at any time in the future can be exactly forecast' (Sawyer, 1988b, p. 100). It is perhaps to avoid such ambiguity that Davidson (1996) has broadened his discussion and further refined his discussion of ergodicity and nonergodicity by embedding it in the more general distinction between immutable and transmutable processes. Davidson has defined nonergodicity in terms of the *absence of governing ergodic processes and immutable laws;* that is to say, Davidson rejects the idea of governing transition probabilities underpinning the movements between states of nature. Thus there is a sense in which Davidson's definition of nonergodicity is similar to the second way of defining nonergodicity, discussed above, but, more saliently, moves beyond the idea that stochastic processes characterise human behaviour, espousing a creative, novelty-inducing conceptualisation of agency.

28 This forms the basis for Davidson's (1982–3) assertion that the rational expectations hypothesis is 'a fallacious foundation for the study of crucial decision-making processes' (see also Davidson, 1996, p. 493).

29 As Davidson (1996, p. 482) highlights, 'This nonergodic view of modelling uncertainty has been described by Hicks (1977, p. vii) as a situation where agents "do not know what is going to happen and know that they do not know what is going to happen. As in history!" Hicks (1979, p. 129) then declared that "I am bold enough to conclude from these considerations that the usefulness of 'statistical' or 'stochastic' methods in economics is a good deal less than is now conventionally supposed."'

30 'Mainstream micro as well as macro theorists ignore this element of cruciality in almost all decisions. Orthodox theorists assume the ability to re-contract without costs if one does not initially trade at the general equilibrium prices that embody the objective reality governed by the real parameters of a predetermined economic system' (Davidson, 1996, pp. 500–1).

31 As Arrow and Hahn (1971, p. 361) point out, if money (and therefore the demand for liquidity) can affect real outcomes, then all general equilibrium existence theorems are jeopardised.

32 It is often ignored that even Davidson himself entertains this possibility. He has noted that 'In the real world, some economic processes may be ergodic, at least for short sub-periods of calendar time, while others are not. The problem facing every economic decision-maker is to determine whether (a) the phenomenon involved is currently being governed by distribution functions which are sufficiently time invariant as to be presumed ergodic – at least for the relevant future, or (b) nonergodic circumstances are involved' (Davidson, 1988, p. 163). Thus there is a sense in which the concerns voiced by both Mearman (2006) and Hodgson (2006) regarding the possibility of partial closure and therefore the role of formal methods are implicitly accepted by Davidson.

33 However, to say that it would not be unreasonable is not to say that one would accept the narrow view of human agency implied by this framework. Even seemingly closed, ergodic processes in the social realm have to be sustained by agency, choice, conventions and social structures (see Lawson, 1997a).

34 There is a sense in which the definition of the long run changes upon recognition of the transmutable nature of economic processes. Clearly, the definition of the long run defined as an asymptotic end-state of a process of learning makes little sense if the process is continually usurped by the extant agency of creative novel choice. Strictly speaking, we should replace the terminology of the long run with history (Robinson, 1980). However, this distinction would further confuse matters and draw attention away from the essential stress on the distinction between creativity and computational constraints.

35 It is for this reason that Davidson advances the notion of sensible expectations. Sensible agents recognise that the future substantially differs from the past and entertain this possibility in decision-making – rational Walrasian intertemporal optimisation is not possible and it is for this reason that it becomes reasonable to hold non-interest-bearing assets such as money as a hedge against uncertainty.

36 As Sawyer (2000, p. xv) notes, 'this laconic statement, on which Kalecki did not elaborate, can be interpreted as undermining the predominant [ergodic, closed-system] equilibrium approach to economic analysis whereby there is a long-period equilibrium around which the economy fluctuates or towards which the economy tends and which is unaffected by the short period movements of the economy'.

37 Although, strictly speaking one might accept that ultimately the concept of the long run appears a misleading focus for historical analysis in which uncertainty and expectations matter, and should be rejected for a historical and processual approach to the study of economic phenomenon. However, as noted above, such a view is implied by Kalecki's reformulation. Moreover, the notion of a 'long run' may be retained here to promote dialogue across different research traditions.

38 This does not entail that one must reject the concept of bounded rationality; *rather, it implies that the distinction should be observed.*

Part III

The future of Post Keynesianism

7 Whither Post Keynesianism?

Lord Keynes, in a famous forecast, thought the subject would eventually become unimportant – in social significance it would rank about with dentistry ... But though in a sense Keynes was right about the subject in decline, in a larger sense he was wrong ... the future of economics could be rather bright. It could be in touch with the gravest problems of our time. Whether this is so – whether economics is important – is up to economists. They can, if they are determined, be unimportant; they can, if they prefer a comfortable home life and regular hours, continue to make a living out of the infinitely interesting gadgetry of disguise...

Or economists can enlarge their system. They can embrace, in all its diverse manifestations, the power they now disguise.

J.K. Galbraith (1973b, pp. 341–3)

Economics that assumes transformation, change, can never be as tidy, secure and elegant as that which assumes and cultivates unchanging verity.

J.K. Galbraith (1991, p. 41)

INTRODUCTION

In the earlier parts of this book we have argued that Post Keynesian economics is methodologically coherent and should be characterised as an open-system, historical approach, which underpins its recognition of the salience of uncertainty and the principle of effective demand. Drawing on this perspective, this chapter explores the not unrelated claim that Post Keynesian economics is in demise and that its impact upon the wider economics profession remains critical, unconstructive and marginal. Here, however, we reject this view, arguing that those who expound the view of the demise of Post Keynesianism are mistaken and their arguments misconceived – with the source of this confusion primarily the different methodological outlook held by Post Keynesians and the mainstream. Accordingly we suggest that the future of Post Keynesians lies in a new dialogue with other approaches that develop analysis consistent with the emphasis of open-systems processes.

Pronouncements regarding the demise of Post Keynesian economics are based upon two distinct but related hypotheses that we shall label the internalist thesis and the externalist thesis. The internalist thesis relates to the accusations aimed at

Post Keynesianism of an unhealthy preoccupation with negative and unconstructive critiques of orthodox economics, displaying insularity and incoherence, accusations that have led to the marginalisation of Post Keynesianism. The externalist thesis relates to the broader malaise in, and status of, economics in general and the declining interest in economics as a discipline worthy of study, with the concomitant implications for any branch of economics such as Post Keynesianism. Over the last twenty years we have witnessed a relative decline in the numbers studying economics at further and higher educational institutions and an expansion of interest in business-oriented programmes, which are more practically related.

In rejecting the internalist thesis, following the arguments of Chapters 3 and 4, we argue that Post Keynesianism is coherent at a methodological level and that its ontological view underpins its recognition of the importance of the principle of effective demand. Moreover, we argue that Post Keynesian economists' failure to engage with the mainstream is primarily methodological. Post Keynesians are committed to open-systems theorising, whereas orthodox theorists are wedded to the precepts of closed-systems theorising. While it is far from true that Post Keynesianism is negative and unconstructive, it logically follows that the opportunity for extensive dialogue is limited, but neither impossible nor undesirable (as, perhaps, the latter half of this book indicates). With respect to the externalist thesis, we note that the wide dissatisfaction with orthodox economics is rooted in the general lack of realism, the excessive and unnecessary mathematisation, and the narrow and outmoded conceptions of empirical research. Similarly it is argued that this debacle is at source methodological: as Lawson (1997a) has argued it relates to the fallacy of applying closed-systems reasoning to the study of open systems.

After rejecting claims that we are witnessing the demise of Post Keynesian economics, we instead question whether orthodox economics as conventionally understood is in crisis and dying (Robinson, 1972; Bell and Kristol, 1981; Ormerod, 1994, 2000; Heilbroner and Milberg, 1995; Cassidy, 1996; cf. Dasgupta, 1998). Moreover, the origin of this crisis is firmly located in the inappropriate employment of closed-systems thinking to predict open-systems outcomes (Lawson, 2004b, 2005c, 2006c). This allows us to clarify the choice as to its future that Post Keynesianism is presented with: either it can attempt to engage the mainstream, which raises problems of methodological incomm ensurability and isolationism, or it can look to other approaches which are compatible with open-systems theorising. We conclude by advocating the latter.

THE DEMISE OF POST KEYNESIANISM? INTERNAL FACTORS

As noted above, the internalist thesis relates to three principal charges. Post Keynesianism, it is argued, (i) exhibits an unhealthy preoccupation with negative and unconstructive critiques of orthodox economics, (ii) is insular, and (iii) is incoherent. While Post Keynesian economists have made extensive contributions to the history of economic thought, the methodology of economics and economic theory, the impact of these contributions remains marginal. Post Keynesian economics does not appear in the programmes of leading economics conferences and there are few explicitly Post Keynesian articles published in the Diamond list of high-ranking journals. This has accompanying implications for the appraisal of Post Keynesians' research output (as well as that of other heretics).[1] As a result, the demand for Post Keynesian economists is low. Few Post Keynesian economists are hired within economics departments, which means that few courses are being taught in Post Keynesian economics (Lee, 1995b).[2]

There are several plausible explanations for this marginality that relate to the internalist thesis. One explanation, alluded to above, is that Post Keynesian economists are only engaged in negative critique, and that they are hostile to mainstream economists and/or are perceived as such. Indeed, they are widely perceived as not wishing to communicate with mainstream economics. While this view is erroneous, Post Keynesianism must bear some of the responsibility for this state of affairs, which is rooted in the inception of the Post Keynesian label.

The common unifying feature of Post Keynesianism in its formative years was its rejection and unified opposition to mainstream economics (Davidson, 1993b). Post Keynesians united around the maxim 'the enemy of my enemy is my friend', exhibiting a distaste for *laissez faire* policies rather than representing a distinct approach to economics. During the initial years, Sraffians were subsumed under the Post Keynesian label. However, it is the inclusion of the Sraffian strand that has generated much confusion, especially within the mainstream. The Sraffian strand openly adopts many of the precepts of a closed-system modelling strategy and would appear well placed to engage in a dialogue with mainstream economics. Indeed, the Cambridge controversies would appear to demonstrate this point (see Harcourt, 1972). The capital controversies debate, however, was largely viewed by the mainstream to be negative in critique and openly hostile (this is not surprising as the controversies represented an internal critique). It is largely because of this episode that Post Keynesian economics acquired the label of 'not bringing much to the table' and 'engaging in negative debate'.[3] Sraffians, while adopting the common language of closed-system mathematics, were widely perceived, especially by the mainstream, as uninterested in *constructive* debate (Hahn, 1975, 1982).[4]

However, as argued above, it was clear quite early on that within this broad church a tension existed between those strands who espoused either an open or a closed-system approach to the study of economic phenomena. It is now widely recognised that while Sraffians share many common political points of emphasis with the other strands of Post Keynesianism (Davidson, 1981, pp. 154–5), the assumption that dominant forces exist which move the economy towards a normal or long-run period position, a characteristic of closed-system modelling, sits uncomfortably with an 'open' world characterised by 'fundamental' uncertainty and institutions such as money-denominated contracts (Carvalho, 1983–4, 1984–5, 1988, 1990; Hodgson, 1989; Arestis, 1996a).[5] As a result Roncaglia (1995; cf. Mongiovi, 1994, 2000) has called for the abandonment of the project to integrate Sraffian and Post Keynesian analysis. This is a view that we endorse here (see para 1 above).

It is this dawning realisation, that Sraffians are methodologically incompatible with other traditions within Post Keynesianism, which has led to the Sraffians being no longer viewed as part of the core of the Post Keynesian programme. This relates to a core argument of this book, that the inclusion of the Sraffian school under the Post Keynesian umbrella is highly contentious, especially given its closed-system methodology. The time has come for Post Keynesianism to formally part company with the Sraffians and jettison the burdensome accusation (more mainstream stereotype) of negative critique, which is chiefly identified with their contribution.[6] While Sraffians and Post Keynesians can be united under the 'political economy' label (see above), it is now clear that theoretical coherence should not be sacrificed for political convenience.[7] As noted above the coping stone of Post Keynesianism is its commitment to open-systems reasoning. And, as such, any attempts to develop (coherent) links to other approaches must be within this framework. We will return to this below.

A second explanation for the marginality of Post Keynesianism voiced in the mainstream is that its proponents want to communicate with the mainstream but are unable to do so (cf. Hey, 1995). They are charged with accusations of insularity and narrow-mindedness. There are several possible reasons for this (perceived) failure to communicate. Firstly, Post Keynesians may have (or may be perceived to have) an inadequate knowledge of developments in mainstream economics.[8] They are considered to lack scholastic rigour.[9] This is perhaps illustrated by the fact that many of the characteristic themes of Post Keynesian economics have (at a superficial level) comparable developments in mainstream economics. However, Post Keynesian economics is perceived to be uninformed of such developments (and vice versa). For example, the Kaleckian emphasis on oligopolistic competition parallels New Keynesian models of imperfect competition; however, little reference is generally made to these developments. Secondly, Post Keynesian economists are seen to be more concerned with critique, methodology and the history of economic thought, rather than the development of economic theory and policy.[10] Finally, and linked to the second reason, the style of Post Keynesian economics is seen to be more literary, with limited use of formal analytical techniques such as mathematics and econometrics.[11]

However, none of these charges stands up to close scrutiny. There is evidence that this failure to communicate reflects a reluctance on the part of the mainstream to engage in debate. The *Journal of Post Keynesian Economics* has been keen to initiate several forums that engage the mainstream in debate on, for example: the distinction between asymmetric information and 'fundamental uncertainty'; the difference between mark-up pricing and marginal cost pricing; the crisis in methodology; this is in addition to sponsoring several policy debates (see also Rotheim, 1998). It is not the case that Post Keynesians are not interested in applied economics or policy.[12] It should be noted, however, that Post Keynesian conceptions of applied research are broader than most mainstream conceptions (which tend to be confined to econometric research). Moreover, it is immediately apparent when reviewing recent contributions in the *Journal of Post Keynesian Economics* that Post Keynesians do use formal analytical techniques. However, their role is illustrative rather than demonstrative, often being relegated to appendices.[13] Given that Post Keynesian economists have difficulty publishing in mainstream journals (largely reflecting academic prejudice and a misunderstanding of Post Keynesian methodology), it would appear correct to suggest that it is mainstream economics that possesses an inadequate knowledge of developments in Post Keynesianism, and not vice versa.

A third and perhaps more substantive explanation for the marginality of Post Keynesianism and the (perceived) failure to communicate, is that Post Keynesian economists have no wish to engage in debate with mainstream economists. This explanation is at root methodological. As noted above, a distinguishing feature of the methodological contributions of Post Keynesian economists is their commitment to thinking seriously about uncertainty. Post Keynesian economists' failure to successfully engage in debate with the mainstream is primarily methodological. Post Keynesians utilise open-systems theorising, whereas orthodox theorists are wedded to the precepts of closed-systems theorising. While it is far from true that Post Keynesianism is negative and unconstructive, it logically follows that the opportunity for extensive dialogue is limited (but not impossible). Post Keynesians have attempted to engage the mainstream but have largely been unsuccessful in advancing serious discussion. This reflects the fact that Post Keynesians do not talk the same methodological language as mainstream economists. Post Keynesians may not be best placed to sit down and talk at the mainstream table. However it may not be the only table to sit at. It might be the case that mainstream economics is in decline, and that alternative tables should be sought if Post Keynesianism is to avoid stagnation and grow and evolve. It is to these issues that we now turn.

THE DEMISE OF POST KEYNESIANISM? EXTERNAL FACTORS

Let us take stock of the argument thus far. Post Keynesianism, some critics argue, is in decline. Post Keynesian economics is incoherent and has failed in its attempt to provide an alternative and/or engage mainstream economics. We have suggested, however, that none of these charges stand up to close scrutiny. Post Keynesians have a coherent methodological outlook and have indicated a willingness to engage the mainstream in positive productive debate. However, it is clear that Post Keynesianism has failed in this second respect. The impact upon mainstream economic thinking has been marginal. One could argue that the increasingly marginal status of Post Keynesian economics should be viewed as a challenge to further engage with orthodoxy. In this section we question whether this represents a wise strategy given the increasing malaise of mainstream economics, i.e. the externalist thesis.

The externalist thesis refers to the low regard of economists and the (relative) decline in interest in economics as an academic discipline. This malaise has obvious implications for any school of thought within economics such as Post Keynesian economics. If economics is in decline, then whither Post Keynesian economics? Does the fact that economics departments are hiring fewer and fewer

Post Keynesian economists just not reflect the diminished status of, and declining interest in, economics in general?

The assertion that the status of professional economists has never been lower is perhaps only mildly contentious.[14] While economists have ignored Keynes' advice to become more humble, like dentists, they have acquired their widespread disdain.[15] Take, for example, the not unusual contemptuous comments reserved for economists by Simon Jenkins in the London *Times*:

> Economics is an accessory after the fact of economic crime. It peddles bogus objectivity, such as statistics purporting to measure unemployment or productivity or price inflation. It peddles no less bogus models of money supply, employment and growth. The thousands thrown out of work as a result of modelling errors in the past five years might be a little consoled if they knew someone else suffered for contributing to their misery, and for the dud growth forecasts that prolonged it.
>
> (*The Times*, 3 February 1993)

It is clear that economists in general have acquired an 'image problem'! That there is a declining interest in economics as a discipline worthy of study is, perhaps, more contentious. Take the United Kingdom for example.[16] Over the last twenty years we have witnessed an unprecedented expansion of higher education, and change in its delivery and structure. In 1980 the total number of first degrees obtained for all subjects from 'old' universities was 66,540.[17] By 1993 this figure had risen to 95,696, a 44 per cent increase (the majority of this increase occurring between 1989 and 1993). Similarly, in 1980, the total number of higher degrees in all subjects obtained from 'old' universities was 18,546. By 1993 this figure had risen to 57,635, an exceptional 211 per cent increase. But what of economics? Over the same period the total number of first degrees in economics had *risen* from 2117 to 2790 while the number of higher degrees rose from 631 to 1663. This hardly represents the death knell for economics!

However when the *relative* increase in these student numbers is considered, the externalist thesis gains more credence. Over this period there was a 32 per cent increase in the number of first degrees in economics awarded and a 164 per cent increase in the number of higher degrees awarded. The growth in numbers of those studying economics clearly lagged behind the growth in all subjects university wide. This slow growth perhaps would not cause great concern in itself. However, when one considers which has happened in business management studies, which many in the university sector regard as a close substitute for economics, the externalist thesis comes sharply into focus. Between 1980 and 1993 the total number of first degrees in business management studies (excluding accountancy-related degrees) sharply increased from 1041 to 2202, while the number of higher degrees (including MBAs) rose from 1084 to 6348. This represents a 112 per cent increase in the number of first degrees in business management studies awarded and a staggering 486 per cent increase in the number of higher degrees. The growth in numbers of those studying management studies massively exceeded the growth in all subjects at the university level.[18] In the race to entice students onto courses, business studies seems to be clearly winning.[19] Is this a case of the marketplace delivering its verdict upon the relevance of economics?

The situation is no better in America (Parker, 1993). In 1991, the *Journal of Economic Literature* published the findings of a study by the *Commission on Graduate Education in Economics* (COGEE) of the *American Economic Association*. The survey focused on 91 American university economics departments which were responsible for the production of approximately 90 per cent of the country's PhD. economists. The results suggest some cause for (mainstream?) concern. Ignoring questions as to whether its method and content are rigorous and robust, economics, in America, is clearly under-performing within the academic education marketplace (Parker, 1993). COGEE's report (statistical annex) highlights the fact that enrolments in economics graduate programs, after increasing threefold during the 1960s, stagnated for a quarter century, with the annual number of MAs and PhDs constant at just over 2800. The situation in America parallels the United Kingdom experience. While economics graduate programs have declined, competing academic industries such as business administration and public policy have blossomed. As well as the 70,000 new MBAs conferred each year in America, business and public policy schools currently award 5700 new MAs and PhDs – double the number of (new) economists produced each year in America (Parker, 1993).

Moreover, while economics has witnessed a fall in its academic market share, it has also faced, in a manner not too dissimilar to other failing industries, an increase in the complaints regarding the quality of its product, its core theory, and the nature of how it is taught (Parker, 1993; Lee, 1995b; Cassidy, 1996; Galbraith, Jr, 1996). Given the widespread dissatisfaction with economists and the diminished interest in economics as an academic subject, the externalist argument that economics is in demise and that any school of thought within economics, such as Post Keynesianism economics, will also inevitably decline seemingly carries force (cf. Harcourt, 1992b). However, this represents a misunderstanding of the processes that have led to the decline in economics. We should be more categoric. It is not economics *per se* that is in decline, but *mainstream economics*. The demise and diminished influence (rumours of its death may be somewhat premature) of mainstream economics need not be of major concern to Post Keynesians (we discuss the choices open to Post Keynesians below).[20] The reasons for the demise of econonics are primarily methodological. As should be apparent from the comments above, it is the lack of predictive and quantitative success that has plagued the economics profession and underpinned claims regarding its demise (Ormerod, 1994; Lawson, 1997a). As Ormerod (1994) notably argued, a case may be made for the death of economics itself.

As noted above in Part I, mainstream economics is based upon a closed-systems methodology. Many of the theoretical structures and predictions of mainstream economic theory, and the quantitative techniques employed, are founded upon this closed-system methodology. The poor forecasting performance of a substantial number of econometric models and the fictitious idealisations of core theory have been responsible for the loss of faith in the economics profession. The well-known derisory jokes about economists, who are wonderfully lampooned by Galbraith (1994) in his novel *A Tenured Professor*, are cited by Post Keynesians as *prima facie* evidence that a closed-system approach to the study of economic phenomena is limiting and a realist open-system approach is relevant.[21] The failure of econometrics to robustly forecast the future has been cited by Post Keynesians as justifying the economics of Keynes and an open-system approach that focuses on explanation rather than prediction. It is the lack of relevance of much mainstream economic theory as well as its poor forecasting performance that has resulted in an increased interest in more practically related, business-oriented programmes. It is not economics *per se* that is in demise but, specifically, closed-systems theorising. It is evident, however, that a range of directions, strategies and opportunities is available to Post Keynesians which must be seized upon if the subject is to flourish, and it is to this we now turn.

THE FUTURE OF POST KEYNESIANISM

Fortunately, Post Keynesians are not alone in recognising that the future is uncertain and open. There are other schools of thought that have sympathies with this vision.[22] The future of Post Keynesianism rests upon choosing one of two available strategies. Either it can attempt to engage with mainstream economics (or more specifically with neoclassical economics) or, as argued here, it can seek links to other traditions with which it may be methodologically compatible, and engage in a more productive debate than that which has previously been possible with the orthodoxy.[23] The Post Keynesian approach, with its vinculum of open-system theorising, may be methodologically incapable of establishing a common dialogue with mainstream economics. But, as argued over the previous sections, mainstream economics may not be the best table at which to sit and engage in academic debate, especially considering its relative demise. Mainstream economics and Post Keynesian economics may be regarded as methodologically incommensurate, with only limited capacity to engage the orthodoxy. However, there may be other tables at which Post Keynesian economics may be more welcome to sit, and to which it has much to bring.

As argued above in Part I, one of the defining features of Post Keynesianism is that it possesses a clear understanding of the importance of the principle of effective demand and of the macroeconomics of monetary economies existing in transmutable, historical time – a major contribution to open-systems thinking and the basis for gains for trade with other open-systems approaches. In developing a more comprehensive and integrated contribution Post Keynesians should examine the potential for debate with other heterodox traditions.[24]

Post Keynesians are recognising and rising to this challenge and many have started to make positive contributions to the various sub-disciplines of economics (e.g. Holt and Pressman, 2001; Downward, 2004; Earl, 2005; cf. Fontana, 2005). For example, both Mark Lavoie (1994) and Peter Earl (1983, 1986, 1991, 1998) have done much to advance an approach to consumer choice which, notwithstanding some necessary caveats, appears to be broadly compatible with the methodological approach advocated here and should inform the articulation and further investigation of a Post Keynesian approach to consumer choice (the Institutionalists could also inform such developments here; see Hamilton, 1987). Post Keynesians have also started to research empirically and identify the symbiosis and contractual nexus of various technostructures and how they can affect the content of advertising and influence consumer demand in ways that may conflict with the wider public interest (cf. Anderson and Dunn, 2006; Dunn and Anderson, 2007). In Chapter 11, for example, we consider what a Post Keynesian approach to health economics might look like. Similarly, Downward (2004) has sought to develop a Post Keynesian approach to the study of the leisure industry, noting the many insights and positive contributions that Post Keynesians have made and can make. And there is a growing contribution to green economics that links the Post Keynesian approach to macroeconomics and employment policy to environmental issues and the development of sustainable policies (see Forstater, 2003, 2004, 2006; Lawson, 2007b). It may also be possible to develop an approach to feminist economics based on an open systems methodology (see, for example, Lawson, 1999c, 2005a, 2007a).

It is also possible to cast the net even further. There are other approaches and areas of potential synergy that will aid Post Keynesianism's continued development and could potentially inform the development of Post Keynesian microeconomics. As noted above, links have been made recently to the (old) Institutionalist tradition (Hodgson, 1989, 1999c, 2000c, 2004; Samuels, 1995).[25] Institutionalism has been linked to Post Keynesianism primarily because it emphasises the transformational nature of economic reality by, for example, highlighting the malleability of preference systems (Hodgson, 1988, 1989, 1998c, 2000a,b, 2001b, 2004).[26] This seems to parallel the Post Keynesian methodological emphasis on a creative, holistic, transmutable reality while at the same time providing for an endogenous theory of expectation formation and the emergence of uncertainty-mitigating (but not eliminating) institutions (Hodgson, 1985, 1989, 1997b; see also Chasse, 1991).[27] Likewise, if Post Keynesians can be described as committed to aspects of the Critical Realist programme, then so can Institutionalists (see C. Lawson, 1994; C. Lawson, *et al.*, 1996a,b; Lawson, 1997a, 2006b).

The institutional approach focuses on evolution and process examining the dynamic interactions between socio-economic groups within economic systems (Hodgson, 1998c; Tool, 1988a,b). The fundamental proposition is that it is the whole organisational and social provisioning structure of the economy that allocates resources and income. The concept of institutions employed by Institutionalists is broad and holistic, referring to the habits, routines and customs employed by both firms and households, and extended to include other institutions such as the government and, say, the banking system (cf. Hodgson, 1988, 1997b; Samuels, 1989; Samuels and Lee, 1994; Lee, 1988). As Arestis (1996a; see also Lee, 1998) notes, the Institutionalist framework may considerably improve the microeconomics of Post Keynesianism.[28] As argued above in Chapter 2, the broad policy agenda of Post Keynesian economics would be policies and institutional arrangements supportive of high levels of aggregate demand in pursuit of the objective of full employment. Post Keynesians are institution builders, as it is institutions that can provide stability in the face of uncertainty and, if designed correctly, stability to achieve near-full employment.

In addition to the Institutionalist tradition, there already exists a variety of approaches that are (potentially) compatible with the methodological perspective outlined above. The potential exists for broader discussion and more fruitful exchange of ideas in areas that have not been previously attempted or sought. For example, the post-Marshallian analysis of authors such as Andrews (1949a), Richardson (1960) and Loasby (1976, 1991) provides a good link between the micro-economics of Keynes, which is embedded in Marshallian economics, and an approach to the firm and to innovation which is conducted in terms of open-system theorising (see Finch, 1999, 2000). Moreover, post-Marshallians, like many Post Keynesians, draw upon a broad array of empirical approaches such as case studies and questionnaires (cf. Downward, 1999; Lee, 2002). That too has led to their marginalisation *vis-à-vis* the mainstream. This clearly reflects a methodological incommensurability epitomised by their historical approach.

Links may also be made to the Austrian school (cf. Wynarczyk, 1992, 1999). There are clear gains from trade to be had between the Austrian theory of praxis and the Post Keynesian 'emerging theory of agency' and conception of transmutable processes (Lawson, 1997a). Austrians propose an organic approach to learning, insisting on the assumption that individuals learn something from the passing of time, not least that the outcomes of market processes are *uncertain* (O'Driscoll and Rizzo, 1995). According to Austrians, it is the world of ignorance and differentiated knowledge that provides the praxeological basis for want satisfaction and value theory. This closely mirrors the Post Keynesian stress on the transformational capacity of agents. However while Austrian ideas tend to be acknowledged by Post Keynesians, their right-wing associations tend to discourage their serious study. This is perhaps surprising given, as Rizzo (O'Driscoll and Rizzo, 1995, p. xvii) himself acknowledges, Austrians (notwithstanding their substantive differences) share similar philosophical foundations with, among others, both Institutionalists and Post Keynesians (cf. Wynarczyk, 1992, 1999; Clark, 1987–8, 1989, 1993). Political affiliations should not preclude serious study of Austrian ideas. There would appear to be much opportunity for cordial debate examining the differences and similarities between the Post Keynesian distinction between 'ergodic' and 'nonergodic' processes and the concomitant implications for Austrian ideas such as 'pattern coordination' (cf. Davidson, 1989c, 1993b). Moreover there is a clear need to examine in more detail the interesting Austrian juxtaposition between Keynes' 'palatable' theoretical system and his 'unpalatable' policy prescriptions, and thus we focus, in Chapter 8, on one of the principal sources of disagreement.

Further links to other traditions also obtain. Davidson (1996) has conjoined the specific Post Keynesian view of time, nonergodicity, that underpins the

Post Keynesian commitment to open-system theorising, to Schumpeterian entrepreneurship (as noted in Chapter 5 above). Uncertainty (nonergodicity) is fundamental to the study of contemporary society because '[t]he fundamental impulse that sets and keeps the capitalist engine in motion comes from new consumer's goods, the new methods of production or transportation, the new forms of industrial organisation that capitalist enterprise creates' (Schumpeter, 1943, p. 83). Such innovations are interpretable as *new* knowledge and are associated with tremors, shocks and surprises, i.e. a transmutable conception of the competitive process (Dequech, 1997b). This opens the door for a fruitful exchange with the neo-Schumpeterian school which itself makes reference to the concept of nonergodicity (Dosi, 1982, 1988a,b; Dosi and Egidi, 1991; Dosi and Orsenigo, 1988; see also Lazonick, 1991). That the scope and potential for such an exchange exists is demonstrated by Crocco (1997), who recently attempted to synthesise Keynes' approach to decision-making under uncertainty with the neo-Schumpeterian approach to innovation and entrepreneurship. Moreover, this is also suggestive of further links to the evolutionary school to which many neo-Schumpeterians and post-Marshallians tend to be aligned (see Nelson and Winter, 1982; cf. Northover, 1999; Finch, 2000). In Chapter 5 we considered Keynes' discussion of uncertainty and the extent to which this is embedded in a view of the dynamics of the competitive process. We argued that aspects of Keynes' discussion are ahistorical and need to be combined with perspectives such as Schumpeter's that provide an explanation of the importance of uncertainty and its emergence.

There are also potential synergies with Post Keynesianism and the increasingly more popular resource based view of the firm (Foss, 1993, 1994a,b, 1996a,b, 1997a,b; Langlois, 1984, 1988, 1995a,b; Langlois and Foss, 1998; Langlois and Robertson, 1995; Glaister, 1996; Chandler, 1962, 1977, 1990, 1992; Lazonick, 1991). For example, in Chapter 10 below we advance a definition of the firm as *a means of coordinating production from one centre of strategic decision-making in an uncertain (nonergodic) environment*. The resource based view of the firm that descends from Penrose (1955, 1959), which describes how the access to routines and capabilities enables a flexible response to an uncertain future, may benefit from the technical definition of uncertainty offered by Post Keynesians (see Foss, 1997b,d; cf. Langlois and Everett, 1992). The specific Post Keynesian view of time, nonergodic open-system processes, may contribute to a clearer understanding of the need to access routines and capabilities (see Dunn, 2000b, 2001e; cf. Hodgson, 1999b). In return, the resource-based view of the firm may facilitate the opening up of the Post Keynesian black-box approach to organisation (Dunn, 2000b). Moreover, the degree of compatibility of the resource-based view of the firm with Institutionalist and post-Marshallian perspectives (Hodgson, 1998a,b) further underscores our claim that there is a methodological commensurability between Post Keynesianism and other traditions.[29]

We may, however, wish to cast this (methodological) net further than one may have thought wise. The neo-Institutionalists may be characterised as embracing an open-systems methodology (Foss, 1994b). Whatever the status of this claim, which is challenged by Post Keynesians (see Davidson and Davidson, 1984;

Dunn, 2000b; cf. Pratten, 1997), there does appear to be enough common ground for a constructive debate. Indeed Shapiro (1991) sought to develop an approach to the firm that builds upon the contributions of neo-Institutionalists such as Williamson (1975, 1985, 1996), using a Post Keynesian framework. This underscores the need for a more fully articulated Post Keynesian contribution to the theory of the firm – a point developed in Chapters 9 and 10 (see also Dunn, 2000b, 2001a,b,c, 2005).

Moreover, the frequently referred to desire to explain and understand the essentials of actual real-world processes and the use of grounded theory by scholars located within business schools, such as marketing and strategic management theorists (among others), suggests a loosely defined, common methodological base that may allow Post Keynesian contributions to flourish and develop (see, for example, Rassuli and Rassuli, 1989; Earl, 1986, 1991, 1995, 1999; Lee, 2002). Indeed, a prime focus of the literature on the role of management and the formulation of business strategy, is that of choice and decision-making in a complex environment (Rumelt, *et al.*, 1991). This literature, while stressing the complex and uncertain nature of the environment within which the modern corporation operates, does not clarify exactly what it understands by such terms (see, for example, Earl, 1984, 1992a,b). The concepts of immutability and transmutability used by Post Keynesian economists can provide a technical approach that would underpin a more rigorous discussion of the salience of uncertainty for the study and analysis of the role of management and strategy as it pertains to the firm (see Chapter 10 and Dunn, 2000b, 2001a,b).

Post Keynesians also have much to contribute in advancing an understanding of the difference between 'bounded rationality' and 'fundamental uncertainty' in management circles. Management and organisational theorists may well wonder what all the fuss is about; is not fundamental uncertainty just reinventing the 'bounded rationality' wheel? However, a moment's reflection suggests that Post Keynesians have much to contribute. Simon's (1959) concept of bounded rationality, and the subsequent decision-making process he describes (satisficing), has come to be identified with the informational processing capacities of economic agents. As discussed in greater detail in Chapter 6, it is the *complexity* of an environment, however defined, that requires agents to make procedurally rational choices. The concept of strategy emanating from the bounded rationality literature is identified with the *informational processing abilities* of agents. This stands in contrast to the stress placed by Post Keynesians on the open nature of the environment within which economic agents operate. As we argued in Chapter 6, in an open, nonergodic (transmutable) environment the processing capacities of agents will affect the *nature* of choice but not the *fact* of choice. Post Keynesians advance a distinct conception of crucial decision-making which *need not* be tied to any conception of the processing abilities of agents (although we may wish to link it with other approaches in a realistic description of decision-making).[30]

There are further potential synergies with business and organisational theorists. Given that management theorists, like Post Keynesian economists, rely on a broad range of quantitative and qualitative techniques, business schools may yet provide

Post Keynesian economics with an opportunity for extensive dialogue and thus constitute a major lifeline. Moreover, this represents an opportunity for a wider acceptance of Post Keynesian ideas and not just a means of survival. It should not be surprising that an increasing number of recent Post Keynesian appointments have occurred within business schools. If Post Keynesians positively engage with business school theorists we may yet see an increasing demand for their services (especially as there is an expansion in this sector; see above). What we may broadly label the business school approach may yield a rich stream of potential gains from trade (see, for example, the contributions in Earl, 1996a).

CONCLUDING COMMENTS

Those who expound the view that Post Keynesian economics is a degenerating research programme are mistaken and their perception misconceived. Building on the arguments advanced in previous chapters, we have argued that the main source of this confusion is methodological. Post Keynesianism, we have argued, is committed to open-system theorising which (i) is characterised by its stress on agency, transformation, organic interdependence and explanation, and (ii) underpins its recognition of the importance of the principle of effective demand. Defining Post Keynesianism in this manner has allowed us to further clarify the confusions that surround charges of incoherence, insularity and a fixation with negative critique. Moreover, we have argued that, rather than witnessing the demise of Post Keynesian economics, it is mainstream economics that is in trouble. The origin of these problems has been located in the inappropriate employment of closed-systems thinking to forecast open-system outcomes. This, we have argued, leaves Post Keynesianism with a serious dilemma; either it can attempt to engage the mainstream, which raises problems of methodological incommensurability, or it can look to other approaches that have potential compatibilitiess with open-system theorising. We concluded by suggesting that the latter represents the most sensible strategy and will contribute to the further development of Post Keynesianism, if not its prosperity. The rest of this book attempts to explore more fully the implications of adopting an explicitly ontological orientation and to further consider some of the synergies and insights that Post Keynesianism has to offer.

NOTES

1 The situation is especially acute in the UK (see for example Hodgson and Rothman 1999; Lee and Harley, 1998; Harley and Lee, 1997; Lee, 2007).

2 In terms of this chapter Lee's thesis deals with aspects of the internalist thesis. Mainstream hostility to Post Keynesianism generally stems from internalist concerns. It is for such reasons that Post Keynesian and other heterodox economics journals have been excluded from the core journals list by which research output is typically appraised. Moreover, in the UK the institutional mechanism of the

Research Assessment Exercise, which is a closed, undemocratic, peer review process, is implicitly denying a role for Post Keynesian and heterodox economics (Lee and Harley, 1998, p. 43). In terms of this chapter one could argue that one way of getting around such institutional constraints is to engage with other potentially compatible traditions and/or move into a more pragmatic and less restrictive business school setting (see below). Nevertheless, this dim outlook might be thought to have improved with at least two (out of ten) explicitly heterodox economists appearing on the 2001 Research Assessment Exercise panel (namely Lord Desai and Professor Philip Arestis). This situation has since changed for the worse with no heterodox economists on the 2007 RAE panel and their future prospects dim (see Lee, 2007).

3 The Sraffians, via the capital controversy, did engage with the mainstream and, in intellectual terms, won. However, this it has had no impact upon the way (aggregate) capital is treated or measured in the mainstream. This raises the question as to whether the mainstream really is receptive to a serious dialogue with alternative traditions, regardless of the methodological considerations outlined above; see Hodgson (1997a) for a discussion.

4 A more sympathetic appraisal of this episode in the history of economics would be that the Sraffians were seeking to establish what propositions could be made regarding aggregate capital and the rate of profit and, by implication, to challenge the conventional wisdom's of both neoclassical and Marxian economics (cf. Steedman, 1977).

5 As Hodgson (1989, p. 97) notes, 'a gulf divides the Sraffian theorists from others like Simon and Shackle who emphasise problems of uncertainty and argue that the economy cannot be captured by a static analysis'.

6 Sraffians have made constructive contributions by extending the theoretical framework to take into account international trade (see Steedman, 1999; Giammanco, 1998; Steedman and Metcalfe, 1981).

7 The same might also be said for Marxism. Hodgson (1999a, p. 41) has accused Marxian as well as Sraffian and neoclassical economics of eschewing a concern for 'the problems of uncertainty in addressing the future, and of decision making in a dynamic context'. Moreover, Davidson (1996; see also Pratten, 1996a) seems to echo these concerns, associating the classical system with a closed ergodic methodology. 'Centres of gravity', 'laws of motion' and 'natural laws' suggest an immutable conception of economic processes which is incompatible with the transmutable conception advocated by Post Keynesians. Notwithstanding such considerations, further debate is clearly needed and a renewed exchange of ideas between Marxism and Post Keynesianism, such as that recently attempted with the Institutionalists, might be warranted (see Dugger and Sherman, 1994).

8 This reflects a misconception rather than a statement of fact (Lee and Harley, 1998, p. 29). A characteristic of most Post Keynesian writers is that they are well versed in orthodox approaches – not least because they have to teach it! Rather, the reverse is true; mainstream economists are depressingly ignorant about non-mainstream theory (indeed, many core mainstream journals form a closed, self-referencing system in direct contrast to non-mainstream journal. see Lee and Harley, 1998). In light of this it is not surprising that one of Lee's (1995b) main criticisms of Post Keynesian economists is that they spend too much time (if not all their time!) teaching mainstream economics and not enough teaching heterodox approaches!

9 This view has long been entrenched in the mainstream, as Lee (2000a,b) makes clear. It is because of this prejudice that Post Keynesian economics does not appear on the programmes of the *Royal Economic Society* or the *American Economics Association*: mainstream economists have deliberately excluded them.

10 Blaug's (1992, p. 197) comments are typical when he notes that 'one sometimes gets the feeling that [Post Keynesian] macroeconomists are more concerned with exegesis of *The General Theory* than with advancing knowledge of how the economy actually works'.

11 The recent debate on formalism in the *Economic Journal* illuminates this point (see Backhouse, 1998; Chick, 1998; Krugman, 1998b).
12 The Knoxville conferences and the *JPKE*, for instance, are filled with papers on applied topics and policy. Moreover a leading Post Keynesian edits the avowedly empirical journal, the *International Review of Applied Economics*.
13 Post Keynesians do not reject formal methods. Rather their use is kept under continual scrutiny as to its ability to illuminate real-world processes (cf. Downward, 2003; Mearman, 2002a).
14 Lawson (1997a, p. 3), among others, provides a degree of evidence for this view.
15 Keynes (1930c, p. 373) commented: 'If economists could manage to get themselves thought of as humble, competent people, on a level with dentists, that would be splendid!'
16 It would be interesting to make further international comparisons of the trends outlined. However, it is not the intention here to examine in detail the health of economics. Others are welcome to examine in more detail the status of this claim.
17 All the figures relating to the expansion in higher education refer to 'old' universities. The period considered is prior to the change in status of former polytechnics. This facilitates 'like for like' comparisons and does not distort the trends identified. No doubt if the former polytechnics were included in this analysis the trends referred to would be more acutely marked, considering their more practical orientation. These statistics are taken from the University Grants Committee (UGC) publication, *University Statistics*.
18 The picture considerably worsens when one considers the situation in further education. Examining statistics taken from the Department for Education and Employment annual publication, *Statistics of Education: Public Examination GCSE/GNVQ and GCE in England*, one finds that in 1989 the number of candidates taking advanced-level examinations in economics in England was 45,710. The number of candidates taking advanced-level examinations in business studies was only 9508. By 1997 this picture had completely changed. In 1997 the number of candidates taking advanced-level examinations in economics had fallen by 63 per cent to 17,130. Meanwhile, the number of candidates taking advanced-level examinations in business studies had dramatically increased by 144 per cent to 23,211. By 1997 more people were studying business studies than economics, a situation inconceivable eight years earlier (see also Anderton *et al.*, 1998).
19 It is clear that even within the mainstream there is a recognition that there may be some cause for concern, especially in terms of the knock-on effect for the recruitment of professional economists. Professor Stephen Machin circulated a questionnaire to Universities in which he notes: 'the Economic and Social Research Council wishes to investigate whether there might be a long-term problem in terms of the training and retention of high calibre economics researchers and teachers, and has commissioned a report into the current and projected future demand for Ph.D. studentships in economics ... The main objective of our study is to establish the reasons for the fall in demand from UK applicants for doctoral students' (see also *The Economist*, 1998; Munford, 1999; Propper and Dasgupta, 2000; Machin and Oswald, 2000).
20 Parker (1993) forcefully makes the point (if slightly overstating it):

> Economists no longer command the prestige they once did. Some of the most influential people 'doing economics' today are noneconomists. Much of what economists do is being done more effectively outside economics departments, in schools of public policy, business schools, and beyond the academy's walls. It is being done by demographers and pollsters, sociologists and historians, and even journalists... With decreasing respect or need for economists in the outside world and declining enrolments in the grad schools, economics teaching may have to face the brutal inevitability of a diminished role.

21 Even the high priests of econometrics are forced to acknowledge the debacle that is econometric forecasting (see, for example, Hendry and Doornik, 1997, pp. 437–8).

22 Having defined Post Keynesian economics in methodological terms, we can 'cherry pick' ideas and concepts from other schools, provided only that the ideas do not in some sense contravene the open-systems approach.

23 One eminent Post Keynesian commented privately that 'for Post Keynesians to withdraw from the table of the "dying" mainstream to get a seat at the table with "old" or even "new" Institutionalists or even Austrians is like jumping out of the frying pan into the fire'. However, this points to a third option, one of non-engagement and insularity, but this, as is clear from the externalist thesis, is a non-option.

24 Lee (1998) is perhaps unusual in that he has already explored areas of potential synergy with other approaches, although not explicitly drawing upon their common methodological base. We return to this in Chapter 9 below.

25 Brazelton (1981) represents an early attempt to link Institutionalism to Post Keynesianism. However, while Institutionalists were quite open early on to the possibility of a synthesis, it is far from clear that Post Keynesians were quite so enthusiastic. This situation has now changed (see, for example, Arestis, 1996a; Davidson, 1996; Hodgson, 1989; Lawson, 1997a; Lee, 1998; cf. Silk, 1989).

26 See also Klein (1988, 1990, 1992, 1994), who considers the nature of Institutionalism and its links with other traditions.

27 Indeed Davidson (1996) characterises the (old) Institutionalists as possessing a transmutable conception of economic processes, in accord with the methodological view outlined above.

28 The Institutionalist literature has also considered the Marshall–Keynes–Institutionalist nexus. See, for example, Jensen (1983, 1990), Birch (1985), Brandis (1985), Parker Foster (1986, 1990, 1991) and Chase (1992).

29 One should note that key proponents of this approach, such as Foss and Langlois, possess strong links to the Austrian school, underscoring the need for extensive debate on a range of issues.

30 Earl (1984, 1990, 1994, 1995, 2000) is quite unusual in that he has attempted to fuse Post Keynesian–Shacklean insights into a more behavioural and psychological framework. While Earl, as we argue in Chapter 6, is occasionally guilty of conflating the concepts of uncertainty and bounded rationality, his approach echoes the type of progressive debate and interchange that is likely to facilitate the further development of Post Keynesian microeconomics.

8 The Austrian question

Amateur defenders of the market, enchanted to discover, as did Adam Smith two centuries ago, that good seems to proceed from evil, have often gone on to conclude that avarice is an original virtue.

(Galbraith, 1973b, p. 61)

INTRODUCTION

In the previous chapter we argued that the future of Post Keynesian economics rests in an extended dialogue with those that appear to employ similar methodological precepts. In Chapter 6 we highlighted how the distinctive Post Keynesian view of time, which is embedded in its methodology, can be marshalled to underscore and clarify the distinction between bounded rationality and fundamental uncertainty. Here we attempt to develop this line of argument by further developing in detail the arguments and implications of the last few chapters, and by exploring and clarifying some of the important synergies and differences with the Austrian school. As we have argued in Chapter 7 there are indeed substantial gains from trade to be had if both Austrians and Post Keynesians communicated on a range of issues such as methodology, praxeology, dispersed knowledge, learning, entrepreneurship, speculation, price theory, market process, uncertainty, co-ordination, effective demand, money – its evolution and its endogeneity – and the importance of power (Lawson, 1994a; O'Driscoll and Rizzo, 1995; cf. Kregel, 1986; Bellante, 1992). However, if Post Keynesians are to engage with the Austrians more seriously than they have done in the past, the fundamental stumbling block of the (implicit) omniscience ascribed to the market process must be broached. That is to say, one of the key differences between Austrians and Post Keynesians centres on their questions of differences in methodology and in the recognition of the salience of 'fundamental' uncertainty! This chapter seeks to further outline the methodological and axiomatic similarities of Austrian and Post Keynesian economics so as to underpin further, more enlightened, debate.

While one would not deny a 'common overlap' and some 'evolving intellectual affinities' between some kaleidic Austrians and some Post Keynesians, nor that Davidson (1989c, 1993b) advances 'a very forced and unsympathetic and uncharitable' appraisal of O'Driscoll and Rizzo, many Post Keynesians would still take issue with the central and more controversial claim that 'Austrian Economics shares all the axioms highlighted by Davidson as the sole preserve of Post Keynesianism so that on his own terms Austrian economics cannot be reduced to an inferior representation of the mainstream' (Wynarczyk, 1999, p. 32).[1] As the debate in the *Journal of Economic Perspectives* (Rosen, 1997; Yeager, 1997) highlights, it is far from clear that Austrians wish to draw attention to their axiomatic and methodological differences with the mainstream and thus there is an issue about whether they do recognise the import and salience of the distinctive Post Keynesian view of time. This chapter attempts to clarify one of the fundamental differences between 'market equilibrating' Austrians and 'transmutable' Post Keynesians, centring on the status, role and omnipotence ascribed to the market process and building on the discussion in the previous chapters.[2]

THE INCOHERENCE OF AUSTRIAN ECONOMICS?

Before we deal with the claim of a shared axiomatic base in more detail we should first contest the associated but separate claim that Austrianism 'appear[s] far more developed as a school ... than Post Keynesianism where question marks remain over its status as an alternative "School" of thought' (Wynarczyk, 1999, pp. 34–7). Such pronouncements are far from uncontentious and we would rather suggest that in fact the reverse is true – that Post Keynesian economics is more coherent and developed as a school than Austrian economics.

These differences are considered by Vaughn (1994), who argues that Kirzner initially saw his project as improving neoclassical economics and providing a 'story' as to how markets adjust, whereas the kaleidic Lachmann-inspired wing (including Shackle and Loasby) seems to have been reaching out to Post keynesians such as Davidson.[3] Indeed, in their debate with Davidson (1989c, 1993b) *both* Prychitko (1993) and Torr (1993) acknowledged the tension between the kaleidic wing of Lachmann, Shackle and Boulding, with their stress on divergent and disequilibrating expectations, and the more dominant, market-as-an-equilibrating-process axis of Mises, Hayek and Kirzner (see Vaughn, 1994, for a detailed discussion of the different factious Austrian traditions). Indeed, a key argument of this chapter is that the 'market equilibrating' strand should undertake a more serious discussion of uncertainty.

In addition to the high-profile *Journal of Economic Perspectives* exchange alluded to above, Austrianism's coherence, contribution and core have been subject to a degree of inauspicious internal and external scrutiny (see, for example, the various debates and rejoinders: Caplan, 1999; Block, 1988, 1999; Tullock, 1988, 1989; Salerno, 1989; Timberlake, 1987, 1988; Rothbard, 1988; Yeager, 1987, 1988; Krugman, 1998a; Garrison, 1999; as well as the assessments by Selgin, 1988; Dow, 1996a; Demsetz, 1997; and Vihanto, 1999). In sharp contrast, however, Post Keynesianism coheres around the commitment to incorporating uncertainty into its theorising and in its methodological stress on agency, transformation and emergence, organic interdependence and explanation. This *a posteriori* methodological approach, which, as argued in Chapter 4, underpins the principle of effective demand, would appear to be at variance with the *a priori*sm, reductionism and methodological individualism that characterises much Austrian theorising and would further undermine the suggestion of a common methodological and axiomatic base, to which we now turn (cf. Lawson, 1994b, 1996c, 1997a).[4]

A COMMON METHODOLOGICAL BASE?

It is not clear that Austrians reject *a posteriori* the assumption of immutability, i.e. reject on empirical grounds the assumption that social processes exhibit a high degree of closure. Even sympathetic kaleidic Austrians, in debate with Davidson were forced to concede that 'most Austrians hesitate to accept nonergodic constructs' (Prychitko, 1993, p. 375) and accepted that one of the main *lessons that Austrians could learn* from Post Keynesians centred on the 'question of ergodicity' (Torr, 1993, p. 404). While it is clearly true that Austrians talk about and recognise the pivotal Post Keynesian themes such as the importance of historical time, radical uncertainty and expectations and appear to have a degree of methodological similarity that might underpin a more fruitful dialogue than has been attempted in the past, the failure to address the *general* Austrian *a priori* insistence that the market represents a paragon of allocative virtue (cf. Littlechild, 1986) ultimately usurps the argument that the majority of Austrians share the same philosophical (open-system) 'world view' as Post Keynesians.[5] In avoiding this fundamental issue we miss an opportunity to promote further dialogue around Austrian ideas.

Davidson's core contention is that the *a priori* Panglossian assertion of the innate superiority of markets *vis-à-vis* other modes of resource allocation is implicitly underpinned by the assumption of an ergodic, immutable, closed theoretical system (a point that Prychitko, 1993, p. 375 accepts). Moreover, the metaphors of discovery, actors and equilibrium, so cherished by the majority of Austrian economists, are suggestive of a predetermined immutable reality that some contend they reject (see Kirzner, 1973, 1985, 1997, 1999; cf. Clark, 1987–8).[6] It should not be surprising that the majority of Austrians, who typically follow the Mises–Hayek–Kirzner story, treat profit opportunities as pre-existing and waiting to be unearthed and utilise the 'static' concepts of Pareto optimality and general equilibrium as benchmarks against which entrepreneurial actions are compared. Post Keynesians, in sharp contrast, typically employ the metaphors of creativity, agency and history and reject the concept of Pareto efficiency as an inappropriate mode of analysis for a world with a fixed past and an unknowable and yet-to-be-created future (cf. Kregel, 1986). As Dow (1996a, p. 115) points out, 'equilibrium rules out the exploitation of new opportunities, and thus creativity; it rules out precisely what many neo-Austrians see as the moving force behind competition'. Any attempt to demonstrate that an unfettered laissez-faire system is at, or tends towards, a predestined optimal full-employment equilibrium, is in essence founded on the assumption of immutability.

If Austrians do indeed share the same methodological foundation as Post Keynesians, then they should follow Post Keynesians and reject at the outset the *a priori* elevation of any institution above any other. While Austrians might espouse sympathies with an open-systems view of economic processes, if they are to avoid being denigrated as ideological they must adopt and develop theory that is *consistent* with this view. As Davidson (1989c, p. 473) correctly notes, 'If two schools share the identical axiomatic foundation ... then if they ask the same questions, they should reach the same answers, unless one school has made a mistake in logic and/or has introduced *ad hoc* constraints on the operation of the system'. Wynarczyk (1999), for example, unfortunately sidesteps such central issues in an otherwise worthwhile endeavour to promote an increased dialogue between Austrians and Post Keynesians. The theoretical and policy differences that Wynarczyk alludes to represent either faulty logic or methodological differences. Austrians must either abandon their *a priori* elevation of the market and reject the assumption of immutability, or recognise that they share a very different methodological base to Post Keynesians.[7]

THE MARKET IS NOT AN OMNIPOTENT *DEUS EX MACHINA*

In order to re-assert the primacy and efficacy of an unhindered market process Austrians augment simplistic Spencerian–Darwinian (ergodic) natural selection arguments with avarice.[8] Keynes' (1926, pp. 282–3) comments on *The End of Laissez Faire* are timeless in this regard and paint a not unfair caricature of many contemporary Panglossian Austrian economists:

> Economists, like other scientists, have chosen the hypothesis from which they set out, and which they offer to beginners, because it is the simplest, and not because it is the nearest to the facts. Partly for this reason, but partly, I admit, because they have been biased by the traditions of the subject, they have begun by assuming a state of affairs where the ideal distribution of productive resources can be brought about through individuals acting independently by the method of trial and error in such a way that those individuals who move in the right direction will destroy by competition those who move in the wrong direction. This implies that there must be no mercy or protection for those who embark their capital or their labour in the wrong direction. It is a method of bringing the most successful profit-makers to the top by a ruthless struggle for survival, which selects the most efficient by the bankruptcy of the less efficient. It does not count the cost of the struggle, but looks only to the benefits of the final result which are assumed to be permanent. The object of life being to crop the leaves off the branches up to the greatest possible height, the likeliest way of achieving this end is to leave the giraffes with the longest necks to starve out those whose necks are shorter.[9]

However, Post Keynesians argue that the love and pursuit of monetary accumulation is inextricably linked to the incessant drive to introduce novel product innovations and technological revolutions and the transformation that this induces (Keynes, 1926; Davidson, 1996; Dequech, 1997b). Such revolutions and innovations generally result in a future inconceivable at the point of origination. Indeed, as argued in Chapter 6, in a nonergodic environment it logically follows that simplistic market-based selection of the fittest arguments must be rejected.[10] If the future cannot be known in advance of its creation – if economic process are fundamentally open – then the market (or governments for that matter) cannot select and learn the optimal rules and routines that characterise the environments because *they are not yet there to be discovered*. This is the market consequence of the argument developed in Chapter 6. The environment is not stable long enough to permit the asymptotic end-state of a process of learning to be reached. What appears to make sense to market agents at one point in time will not make sense over all time. In the Austrian approach the coordinating function of the entrepreneur is clearly over-stressed and the allusion to the creative capabilities of entrepreneurs misleading. The expectation of future coordination failures, allied to the capacity to make 'imaginative, bold leaps of faith, and determination' in the creation of the future, must surely open up the possibility that entrepreneurs generate, rather than correct, error. Moreover, the *a posteriori* existence of widespread unemployment *prima facie* underpins such claims.

An environment that exhibits transmutability over time destroys Pareto efficiency (not to mention other modes of efficiency). If processes are fundamentally open – if it is impossible or difficult to isolate the objects of enquiry and guarantee their constancy – then it is impossible for economists, entrepreneurs and governments to evaluate the impact *ex ante* of price and non-price modes of competition and new policy,[11] such as research and development, persuasion, product and production innovation, aggregate demand expansion, that impinge on the process of allocating and creating resources to assure *ex post* optimal arrangements eventuate. Counter factuals that relate to moving from one state of the world to another one can only be assumed – they cannot be predicted.

Market uncertainty resulting from situating entrepreneurship within historical time, constructed as a stream of novel events existing in historical time, cannot lead to *ex ante* optimisation *even in the long run*. Kirzner's (see Selgin, 1988, p. 44) famous trite observation that 'Paris gets fed', invoked to exemplify the Austrian belief that the market can indeed efficiently solve complex coordination problems, only deals with half of the story. The feeding of Paris involves much more than the operation of the market, such as the production processes within firms, the distribution network (much of which takes place within firms), agreements between firms especially along the supply chain, regulation by government and so on (Sawyer, 1993).[12] Moreover, Paris also suffers from homelessness, poverty, student riots, revolutions, liquidity crises and unemployment. Indeed, it is such 'generalised features of experience' and considerations that have underpinned the view amongst some Post Keynesians that while Austrians (and others) talk incessantly about the market they never define what they mean by it nor its nexus to uncertainty, accumulation and the rules, routines and institutions that characterise it.[13]

MONEY AND GOVERNMENTS MATTER

While Hayek's (1937) famous essay on 'Economics and knowledge' criticised (quite rightly) 'mainstream' theory for abstracting from the process of dispersed and differentiated learning, Post Keynesians would more radically criticise both for neglecting the essence of nonergodic, historical time and its nexus to a monetary production economy.[14] Post Keynesians, and some kaleidic Austrians such as Shackle and Lachmann, focus on the inability of the market to harness dispersed knowledge about a kaleidic future *that has yet to be created*. It is the fact of uncertainty and the salience of historical time which, in conjunction with the essential properties of money, that of zero elasticity of both production and substitution, represents a necessary and sufficient condition for the existence of unemployment. Unemployment develops as the demand for liquidity expands in response to an increase in dispersed 'fundamental' uncertainty. As Hahn (1977, pp. 31, 39) stated, an unemployment equilibrium can occur as long as there are 'resting places for saving other than reproducible money … if we study an economy which is not a barter economy … then any non-reproducible asset allows for a choice between employment-inducing and non-employment inducing demand'.

As the individuals become more uncertain about the future it makes sense for them to hold non-reproducible, non-substitutable, liquid assets whereby, in the act of deferring contractual commitments, they are saved to make a decision another day. However, such decisions do not necessarily make sense from the point of view of the whole economy. It is this recognition of the substantive role for money in a credit production economy, in which goods buy money and money buys goods but goods do not buy goods, that undermines the *a priori* demonstration of the effectiveness of the market in coordinating economic activity. Davidson (1996, p. 20) notes correctly that Arrow and Hahn (1971, p. 361) have demonstrated that:

> [A]ll general (full employment) equilibrium existence proofs are jeopardized in a world with fixed money contracts over time; no general equilibrium may exist. A nonergodic setting provides the analytical basis for the use of fixed money contracts and therefore provides for the possibility of the existence of long-period unemployment equilibrium – and the possibility of the non-existence of a general (i.e. full employment) equilibrium in the absence of deliberate government policy to assure there is never a lack of aggregate effective demand.

It is for these reasons that Post Keynesians develop theoretical structures that highlight how political and economic institutions can act as a channel for effective demand and influence the amount of activity in an economy, and why they explicitly consider the distributional *and normative* implications of their analysis (Galbraith, 1975; Arestis and Sawyer, 1998, 1999; Davidson and Davidson, 1996; cf. Keynes, 1934).

The fact that the solution to such problems, as Keynes (1926) noted, 'lies outside the operations of individuals' relates to Keynesian identification of the importance of the fallacy of composition (which is committed when a conclusion is drawn about a whole on the basis of the features of its constituents when, in fact, no justification is provided for the inference) and its nexus to a monetary economy existing in historical time (see also Lawson, 1997a, who highlights the relationship of policy to emancipatory goals).[15] The answer to Wynarczyk's (1999, p. 32) question 'why a nonergodic environment implies intervention' is based upon an elaboration of this fallacy (see Dequech, 1997a,b, 1999b).[16]

While Post Keynesians would accept that neither governments *nor individuals* are omniscient or omnipotent (cf. Buchanan, *et al.*, 1978), they would still argue that governments differ from individual agents in many important dimensions, not least in terms of its democratic accountability, its relative immortality, the fact that it can borrow at rates substantially below those at which individuals can, and its legal authority to levy taxes, print money and enforce contractual (debt) obligations (Keynes, 1930a; Davidson, 1994, Chapter 6, 1999c; Wray, 1998).[17] It is these characteristics that underpin its ability to pump-prime effective demand and repay and sustain loans and finance deficits above and beyond the level that we might think prudent from an individual point of view (see Arestis and Sawyer, 1997a, 1998 for a more detailed elaboration of a set of 'Keynesian policies for the new millennium'). As Davidson (1996, p. 21) notes, in a world of transmutability

> plagued by persistent long-period underemployment equilibrium, society can intelligently control and improve the performance of the economy by developing governmental policies to influence, directly or indirectly, entrepreneurial animal spirits sufficiently to offset agents' excessive aggregate demand for liquidity. Keynes' suggestion (1936, pp. 377–9) that policies be designed to assure that there is never a lack of effective demand does not require a prescient government. All that is necessary is the development of institutions that act as a balance-wheel by providing a guiding influence (a) in stimulating effective demand whenever the private sector displays a propensity to produce a lack of effective demand and (b) in reducing demand whenever over full employment conditions prevails.

Post Keynesians, like 'kaleidic' Austrians, recognise the associated problems with fine-tuning and hydraulic Keynesianism and the importance and influence (sometimes positive, sometimes negative) of government activism and regulation upon entrepreneurial confidence and expectations given their transmutable conception of economic agents (see Lawson, 1997a, especially Chapter 18). However, such caution and humility in policy-making does not undermine the fact that a monetary production economy passing through real time is unlikely to generate a high and stable level of employment and thus there is *prima facie* evidence that, as mass unemployment develops, there develops a role for what Arestis and Sawyer (1998, p. 187) refer to as 'coarse' tuning, whereby 'over the medium term the government seeks to ensure an adequate level of aggregate demand through the usual channels of the balance between taxation and government expenditure and … through the balance between savings and investment'.

CONCLUDING COMMENTS

In summary, the Post Keynesian recognition of the fact that economic processes are transmutable challenges the *a priori* assumption of market efficiency adhered to by many Austrians. Post Keynesians reject the assumption of governing ergodic processes on both *a posteriori* empirical grounds: the fact that most macroeconomic time series are non-stationary, a sufficient but not a necessary condition for the existence of nonergodic processes, as well as a hermeneutic recognition that agents can make crucial decisions, including those clustered in organisations such as firms and governments, that can make a difference *in the long run* (Davidson, 1996; Dunn, 2000b). It would not be unfair to suggest that the majority of Austrians (implicitly) assume the conditions of closure – that is, the ability to isolate and guarantee constant the objects of enquiry – when they argue that 'the love of money, acting through the pursuit of profit, as an adjutant to natural selection, to bring about the production on the greatest possible scale of what is most strongly desired as measured by exchange value' (Keynes, 1926, p. 284). Post Keynesians, and some kaleidic Austrians, categorically reject the *a priori*st assertion of the efficacy of the market espoused by the Austrian Panglossians.

NOTES

1 Wynarczyk (1992) has also suggested that there exists a degree of intellectual overlap with the Institutionalists. Clark (1989, 1993) contests such a claim in a manner that suggests that the Institutionalists are closer to the Post Keynesian open-system view than the Austrians. Clearly, this underscores the need for an increased dialogue on such issues and this book, as a whole, should be viewed as a contribution to this debate.
2 The focus is on the areas of apparent significant overlap, i.e. the contention that both accept the importance of uncertainty for economic analysis. That is why we do not consider other important and related Post Keynesian criticisms of Austrianism such as their adherence to methodological individualism (briefly alluded to below), deductivism and neglect of the power and role of large organisations. (see Chapter 7 and Dixon, 1986).
3 Loasby (1983, p. 218) also acknowledges this when he notes that Kirzner shows a 'reluctance to accept fundamental uncertainty'.
4 Indeed, many Post Keynesians would view the acceptance or rejection of methodological individualism as perhaps the principal divide between themselves and Austrians. As Keynes (1926, p. 288) pointed out, 'Experience does not show that individuals, when they make up a social unit, are always less clear-sighted than when they act separately.'
5 Although Wynarczyk appears to have forgotten Menger's scathing methodological attack on the Gustav Schmoller and German historical school in the *Methodenstreit* (see Selgin, 1988; Hodgson, 2001a).
6 Post Keynesians, following Paul Davidson, would dismiss the heuristic significance of equilibrium as a misleading focus for historical analysis. While the Post Keynesians occasionally invoke the concept of equilibrium in the generic sense *à la* Marshall to refer to a position of no tendency to change, they reject unequivocally the conventional association of equilibrium with market clearing and logical time (Davidson, 1993b).
7 See Selgin (1988), who argues contra Wynarczyk that the axiomatic foundation of Austrianism rests upon the enunciation of 'praxeology', the axiom of action. The metaphor of action, as opposed to agency which Post Keynesians typically adopt,

is suggestive of a pre-determined, immutable world which is played out according to preordained laws.

8 We use the term 'Spencerian–Darwinian' here to refer to the 'bastardisation' and simplification of evolutionary arguments typically invoked to justify the a *priori* elevation of the market as the premier 'social' institution. Hodgson (1993, Chapter 13, 1994; see also 1999a) suggests that such simple appeals to the evolutionary selection mechanisms in order to assert the superiority of the market process are both common and misleading. Hodgson demonstrates that the view that evolutionary processes lead generally in the direction of optimality and efficiency is in fact fallacious.

9 Keynes (1926, p. 276) further noted that: 'The economists were teaching that wealth, commerce, and machinery were the children of free competition – that free competition built London. But the Darwinians could go one better than that – free competition built man. The human eye was no longer the demonstration of design, miraculously contriving all things for the best; it was the supreme achievement of chance, operating under conditions of free competition and laissez-faire. The principle of the survival of the fittest could be regarded as a vast generalisation of the Ricardian economics. Socialistic inferences became, in the light of this grander synthesis, not merely inexpedient, but impious, as calculated to retard the onward movement of the mighty process by which we ourselves had risen like Aphrodite out of the primeval slime of the ocean'.

10 Sophisticated evolutionary arguments (e.g. Hodgson, 1993) are consistent with the nonergodic approach. However, to reject the ergodic axiom does not necessarily entail a rejection nor an unequivocal acceptance of the evolutionary mode of theorising (although Davidson, however, continues to use the metaphor of evolution).

11 Post Keynesians prefer to refer to the transformative development and initiation of (government) policy initiatives as activism, as opposed to intervention, as the latter carries with it the associations with an external *deus ex machina* imposed malevolently upon a natural law process.

12 Consider also the Austrian view of industrial policy. For example, O'Driscoll and Rizzo (1995, Chapter 7) conclude, in a manner reminiscent of the socialist calculation debate, that the information required for 'optimal regulation' of pollution control and monopolies can only be supplied by market processes themselves. The large modern corporation is best left alone. This conclusion, however, is typical of Austrian economics which in general tends to neglect the behaviour and processes associated with large firms. Yet, as argued in the next chapter, in an uncertain world it is firms and not omniscient, omnipotent Walrasian auctioneers who set prices. And surely the fact of price setting conveys *some* notion of power. O'Driscoll and Rizzo have little to say about the relationship between price-setters and price-takers, nor about the changes through time in the roles of market participants – a surprising omission for those expressing a concern with processes.

13 Indeed, it has been widely acknowledged that the theory of the firm was a notable lacuna in Austrian theory generally (O'Driscoll and Rizzo, 1985, p. 123; Loasby, 1989, p. 157; Langlois, 1992, p. 166; Foss, 1994a, p. 31). There have been some moves to integrate the firm into a more comprehensive view of the market process (see, for example, Foss, 1997c; Yu, 1999; Dulbecco and Garrouste, 1999; Klein, 1999; Kirzner, 1999; Witt, 1999; Ioannides, 1999; and Lewin and Phelan, 2000). However, while many of these interesting developments have much to contribute to Post Keynesian microtheory they have yet to fully grasp the nonergodic 'nettle' and explore the ramifications for the theory of the firm and concomitantly the continued pre-eminence and status of the market.

14 For Keynes' account of the importance and relevance of the distribution of uncertainty see Cameron and Ndhlovu (1999). On the Hayek/Keynes overlap see Lawson (1994b, 1996c).

15 To quote Keynes' (1926, p. 292) views on the nature and role of government intervention at length: 'We must aim at separating those services which are technically social

from those which are technically individual. The most important Agenda of the State relate not to those activities which private individuals are already fulfilling, but to those functions which fall outside the sphere of the individual, to those decisions which are made by no one if the State does not make them. The important thing for government is not to do things which individuals are doing already, and to do them a little better or a little worse; but to do those things which at present are not done at all, [i.e.] great inequalities of wealth … unemployment of labour … the disappointment of reasonable business expectations [etc.] … [T]he cure for these things is partly to be sought in the deliberate control of the currency and of credit by a central institution, and partly in the collection and dissemination on a great scale of data relating to the business situation, including the full publicity, by law if necessary, of all business facts which it is useful to know. These measures would involve society in exercising directive intelligence through some appropriate organ of action over many of the inner intricacies of private business, yet it would leave private initiative and enterprise unhindered. Even if these measures prove insufficient, nevertheless, they will furnish us with better knowledge than we have now for taking the next step.

My second example relates to savings and investment. I believe that some co-ordinated act of intelligent judgement is required as to the scale on which it is desirable that the community as a whole should save, the scale on which these savings should go abroad in the form of foreign investments, and whether the present organisation of the investment market distributes savings along the most nationally productive channels. I do not think that these matters should be left entirely to the chances of private judgement and private profits, as they are at present.

My third example concerns population. The time has already come when each country needs a considered national policy about what size of population, whether larger or smaller than at present or the same, is most expedient. And having settled this policy, we must take steps to carry it into operation. The time may arrive a little later when the community as a whole must pay attention to the innate quality as well as to the mere numbers of its future members'.

16 However, to 'show' that markets 'work best' requires additional, auxiliary, assumptions beyond ergodicity *per se*. For example, the market failure literature 'shows' that even in an ergodic world market outcomes can be improved upon. I would like to thank Malcolm Sawyer for reminding me of this point.

17 Indeed, as Keynes' (1926, pp. 287–8) mordant assessment concluded: 'It is not true that individuals possess a prescriptive 'natural liberty' in their economic activities. There is no 'compact' conferring perpetual rights on those who Have or on those who Acquire. The world is not so governed from above that private and social interest always coincide. It is not so managed here below that in practice they coincide. It is not a correct deduction from the principles of economics that enlightened self-interest always operates in the public interest. Nor is it true that self-interest generally is enlightened; more often individuals acting separately to promote their own ends are too ignorant or too weak to attain even these'.

9 Post Keynesian pricing theory

Identifying an open systems core

A great deal of work remains to be done to establish a macro–micro analysis of prices appropriate to the modern world.

Joan Robinson (1977, p. 1327)

The task of deciding how resources should be allocated is not fulfilled by the market but by the great corporations who are in charge of the finance for development.

Joan Robinson (1977, p. 1337)

INTRODUCTION

In previous chapters we have considered the general methodological foundations of Post Keynesian theory and its nexus to uncertainty. Nevertheless, although we have argued that Post Keynesianism is coherent, principally at the methodological level, and defined by its recognition of the importance of uncertainty and its nexus to the elaboration of the principle of effective demand, it will no doubt be unclear to the reader how this relates to what is commonly associated with its microeconomic core. While Post Keynesian micro-theorists recognise the embeddedness of the firm and its pricing practices in history they have not, generally speaking, explicitly linked their discussion to attempt a methodological delineation of its core in order to underpin its drive towards coherence. This chapter attempts to consider the relationship between what is frequently identified as part of the core of Post Keynesian price theory and its nexus to its conceptualisation of uncertainty.

In this chapter we begin this process by reviewing some of foundational issues and debates that have exercised Post Keynesian micro-theory recently, and argue that these can be made intelligible by drawing on the methodological framework and view of time outlined earlier in the book. We appraise recent attempts to identify the core of Post Keynesian micro-theory, drawing on the methodological discussion and definition of Post Keynesianism advanced earlier. This discussion yields an assessment that many of the conclusions that Post Keynesian micro-theorists reach would be strengthened by an explicit recognition of the nexus of uncertainty to its underdeveloped microeconomic core.

THEORIES OF PRICING AND THEORIES OF PRICE

Post Keynesians bridging the traverse between the macro-and microeconomic fields typically draw upon the Marshallian-inspired writings of Keynes and/or the more explicitly radical approaches such as those of Marx, Kalecki and Sraffa (cf. the argument of Part I above). Historically, Post Keynesian micro-theorists have developed theories of pricing. As Sawyer (1995, p. 170) notes:

> [Much] of the Post Keynesian literature has been concerned with the former, that is with theories of how prices are set at the level of the firm or industry. Consideration of the setting of prices may involve some generalisation of the procedures used for pricing, or theorising at the level of the firm or industry. These theories are microeconomic in orientation, though most Post Keynesian authors have been aware of the macroeconomic implications of and impact on pricing. When the configuration of prices which satisfy some economy-level steady-state condition (perhaps based on a theory of pricing) is derived, then such a theory of price has been generated. Theories of price, of which the Sraffian approach is the most relevant for our discussion, are not concerned with the process of price formation but rather with a configuration of prices which conforms to some system-level requirement (e.g. of an equalised rate of profit).[1]

However, apart from Kalecki, those traditionally cited at the heart of Post Keynesian microeconomics do not possess a coherent and fully developed analysis of the *process* of pricing and its embeddedness within a broader conceptualisation of Post Keynesianism. This has clearly undermined Post Keynesian attempts to present itself as a positive, coherent and comprehensive paradigm capable of illuminating reality. What is more, the fact that Sraffian theories of price tend to eschew a concern for pricing processes underscores the argument developed above and adhered to throughout, that the Sraffians should no longer be thought of as part of the Post Keynesian (microeconomic) core.

Similarly, Lee (1994, 1995a, 1998) has forcefully argued that other Post Keynesian macro- and micro-theorists need to stop talking about the importance of history and practise what they preach and recognise the diverse set of contributions made on the nature of actual pricing procedures. It is for such reasons, in addition to the other associated reasons outlined in Chapter 7, that many Post Keynesians are beginning to acknowledge the contribution of Institutionalists, especially with respect to developing a multi-dimensional approach to pricing and the firm (see, for example, Arestis, 1992, 1996a; Lee, 1994, 1995a, 1998; Samuels, 1995).[2] Indeed, Arestis (1996a, p. 114) suggests 'that the Institutionalist approach strengthens ... the underdeveloped nature of Kalecki's and Keynes' microeconomic analyses despite attempts that have been made to overcome this weakness'. Indeed, as argued in Chapter 3, given that Institutionalists tend to firmly locate their analysis in history, implicitly recognising the fundamental asymmetry between an unalterable past and an uncertain yet-to-be-conceived future, their approach seems to accord a degree of compatibility with Post Keynesianism (see Hodgson, 1988, 1989, 2001a,b,c).[3]

POST KEYNESIAN PRICING THEORY

Some commentators would argue, in a manner reminiscent of attempts to define Post Keynesian economics more generally, that what unites Post Keynesian writings on pricing and the firm is perhaps an opposition to some (loosely) defined mainstream viewpoint. We would, however, take issue with this view. A key tenet of explicitly Post Keynesian contributions to pricing theory is that prices fulfil other roles than the narrow allocative one ascribed to it by neoclassical theory (Sawyer, 1995; Lavoie, 1992; Shapiro, 1995; Lee, 1998; Reynolds, 1987; Downward, 1999). In the conventional wisdom, the function of price is typically allocative (Sawyer, 1993). Prices allocate resources and price changes (signals) coordinate economic activity. Time, as exemplified by general equilibrium models, is effectively suspended and a disinterested and anonymous auctioneer adjusts prices until market demand and supply are equated and the process of resource allocation can commence.

However, such a narrow concept of the role and function of prices is rejected by Post Keynesians, who argue that prices in themselves cannot convey the requisite amount of information that is commonly attributed to them. If the product or commodity is not well defined, then additional 'information on the nature of the product is required, and knowledge of the seller and conditions of sale may also be useful' (Sawyer, 1993, p. 35). Moreover, the fact of a price change, while useful in itself, does not convey information of the reasons for the price change which may be temporary or permanent and arise from changes in consumers' tastes and incomes, product innovations, technological innovations, government intervention and regulation, demand and so on. Clearly the underlying reasons, processes and mechanisms that affect price changes represent useful information to market participants which would allow them to broach and plan for an uncertain future.

Post Keynesians observe that when prices are set by firms, and not by some anonymous and disinterested auctioneer, then prices will reflect the objectives of the strategic decision-makers and have a variety of different roles beyond, and in addition to, a purely allocative one. This leads us to the positive contribution and distinctiveness of Post Keynesian pricing theories. *A distinctive feature of the Post Keynesian approach to pricing is that it is firm-based and that it influences and impinges on, among other things, the distribution of income.* As Shapiro and Mott (1995, p. 25) point out, 'the importance of enterprise decisions distinguishes [Post] Keynesian theory and ... these decisions affect the prices of products as well as their rates of production ... it is not the auctioneer but the product's producer that decides the product price'.

Sawyer (1993), drawing on Gerrard (1989), outlines at least five roles of prices that inform this strategic conceptualisation of firms and their associated pricing processes: the financial, conductive, rivalrous, positional and allocative functions.[4]

The financial role relates to the overriding objectives of the firm such as the pursuit of profit, growth, technological virtuosity and means to achieve and realise these goals. Post Keynesian theorists such as Galbraith (1967) and Eichner (1973, 1976; see also Reynolds, 1987) depict the firms as altering prices and thus profit margins so as to generate an internal flow of funds to facilitate and secure investment. These approaches exemplify the financing role of prices. The conductive role relates to the process by which the costs of production, including labour (wage) costs, are encapsulated in price-setting behaviour. Prices that are set by some mark-up over costs such as the full cost principle, by administered pricing, or cost-plus pricing typify the conductive role of prices. Similarly, the conflict theory of inflation developed by Post Keynesians (see Sawyer, 1982, 1989, 1992b; Davidson, 1994; Lavoie, 1992; Galbraith, 1973b,c) outlines a clear view of the inflationary process as reflecting conflict over the distribution of income and being underpinned by the (money) wage demands of workers which are channelled through the pricing and finance process into rising prices. The 'rivalry' role reflects the combative and interdependent nature of pricing and the 'marketing' need to position the firm and product in relation to rivals (see Rothschild, 1947; Gerrard, 1989; Rassuli and Rassuli, 1989). The notion of a limit price set to deter and inhibit potential entrants would be an example of the 'rivalry' role of price. Similarly, the strategies of 'predatory pricing', 'loss leaders', 'persuasion and exhortation' and 'multi-product pricing' all fulfil 'rivalrous' roles designed to affect the future position, dominance and continued viability of the firm (cf. Galbraith, 1973b, pp. 126–137). The positional role of pricing refers to the ceremoniously and socially comparative function of prices and reflects the need to maintain wage relativities between different groups of workers (Henry *et al.*, 1976; Sawyer, 1982, 1989) or engage in conspicuous consumption, emulation and so on (Veblen, 1899; Galbraith, 1958, 1979, Chapters 11 and 12; Earl, 1983, 1986, 1995).

These multi-faceted functions of price arise in the context of a strategic and intentional view of the pricing process which is embedded in historical time. And 'it follows that prices are no longer of unique importance in telling how resources are distributed' (Galbraith, 1973b, p. 127). Firms are viewed as price makers, actively coping with history, and this view stands in direct contrast to the disinterested and disembodied fictional Walrasian auctioneer. It is a conceptualisation based on an *a posteriori* assessment that typically firms possess power and have the capacity to make real choices that can affect and influence, in a real sense, the firm's evolution, the nature of the competitive process and the resulting course of history.

According to this perspective, the allocative role from the Post Keynesian perspective is a residual by-product of the other four roles. To paraphrase and quote Galbraith (1973b, p. 127), in the Post Keynesian system 'the role of prices is greatly diminished. They are much more effectively under the control of the firm'. *Prices reflect the strategic objectives of the firm*. Any constancy of price in the face of in changes in demand reflects the functions of price and the objectives and decisions of the firms themselves. From this perspective it is fallacious to interpret any constancy of prices as rigid prices, i.e. fixed by an external agency to induce disequilibrium trading (as typified by the re-appraisal of Keynesian economic literature; see Sawyer, 1995). Any constancy of price reflects the decisions of strategic decision-makers within the firm and is likely to reflect the (strategic) costs of making price changes or the fact that the underlying conditions and mechanisms that underpin the pricing process remain unchanged. As Sawyer notes, 'When producers are price makers, then firms charge the prices they wish to charge even if those prices may not be the ones they would have wished to charge had they been fully informed' (Sawyer, 1995, p. 173). From this perspective the prices set are not disequilibrium prices; rather, they are more akin to equilibrium prices in that firms set prices in the expectation that they will meet whatever demand is forthcoming at that price (with stock changes being a principal means of absorbing any fluctuations).

However, when Post Keynesians refer to prices as being tantamount to equilibrium prices they are referring to the generic conceptualisation of equilibrium as a position from which there is no tendency to change – that 'there are no market forces inducing buyers and sellers to change their offers at the going price – *even if markets do not clear*' (Davidson, 1981, p. 153).[5] In the Post Keynesian tradition it is firms and not impersonal market forces that set prices, and these prices reflect their strategic interests. Indeed, as Galbraith (1967) argues, producers may actively attempt to mould preferences to ensure whatever is supplied is ultimately demanded and thus to ensure that the large capital outlays associated with modern production are eventually recouped (see also Chapter 10 below). Individual markets may or may not clear, in the sense that demand may or may not be met by supply, but from a Post Keynesian perspective this falls out as a residual from the interaction between the price setting and market processes. This relates to the Post Keynesian explanation of unemployment which, as elaborated in the first half of this book, is linked to monetary considerations and is not an imperfectionist account.

It is from this perspective that Post Keynesian micro-theorists typically argue that the common characteristic of authors that may be ascribed Post Keynesian, or as informing the Post Keynesian view, is the recognition that the prices set by firms in the short run are *non*-market clearing prices (as opposed to not market clearing prices) nor are they intended to be. As Lavoie (1992) and others argue (see, for example, Sawyer, 1985b, 1990; Reynolds, 1987; Arestis, 1992; Lee, 1998; Downward, 1994, 1995, 1999), it is the different conditions of supply which implies that firms need not equate demand to the normal use of capacity when they set prices; rather, they may reflect other objectives and considerations.[6] Prices reflect the other roles of price, and the issue of whether the market clears is a secondary consideration that perhaps makes little sense in terms of a historical process.

TOWARDS A POST KEYNESIAN MICROECONOMIC CORE?

From this starting point, a variety of non-orthodox approaches to pricing can be identified as being broadly compatible in their vision of the firm to provide a foundation for Post Keynesian micro-theory (cf. Sawyer, 1992c; Lee, 1998;

see also Earl, 1983, 1984). These include what we may term: the Cambridge school, which incorporates Kaldor (1959, 1978), Robinson (1942, 1956, 1962b), Kalecki (1939, 1954, 1971) and Kaleckians such as Steindl (1954), Asimakopulos (1975), Cowling and Waterson (1976), Sawyer (1982, 1985b, 2000), Kriesler (1987); the Oxford specialists of the firm such as Hall and Hitch (1939), Harrod (1972), Andrews (1949a,b, 1964) and Brunner (Andrews and Brunner, 1951, 1962, 1975); the administered prices school that extends from Means (1933, 1935, 1936, 1962, 1972) and Lanzillotti (1958, 1964) to perhaps Galbraith (1958, 1967, 1973b) and Baran and Sweezy (1966; see also Sweezy, 1939); and the American Post Keynesian theorists of the 'megacorp' such as Eichner (1969, 1973, 1976, 1985, 1991), Shapiro (1983, 1988, 1994, 1995) and Lee (1986, 1990, 1994, 1995a, 1996).[7] Clearly, this diverse set of authors is wider than those commonly identified with the core of the Post Keynesian research programme. Moreover, while these authors incorporate elements of the 'vision' of Post Keynesian pricing theory outlined in the previous section, there is little systematic evaluation or distillation of this diverse list into a foundational core.

Lee (1998) arranges these diverse contributions into three non-neoclassical doctrines of administered prices, normal cost prices and mark-up prices, associated with the seminal contributions of Gardiner Means, Philip Andrews and Michal Kalecki respectively, to outline the foundations for Post Keynesian price theory.[8] Lee provides a comprehensive examination of the origins and theory of the various doctrines as well as discussing the contributions of the subsequent developers, which include many of those identified above plus less widely cited contributions (within the Post Keynesian tradition at least) of authors such as Jack Downie, Edwin Nourse, Abraham Kaplan, Alfred Chandler, Paolo Sylos Labini, Harry Edwards and George Richardson. Lee marshals an impressive amount of empirical evidence to support his contention that Post Keynesian price theory should be founded upon *all three* of the non-neoclassical doctrines of administered prices, normal cost prices and mark-up prices.

However, while Lee goes some way to advancing his contention, his argument would be considerably fortified if he explicitly addressed the fundamental question of what constitutes Post Keynesian economics.[9] Although Lee acknowledges that coherence is important, he is willing to accept that Post Keynesianism is at the present time what Post Keynesians say it is. This leads to problems. Lee's fundamental argument is that the almost exclusive reliance by some Post Keynesians on the mark-up approach of Kalecki is empirically misleading and unjustified. The central proposition that Lee advances is that 'if realism is a crucial presupposition of their research programme, post-Keynesian (or post-classical) authors should pay more attention to the results provided by various empirical studies, and consequently should pay more attention to the work of authors such as Gardiner Means and P.W.S. Andrews' than they presently do (Lavoie, 1996b, p. 57). Post Keynesians, Lee argues, need to recognise *all* three doctrines of pricing in addition to the broad range of supportive empirical price studies if they are to articulate a non-neoclassical view of pricing which corresponds to actual historical experience.[10] Lee's argument, however, would have been strengthened if it had been more firmly methodologically grounded – something he has latterly sought to address (see Lee, 2002).[11] As we argued in Chapters 3 and 4, the coherence of Post Keynesianism can be methodologically articulated as representing *a commitment to open-system theorising, to taking uncertainty seriously*. Post Keynesianism exhibits, at its core, a stress on agency, transformation, organic interdependence and explanation which underpins its articulation of the macroeconomic foundations of microeconomics and its distinctiveness from other sympathetic approaches.

Approaching Post Keynesianism in this manner allows us to integrate ideas and concepts from other approaches, provided only that the ideas are consistent with an open-system approach – the argument of Chapter 7 above. This is precisely what Lee implicitly does; the administered price, normal cost price and mark-up price theses are all compatible with an open-system, *a posteriori* approach to the study of transmutable economic phenomena.[12] Lee presents detailed evidence that both Means and Andrews advance an approach that is fully consistent with the methodological approach detailed earlier. The businessmen that both Means and Andrews were engaged with were setting their prices 'in [the] face of constant and unforeknowable shifts in market conditions, changes in technical knowledge, financial conditions and politics' (Lee, 1998, p. 87), i.e. in the face of uncertainty.[13] Post Keynesians clearly need to acknowledge the role of administered and normal cost pricing procedures, given that they are compatible with their methodological vision and strategic conceptualisation of pricing and the firm.[14] Moreover, as Lee (2002) argues, the grounded theory approach used by many of these authors is consistent with a realist approach that takes history and transmutability seriously.

Defining Post Keynesianism in this manner would allow Lee to present a firm methodological defence of his insistence that Post Keynesians should pay attention to all three doctrines and not focus almost exclusively upon mark-up pricing. Lee's argument is principally a *realist* one – Post Keynesians who focus exclusively on Kalecki and mark-up pricing ignore a key pricing stylised fact (demi-regularity) that all three doctrines prevail in the real world.[15] Methodologically grounding the discussion further strengthens an already persuasive argument. In an uncertain nonergodic world one would not expect one approach to pricing to dominate. This should be clear from the argument of the previous chapter. There will be no 'natural' forces or market processes forcing firms to adopt one pricing procedure or technique of production. Heterogeneity, not homogeneity, is the more likely outcome in a transmutable economy in which clusters of economic agents collectively create structures that allow the uncertainties of the future to be broached (cf. Robinson, 1977, 1980; Lawson, 1997a). As Robinson (1978, pp. 176–7) has pointed out, 'A debate which consists in defending or attacking "principles", such as the "full-cost principle", "the marginal principle" or the "normal-cost principle", and trying to fit all types of situation into one system is obviously foredoomed to futility.'[16] Although the world is open it is characterised by distinct and reasonably enduring pricing structures which are dependent upon inherently transformative practices. All three pricing doctrines represent *enduring* institutional and firm-based strategic responses to an uncertain future which are specifically designed to mitigate its impact. Such a methodological perspective is fully consistent with the empirical evidence marshalled by Lee and would have made it difficult for self-styled Post Keynesians to ignore Lee's plea. It would also be consistent with its approach to other schools and its wider rejection of simplistic selection of the fittest arguments sometimes invoked by *a priori* proponents of the market.

A METHODOLOGICAL APPRAISAL

As noted above, much of what has been traditionally identified as forming the essence of Post Keynesian pricing theory differs greatly in terms of method, theory, argument and evidence and there has been little consistency or rationale for the citation of a variety of the pricing studies. Downward and Reynolds (1996), responding to Lee (1994, 1995a), made the first explicit attempt to link Post Keynesianism's microeconomic framework to its various methodological debates. They present 'an overview of recent developments in methodological and epistemological discussion in post-Keynesian work ... use[ing] these developments as a basis for judging the contributions to pricing cited in the post-Keynesian literature, as well as Lee's critical comments on them' (Downward and Reynolds, 1996, p. 67). This contribution is embedded in the 'increasing recognition in post-Keynesian work that ... one can characterise post-Keynesian theory as an open-system approach' (Downward and Reynolds, 1996, p. 68). This is extremely salient, given that it parallels the argument advanced here and the next chapter that a Post Keynesian contribution to the theory of pricing and the firm can be defined and articulated in a manner that is consistent with its methodological outlook, i.e. the recognition of the salience of uncertainty underpins a strategic conceptualisation of the firm and its approach to pricing.[17]

Downward (1999, 2000) further elaborates this argument, making a persuasive case that the methodology of Post Keynesianism is realist and that its approach to pricing should reflect this open-system approach and recognise the importance of uncertainty, history, complexity and institutions. Downward then uses this methodological standpoint to appraise traditional accounts of Post Keynesian price theory.[18] Downward suggests that Asimakopulos, Cowling and Waterson, and Eichner (as well as Kalecki's more orthodox contributions)[19] should no longer be *automatically* thought of as constituting the theoretical microeconomic core and that Hall and Hitch, Means and Andrews should replace them.[20]

This goes to the very heart of those typically identified with Post Keynesianism. Recall that the purpose of Eichner's (1976, p. 2) *The Megacorp and Oligopoly* was 'to provide a valid micro foundation for Keynesian – and post-Keynesian – macroeconomic theory ... This purpose is accomplished, first by developing a model based upon assumptions that more accurately reflect conditions in the oligopolistic sector and, second, by relating the variable to be explained to the same key determinant as that found in the basic Keynesian system'. While the typical Cournot duopoly model is deterministic, it does not, according to Eichner, illuminate reality.[21] Nevertheless, according to Eichner (1976, p. 3), more realistic pricing models, 'such as the frequently employed percentage mark-up or cost-plus models, are indeterminate ... [and] lead to a multiplicity of possible price levels (Hall and Hitch, 1939; Lanzillotti, 1958)'. Rather than recognise the openness of economic processes explicitly in formal theory, Eichner preferred to develop an approach to the larger firm that was based on assumptions that accorded with reality but that was nevertheless *deterministic*:

> Aside from its greater compatibility with the Keynesian system the pricing model developed here has several other important characteristics. For one thing ... it is predicated upon realistic assumptions, that is, assumptions descriptive of actual conditions in oligopolistic industries. These assumptions ... pertain to the representative firm in the oligopolistic sector. The assumptions made about the megacorp are three fold: (1) that it is characterized by a separation of management from ownership, with the effective decision-making residing in the former; (2) that production occurs within multiple plants or plant segments, the factor coefficients for each of these plants or plant segments being fixed due to both technological and institutional constraints, and (3) that the firm's output is sold under conditions of recognised interdependence, the members of the industry engaging in what has been termed "joint profit maximisation" ... Another important characteristic of the model developed here is that it leads to a determinant solution. *It is this determinateness, together with the realistic nature of the underlying assumptions, which makes the model unique.*
>
> (Eichner, 1976, p. 3, italics added)

Such an approach risks confusion and contradiction. It has led some commentators to point to an apparent inconsistency between Post Keynesian microanalysis and their macroeconomic insistence on the salience of uncertainty (cf. Reynolds, 1990). As Tarshis (1980, p. 12; cf. Kenyon, 1980; Harcourt, 1980) notes, 'it is hard to reconcile the Post Keynesians' insistence that uncertainty about the future is ever present, with their readiness to forget this whole business when they come to discuss price setting in that very set of market conditions in which uncertainty is likely to be most serious'. In an uncertain world within which 'production and hiring decisions must be made in advance of offer for sale and knowledge of market demand ... (a) a price must be set without the 'correct' price being known; (b) the price could well be set 'too high' or 'too low' [in terms of other competitors]... and (c) others might do the same' (Chick, 1992, pp. 158–9). Clearly the desire and search for determinate conclusions has had its costs, not least in the obscuring of historical processes and undermining attempts to present Post Keynesianism as a coherent alternative to mainstream economics.[22]

It is for this reason that we would agree with Downward (2000, p. 214) that the essentially closed-system pricing models of 'Asimakopulos, Cowling and Waterson and Eichner, cannot form part of the core of post Keynesian pricing theory ... through their core assumptions, the models do not present the pricing decision in an uncertain context; the impact of expectations on pricing decisions is not emphasised; and the rationale for the pricing formula used by firms does not rest in this state of affairs'.[23] Such a conclusion should appeal to, and is not inconsistent with, Lee's (1998) account of the foundations of Post Keynesian pricing theory, but it rests on a more secure methodological foundation which is consistent with its broader vision and its macroeconomics.

REFINING REALIST ASSESSMENTS

However, while one can broadly agree with the core of Post Keynesian price theory that Downward (1999) identifies, there is a clear deficiency in his otherwise erudite appraisal. Like so many other self-professed Post Keynesians, Downward does not recognise the import of Paul Davidson's technical distinction between ergodic and nonergodic processes which underscores the technical distinction between risk, bounded rationality and 'fundamental' uncertainty (see Chapter 6 above). Downward quotes with approval Kay's (1989, p. 190) suggestion that 'some recent developments ... following on the work of Herbert Simon exhibit interesting parallels with post Keynesian economics in terms of issues and concepts identified as having central importance for economic analysis ... even though the substance of analysis may be superficially very different in the respective arenas.' Moreover, he subsequently conflates the two concepts (in a manner not too dissimilar to those identified in Chapter 6), noting that:

> [to] those following in the footsteps of Simon (1957, 1959, 1961, 1979), the essence of understanding organisational, decision making relations lies in an appreciation of the concepts of 'bounded rationality' and 'satisficing behaviour'. These behavioural assumptions stand in sharp contrast to those of neoclassical economics ... but share the emphasis of post Keynesian core assumptions. Bounded rationality implies that individuals, and hence the organisations they are part of, do not have either the information or capability in real historical situations to optimise on decisions. As a result, individual and organisational behaviour can be seen to be a means of coping with this uncertainty in practice or real situations in a satisficing way.
>
> (Downward, 1999, p. 133)

As we have noted above, fundamental uncertainty forms part of the heuristic core of Post Keynesian economics and refers to the nonergodic transmutable nature of historical time and its intrinsic nexus to creative, crucial choice. This is quite distinct from the concepts of bounded rationality and satisficing, which relate to the computational and processing abilities of agents and are implicitly underpinned by the assumption that processes are immutable and potentially subject to the closure conditions discussed in earlier chapters. No amount of processing power will enable one to ascertain the nature of a future that is yet to be originated. Any Post Keynesian account of pricing should recognise this fact and use it to delineate its core and explore gains from trade with other open-system approaches.[24]

Similarly, Lavoie (1992, p. 95) is mistaken to suggest that the Post Keynesian approach to the theory of the firm coalesces around the notion of bounded rationality: 'that the framework developed by all these economists [alluded to above] is quite coherent with the notion of bounded rationality'. Indeed, part of this confusion stems directly from Simon himself. In attempting to encourage his fellow economists to depart from the assumption of substantive rationality, Simon (1959, p. 264) noted that 'There is some empirical evidence that business goals are, in fact, stated in satisficing terms. First, there is the series of studies stemming from the pioneering work of Hall and Hitch that indicates that businessmen often set prices by applying a standard mark-up to costs'. However, this is a clear example of Simon's conflation of the following of conventions and rules of thumb, to which Hall and Hitch allude, with the more precise delineation of satisficing behaviour. The former relates to uncertain and transmutable 'open system' processes and the latter to closed, ergodic ones. While we would agree that, generally speaking, any Post Keynesian approach to the firm should be further developed and extended to embed more centrally the problems of knowledge and uncertainty into its theorising, following the argument developed in Chapter 6, we would issue a strong caveat against making bounded rationality a central organising concept, given its implicit nexus to the assumption of immutability that underpins it.

This is not to say that insights that are gleaned from the notion of bounded rationality should be ignored by Post Keynesians. Rather that they should be reformulated and made consistent, with a stress on the nonergodic nature of historical time. People do follow rules of thumb and do possess limited computational powers but, in the absence of governing ergodic, historical processes, to label behaviour as satisficing is clearly misleading when the optimising counterfactual against which satisficing behaviour is compared is vacuous. There are no omniscient parties who can judge behaviour to be falling short of optimality. Rules of thumb and dispersed and differentiated computational abilities will clearly affect the nature of the history created across firms, governments, countries and continents, etc., but the history that is created is in no sense sub-optimal. The concepts of sub-optimality, satisficing or bounded rationality all imply falling short of some omniscient, maximising substantive rationality which, as argued above in Chapter 6, does not make sense in an uncertain, yet-to-be-imagined world. Clearly such confusions offer *prima facie* evidence of the need to further develop the Post Keynesian microeconomics to incorporate problems of knowledge and uncertainty. Moreover, it would strengthen the Post Keynesian view of the firm as a strategic organisation by outlining a more precise formulation of the concept of choice and strategy and its nexus to a yet-to-be-created future (as we argue in the next chapter).

THE DOMAIN OF VALIDITY OF POST KEYNESIAN PRICING THEORIES

The Post Keynesian approach to pricing, however, is generally viewed as synonymous with oligopoly. Some Post Keynesians assert that the standard neoclassical model is of *limited applicability* in the face of the large-scale dominance of modern oligopolistic corporations; the 'megacorp' in Eichner's terminology.

To use Galbraith's (1973b) terminology, Post Keynesians distinguish between the market and planning systems, with the latter dominating the former:

> In a context where supply is flexible, firms do not necessarily equate demand to the normal use of capacity when they set prices. This in my opinion is what distinguishes the markets in which firms of the post-Keynesian type operate and those in which the standard neoclassical firm still makes sense. The position taken here is that these non-clearing markets are the rule whereas the clearing ones are the exception.
>
> (Lavoie, 1992, p. 95)

Lavoie (1992, p. 96) does, however, recognise that to assert that the Post Keynesian theory of pricing relates to mainly oligopolistic industries is unnecessarily restrictive. Means (cited in Clifton, 1983, p. 24) explicitly suggested that administered pricing should not be confused with monopoly. Moreover, Okun (1981, pp. 175–6) suggests that 'mark-up' pricing is too pervasive across the U.S. to be attributable to monopoly. This conclusion was also reached by Hall and Hitch (1939, pp. 30–1). Moreover, even when large firms do not dominate, variants of the normal cost, mark-up and administered pricing doctrines are still observed as characterising the actual pricing practices of firms.

The Post Keynesian approach starts from the *a posteriori* assessment that in the *majority* of markets short-run pricing depends on costs adjusted according to some principle of either mark-up, administered, or normal cost pricing. Post Keynesians do, however, recognise certain exceptions to this rule (Shapiro, 1995). These distinctions are made in the context of the Post Keynesian recognition of the difference between producible and non-producible commodities which underpins the distinction between demand-determined and cost-determined prices.[25] For example, commodities which are reproducible are more likely to exhibit linear marginal costs up to capacity, i.e. inverted L-shaped average variable cost curves. Products which are not reproducible, i.e. natural resources, require long delays to increase production and are subject to diminishing returns, and this implies traditional U-shaped average cost curves (Marshall, 1920; cf. Loasby, 1976, 1989). This points to an important distinction made by Means (1936, p. 35) that administered prices refer to the shape of the costs 'inherent in [the] modern technology' in use and not market structure. The pricing doctrines identified by Post Keynesians refer to the nature of modern technology and the problems of accumulation and reproducibility under conditions of uncertainty that the firm faces and not the conditions of static monopoly.

Clearly, the discussion above suggests that the domain of validity that must be ascribed to the Post Keynesian doctrines of pricing is quite wide. However, it is clear that not all areas are cost determined and the Post Keynesian analysis of pricing and the firm is not truly comprehensive! One might thus be tempted to conclude, following Lavoie, that the neoclassical concept of perfect competition retains a degree of, albeit limited, relevance. However, we would argue that one of the distinguishing characteristics of the Post Keynesian approach to pricing is that it is firm based – and this has the corollary that the resulting pricing procedures that eventuate will reflect the strategic choices of a subset of those involved in production and thus may or may not result in cost-based pricing (Shapiro and Mott, 1995). As Galbraith (1973b, p. 64) stresses, even small firms set prices strategically and draw upon pricing conventions:

> The small clothing manufacturer or builder uses the union scale which is common to all plus a conventional mark-up as the basis for pricing his product. So do others, and all thus win control (sometimes tenuous) over prices. Physicians, chiropractors, osteopaths, optometrists, lawyers and the building trades control or influence supply by control of educational requirements, apprenticeship requirements or state licensing. Farmers persuade the state to fix prices by government purchase and, through acreage or marketing quotas, to limit supply. Small manufacturers seek publicly enforced retail price maintenance ... All of these efforts reflect the tendency of all producing firms, whether in the market or planning system, to control their economic environment and not be subject to it.

Clearly, the pricing practices employed by firms that are *a posteriori* identified will depend upon the nature of the firm and its embeddedness within the broader social, technological and market structures.

Thus although, generally speaking, Post Keynesians have focused on the pricing mechanisms of the more dominant and influential oligopolistic sectors, this should not be taken as implying that a niche exists for the (ahistorical) neoclassical view of pricing and perfect competition. The neoclassical view of pricing and perfect competition is based on an ergodic, immutable conception of economic processes. As Knight (1921, p. 197) pointed out long ago: 'Chief among the simplifications of reality prerequisite to the achievement of perfect competition is, as has been emphasised all along, the assumption of practical omniscience on the part of every member of the competitive system'. Moreover, as the analysis of authors such as Richardson (1959, 1960), Loasby (1976, 1991) and Hodgson (1988, pp. 187–94) have since established, and need not be rehearsed here, the theoretical foundations of neoclassical theories of the firm and perfect competition are inconsistent and erroneous. In contrast to Lavoie, we would argue that the standard neoclassical theory of perfect competition makes no sense when we follow Knight and Keynes and begin to address problems of knowledge and information. Neoclassical theory, by assuming agents possess perfect information and the capacity to use it effectively, destroys the theoretical basis of competition and the firm (see also Shapiro, 1997; Kregel, 1998a).[26]

In recognising the internal incoherence of the neoclassical competitive model of the firm, post-Marshallian authors, such as Richardson (1959, 1960) and Loasby (1976, pp. 173–92), introduce the distinction between free competition used by Marshall and Andrews (cf. Lee *et al.*, 1986; Clark, 1940) and perfect competition used by the more orthodox approaches.[27] Free competition does not rest on the assumption of perfect information and foresight and is consistent with the methodological outlook ascribed here to Post Keynesianism (cf. Chick, 1992; Davies and Lee, 1988).[28] The concept of free competition refers to the everyday usage of the term to denote rivalry between similarly matched competitors (see Marshall, 1920, pp. 337–50). Under free competition competitors do not collude with competitors on either side, that is buyers compete freely with buyers, and sellers, compete freely with sellers, and the free flow of technical knowledge, not the number of competitors, ensures a conventional and broadly uniform price.

In Post Keynesian price theory the structure of production and costs faced by firms, along with the pricing procedures employed, are ultimately contingent upon the nature of the planning and time horizons that the firm faces and its business strategy – which are themselves conditional on the scale of production and the power (absolute and relative) that the organisation possesses. Thus, as Lee (1998, p. 51) notes, 'if the interaction of technology and organisation created a small sized enterprise with virtually no market power, then ... the enterprise would adopt a very restricted time horizon and devise an appropriate business strategy in light of it which would manifest itself in the structure of production costs and pricing procedures adopted by the enterprise'. Clearly, as the number of similarly matched competitors increases then the degree of rivalry and competition intensifies, limiting (but not eliminating) the power and independence of firms and reinforcing pricing conventions and behaviour. While the pricing processes and objectives adopted in competitive markets may differ from those adopted in more oligopolistic markets both are subject to uncertainty, not least the agency of actual and potential competitors and the uncertainty that this engenders.

THE NEED FOR A POST KEYNESIAN THEORY OF THE FIRM

However, while opening up the orthodox 'black box' approach to price determination *vis-à-vis* Walrasian, neoclassical and Sraffian models, Post Keynesians are generally happy to leave the 'black box' approach to the firm firmly closed (Sawyer, 1990). Post Keynesian price theory, or for that matter Sraffian production theory, cannot be relied upon to provide a theory *of the firm*. Pricing theory, or for that matter price theory, was never intended to be a theory of the firm as an organisation or an institution (cf. Kaldor, 1934). Generally speaking, pricing and price theory have been used as a theoretical link in the explanation of changes in price, quantity, the rate of accumulation, capacity utilisation and other macroeconomic considerations and were never designed to explain industrial structure, let alone serve as a guide to industrial policy or internal modes of organisation. More to the point, using pricing or price theory to explain the boundaries of the firm is just plain illogical, since the firm's boundaries in price or pricing theory are a matter of assumption.

Clearly there is an urgent need, if Post Keynesianism aims to extend its domain of theoretical validity, to articulate more comprehensively a theory of the business enterprise that deals with the questions of the firm's existence, boundaries, internal organisation and competitive advantage, building upon its more fully articulated understanding of the strategic process of price setting. Post Keynesian theorising regarding firms and their internal organisation, the making of investment and employment decisions, inter-enterprise decisions (including cartels and joint ventures), the nature of competitive activities, the coordination of economic activity, the process of innovation and technical change and the conceptualisation of inter-governmental decisions, such as the regulation of markets, tariffs, influencing legislation etc., is *ad hoc* at best, and non-existent generally. While Post Keynesians recognise that 'the enterprise cannot operate without a management – *it is not a production function* – and the knowledge and skills of its managers, as well as those of its engineers and product designers, cannot be changed overnight' (Shapiro and Mott, 1995, p. 37, italics added), generally speaking they have not considered in detail the nature and internal organisation of the business enterprise, its hierarchical structure and concomitant power relationships, its decision-making centres, flows of information, labour processes and so on.

This is not to say that Post Keynesians eschew an understanding of the firm as an organisation. As Sawyer (1994, p. 19, italics added; cf. Eichner, 1976; Lee, 1998; Shapiro, 1983, 1994; Shapiro and Mott, 1995) notes, in the Post Keynesian approach '[t]he firm is viewed as an *organisation* which strives to remain in business over the long term, and hence pays attention to the conditions for survival'.[29] The point is not that developments in the theory of the firm have been completely overlooked nor that no contributions have been made in this area (see, for example, Shapiro, 1983, 1988, 1991, 1994; Phillips, 1985-6), but rather that they have yet to fully recognise that a common methodological and historical base underpins their *a posteriori* recognition of the salience of money, the various pricing doctrines and real-world institutions such as the firm, and to link them together in an integrated and organic fashion around a strategic concept of the firm. Post Keynesian microeconomics remains under-developed. As Lee (1994, pp. 304–5, italics added) notes:

> post-Keynesians have devoted little energy towards articulating a consistent and realistic microfoundation and have largely ignored 'micro' themes and issues, such as the business enterprise, pricing, the organisation, the nature of competitive activities, co-ordinations of economic activity, and innovation and technical change. As a result, there exists no *well-grounded cohesive* body of economic analysis that could be referred to as post-Keynesian microeconomics.

If Post Keynesianism aims to present itself as an alternative to orthodox economics then it surely has to articulate itself more systematically on a wider range of microeconomic issues than it presently does. Moreover, this articulation should be consistent with its methodological presuppositions. A fully constituted Post Keynesian theory of the firm should display, to repeat, a commitment to open-system theorising, stressing agency, transformation and organic, socialised interdependence. This would suggest that Post Keynesian theorists of pricing and the firm should pay more attention to those areas previously neglected. The next chapter attempts to begin this process.

CONCLUDING COMMENTS

It should be clear from the above that a core of Post Keynesian pricing theory can be identified that is consistent with its stress on the uncertain, creative and sometimes destructive nature of the competitive process. The foundations of Post Keynesian price theory are to be found in the non-neoclassical doctrines of administered prices, normal cost prices and mark-up prices associated with Means, Andrews, Hall and Hitch and the non-orthodox writings of Kalecki. Efforts to develop a more comprehensive Post Keynesian economics should start from this foundational core. However, it is clear from this discussion that Post Keynesians focus almost exclusively upon pricing to the exclusion of considerations of the nature of the organisation and its uncertain foundations.

NOTES

1 As Sawyer (1995, p. 171) continues: 'In that dichotomy, the Walrasian general equilibrium analysis provides only a theory of prices, but not of pricing since there are no mechanisms of price setting (unless the auctioneer is so considered). However, the non-neo-classical approach is able to generate both a theory of pricing and of price'.
2 In *Post Keynesian Price Theory* Lee (1998) attempts to develop the *foundations* of a realistic and empirically grounded non-neoclassical approach to pricing that challenges the view, sometimes espoused within Post Keynesianism, that its price theoretic foundations are to be found in either the Kaleckian or Sraffian approach to prices or in some hybrid of the two (see Lee, 1998, pp. 1–17). Lee's (1998, pp. 3–4) objective is to 'move Post Keynesian analysis forward, towards a more comprehensive, coherent, realistic – and, indeed, believable – non-neoclassical theory of prices by setting out its non-neoclassical pricing foundation by developing an empirically grounded pricing model in conjunction with an empirically grounded production schema'.
3 Lee (1994, p. 329) argues quite strongly that 'It must be noted that the failure of the Kaleckian, Weintraubian and Sraffian-inspired pricing models *vis-à-vis* the empirical pricing model can be largely attributed to their ahistorical nature and the fact that they did not correspond to economic reality when initially developed'.
4 Strictly speaking, both Sawyer (1993) and Gerrard (1989) use the term 'strategic' to refer to what we label here as the 'rivalrous' role of price. I have adopted not to follow this classification to help avoid initiating confusion and to reflect the fact that the different roles and functions identified with the price-setting process all reflect a strategic concept of the firm in which the notion of decision-making is real and matters.
5 As Davidson (1981, p. 156) notes, 'Keynes' analytical framework is logically incompatible with all general equilibrium systems for a number of reasons not least being that it is based on a wider definition of equilibrium than merely market clearing'.
6 Lavoie (1992) perhaps represents one of the first attempts to explicitly produce a coherent and comprehensive view of Post Keynesianism as he strives to delineate a Post Keynesian approach to the theory of the firm. Specifically, Lavoie aims to outline a *realistic* view of the firm, and to demonstrate that this view is shared by *all* Post Keynesians; i.e. Lavoie's aim is to argue that Post Keynesians possesses a coherent vision as to the nature of the firm.
7 See Sawyer (1985b, 2000) for a survey of Michal Kalecki's work. For an overview of Means' doctrine of administered prices see Lee (1989, 1990; see also Lee and Samuels, 1992; Samuels and Lee, 1994; Goode, 1994). On the Oxford challenge to marginalism see Lee (1981, 1991) and Lee and Young (1993). For a discussion of Andrews's

contribution see Lee and Earl (1993) and Lee *et al.*, (1986). Lee (1990–91) outlines the significance of these debates and the challenge of marginalism for Post Keynesianism more generally.

8 It should be pointed out that although the title of Lee's (1998) book is perhaps misleading that was not his fault. It was supposed to be titled *The Foundations of Post Keynesian Price Theory,* which would have clearly indicated that it was not a review of Post Keynesian price theory but an attempt to establish its core. In the process of publishing the book Cambridge University Press made the change in title without informing Lee.

9 Lee's view is that Post Keynesian economics has been evolving since 1971 and its core features have yet to be codified. Thus, like many of the books published on Post Keynesian economics over the last decade, Lee attempts to influence its direction and future evolution. However, in the absence of any consensus, Lee chooses to delineate Post Keynesian economics in terms of those economists who call themselves Post Keynesians, who write and publish articles in Post Keynesian journals and/or with Post Keynesian in the title, or are involved with existing and evolving Post Keynesian social structures and networks and are, in essence, defining by their actions what Post Keynesian economics is (Lee, 1998, 2000a,b). Thus he chooses not to fix the definition of Post Keynesianism and anchor it to a specific point in time. While this approach has merit from a historical perspective, it makes it difficult to assess claims of coherence and to outline a conception of Post Keynesian economics that one can either accept or reject. It is for such reasons that we have devoted the first half of the book to arguing that a coherent Post Keynesian approach exists which can underpin a research programme examining a Post Keynesian contribution to the theory of the firm.

10 However, the more interesting question is why this should be the case: why is Kalecki, who as Lee points out is perhaps the most neoclassical of the authors discussed, the inspiration for most Post Keynesian articulations on price theory? The question of why this should be the case is side-stepped. This paradox may reflect the overt links made by Kalecki and his followers between prices and investment, which lie under-developed in Means and Andrews. Whatever the reason for this, however, an attempt at defining Post Keynesianism would have helped the reader assess whether Lee outlines a view of Post Keynesianism that they can recognise and subscribe to.

11 In Lee's defence, his book was largely completed by 1996 before both Sheila Dow (1996a) and Tony Lawson (1997a) raised the methodological stakes in Post Keynesian economics!

12 As Lee has pointed out in private correspondence: 'As for uncertainty, the three doctrines have in one form or another non-clearing markets, non-clearing market prices, perpetual non-equilibrium, monetary economy, social rules, market institutions, business enterprises, pricing procedures based on normal output, and business cycles and the need for national economic planning. All of these attributes presuppose a nonergodic world with radical uncertainty. Just because the term uncertainty was not a term used or discussed by the economists in the book (Lee, 1998), it does not mean that it was absen[t from] their thinking. Besides that Means discussed this issue with Keynes in 1939; and Richardson (1959, 1960) was heavily influenced by uncertainty.'

13 Indeed, as Andrews and Brunner (1951, pp. 8–10) note, 'Keynes is most certainly correct in calling attention to the future uncertainty of the earnings from a business's capital equipment, whose life must extend beyond any horizon of certainty which is visible to the business man who has to make the important decisions concerned with the acquisition and use of the equipment'.

14 Moreover, it is clear that these authors had read Keynes (and Shackle) and proceeded to criticise and develop their microeconomics, explicitly recognising the import of

uncertainty as it bears down upon microeconomics theory. To quote Andrews and Brunner (1951, pp. 11–12) at length: 'The consequence is that Keynes' theories retain the chief characteristic of the older, static, theories – that the rate of investment will depend upon the rate of interest so far as external influences are concerned. Despite all the splendid passages in the *General Theory* where Keynes discusses the effects upon economic affairs of the uncertainty which surrounds business operations, he yet, when it comes to the point, resolves that uncertainty into the formal equivalent of certainty. It is this which enables the rate of interest to maintain the importance which it has in his theory of investment decisions. If it is puzzling that Keynes should have accepted this, in view of his insistence upon the importance of uncertainty, it is even more puzzling that he should have accepted its consequence, that the rate of interest retained its decisive importance in investment decisions ... Until just before the outbreak of the recent war, economists generally still regarded the rate of interest as having a decisive influence on the level of current investment, and as an effective means of hastening or slowing down capital investment according to public policy. The discovery that this was not so was largely the result of some researches by the Oxford Economists' Research Group, the publications of which are listed in the bibliography. It was found on questioning the business men about their behaviour during the trade cycle that they were decidedly not conscious that changes in rates of interest had affected their decisions to acquire new capital assets ... The main reason for the unimportance of rates of interest in this particular field was found to be that the earnings of capital equipment are subject to two considerable sources of uncertainty. The first attaches to the value of the output to which they will contribute. The second, is a consequence of the fact that machinery and other equipment are not only subject to physical deterioration through wear and tear, but become obsolete so that they have to be scrapped in favour of new and superior equipment ... Recently, some economists have begun to allow for the effect of uncertainty in such a way as to show the diminished practical importance of the rate of interest. One example is the article by Dr Shackle ... He .... provides a new formulation in which the future earnings of capital are discounted not only by the rate of interest but also by a term 'U'. This latter is taken as depending upon the psychology of the business man concerned as well as upon the uncertainty attaching to the basic factors which he takes into account in his judgements. Shackle then goes on to warn us that, in practice, U may be so large, and its changes of such an order of magnitude, that the inclusion of the rate of interest in his analysis has only formal significance, and that it will not then, in practice, affect the rate of investment ... Putting the matter bluntly, the position is really that we are left with no effective theory of the determination of the rate of investment – although it is possible to put forward some very broad generalisations which seem to be justified by empirical research'.

15 As elaborated in more detail in Chapters 6, 7 and 8 above, in a nonergodic environment the market cannot select *ex post* optimising configurations such as the most efficient pricing process. Thus Tarshis (1980, p. 11) is wrong to suggest that 'it follows that if the mark-up is properly chosen – say by a Darwinian process in which firms that have somehow made a near-correct choice survive and hence can instruct newcomers – and if changes in the value of *e* are generally small, mark-up pricing with a constant mark-up will yield a price close to "the most profitable one". And the rule is obviously far easier to use!' Similarly, Tarshis (1980, p. 11) accuses Post Keynesians of not detailing why they reject the axiom of maximisation: 'for reasons that remain obscure some Post Keynesian economists assume that firms in a crucial core are part-way philanthropist; that they don't even aim to maximise profits'. It is not the case that Post Keynesians posit philanthropy (satisficing) in the objective functions of managers but rather, as argued in Chapter 4, they make a crucial distinction between striving for profits and maximising profits (cf. Andrews and Brunner, 1962). The pursuit of profits does not entail maximisation of profits in an uncertain world.

16 As Kaldor and Robinson (2000, p. 270) point out in a recently discovered 1941 manuscript: 'It is possible that insofar as the empirical investigation will be found to support or eliminate these theoretical hypotheses at all in different sections of industry, different hypothesis will be found appropriate; it is possible also that no single hypotheses will provide an explanation: which is another way of saying that to formulate a general theory of distribution proves impossible'.

Similarly as Robinson (1977, p. 1332) also later pointed out: 'Innovating firms have to set prices *ex ante*. They may be supposed to aim at a price that will cover average total cost (including the interest bill) at some standard level of utilization of plant, plus an allowance for selling costs, plus an allowance for net profit. As well as the choice of technique, the choice of the standard of utilisation, of selling costs, and the ratio of net profit to price depend upon the policy of the individual firm. There is too great an element of luck in the game for an outside observer to tell which policies are proving the most successful in any particular circumstances'.

17 Downward and Reynolds suggest that 'one of the most positive features of post-Keynesian economics in general, and post-Keynesian price and pricing theory in particular, is that it embraces a wide range of approaches, all of which are entirely consistent with the methodological position outlined above' (Downward and Reynolds, 1996, p. 70).

18 From this perspective Downward (1999) goes on to present a detailed realist investigation into the stylised facts of pricing and the causal mechanisms that underpin them. Challenging the conventional wisdom associated with Critical Realism, Downward makes a convincing case that there *is* a role for econometrics within a radical methodology – one of establishing the nature of the stylised facts (demi-regularities) upon which theorising is to proceed. However, in sharp contrast to many orthodox empirical accounts, which typically eschew and denigrate case study evidence, Downward uses this econometric fact-clearing exercise to inform a more detailed case study examination of the causal mechanisms that underpin his previously identified pricing facts.

19 One must be mindful not to place too much emphasis on the few papers of Kalecki where he made use of the closed-system assumptions of profit maximisation and allied marginalist concepts, and overlook the fact that his post-1943 writings on price were clearly non-marginalist (Sawyer, 1985b; cf. Basile and Salvadori, 1994; Carson, 1994).

20 For example, Andrews and Brunner (1951, pp. 15–16) note, in a manner reminiscent of recent realist contributions (cf. Lawson, 1997a, Chapter 15; Siakantaris, 2000): 'Although economics uses precise measurement when it can, and although the sphere in which quantitative laws can be made is tending steadily to increase, its generalisations are more usually of a qualitative kind and are reached in rather a different way. This is the consequence of the complexity of subject-matter and of the impossibility of making controlled experiments in a laboratory'.

Similarly, as Joan Robinson (1977, p. 1319) noted: 'With the best will in the world, it is excessively difficult to find an agreed answer to any question concerned with reality. Economists cannot make use of controlled experiments to settle their differences; they have to appeal to historical evidence, and evidence can always be read both ways'.

21 Eichner had good reason to dismiss the Cournot model as unrealistic after having completed a case study investigation into the actual historical process by which oligopoly arose in the sugar refining industry (see Eichner, 1969). As Eichner (1976, p. xi) noted, the exercise was important in two major respects: firstly ' it showed how limited in time was the existence of competitive conditions in the American economy's manufacturing sector and, second, it showed how unstable and unviable those conditions were even for the brief period they lasted ... oligopoly must be viewed, not as the perversion which most economists consider it but rather as simply a historical necessity'.

Unfortunately, in the rush to produce a determinate theory of the megacorp, much of this historical approach was obscured from view.

22 As Samuels (1989, p. 537; see also Fusfeld, 1990) notes, 'the price that must be paid in order to reach determinate solutions is complex, but fundamentally it ignores and excludes the processes at work in the real world that produce the actual content of preference functions, social values, power structures, rights, opportunity sets, mutual coercion, freedom, change, knowledge and psychic states'.

23 As Loasby (1967, p. 168) noted in an unjustly neglected article on the theory of the firm: 'The great attraction of perfect competition theory, which was inherited by monopolistic and imperfect competition theories (but which oligopoly theory lacks), was its determinism; it had no need of the individual. It was time he was allowed back.' We would, however, in light of the first half of this book, refine Loasby's assessment by pointing to the fact that it is time that creative capabilities of agents operative within, and enabled by, social structures was let back into economic theory.

24 Notwithstanding such caveats, however, Downward has done Post Keynesian economics a great service in outlining a (methodological) approach which should facilitate the further enunciation of a coherent and comprehensive body of economic knowledge which can be referred to as Post Keynesianism. Moreover, Downward, in characterising Post Keynesian economics as an open-systems approach, paves the way for an increased dialogue, with appropriate caveats, with other like-minded open-systems approaches such as Institutionalists, behaviouralists, resource-based theorists of the firms and marketing and management theorists, to name but a few (see also Chapter 7 above).

25 However, as Joan Robinson (1978, pp. 130–1) points out: 'The theory of markets was [is?] in need of a Keynesian revolution just as much as the theory of employment. Keynes himself threw out some hints and anyone who is acquainted with the conduct, say, of trade in primary commodities, knows that it is dominated by *speculation*, that is by guesses about the future behaviour of demand and of supply. Such markets are made by intermediaries (often on several layers) between original producers and final buyers. Uncertainty tends to make markets unstable since a rise of price is often a signal for buying in stocks and a fall for selling out. The prices of manufacturers are less volatile. The large powerful firms deal directly with retailers and set prices according to a more or less long range policy. Even they, however, cannot know the future; they work on estimates. The system of so called 'full-cost pricing' means calculating expenses, including amortization allowances, per unit of output on the basis of an assumed average level of utilisation and length of earning life of plant and then adding a margin for the level of net profit that it seems prudent to go for. When actual utilisation over the life of plant exceeds the standard, net profit exceeds the calculated level, and conversely'.

26 Indeed, the whole concept of marginal productivity is pretty nebulous in the context of an uncertain process of production taking place in historical time (see Shackle, 1983–4, pp. 244–5). It is for such reasons that entrepreneurs rely on the various conventions elaborated in the various pricing doctrines rather than engage in marginal mysticism.

27 Moreover competition has many guises beyond pure price competition. As Robinson (1978, pp. 171–2) notes: 'The very fact that markets are not perfect means that competition may take many forms. The main vehicles of competition may be summarised as: (1) imitation of products; (2) differentiation of products – and these may be in respect of qualities which affect practical usefulness or pleasure to the consumer, qualities which appeal to snobbishness or to pseudo-scientific notions, or simply methods of packing and labelling articles; (3) services of all kinds, prompt delivery, long credit; (4) advertisement; (5) pure salesmanship, in the sense of the persuasiveness of travellers, etc.; (6) higher price – giving the impression of better quality; (7) lower price. The multi-dimensional nature of competition is illustrated by the fact that rings

formed to limit competition, which begin by agreeing only on a price list for their products, often go on to limit terms of sale, permissible types of advertising appeal and the specification of products, so that sometimes competition in pure salesmanship is all that is left unregulated, and rival travellers are found making offers to potential customers which are identical in all respects except the names on the labels of the goods'.

28 As Shackle (1972, pp. 286–7) notes, 'the *Principles* is a relentless effort to bring into one fabric of argument the two incompatibles ... the mutually repellent strands of rationality and novelty ... the economist must study change. Yet he must be a seeker of principles ... the *Principles* is, in the main, an intense and unremitting struggle with this central theme'.

29 However, Sawyer adds: 'in both approaches considered the firm is sometimes represented as a "black box".'

10 A Post Keynesian approach to the theory of the firm

Its [the firm's] existence in the world is a direct result of the fact of uncertainty.

Frank Knight (1921, p. 271)

With uncertainty entirely absent, every individual being in possession of perfect knowledge of the situation, there would be no occasion for anything of the nature of responsible management or control of productive activity.

Frank Knight (1921, p. 267)

A firm is likely therefore to emerge in those cases where a very short-term contract would be unsatisfactory ... It seems improbable that a firm would emerge without the existence of uncertainty.

Ronald Coase (1937, pp. 337–8)

INTRODUCTION

In the first half of the twentieth century both Knight and Coase suggested that without uncertainty there would be little need for the firm or, for that matter, the strategic control of production. However, Coase largely dismissed Knight's account of entrepreneurship and the firm and a major opportunity to integrate the study of uncertainty into the theory of the firm was lost. More recently, Cowling and Sugden (1987, 1993, 1998) have returned to the notion of strategy while reflecting on developments in the theory of the firm stemming from Coase. They have concentrated on Coase's original starting point, the notion of economic planning, and provide an alternative approach and definition of the firm, as a 'means of coordinating production from one centre of strategic decision making'. However, they fail to appreciate the key insight, recognised by Knight and Shackle (1955, p. 82), that 'uncertainty is inherent in production' and to examine the implications for coordinating decision-making.

This chapter proposes an extension to the definition of the firm advanced by Cowling and Sugden by arguing that centres of strategic decision-makers coordinating production operate under conditions of fundamental uncertainty or nonergodicity. This extension reinforces many of Cowling and Sugden's central conclusions and, more importantly, extends and clarifies their notion of strategic decision-making. Cowling and Sugden's approach also implicitly suggests a focus on the role of money in production, given that 'In the strategic decision-making approach what others have referred to as market exchanges falling outside the ambit of the firm, notably subcontracting relationships, are incorporated inside the firm' (Cowling and Sugden, 1998, pp. 60–61). From a Post Keynesian perspective, we argue that this link should be made explicit and that, by embedding Cowling and Sugden's discussion in terms of uncertainty, we underscore the fact that market exchanges are conducted in terms of money-denominated contracts as a planning response to an unknowable future (Galbraith, 1967; Davidson, 1972).

The definition of the firm advanced in this chapter also has implications for Post Keynesianism. We suggest that our extension to Cowling and Sugden offers a way of integrating Post Keynesian monetary economics, which is largely Keynesian, more fully with its analysis of the firm, which is broadly Kaleckian, by making explicit the contractual nature of the firm and its nexus to strategic nodes of power, uncertainty and money. This promotes further coherence across the different Post Keynesian traditions and provides a good example of open-systems theorizing.

The chapter begins by outlining the transaction cost approach to the theory of the firm that descends from the seminal contribution of Coase (1937). We then consider the essence of 'transaction costs', noting that it primarily refers to informational problems and some radical conceptualisation thereof. The next section considers the critique of the transaction cost approach by Cowling and Sugden (1987, 1993, 1998). We then extend Cowling and Sugden's contribution to the theory of the firm to account for fundamental uncertainty (nonergodicity). Finally, it is argued that this extended definition might provide a basis for a further integration of the 'Keynesian' and 'Kaleckian' strands of Post Keynesianism.

THE CONTRACTUAL APPROACH TO THE THEORY OF THE FIRM

Coase (1937) attempted to provide a definition of the firm that permitted its nature to be more fully understood. According to Coase, markets and firms are alternative means of coordination. Firms represent the internal supersession of the market mechanism by command. As markets and firms are alternative mechanisms for resource allocation, a choice is offered. The allocation of resources by planning or command, as opposed to movements in the structure of relative prices, is conditional on the fact that the use of the price mechanism is costly. In finding what are the relevant prices, undergoing a process of negotiation and in engaging in contractual behaviour, resources are consumed. Command, with one party obeying the direction of another, reduces the need for costly continual renegotiation and reformulation of contracts. Economic institutions such as the firm economize on, but do not eliminate, contracting costs that arise from using the market. Firms succeed where markets fail; that is, 'in the beginning there were markets'.

Williamson (1975, 1979, 1981, 1985, 1987) has labelled such contracting costs as transaction costs. Williamson (1981) highlights five core methodological elements associated with the transaction cost approach:

1 The basic unit of analysis is the transaction (that is, exchange).
2 Agents exhibit bounded rationality and act opportunistically.
3 The critical dimensions for describing transactions are (a) the frequency with which they occur, (b) the uncertainty to which they are subject, and (c) the degree to which transactions are supported by specific investments.
4 The criterion employed to explain the choice between alternative modes of contracting is a purely instrumental one of economising on transaction costs.
5 The assessment of differences in transaction costs is a comparative institutional undertaking.

A transaction occurs 'when a good or service is transferred across a technologically separable interface' (Williamson, 1981, p. 1544). These transaction costs refer to three sequential aspects of the exchange process, namely search and information costs, bargaining and decision costs, and policing and enforcement costs (Dahlman, 1979).

Williamson employs two principal behavioural assumptions, bounded rationality and opportunism. The notion of bounded rationality, as developed by Herbert Simon (1957, 1959, 1976), refers to conduct that is 'intendedly rational behaviour but limitedly so' owing to knowledge and computational constraints on individual economic agents. As a result, all complex contracts are inevitably incomplete and future states of the world cannot be fully specified (Radner, 1968; cf. Dunn, 1999, 2000b). Opportunism refers to 'self-interest seeking with guile'. The import of this assumption is that agents can be selective in their information disclosure and can distort information in such a way that contracts-as-promises lacking credible assurances are ultimately naive. For Williamson, such considerations suggest that transactions should be contrived so as to economise on bounded rationality and protect the transaction from the hazards of opportunism; that is, to reduce the behavioural uncertainties that surround transactions.

In terms of the critical dimensions that describe a transaction, transaction-specific investments or asset specificity is seen as the most important and distinctive. Asset specificity refers to the extent to which an asset can be redeployed to alternative uses without a reduction in its productive value. Asset specificity is critical in that, once an investment has been undertaken, the buyer and seller become locked into a transaction for a considerable period thereafter, a situation of *ex post* bilateral dependence. Such dependence is exacerbated by problems of information impactedness that arise in light of the complexity and opportunism that surround a transaction-specific investment. The asset specificity principle transforms the exchange relation 'from a large-numbers to a small-numbers condition during the course of contract execution' (Williamson, 1981, p. 1547).

The situation whereby market transaction costs are greater than those incurred by superseding the market arises as a result of the coexistence of asset specificity, bounded rationality and opportunism. The market is superseded by the firm by virtue of its ability to reduce or economise on market transaction costs arising from these constituent elements. The coexistence of these three factors represents a necessary condition for hierarchical modes of organisation (firms) to be economically viable and for the study of economic institutions to be meaningful. In situations where bounded rationality, opportunism and asset specificity are pervasive, hierarchies replace markets. As Pitelis (1991, p. 12) notes, 'the advantages of internal organisation are that they facilitate adaptive, sequential decision making in circumstances where complex, contingent claim contracts are not feasible and sequential spot markets are hazardous'.

The presence of an authority relation represents the capacity to stop protracted disputes and, as well, the potential to promote cohesion: members of a hierarchy might identify with the objectives of an organisation, thus reducing the desire to engage in opportunistic behaviour. However, as the problems of asymmetric information cannot be solved fully by the employment relation, the firm has to provide an incentive structure to induce worker cooperation. This yields the replacement of the external labour market by an internal labour market. The bargaining costs associated with asset specificity can be reduced through the use of an authority relation and by assigning a wage for a position or job as opposed to an individual. In internal labour markets a wage is attached to a position and not an individual worker.[1] Although workers accept a loss of freedom in the acceptance of an authority relation and monitoring framework, they still retain the right of exit. This provides a check on employers indulging in opportunistic behaviour. Employers' opportunism is further attenuated for reasons of reputation and by the monitoring of employers by employee organisations such as trade unions.

The transaction costs or markets versus hierarchies framework provides an *ex post* rationalisation of various institutional structures such as the 'employment relation', the degree of vertical integration, the evolution of multidivisional (M-form) corporate structure and transnational corporations. It permits an opening up of the previously closed neoclassical 'black box' view of production and suggests a focus upon the institutions of corporate governance. Pitelis (1991) notes, however, the primacy of the 'employment relation', in that only it can explain the emergence of hierarchy from markets. Other institutional arrangements presuppose the existence of firms: the choice is then one of hierarchies versus hierarchies; firms vertically integrate up to the point where it is equally costly not to. So how does the transaction cost framework address the principal question raised in Marglin (1974): why did the authority-based factory system succeed the putting-out system?

For Williamson the emergence of the factory system is an example of efficient transaction cost economising. Williamson's principal claim is that employees have tacit skills which, in conjunction with opportunism and bounded rationality, give rise to high market-based transaction costs; that is, the result would be protracted haggling. In terms of an explanation of the emergence of firms, it is evident that, from an employer–merchants perspective, some of the problems of the putting-out system could be resolved by installing an authority relation (Pitelis, 1991). It may be the case that monitoring does result in enhanced productivity and that such a movement from a market to a hierarchy does (superficially) appear to be in line with efficiency arguments. Yet, before we critically evaluate this *ex post* transaction cost rationalisation, we must attempt to clarify more fully the essence of transaction costs.

CLARIFYING TRANSACTION COSTS

It has been noted that in Williamson's discussion of transaction costs he has failed to provide a precise definition of what the term means (Hodgson, 1988). Dahlman (1979, p. 148), as noted above, in attempting to apply some precision to the concept of transaction costs, has related them to three sequential aspects of the exchange process: search and information costs, bargaining and decision costs, and policing and enforcement costs. These three aspects of transaction costs denote more simply a resource loss due to information inadequacies.

But what is the nature of these informational inadequacies? Following Stigler (1961; see also Hodgson, 1988, 1999b), can we not ask whether it is not the case that such informational problems could be accommodated within the standard 'marginal apparatus', given that they can be characterised by a probability distribution? Why should we treat information as distinct from other commodities? Why would agents not collect information until the marginal benefit of such information is equated to its marginal cost? And thus, if information can be conceptually treated as being just like any other commodity, why should we view firms as distinct from other modes of organisation? Even the assertion that there are substantial informational economies of scale will not help. 'If informational economies of scale are substantial, why is it that such syndicates of independent producers should not arise to minimise the information costs that they would each face on their own, and thus obviate the need for the firm?' (Hodgson, 1999b, p. 205).

The intuitive response to such 'Stiglerian posturing' may be put quite simply: if we lack a piece of relevant information, how can we assess its marginal return? 'The very fact that information is lacking means at most such expectations are hazy and ill-defined' (Hodgson, 1999b, p. 205). This response suggests some radical conceptualisation of the informational problems faced by agents along the lines developed by Post Keynesians. A lack of information, associated with a probabilistic framework, is not a necessary prerequisite for us to rationalise salient institutions such as firms or money (Loasby, 1976; Davidson, 1977):

> There is no need for a theory for non-market forms of organisation in the general equilibrium model. Even the probabilistic version of general

> equilibrium theory, which implies informational problems of a stylised and limited kind, provides no reason why firms, as such, should exist.
>
> (Hodgson, 1999b, p. 206)

Recognition of such considerations focuses our attention more fully on the nature of information problems faced by economic agents such as the firm.[2] Langlois (1984) suggests that it is instructive to distinguish between (probabilistic) risk and (fundamental) uncertainty by introducing the concepts of 'parametric' and 'structural' uncertainty (see also Hodgson, 1988, 1999b). However, the concepts of 'parametric' and 'structural' uncertainty are vague and imprecise. This has meant that, when the importance of uncertainty to the study of the firm has been recognised (see, for example, Loasby, 1976; Langlois, 1984, 1988; Langlois and Everett, 1992; Hodgson, 1988, 1999b; Kay, 1984), the salience and distinctiveness of the concept of fundamental uncertainty has not always been fully appreciated – not least its ability to explain the existence of long-run transaction costs (Dunn, 1996, 1997, 1999).

As noted in Chapter 6 Post Keynesians technically differentiate situations of (probabilistic) risk and (fundamental) uncertainty by drawing upon the distinction between ergodic and nonergodic processes, with the latter providing a radical conceptualisation of uncertainty. This distinction is instructive in providing a precise technical delineation of the nature of the informational problems confronted by economic agents. Ergodic processes ensure that 'the probability distribution of the relevant variables calculated from any past realisation tends to converge with the probability function governing the current events and with the probability function that will govern future economic outcomes' (Davidson, 1988, p. 331). Under a situation of nonergodicity, such convergence does not exist; statistical distributions of the past provide no guide to the course of future events. Uncertainty prevails.

The source of transaction costs and thus the *raison d' être* for firms and contractual behaviour must be embedded in some non-probabilistic concept of uncertainty (see Dunn, 1999, 2000b).[3] This echoes Post Keynesian claims that the institution of money as a distinct economic category can be understood only in the context of a nonergodic environment; that is, under conditions of fundamental uncertainty (Davidson, 1982–3). As Hodgson (1999b, p. 207) notes, 'there is a prima facie case for seeing the concept of uncertainty as a necessary – but not sufficient – concept to explain the existence of any kind of firm'. We now turn to Cowling and Sugden, who attempt to address the sufficient conditions that characterise the firm as a distinct economic category.

A RADICAL CRITIQUE

In his approach to the theory of the firm, 'Williamson poses two basic questions: (a) why markets versus hierarchies, i.e. why carry out a transaction in a hierarchy rather than in a market? (b) what organisational form within a hierarchy, i.e. why carry out a transaction in a hierarchy in one way rather than in another?' (Cowling and Sugden, 1998, p. 72). Williamson's answer, to both questions, concentrates on the transaction costs (and their alleged causes; see above) associated with using either markets or hierarchies. When transacting in a market is more costly than in a firm, hierarchies efficiently replace markets.

However, this contractual approach to the theory of the firm exhibits an excessive concern with markets and exchange, to the neglect of the main activity of firms, the organization and execution of production (Coase, 1991; Simon, 1991; Cowling and Sugden, 1993, 1998; Fourie, 1993). The focus in the contractual approach still resides on exchange; that is, 'in the beginning there were markets'. As Fourie (1993) notes, without prior production, that is firms, there can be no market transactions.[4] This distinction directs attention to the different focus of firms (production) and markets (exchange), with the emphasis on the primacy and salience of the former conceptually.[5] Is it not preferable, as Cowling and Sugden suggest, that rather than view the firm as being incorporated into the market 'we may see the modern corporation as incorporating more of the market into the organisation'.[6]

The notion that the firm is an alternative mechanism for resource allocation may initially appear attractive. Yet such a dichotomy between market and non-market activity may be unwarranted and misleading. We would follow Cowling and Sugden (1998, p. 62) and 'question at the outset the focus on market versus non-market activity'. Focusing on the type of transaction used in production, be it market, non-market or some composite form, precludes consideration of the nature of the transaction.

For Cowling and Sugden, contemplation of the nature of the transaction directs analysis to the nature of control, that is the power and ability to make strategic decisions and to take a firm in a direction that may or may not be in the interests of others. This does not entail that production is solely determined by strategic decisions; rather, they constrain operational and working decisions (and vice versa). Those that undertake the strategic decisions represent the apex of the hierarchical system of decision-making and give rise to a firm's broad direction (see Pitelis and Sugden, 1986). The actual outcome of production, however, results from the interaction of the three tiers of decision-making: strategic, operational and working levels. One could suggest that there are no strategic decisions to be made: that competitive product markets force firms into a line of action consistent with loss avoidance.

Cowling and Sugden (1998, p. 66) argue, however, that 'mainstream industrial economics rejects this characterisation', that product markets are typically not competitive and, as a result, this is an empirically invalid objection.[7] To summarise, Cowling and Sugden suggest that the characteristic of a transaction within a firm is that it is subject to strategic decision-making from one centre.[8] In their view, the essence of the firm is not to do with a set of transactions but with strategic decision-making. This, Cowling and Sugden (1998, p. 61) suggest, returns the focus of the firm to Coase's real starting point, the notion of planning, and this 'concern with planning points to the particular relevance of strategic decision-making in today's large corporations'. In light of this, Cowling and Sugden propose a definition of the firm that highlights its essence as a 'means of coordinating production from one centre of strategic decision-making'.

There are several implications of this definition worth dwelling on. In the contractual approach to the theory of the firm, it is presumed that interfirm contact comes under the ambit of the market mechanism and is competitive. Yet, as Sawyer (1993) notes, firms may engage with others in non-competitive activities such as tacit collusion. The salience of Cowling and Sugden's definition is the implication that a firm incorporates all market and non-market transactions coordinated from one centre of strategic decision-making; that is, subcontracting relationships fall within the scope of a single firm. Arguably, the markets versus hierarchies dichotomy is misleading. Intra-firm transactions may be conceived as being constituted as either a market or a non-market transaction, given that production is coordinated from one centre of strategic decision-making. Inter-firm transactions represent market transactions, although different in character to intra-firm market transactions. Inter-firm (market) transactions take place between two centres of strategic decision-makers. Intra-firm (market) transactions emanate from one centre of strategic decision-makers. Consequently, Cowling and Sugden ask, not why 'markets versus hierarchy', but 'why are some activities coordinated from one centre of decision-making and some others not?'

The implications are striking. By focusing on the type of transaction, market or non-market, one may fail to appreciate fully the scope of a firm's production and the subsequent extent of concentration within an economy. Such a definition of the firm shifts the analytical focus away from an excessive concern for property rights to one where power and distributional considerations are centre stage.

The response to Williamson's second question, 'What organisational form within a hierarchy?', will depend ultimately on the objectives of those making strategic decisions. A key aspect of Cowling and Sugden's definition is that capitalist firms disallow Pareto efficiency. The firm is not viewed as an optimal outcome from a collective choice process as typified in the contractual approach (cf. Fitzroy and Mueller, 1984). Strategic decision makers may effect decisions that yield advantages, that is distributional gains, at the expense of others through the exercise of power. This contradicts the conventional wisdom that firm emerge as an efficient response to transactional market failure. Given that efficiency may be sacrificed for distributional gains, interference with the degree of discretion exerted by strategic decision makers may augment economic efficiency as well as alter the distribution of wealth. 'How else can one explain why unionisation, a most significant form of constraint on managerial prerogative, can actually increase productivity as well as wages?' (Fitzroy and Mueller, 1984; p. 75; see also Freeman and Medoff, 1984; Belman, 1992). Transaction cost theorists typically employ 'evolutionary' arguments to explain the replacement process of markets by firms as a 'comparative static' one of efficiency calculus. According to Cowling and Sugden, and most Post Keynesians, it would be more appropriate to view competition as a process that culminates in monopoly and a wasteful use of resources (Marx, 1976; Baran and Sweezy, 1966; Cowling and Sugden, 1987; Rutherford, 1989).

Exploring these points, Cowling and Sugden focus on the movement from the putting-out system to a factory-based system in the English textile industry during the Industrial Revolution. They suggest that this can be seen as contradicting the Pareto criterion, in that the move from one organisational form to another is made at the expense of one group (workers) for the benefit of another (strategic decision-makers, such as capitalists). Transaction costs remain important in the study of 'what organisational form within a hierarchy?', but as a delineation of the essence of the firm it does not go far enough (Cowling and Sugden, 1998, pp. 73–4). For Cowling and Sugden, such a movement is efficient in the distributional sense in that it enhanced the gain of the decision-makers at the expense of workers. It is not, however, necessarily Pareto efficient. According to Cowling and Sugden, hierarchy emerged for power-distributional reasons and not for narrow efficiency reasons (Marglin, 1974).[9] The focus on the role of strategic decision-makers suggests that the choice of organisational form will be one that suits strategic decision-makers. The benefit to strategic decision-makers is thus the critical factor.

This discussion, however, points to a confusion evident in Cowling and Sugden. As noted above, they explicitly relate their concept of strategy to non-competitive product markets. Yet in demonstrating how their (strategic) decision-making approach to the firm destroys Pareto efficiency, they refer to Marglin's (1974) discussion of the movement from putting-out to the factory system. 'According to the strategic decision-making (but unlike the pure Coasian) approach this was a change in the organisational form within a firm' (Cowling and Sugden, 1998, p. 73). Now the movement from putting-out to the factory system occurred in an environment that is widely considered to have been in some sense competitive. This creates many new questions. Are all (capitalist) contexts non-competitive or, if they are not, why did the firm succeed the factory system which succeeded the putting-out system? Moreover, is power synonymous with strategy?[10] Such conundrums are avoided in the Post Keynesian framework proposed below.

A POST KEYNESIAN CONTRIBUTION TO THE THEORY OF THE FIRM

Cowling and Sugden, in emphasizing the overriding importance of the role of strategic decision-making, fail to enquire as to the source and essence of transaction costs. As a result, the implications of a nonergodic environment in the context of the firm are little explored. The discussion above suggests that a theory of the firm would do well to note the role played by strategic decision-makers, uncertainty and transaction costs in addition to pure production costs in the context of production (see also Dunn, 1999). We propose here to extend Cowling and Sugden's contribution by defining the firm as a *means of coordinating production from one centre of strategic decision-making in a nonergodic (transmutable) environment.* As we shall see, this extension reinforces several of Cowling and

Sugden's central conclusions and facilitates a better understanding of the role of money in production.

Although Cowling and Sugden propose a historically specific analysis, an appreciation of the nature of a nonergodic environment in which decisions, strategic or otherwise, are made represents a significant extension and refinement of their concept of strategic decision-making. In an uncertain world, decisions have to be made. The past cannot be relied upon as a guide to the future, a fundamental feature of ergodic environments:

> If … the concept of uncertainty involves important nonergodic circumstances, then there currently does not exist information (complete, incomplete, distorted or otherwise) that will aid human beings to discover the future. Instead human beings will have to invent or create the future by themselves by their actions within evolving and existing organisations.
>
> (Davidson and Davidson, 1984, pp. 329–30)

Strategy, according to this perspective, refers to the process by which those at the pinnacle of a hierarchical decision-making process attempt to mitigate the impact of this uncertainty by attempting to control for as many factors as possible that impinge on the process of production. The practice of strategic decision-making is the practice of dealing with uncertainty. The concept of strategy employed here is linked to the nature of the environment, of time, and not to 'market structure' (see also Dunn, 2000b, 2001a,c).

In emphasising the fact that strategic choices have to be made, and consequently emphasising the coordinating role of strategic decision-makers in production, Cowling and Sugden are somewhat forced, given their definition of the firm, to limit their contribution to situations in which product markets are not typically competitive:

> For some economists the idea of making strategic decisions would not be meaningful: a typical view is that firms operate in a more or less perfectly competitive environment, which if true implies that strategic decision makers would be forced into the only course of action enabling a firm to avoid losses and stay in business.
>
> (Cowling and Sugden, 1998, p. 66)

Following mainstream industrial economics, Cowling and Sugden reject this characterisation, suggesting that in reality product markets are not typically competitive. Their notion of strategy is thus linked to the structure of the market and the resultant discretion permitted in the conduct of firms and the objectives of strategic decision-makers. Cowling and Sugden, by refusing to focus on the type of transaction used in production, propose an unnecessarily restrictive concern with non-competitive product markets. However, as noted above, strategy is an inevitable consequence of a nonergodic environment. Market structures may indeed reflect the responses of strategic decision-makers to an uncertain environment, given that size (both absolute and relative) helps to reduce the impact of uncertainty on the firm (see Galbraith, 1967; Rothschild, 1947; Dunn, 2001a,c). But competitive markets do not remove the need for strategy. As Knight (1921, pp. 226–7) notes, in even what we may consider to be a competitive context:

> The business man himself not merely forms the best estimate he can of the outcome of his actions, but he is likely also to estimate the probability that his estimate is correct. The 'degree' of certainty or of confidence felt in this conclusion after it is reached cannot be ignored, for it is of the greatest practical significance. The action which follows upon an opinion depends as much upon the amount of confidence in that opinion as it does the favourableness of the opinion itself.

Competition, structural or behavioural, in an uncertain environment cannot force a course of action, a strategic decision, to be made, that *ex post* is consistent with loss avoidance or, for that matter, the maximisation of any from a range of objective functions we may wish to choose (Robinson and Eatwell, 1973, p. 236). If we do not know what the future will bring or is likely to bring, that is, in a nonergodic environment, history, be it subjective or objective, will not tell us what to do. However, the environment in which an agent operates is not unimportant. The reverse is true. The social context acquires a heightened relevance. The psychology of the business environment will affect the nature of strategic decisions.

At this point parallels could be drawn to modes of behaviour invoked by Herbert Simon's (1957, 1959, 1976) notion of 'satisficing', proposed in light of his introduction of the concept of bounded rationality. As noted in Chapter 6 above, however, Simon's concept of bounded rationality and the subsequent decision-making process has come to be identified with the informational processing capacities of economic agents. It is the complexity of an environment, regardless of whether it be ergodic or nonergodic, that requires agents to make procedurally rational choices (see Simon, 1976). Strategy here is identified with the informational processing abilities of agents. This is in contrast to the stress placed here on the uncertain or nonergodic nature of the environment within which agents operate (Dunn, 1999). For example, Cowling and Sugden are concerned with non-competitive product markets because in an ergodic environment competitive product markets will force substantively rational agents into a course of action consistent with avoiding losses and remaining in business. There will be no room for strategic choices to be made. In a nonergodic environment substantively rational agents will still have to make (strategic) decisions, for reasons outlined above. In a nonergodic environment, the processing capacities of agents will affect the nature of choice, but not the fact of choice. Our notion of strategic decision-making need not therefore be tied to any conception of the processing abilities of agents, although we may wish to link it with other approaches in a realistic description of decision-making.

Emphasising that strategic decisions need to be made, whatever the nature of product markets, reinforces Cowling and Sugden's suggestion that firms disallow Pareto efficiency, not to mention other modes of efficiency. Situations of strategic decision-making under conditions of nonergodicity make it impossible to assess the impact *ex ante* of price and non-price forms of competition, such as research and development, advertising, product and production innovation, that consume resources[11] in the market process.[12] With a focus on the effects of history and path dependence, that is in the face of a nonergodic environment, the assessment of transaction costs by strategic decision-makers becomes an evolutionary dynamic assessment as opposed to a comparative static assessment. As Langlois (1984, p. 38) notes, "we need to be especially careful in judging organisational efficiency in terms of the environment at any moment in time – for if that environment is likely to change, an organisational mode adapted to the environment of the moment may well be maladapted in some larger sense".

Hodgson (1988, 1999b) makes a similar point, arguing that the assessment of transaction costs should be an evolutionary assessment rather than a comparative static assessment that is typical of the orthodox approach. The basis for such a diagnosis is Hodgson's suggestion that Simon's concept of bounded rationality is inconsistent with Williamson's (1981, p. 1544) desire to make '[t]he study of transaction-cost economising ... a comparative institutional undertaking'. Especially as, for Williamson (1985, p. 32), 'Economising on transaction costs essentially reduces to economising on bounded rationality'. As Hodgson (1999b, p. 207) notes:

> Simon's argument, of course, is that a complete or global rational calculation is ruled out, and thus rationality is 'bounded'; agents do not maximise but attempt to attain acceptable minima instead. But it is important to note that this 'satisficing' behaviour does not arise simply because of inadequate information, but also because it would be too difficult to perform the calculations even if the relevant information was available ... Contrary to [the orthodox] 'cost minimisation' interpretation [of Simon's work], the recognition of bounded rationality refers primarily to the matter of computational capacity and not to additional 'costs'.

However, to reject the 'comparative static, efficiency calculus assessment of organisational forms' framework employed by Williamson and the like, we do not require Herbert Simon's concept of bounded rationality. Williamson's use of the concept may indeed be inconsistent with Simon's proposed use of the concept, but to suggest that the assessment of transaction costs is a dynamic evolutionary exercise requires no behavioural assumptions about the informational processing capacities of agents. The fact that the assessment of transaction costs is a dynamic evolutionary exercise is an inevitable consequence of a nonergodic environment. As noted above, the informational processing ability of economic agents is irrelevant to situations where there is insufficient information to process, when the past cannot be relied upon as a guide to the future, when 'there is no scientific basis on which to form any calculable probability whatever' of the relevant outcomes (Keynes, 1937, p. 114).

Furthermore, in an uncertain environment, the centrality of control and power is given renewed importance. The necessity of planning and acquiring control of strategic cost factors is essential in mitigating the impact of an uncertain environment (see Rothschild, 1947; Galbraith, 1967; Dunn, 2001a,c). Control represents the means to achieve survival. As Lavoie (1992, pp. 99–100) notes:

> Power is the ultimate objective of the firm: power over its environment, whether it be economic, social or political ... The firm wants power over its suppliers of materials, over its customers, over the government, over the kind of technology to be put in use. The firm whether it be a megacorp or a small family firm, would like to have control over future events, its financial requirements, the quality of its labour force, the prices of the industry and the possibility of take-overs. 'The firm is viewed as being able to exercise a degree of control over its environment through R&D, market development, interfirm co-operation, entry deterrence' (Davies and Lee, 1988, p. 21). In a world without [fundamental] uncertainty, the notion of power dissolves and loses much of its importance. In such a world, for instance, firms always have access to all of the financial capital that they require provided their investment project is expected to be profitable. The source of financing is immaterial.

This is related to the point made above. If, as Malcolmson (1984) suggests, firms acquire monopoly power by 'economising' on market transaction costs, it follows that the notions of market power, transaction costs and uncertainty are inseparable. Market (and firm) structure must be viewed as the evolutionary response of strategic decision-makers to a nonergodic environment. This is the logical consequence of the above discussion on the source of transaction costs. Moreover, the Post Keynesian approach has much to offer to the study of such processes. In the Kaleckian and Eichnerian approaches to the firm, the role and relation of strategic decision-makers to the external environment, that is, in the context of price determination, investment behaviour and the links to the macroeconomy, are well understood (Sawyer, 1993, 1994).

This leads us, however, to the most important contribution from a Post Keynesian perspective. That is the focus, role and *raison d'être* given to money in terms of production in a nonergodic environment (Davidson, 1972, 1977, 1988). In their delineation of the firm as a distinct economic category, Cowling and Sugden fail to allow for a substantive role for money in the process of production. Although they note that, in their strategic decision-making approach, what others have referred to as market exchanges falling outside the ambit of the firm, notably subcontracting relationships, are incorporated inside the firm (given that they are coordinated from one centre of strategic decision-making), they still do not explicitly introduce money and its analytical properties into their theoretical schema.[13] In fact, this criticism generalises for most contractual treatments of the firm (Davidson and Davidson, 1984, p. 333). This is symptomatic of the markets versus hierarchies dichotomy, a dichotomy Cowling and Sugden are keen to avoid, whereby money is viewed as crucial to market behaviour, and firms represent islands in which monetary or market exchanges are excluded.

Money is essential in the conduct of market exchange and plays a significant role in the contracting that allows the formation of the hierarchical relation. Money is essential because it economises on the transaction costs associated with barter:

> The use of money in exchange transactions presupposes a certain degree of organisation of trading activity. Such organisation is socially beneficial because it enables individuals to channel into production or leisure labour and resources that would otherwise be devoted to search and bargaining activity. Barter would always be possible in a world with organised markets, but it would never in any circumstances be efficient as long as organised markets continued to function … [G]oods buy money and money buys goods – but goods do not buy goods in any organised market.
>
> (Clower, 1969, pp. 13–14)

As Davidson (1972) makes explicitly clear, it is only in monetary economy that an extended system of production and a highly specialised division of labour can evolve. As a result, the primacy of production as opposed to exchange, both historically and theoretically, is emphasised, with its nexus to money and money contracts. To reiterate, insufficient attention is paid to the role of money in the context of production. The circuit of money or capital is integral to any understanding of the firm and the nature of production. We may recall Keynes' (1979, p. 81) recognition of Marx's 'pregnant observation' that:

> the nature of production in the actual world is not, as economists seem often to suppose, a case of C – M – C′, i.e. of exchanging commodity (or effort) for money in order to obtain another commodity (or effort). That may be the standpoint of the private consumer. But it is not the attitude of business, which is a case of M – C – M′ i.e. of parting with money for commodity (or effort) in order to obtain more money.

By focusing on the role of money in production, we note that, in the circulation of finance, money represents and expresses the power relationship contained in production. It is the existence of money contracts in a nonergodic environment that creates the possibility of conflict, *ex post* to contract formation, a situation not generally acknowledged in neoclassical and Williamson-type approaches (Davidson and Davidson, 1984). Moreover, having made explicit the role of money in production, we must contemplate its nexus to the strategic decision-makers and how it relates to their objectives (growth maximisation, the role of profits, prestige, psychological love of money). Despite Cowling and Sugden's emphasis on the role of power within the firm, which they suggest has been ignored in the mainstream literature, they fail to highlight money's nexus to hierarchy.

However, consideration of the 'essential properties of money', the reasons for money's 'moneyness', and the fact that the existence of money as a human institution can only be rationalised in the context of a nonergodic environment, directs us to liquidity considerations as they bear down and impinge on production (Davidson, 1972, 1977).[14] That is to say, money's nexus to production derives from the fact that:

> In all modern market-orientated production economies, production is organised on a forward money-contracting basis … Since production takes time, the hiring of factor inputs and the purchase of materials to be used in any productive activity must precede the date when the finished product will be at hand. These hiring and material-purchase transactions will therefore require forward contracting if the production process is to be efficiently planned. The financing of such forward production-cost commitments … requires entrepreneurs [or strategic decision-makers] to have money available to discharge these contractual liabilities at one or more future dates before the product is sold and delivered, payment received, and the position liquidated.
>
> (Davidson, 1981, p. 165)

The salience of such considerations seems little understood, especially as it impinges upon the theory of the firm. For example, in the contractual approach to the firm, there is little regard for the way liquidity constraints affect the scope of the firm (cf. Coase, 1937, p. 340). In noting that certain market transactions are costly and thus noting the cost advantages of internal organisation, what factors limit the expansion of the firms? The typical reply is to suggest that we may list

> three main factors which would limit the expansion of a firm. Economies of scale in the production of an input … [that is] when the production of an input is subject to economies of scale, but the users of the input make small use of the input (relative to the minimum efficient scale). A loss of control by the managers of the firm as the firm expands, particularly as that expansion involves not only increased size but also a larger range of activities. The comparative advantage held by specialist firms and a reluctance of those firms to be taken over.
>
> (Sawyer, 1985a, p. 200)

However, as opposed to mainstream analysis, we suggest this can be explained by the nonergodicity of the competitive process and the creative crucial decisions of strategic decision-makers and thus need not find its origins in the bounded rationality of agents and the fact that they indulge in opportunistic behaviour. This is due to the integrated Post Keynesian approach that links a micro-strategic conceptualisation of the firm to the macroeconomy. Post Keynesians have been willing to go beyond the typically partial analysis of industrial economics in examining the link between the way the macroeconomy affects firms and vice versa (see Sawyer, 1990). However, such insights have not generally been explicitly embedded in a contractual approach to the firm.

THE THEORY OF THE FIRM AS A CONTRIBUTION TO POST KEYNESIANISM

It should be recognised that the definition of the firm advanced here contains the notion that some organisational forms are more costly than others. However, as opposed to mainstream analysis, we see this as a result of the transmutability of the environment, i.e. the creative and crucial decisions of strategic decision-makers, and not as a result of the fact that agents are subject to bounded rationality or indulge in opportunistic behaviour. We may, however, retain the notion of asset specificity, given that it has links to, and is suggestive of: the Post Keynesian emphasis on the irreversibility of time, that is nonergodicity; differentials in productive efficiency as a result of different vintages of capital investment; the capital controversies; and notions of learning by doing and cumulative causation.[15]

Moreover, the definition of the firm advanced above, by focusing on fundamental uncertainty and power, provides a link between the Post Keynesian theories of income distribution and industrial structure and the macroeconomics of a monetary economy. That is, our definition of the firm suggests a focus on the important decisions made by strategic decision-makers: investment behaviour, under conditions of nonergodicity (cf. Keynes, 1936, Chapter 12, 1937). It allows a marriage of the key themes of reproducibility and liquidity in a microeconomic context of accumulation and nonergodicity. As noted in the previous chapter, the Post Keynesian 'black box' of production may be opened up and an explicit focus can be given to the fact that firms operate under conditions of uncertainty, a point not generally theorised upon. Post Keynesian contributions on the theory of the firm focus on the role and power of strategic decision-makers, with the implications for firm objectives, pricing behaviour, levels of investment and savings and their consequences for the distribution of income, level of growth and the level of aggregate demand in the macroeconomy. These contributions, as Davidson (1992) notes, leave an underdeveloped role for the monetary sector.

However, for Post Keynesian monetary theorists, money enters in an essential and peculiar manner as a result of its essential properties in contemplation of a nonergodic environment (see Davidson, 1972, 1977). As production takes time and planning, money-denominated contracts represent the means by which uncertainties about the future may be mitigated and money enables the discharge of such contractual arrangements. Contractual behaviour, internal organisational change, institutional development and money and financial innovation allow the constraints imposed by an uncertain environment to be reduced. That is, attempts will be made to remove and mitigate constraints or barriers to accumulation and reproducibility that bear down on strategic decision-makers, e.g. uncertainty. Moreover, it is the institution of money that will be pivotal to such developments. By focusing on a definition of the firm that encompasses the notion that strategic decision-makers are coordinating production under nonergodic conditions, we are provided with a link between the way in which we can account for institutional organisations (and their internal structure), such as firms, and how we can account for money and its distinctiveness. In recognising the role that strategic decision-makers have in eliciting the response of institutional organisations such as firms, we avoid the reduction of all choices as ones solely concerned with uncertainty, and the associated problems of such reductionism.

Additionally, the focus and development of a contractual theory of the firm may provide a more rigorous theoretical explanation of the postulate of a preference for internal as opposed to external finance by Post Keynesian theorists of the firm. Here the transaction costs of using external finance become a prime consideration (Sawyer, 1989, p. 184). Post Keynesians generally recognise the links between uncertainty, power, decision-making and financing arrangements, but fail to enquire systematically what this means for a firm's organisational structure: its pricing procedures, its relationship to labour, its investment procedures, its attitude towards inter-firm cooperation, the motivation of its owners and so on. Lavoie (1992, p. 100) is typical when he suggests that it is only 'in a world where fundamental uncertainty prevails, [that] firms must find means to guarantee access to financial capital, all of their material inputs, or critical information'. However, he subsequently presents a technical 'black box' approach to the firm under conditions of certainty equivalence, largely derived from the Kaleckian tradition.

Similarly, in all Davidson's discussion of the role of money in a nonergodic world, in which production takes time and is conducted in terms of money-denominated contracts, he fails to examine the implications for the theory of the firm; that is, that its contractual nature and modes of internal organisation should be addressed more fully. Thus, while Post Keynesians have opened up the orthodox 'black box' approach to price determination as contained in Walrasian and neoclassical models, they have generally been happy to leave the 'black box' approach to production relatively closed. In a nutshell, Post Keynesian theorising on the internal organisation of the firm is *ad hoc* at best and non-existent generally. That is not to say that Post Keynesians reject a focus on the 'firm as an organisation' (Sawyer, 1994, pp. 10, 19); rather, that they have yet to theorise about it. Focusing on the informational problems faced by (strategic) decision-making agents within firms facilitates the further opening up of this 'black box' and provides a bridge between the Keynesian and Kaleckian strands of Post Keynesianism which will further allow it to refute accusations of incoherence.

CONCLUDING COMMENTS

In this chapter we have advanced an extension to the definition of the firm proposed by Cowling and Sugden that accounts for the fact that strategic decision-makers engaged in the coordination of production operate under conditions of 'fundamental uncertainty'. We have argued that theorists of the firm should account for the fact that uncertainty bears down upon those strategic decision-makers engaged in the production of commodities and that such decision-makers will respond to the nature of the environment they face in their choice of organisational form. Moreover, as we have seen, the import of this extension is threefold. First, such considerations reinforce Cowling and Sugden's main conclusions while making explicit the informational basis of the firm and the need for strategy. Second, this extension facilitates a more adequate treatment of the role of money in production, a feature underdeveloped in the literature on the theory of the firm. Third, by directing the focus onto uncertainty, money and power in production, our definition of the firm brings together central themes from the Keynesian and Kaleckian traditions of Post Keynesianism and further promotes steps towards coherence. This amounts to a positive contribution to both the theory of the firm and Post Keynesianism, providing a new agenda for future research.

NOTES

1 This represents an important critique of the marginal productivity theory of income distribution, but its implications as such have generally been ignored by transaction cost theorists.
2 Langlois (1984, p. 28) notes that 'having collapsed all such costs into the lack-of-information category, we now need to make new distinctions within this category if we are to explain internal organisation modes'.
3 However, there are important caveats to such a strict conclusion (cf. Langlois, 1984, p. 30).
4 This argument rests on the assumption that we may treat 'production' and 'firms' as synonymous. Here we note the essence of this point, the primacy of production. As Hodgson (1999b, pp. 79–81) suggests, we may wish to clarify more precisely what we mean by the firm, especially in the context of differentiating between several modes of production such as feudalism, capitalism and so on. Although important, this clarification does not alter the argument here.
5 Pitelis (1991) suggests that it is not even clear that, historically, markets predate hierarchies.
6 Because of the focusing on the primacy of transaction costs associated with market exchange, the features associated with production, that is planning, innovation, the management of technical change and so on, are lost, along with the associated time-scales that are involved. Such considerations suggest a wider range of functions that firms provide (see Sawyer, 1993; Hodgson, 1999b).
7 'For example Tirole (1988, p. 3) refers to "most real markets" being imperfectly competitive, and he expresses the view that "analyses that rely on models of perfect competition may be quite unsatisfactory from a positive and normative perspective"' (Cowling and Sugden, 1998, p. 8).
8 This view has some 'similarities to Coase (1937), given the latter's focus on hierarchical direction … However our concern with strategic decision-making as against a hierarchy which (according to Coase) "includes … management … foremen and … workmen" is arguably a discriminating focus on the prime determinants of a firm's activity' (Cowling and Sugden, 1998, p. 10).
9 Even if it can be demonstratively proved that both groups gain financially we still must assess the psychic or utilitarian costs that are incurred in such a transition, a point underdeveloped in the literature (see Sugden, 1983).

10 On this latter question, Marxists presumably would reply 'maybe not'. Marx examines the nature of exploitation in a competitive environment. Capitalists by their nature possess power, the ability to extract a surplus from the workers, but it is the competitive environment that compels them to exercise this power to the full. Individual capitalists have no alternative but to accede to the demands of accumulation.

11 We suggest here that the Walrasian fiction that allows the costless movement along demand and cost curves due to the price-setting function of the auctioneer is irrelevant to any Post Keynesian conception of the firm. See Dutt (1992) and Chick (1992) on the small firm under uncertainty.

12 'An efficient analysis of organisational forms is thus a kind of *ex post* reconstruction. It is an attempt to demonstrate the rationale for what exists by superimposing after the fact an axiomatic framework on a structure that could not have been predicted *ex ante* from such a framework … This does not mean … that we can ever portray an organisational mode as optimal, except in a very narrow sense of the term' (Langlois, 1984, p. 37).

13 There are no references to money as it affects the firm and production in Cowling and Sugden (1998).

14 Money's essential properties are that it possesses a zero (or negligible) elasticity of production and a zero (or negligible) elasticity of substitution, along with low (or negligible) carrying costs (see Keynes, 1936, pp. 230–1).

15 'Investment in firm-specific human capital makes both labour and management dependent on each other. Asset specificity makes less palatable those alternatives, which would involve both parties in capital-asset valuation losses. Opportunism is therefore discouraged and co-operation encouraged, as the existence of firm-specific assets makes both parties aware that their opposite is similarly constrained … Bargaining situations where one or both parties cannot be credibly constrained are unstable, because there are no assets uniquely specified to them that can be lost if either side withdraws from cooperative activity. Asset specificity can therefore play a useful role in creating an environment for contractual agreements in a nonergodic world … Without clearly realising it, Williamson has located one of the Achilles' heels of neoclassical economics and its efficiency approach – namely, the implicit assumption that all assets are not agent specific. Neoclassical theory always presumes that all assets are liquid and readily resaleable for use by others. In a neoclassical world, capital is liquidity fungible if not malleable' (Davidson and Davidson, 1984, pp. 331–2).

11 A Post Keynesian approach to health economics

We have ... to consider the condition on which depend health and strength, physical, mental and moral. They are the basis of industrial efficiency, on which the production of material wealth depends; while conversely the chief importance of material wealth lies in the fact that, when wisely used, it increases the health and strength, physical, mental and moral of the human race.

Alfred Marshall (1920, p. 193)

INTRODUCTION

Post Keynesian economics has no specific association with health economics. In one sense this is perhaps unsurprising. Health economics is typically viewed as a branch of microeconomics. Conversely, Post Keynesian economics is viewed by many as a distinct approach to macroeconomics. It has, however, always invoked a strong microeconomic analysis and, as noted above in Chapter 7 many Post Keynesians have begun to make positive contributions to the various sub-disciplines of economics. Nevertheless, no attempt has been made to consider what Post Keynesian economics might have to offer health economics. This is perhaps rather more surprising given that health expenditure has become a prime component of fiscal strategy with its concomitant implications for productivity, employment and income distribution in most advanced industrialised societies. The purpose of this chapter is thus to attempt to delineate the elements of a Post Keynesian approach to health economics.

The outline of the chapter is as follows. In the subsequent sections we consider, at a general level, the potential theoretical import of Post Keynesianism for the economics of health and healthcare policy. We broadly follow the taxonomy first introduced by Williams (1987) and subsequently used as a frame of reference in the prominent *Handbook of Health Economics* (Culyer and Newhouse, 2000) and by those considering the state of health economics in general (see Maynard and Kanavos, 2000; Edwards, 2001). We consider the potential Post Keynesian contributions to particular areas of health economics including health and its influences, the demand for and supply of healthcare, and industrial organisation in the health sector. We also consider the role of health expenditure as an element of macroeconomic policy. We conclude that Post Keynesian economics has the potential to make useful contributions to the evolving paradigm that is health economics.

WHAT IS HEALTH? WHAT IS ITS VALUE?

Post Keynesianism starts from the proposition that everyone should be given the opportunity to participate fully and flourish in society. Such emancipatory considerations underscore the Post Keynesian commitment to activist employment policy. In doing so it moves beyond traditional economic concerns, such as producing more goods more efficiently and maximising utility, focusing instead on the promotion of opportunities and the pursuit of equity (see, for example, Galbraith, 1973b).

Similarly, a basic tenet of any Post Keynesian approach to health would be that access to health and healthcare, like access to employment, is a basic right, underpinning the potential of humans to effectively contribute to society. Post Keynesians therefore would accept that health is not simply a commodity like any other. As a component of human potential, health is a crucial ingredient of economic growth and social development, underpinning civility, productivity, and national economic success (cf. Marshall, 1920, pp. 193–203). In terms of health policy, this would entail an acceptance of the need for an equitable distribution of, and access to, healthcare resources. Making equitable provision for healthcare allows humans to realise their potential and to participate fully in economic life and society (cf. Sen, 2002). This objective can be operationalised in various ways, e.g. by ensuring equal access for equal need, or reducing avoidable health inequalities (see Hauck *et al.*, 2002).

Healthier workers are more productive, earn higher wages, and are less likely to miss work because of illness.[1] Of course, as far back as Mushkin (1962), microeconomists have recognised that health can be viewed as investment and as underpinning productivity. Only recently, however, have macroeconomists explored the implications for economic growth (see Bloom *et al.*, 2001b). Such treatments, however, typically ignore the relationship between unemployment and health. Post Keynesians would develop a distinctive macroeconomic perspective on such issues, arguing for the general tax financing of healthcare provision on the grounds of equity as well as cost (on the latter, see the discussion below).[2]

WHAT INFLUENCES HEALTH (OTHER THAN HEALTHCARE)?

At root, a Post Keynesian conceptualisation of health would challenge the dominant atomistic, asocial and ahistorical conception of the individual, arguing that the whole is sometimes greater than the sum of its parts. As Davis (2003, p. 11) points out, 'Most economists … do not believe that individuals are changed by the nature of the economic process, and much less believe that their status as individuals might itself be affected by that process, or that individuals and the nature of individuality might be *endogenous* to the economic process'. In contrast, Post Keynesians reject methodological individualism and understand the need for well-developed theories of the individual (Chick, 1995; Davis, 2003). They argue for an organic, socially embedded view of the individual and would recognise that human agency, structures, social positions and history all matter to health and healthcare systems (Lawson, 2003).

Informed by this perspective, Post Keynesians, like many (practising) health economists, would list a broad array of factors among the determinants of health and its distribution such as: genetics, the socio-economic environment, the physical environment, and individual responses and interactions. Such factors, however, are not easily accommodated in the *methodology* of mainstream economic theory, which typically eschews concern for history or wider social processes. They require attention to the path-dependent actions of agents (and groups of agents) in creating, reproducing and transforming health and healthcare institutions over time. Post Keynesians would attempt to incorporate such considerations into their conceptualisation of the nexus between health, history and the economy. And they would also point to the relevance of a range of empirical evidence including the role for qualitative analysis (see Downward *et al.*, 2002; Downward and Mearman, 2006; cf. Coast, 1999).

To focus on the transformation and reproduction of health and healthcare institutions is to focus on path dependence in both the socio-political *and health* domains, i.e. on the virtuous and vicious cycles of cumulative causation that reinforce and underpin many social and health disparities (cf. Veblen, 1898; Myrdal, 1957). In underdeveloped economies, for example, poverty, poor health and disease combine to slow the progress of economic development. The high rates of disease and child mortality in developing countries are compounded by families' attempts to compensate by having more children, intensifying their poverty. This results in a vicious downward cycle. Having more children, reduces families' ability to provide for the health and education of each child. Lower educational levels undermine trust in healthcare communications and thus the efforts of healthcare professionals.

Reductions in avoidable disease and increases in years of healthy life expectancy would accelerate economic growth of many underdeveloped regions of the world (WHO, 2001). The economic loss to society of shortened lives due to early death and chronic disability is hundreds of billions of dollars per year and a significant percentage of national income in low-income countries. The AIDS epidemic in Africa, for example, means that many individuals of prime working age are unable to contribute to economic growth. Moreover, this is not just a question of undermining individual worker productivity. Rather, such factors combine to mean that whole sectors of the economy are decimated through social, economic and epidemiological interdependence. As the WHO (2001) notes, 'whole industries, in agriculture, mining, manufacturing, and tourism, as well as important infrastructure projects, are undermined by a high prevalence of disease. Epidemic and endemic diseases can also undermine social co-operation and even political and macroeconomic stability'.

DEMAND FOR HEALTHCARE

Healthcare is characterised by problems of knowledge, as well as imperfect and asymmetric information, problems which are compounded by the potentially disastrous and often irreversible consequences of decisions based on that information. Such considerations challenge many of the basic tenets of neoclassical economics: global rationality, utility maximisation, individual sovereignty, consequentialism and welfarism, and their application to healthcare (cf. Davis, 2001, 2003). Yet, with some notable exceptions (Evans, 1983; Donaldson and Karen, 1993; Rice, 2002), there has been little development of alternative approaches to healthcare demand, with most economists content to make piecemeal and *ad hoc* refinements to the dominant framework. Lavoie's (1994) Post Keynesian approach to consumer theory, however, offers the prospect of a more realistic view of healthcare demand, one that captures many of the concerns voiced by non-economists as to how healthcare choices are analysed. This analysis of consumer choice could be adapted to study healthcare demand in the following ways.

First, the Post Keynesian approach to choice recognises the importance of distinguishing between needs and wants (Boulding, 1966). This distinction is recognised by some health economists, who argue that need relates to the ability to benefit from healthcare interventions, whereas demand is a function of preferences and ability to pay (Culyer, 1995). Most neglect, however, to consider the broader ramifications of this distinction (for a more general discussion of the various methodological considerations that this raises, see Lawson, 2003).

Post Keynesians begin with the principle of satiable needs, a recognition that (a) there is a fundamental distinction between wants and needs and (b) there are threshold levels of consumption, i.e. that beyond certain points, price will have no bearing on the decision to consume. Post Keynesians argue that there is a hierarchy of needs in which some are more basic and fundamental than others. This implies that needs and wants must be satisfied reflecting some degree of prioritisation, with some needs becoming satiated before others. All humans need food, warmth, shelter and the suppression of pain and no amount of persuasion will induce alternative demands. 'Though a hungry man cannot be persuaded between bread and a circus, a well nourished man can. And he can be persuaded as between different circuses and different foods. The further a man is removed from physical need the more open he is to persuasion' (Galbraith, 1967, p. 207). This perspective is especially relevant to the demand for healthcare services.

Health needs relate to the existence of effective interventions that can improve health. And when those needs are proximate, such as the closeness of physical pain, they must be addressed in a way that is beyond the hedonistic conception. No amount of relative price movements may induce the requisite psychic balm or induce additional consumption to assuage such a state of affairs. Or, to phrase it differently, very poor health, e.g. acute pain, drastically alters one's interest in other types of consumption. This may go part of the way to help explain why much of the evidence suggests that the price elasticity of the demand for medical care appears very low. It also suggests that the nomenclature of consumers may be misleading when considering the demand for healthcare. There are only so many times that one can have one's hip replaced or be inoculated. And sharp falls in the price are unlikely to induce additional consumption.

What is more, the whole notion of needs further reinforces the conception of health articulated above. In acknowledging and identifying certain basic and universal needs, it follows that Post Keynesians would be keen to secure universal access to a basic set of health services. What is more, the identification of inalienable basic needs and rights would lead Post Keynesians to advocate some external valuation of the minimum basic health benefits package that all members of society would have access to (cf. Galbraith, 1973b).

Second, Post Keynesians would invoke the principle of separability of needs which governs the allocation of resources across different budget needs. Consumers typically allocate a portion of expenditure across needs and wants in a hierarchical way (the principle of the subordination of needs), with the effect that income effects predominate relative price effects (the principle of the growth of needs). That is to say, consumers divide their expenditure between needs and wants in a hierarchical way, satisfying the more basic needs first. This perspective may help explain the seemingly contradictory findings concerning the effect of income on healthcare expenditure (Gerdtham and Jonsson, 2000).

It has been well documented in the health economics literature that cross-sectional estimates of the income elasticity of healthcare expenditure are typically less than one while time-series estimates suggest an elasticity of greater than one. As Blomqvist and Carter (1997) acknowledge, 'the discrepancy between income elasticities estimated from individual or family data and those estimated from aggregative cross-sectional or time-series data is not easily explained'. The tendency has been to devise elaborate explanations of these differences and to conclude that the long-run time-series estimates reflect long-run behaviours and that health is therefore a luxury good.

In contrast, Post Keynesians would argue that the causality is reversed. Rather than higher income inducing additional expenditures, higher income at the national level means that that basic medical needs can be attended to that would otherwise go untreated. This helps explain why the positive macroeconomic correlation between national income and health outcomes is strongest in less developed countries and tends to disappear and become weaker at higher income levels. The Post Keynesian explanation of this fact is embedded in a recognition that as income increases beyond some poverty threshold the diseases associated with poverty can be addressed.[3]

Third, Post Keynesians would stress the complexity that pervades healthcare decisions. They assume economic agents are procedural rational, which embodies the proposition that in response to complexity consumers will rely on habits, routines, rules of thumb, social conventions and/or exhibit myopia (Lavoie, 1994). In the medical literature the importance of adaptive, emergent processes and adherence to simple rules in healthcare has been recognised (Plsek and Greenhalgh, 2001). There is much *prima facie* evidence that patients behave in a procedurally rational manner, i.e. use rules of thumb to make healthcare decisions.

For example, those faced with decisions about the consumption of healthcare services do not appear to use objective, publicly available data on healthcare quality to inform their decisions even though it would seem (globally) rational to do so. As Marshall *et al.* (2003, p. 141) note, the use by individuals of much public reporting of healthcare performance data is limited: 'the public does not search it out, does not understand it, distrusts it, and fails to make use of it'. Instead, they tend to rely on simple decision rules and social networks when making healthcare choices in attempting to navigate and engage the complex healthcare system. Saliently, the policy response to this lack of user interest has been to present healthcare information in simpler, more accessible ways, i.e. to reduce the complexity of the information and make it more useful to procedurally rational agents.

Fourth, Post Keynesians would argue that health and the resultant demand for healthcare are influenced by, and contingent upon, social processes. Neoclassical economists have little to say about the formation of consumer preferences and its links to health and healthcare consumption. Post Keynesians would point to the principle of non-independence which refers to the socially embedded nature of the individual (see Lavoie, 1994; Davis, 2003). What is more, the principle of non-independence points towards a more methodologically grounded account of the prospect of supplier-induced demand in healthcare which saliently questions the orthodox presumption of the independence of supply and demand (this phenomenon has been subject to detailed investigation in the US literature. For a discussion, see McGuire, 2000). From this perspective, health is contingent on agents' consumption decisions which reflect the nature and structure of society. Individual health and health-related tastes are not exogenous but learned and shaped by cultural, institutional and socio-economic processes, and by particular influences such as advertising and healthcare physicians.

Some cultural patterns of consumption, for example, are linked to improved health outcomes, such as the fish-heavy diet of the Japanese, the French and their red wine, and the so-called Mediterranean diet. Conversely, the high saturated-fat content of the Scottish diet has been linked to poor health. Public health programmes attempt to alert consumers to the health consequences of their consumption habits, but receptiveness to such warnings tends to be contingent upon a mix of education and income (Fine, 2002). Moreover, the demands of accumulation and the wider economic superstructure influence consumption patterns. The food, tobacco, automobile and alcohol industries, for example, use sophisticated marketing techniques to increase sales. The resulting augmented consumption patterns can have harmful health effects (Fine, 2002). Similarly, social and economic pressures to increase working hours and augment incomes have been linked to the increase in psychological disorders. Indeed, many modern health problems should be seen as consequences of various economic modes of organisation and the behaviours that they encourage. As Galbraith (1973, p. 297) presciently argued:

> Virtually all of the increase in modern health hazards is the result of increased consumption. Obesity and associated disorders are the result of

> increased food consumption; cirrhosis and accidents are the result of increased alcohol consumption; lung cancer, heart disease, emphysema and numerous other disabilities are the result of increased tobacco consumption; accidents and resulting mortality and morbidity are caused by increased automobile use; hepatitis and numerous disabling assaults are often caused by increased drug consumption; nervous disorders and mental illness follow from efforts to increase income, observation of the greater success of others in increasing income, the fear of loss of income or the fear of the various foregoing physical consequences of high consumption. At the same time medical and hospital care is not part of the development which induces these disorders. It lags systematically behind – for a large part of the population, including many who are relatively affluent, its availability is uncertain and its cost alarming or prohibitive.

Finally, Post Keynesians would acknowledge the many uncertainties that plague healthcare. Arrow (1963) identified two main types of uncertainty in healthcare: uncertainty in the demand for healthcare, and uncertainty about the effectiveness of treatment. In terms of healthcare demand, for example, the conventional wisdom is that at the individual level illness and injury are highly stochastic events and thus health expenditure has a large random component. Post Keynesians, following the arguments put forward here, would seek to move beyond stochastic conceptualisations of uncertainty (Davidson, 1991b). They would point to the relevance of path-dependent processes and argue that conceptualising healthcare uncertainty as ergodic risk suggests that the decisions made by economic agents cannot make a difference in the long run. In contrast, the assumption of transmutability means that the decisions taken by agents can make a difference in the long run, affecting both health outcomes and health-related expenditures, reinforcing the principle of non-independence outlined above.

There is ample evidence of processes that exhibit transmutability in the health domain. Many diseases exhibit path dependence. Chronic diseases, which account for a high and growing proportion of healthcare expenditures, are typically (though not always) irreversible, and their emergence embodies a mixture of genetic, personal, emulatory and socio-economic factors. Similarly, healthcare interventions which are typically aimed at improving the health status of individuals are uniquely irreversible. They are instances of what Shackle (1955) referred to as crucial experiments. The adverse side-effects of some medications cannot be reversed. And once a hip has been replaced the operation cannot be undone (although it may be re-done), notwithstanding whether it was a success or a failure. Moreover, many branches of the science of health are devoted to transforming and influencing the course of history, at the individual and the societal level. For example, epidemiology – the study of disease – is about assessing risk *and changing it*. It is accepted that assessments of medical risk are not constant over time and are subject to modification as a result of changed behaviours and habits (see Brindle *et al.*, 2003, for example).

SUPPLY OF HEALTHCARE

Broadly speaking, the economics literature identifies two principal modes of organisation for allocating resources: decentralised *markets,* which allocate resources through competitive processes and impersonal exchange relationships, or *hierarchies* that depend on managerial fiat and various control mechanisms to allocate resources. In theory the preferred mode of transactional governance is that which economises on bounded rationality, minimises opportunism and protects asset-specific investments (Williamson, 1985). In the absence of problems of complexity, short-run opportunities for self-seeking behaviour, problems of self-interest seeking and large irreversible investments, an unfettered market may be relied on to allocate resources, i.e. in the beginning there are markets. In most markets, however, such problems are present in varying degrees, giving rise to a variety of hybrid organisations and institutions that seek to allocate resources.

In healthcare the existence of numerous uncertainties, the prevalence of large, asset-specific investments, and opportunities for self-seeking behaviour are typically invoked to explain some of the non-market institutions observed in the healthcare sector (Arrow, 1963; Hansmann, 1996). The numerous types of market failure suggest that, in some areas of healthcare delivery, other governance structures may generate lower transaction costs than unfettered markets. A rationale for the prevalence of non profit entities in healthcare provision is that such organisations have less incentive to maximise the economic rents that may be had by exploiting consumer ignorance (Hansmann, 1996).

A Post Keynesian approach to the supply of healthcare would highlight the limits of traditional theoretical conceptions of the role, rationale and origins of alternative governance structures. First, Post Keynesians would reject the narrow conceptualisation of human behaviour that underpins most comparative analysis of institutional forms in favour of a broader view of human motivations (cf. Chick, 1995; Lawson, 2003; Davis, 2003). They recognise that human behaviour is not always driven by pecuniary motives. They do not deny the importance of self-interested behaviour, but argue that policy makers need to recognise that behavioural norms may differ across, and be reinforced by, cultures and institutions.

The need for a broader conception of human behaviour is recognised by some health analysts, underpinning, for example, Le Grand's (1997, 2000) distinction between intrinsic and extrinsic motivations, or between knightish and knavish behaviour. Policymakers have also increasingly recognised the need for a broader conception of human motivations (cf. Department of Health, 2000, p. 57). But they have also recognised that in some areas financial incentives can have a role and can contribute to improved service delivery (Department of Health, 2002).

Second, Post Keynesians would also recognise the role that trust plays in the provision of healthcare. Trust is a socially embedded quality that manifests itself in the expectations of others, affects the interactions between patients and providers and facilitates the development of networks as modes of allocating resources. Different motivations, such as professional and clan ethos, might underscore the value of networks, trust and collaboration in underpinning service delivery (Ouchi, 1980; Thompson *et al.*, 1991). Networks which rely on social relationships that involve trust and cooperation can be effective in allocating healthcare resources (Institute of Medicine, 2001; Department of Health, 2000). Post Keynesians also recognise the role that institutions can play in building and sustaining trust. While it may be hard to measure, the importance of trust for health cannot be dismissed (McMaster, 2001).

Third, and perhaps most importantly, Post Keynesians would emphasise the role of history. They would point to the long-run relevance of certain institutional forms that minimise transaction costs and supersede the market, and would not take it for granted that hierarchical modes of allocating healthcare resources will dissolve into market-based governance structures in the (very) long run (cf. Dunn, 2000b). Post Keynesians would expect that ongoing experience with a variety of market and non-market governance forms will inform decisions to move from one institutional arrangement to another.

The considerable heterogeneity across healthcare systems is evidence that historical, socio-economic and political processes all affect the organisation of healthcare systems. The existence of what we may loosely characterise as three dominant modes of healthcare provision – socialised, social insurance and private insurance – and the heterogeneity within each mode point to the absence of compelling forces elevating one set of institutions above others (an implication of the discussion in Chapter 6). Most healthcare systems contain a variety of allocative and incentive mechanisms. Each system is the reflection of a range of social values and political trajectories – of history – rather than a homogenous response to a set of market failure problems. The prevalence of universal coverage healthcare systems, for example, cannot be fully understood or explained in terms of the standard insurance model approach to health (Evans, 1983).

MARKET ANALYSIS

Such microeconomic considerations can be extended to the study of pricing, as well as to other parts of the healthcare sector such as the pharmaceutical industry. Post Keynesians recognise that modern technology requires large, long-term investments in highly specialised capital and labour, as well as effective group decision-making (Galbraith, 1967; Dunn, 2001a,c). Post Keynesians view the business enterprise as a strategic planning organisation that, in addition to coordinating production, tries to shelter it from market uncertainties.

As noted in the previous section, in more orthodox conceptualisations of the firm planning is solely conceived as coordinating production. From a Post Keynesian perspective, planning is also about preparing for, and attempting to control, the future. To mitigate the uncertainties that surround large commitments of time and money, the firm must either supersede the market or subordinate it to its own needs (see Dunn, 2001a,c). And the larger the firm, the greater the likelihood that it can successfully mould the future in ways that suit its own interests. Under this conception firms attempt to set prices strategically, reflecting the overriding planning objectives of the firm such as the pursuit of profit, growth and technological virtuosity. Post Keynesian theories of the modern corporation, for example, highlight how firms alter prices and thus profit margins so as to generate an internal flow of funds to facilitate and secure investment (Lavoie, 1992). Prices are set by some mark-up over costs such as the full cost principle, by administered pricing, or by cost-plus pricing (see Chapter 9). This perspective offers the prospect of a potentially fruitful analysis of the firm and price determination in, say, the pharmaceutical industry.

The pharmaceutical industry is characterised by large firms and a vast technostructure that undertakes huge asset-specific investments in drug development over long periods of time, despite considerable uncertainty about future returns. The fully capitalised cost to develop a new drug can be as high as $897 million, according to the Tufts Center for the Study of Drug Development (DiMasi *et al.*, 2003). On some calculations it can take up to fourteenyear from the point of discovery to bring a drug to market. This fourteen-year period consists of a six-year pre-clinical phase (to assess whether the drug is safe enough to test on humans), a six-year clinical phase of human trials, and a two-year review and approval phase. This process involves a great deal of uncertainty. According to the Pharmaceutical Research and Manufacturers of America, which may somewhat overstate the case, only five of every 5000 drugs reach the stage of clinical trials. Of these only 21.5 per cent are eventually approved (Tufts Center for the Study of Drug Development, 2002).

Given the high cost of modern drug production, it is natural that the pharmaceutical industry would seek to influence consumer response and set prices strategically in a way that allows them to recover their costs. Drug firms would like to ensure that what they produce (at great cost) is ultimately purchased. Thus it is no surprise that promotional spending is a large share of the industry's total spending, exceeding R&D costs by a factor of two or more. In 2002, R&D accounted for '14 percent of total revenue in thirteen of the largest research based pharmaceutical companies … while selling and general administration absorbed close to 33 percent' (Reinhardt, 2004, p. 108). Moreover, Direct To Consumer Advertising (DTCA) of pharmaceuticals has become an important element of this strategy, growing from nothing in late 1997, when the US Food and Drug Administration (FDA) eased regulatory restrictions, to US $2.5 billion in 2000 (IMS Health, 2001). Such ramifications have been little explored by the mainstream economics profession.

In mainstream economics, advertising is usually seen as the provision of information to the consumer, rather than as an attempt to alter consumer preferences. Preferences and prices are taken as exogenous, and consumers and their advocates are presumed or assumed to be able to evaluate the veracity of sellers' claims. Proponents of pharmaceutical advertising would argue that it informs and empowers patients, reduces under-diagnosis and under-treatment of disease, de-stigmatises disease and encourages compliance.

In contrast, Post Keynesians would not accept the traditional assumption of consumer sovereignty. Recognising that advertising may have other objectives than the provision of information, Post Keynesians acknowledge the possibility of what

Galbraith (1967) labels the 'revised sequence': the situation in which consumers are manipulated to meet the firm's needs, rather than the other way around.

The health services research community has also recognised this possibility. They have highlighted the social and medical consequences of efforts by the pharmaceutical industry to manipulate consumers and providers. Moynihan (2003a) documents industry efforts to create new diseases by encouraging and lobbying for the systematic definition and classification of new medical disorders. Similarly the industry uses a variety of marketing strategies to create wants for ostensibly healthy people by attempting to medicalise ordinary life. Moynihan *et al.* (2002, p. 886) note the problem of 'disease mongering widening the boundaries of treatable illness in order to expand markets for those who sell and deliver treatments'. Similarly the many instances of corrupting flows of money between the medical profession and the pharmaceutical industry has been recognised as a threat to the doctor–patient relationship and has met with activist response (Moynihan, 2003b).

Such concern with the adverse impacts of the revised sequence may illuminate why New Zealand, the only country other than the United States to allow DTCA of drugs, appears to be on the verge of banning it. Pleas for more lenient regulation of pharmaceutical marketing, for example, should not therefore be understood or seen merely as consumer-driven demand for more information.

Post Keynesians would also identify the symbiosis and contractual nexus of various technostructures and how they can affect the content of medical advertising in ways that conflict with the wider public interest (cf. Anderson and Dunn, 2006). The tobacco industry, for example, has used its leverage with the chemical and pharmaceutical industries to influence the marketing of anti-smoking drugs. Internal documents from tobacco companies show that from the mid-1980s to the early 1990s they successfully lobbied drug companies to drop or modify their marketing of nicotine replacement therapies (Shamasunder and Bero, 2002). The tobacco industry also used its clout as a buyer of agricultural chemicals from corporations that also produce pharmaceutical products to induce them to modify their anti-smoking messages in ways that undermined public health objectives.

Such considerations suggest the need to monitor and regulate some types of advertising. Once policy makers understand the nature and extent of an industry's influence over the public, that knowledge can be marshalled to serve the development of broader social aims. 'This consists in disciplining [an industry's] purposes – in making it serve, not define, the public interest' (Galbraith, 1973b, p. 240). Policy makers should question whether it is efficient, from society's point of view, for the pharmaceutical industry to allocate such substantial sums to marketing and R&D and whether alternative institutional arrangements should be encouraged (for a discussion of such matters, see Reinhardt, 2004).

EVALUATION AT THE WHOLE SYSTEM LEVEL

Post Keynesians would obviously seek to emphasise the macrofoundations of healthcare. The distribution, financing and organisation of healthcare have ramifications for consumption and investment patterns, government spending and even net imports, and thus will affect the distribution and level of aggregate demand. The health sector is one of the biggest industries and employers in most advanced Western industrialised societies. Healthcare spending typically accounts for between 10 to 20 per cent of government spending. In the 1990s, OECD governments spent between 5 and 8 per cent of GDP on healthcare (Table 4). Health spending is rising even higher over the current decade.

The level of healthcare spending is likely to have causal and consequential effects on both the level and distribution of health and the broader economy. For example the level of aggregate demand and its components will affect and reflect the age structure of the population and impinge on the dependency ratio, i.e. the number of people working relative to those that are retired, in ill health and/or are not in the labour market. This will have implications for consumption and saving rates, which in turn impact on the level of effective demand and the level of employment. Assumptions about the level of employment exhibited by advanced industrial systems will also have consequences for health-related expenditures. The precise nature of healthcare financing is also likely to have macroeconomic consequences. These issues are considered in turn below.

First, Post Keynesians acknowledge a positive role for state intervention and activist macroeconomic policy. Keynes' *General Theory* provides a theoretical foundation for the elaboration of the consequences of a monetary production economy for macroeconomic coordination (Davidson, 2002). It outlines a role for governments to assume responsibility to ensure an adequate level and distribution of effective demand and thus employment. In rejecting Say's law, Post Keynesians point to the chronic unemployment and excess capacity that characterise many advanced industrialised countries. They highlight the social consequences of unemployment and how labour market exclusion contributes to poverty and ill health, and how ill health can contribute to labour market exclusion and thus poverty. As Rowthorn (2000, p. 157) notes:

> For people below pensionable age, long-term illness rates range from 3 percent in the most prosperous areas up to 18 percent in the most depressed. The very high rates in depressed areas must surely conceal a greater deal of disguised unemployment. Many of those who are classified as too sick to work are probably capable of holding down a job, but have such poor employment prospects that doctors have certified them as unfit to work as a humane way of providing them with a secure income in the form of sickness benefit. Even where their incapacity is genuine, some of those concerned must have become sick because of the stress and poverty of job insecurity and unemployment.

Poverty and ill health can be part of a downward vicious circle of causation whereby sluggish market adjustments and low levels of effective demand are transformed into structural unemployment, leading to poor health and poverty which in turn threaten to reproduce themselves across generations,

Table 4 Percentage of all healthcare costs (all government-paid healthcare costs) as a percentage of GDP

	1991	*1992*	*1993*	*1994*	*1995*	*1996*	*1997*	*1998*	*1999*	*2000*	*2001*
Australia	8.0 (5.4)	8.1 (5.4)	8.2 (5.4)	8.2 (5.4)	8.2 (5.5)	8.4 (5.6)	8.5 (5.8)	8.6 (5.9)	8.7 (6.0)	8.9 (6.2)	9.2 (6.2)
Canada	9.7 (7.2)	10.0 (7.4)	9.9 (7.2)	9.5 (6.9)	9.2 (6.5)	9 (6.3)	8.9 (6.2)	9.1 (6.5)	9.1 (6.4)	9.2 (6.5)	9.7 (6.9)
France	8.8 (6.7)	9.0 (6.9)	9.4 (7.2)	9.4 (7.1)	9.5 (7.3)	9.5 (7.2)	9.4 (7.1)	9.3 (7.1)	9.3 (7.1)	9.3 (7.1)	9.5 (7.2)
Germany	0.0 (0.0)	9.9 (7.7)	9.9 (7.6)	10.2 (7.8)	10.6 (8.1)	10.9 (8.4)	10.7 (8.1)	10.6 (7.9)	10.6 (8.0)	10.6 (7.9)	10.7 (8.0)
Italy	8.3 (6.6)	8.4 (6.5)	8.1 (6.2)	7.8 (5.9)	7.4 (5.3)	7.5 (5.4)	7.7 (5.6)	7.7 (5.6)	7.8 (5.6)	8.2 (6.0)	8.4 (6.3)
Japan	5.9 (4.6)	6.2 (4.8)	6.4 (5.1)	6.7 (5.3)	6.8 (5.3)	6.9 (5.4)	6.8 (5.3)	7.1 (5.5)	7.5 (5.8)	7.7 (6.0)	8.0 (6.2)
Netherlands	8.2 (5.7)	8.4 (6.1)	8.5 (6.3)	8.4 (6.1)	8.4 (6.0)	8.3 (5.5)	8.2 (5.5)	8.6 (5.5)	8.7 (5.5)	8.6 (5.5)	8.9 (5.7)
Sweden	8.1 (7.2)	8.3 (7.3)	8.6 (7.5)	8.2 (7.1)	8.1 (7.1)	8.4 (7.3)	8.2 (7.1)	8.3 (7.1)	8.4 (7.2)	8.4 (7.1)	8.7 (7.4)
UK	6.5 (5.4)	6.9 (5.8)	6.9 (5.9)	7.0 (5.9)	7.0 (5.8)	7.0 (5.8)	6.8 (5.5)	6.9 (5.5)	7.2 (5.8)	7.3 (5.9)	7.6 (6.2)
US	12.6 (5.2)	13.0 (5.5)	13.3 (5.7)	13.2 (5.9)	13.3 (6.0)	13.2 (6.0)	13.0 (5.9)	13.0 (5.8)	13.0 (5.7)	13.1 (5.8)	13.9 (6.2)

Source: OECD HEALTH DATA 2003, 3rd ed.

Notes

1 Figures in brackets represent all government-paid healthcare costs.

2 According to the OECD System of Health Accounts, total expenditure on health is a measure of the economic resources spent by a country on healthcare services and goods (such as health administration) plus gross capital formation in healthcare industries. Gross capital formation in healthcare industries comprises those expenditures that add to the stock of resources to the healthcare system and last more than an annual accounting period. In general, the OECD data does not include training of health professionals within their healthcare costs (France is the exception). The OECD data technical notes do not cite the inclusion of the cost of liability insurance for healthcare professionals. With regard to health research, in Canada, health research is included within healthcare costs. In the US, non-commercial biomedical research is included within their healthcare costs. Although not specified in the source notes, such research is likely to be included in the other OECD countries' health expenditure data.

reducing opportunities for groups and classes of people to make their contributions to society.

Post Keynesians start from the position that public expenditure should be undertaken for its social value, reflecting (broadly) the principles of functional finance. Public expenditures, which operate through the lens of the welfare state, may serve to prevent downward cycles of cumulative causation that result in poverty and ill health. Although health expenditures are typically absent from debates about the extent, nature and future of the welfare state – which tend to revolve around the nature of government transfers – they represent a prime component of public spending and aggregate demand.

From a fiscal point of view, public health care expenditures can be used to underpin the level and distribution of aggregate demand. Public healthcare expenditures may be a major part of any expansionary or stabilisation policy. They can be used counter-cyclically to support the level of aggregate demand. Similarly, the composition and distribution of public healthcare spending will impact on the structure of aggregate demand across regions. For instance, consider the consequences of reductions in the level of aggregate demand at a regional level:

> This will cause an immediate fall in employment and total income in the region. There will be a short-run multiplier effect on employment as local suppliers lay off workers, and consumer expenditure on housing, shopping, leisure activities and the like is reduced. The scale of this short-run multiplier will be limited by the operation of the welfare state, whose expenditures in the region will help to maintain local demand following a blow to the local economy. Government transfer payments to the newly unemployed will allow them to continue spending, albeit at a reduced rate, on local goods and services. Hospitals and schools will continue to operate as normal, providing jobs for those who work in them and supply them.
>
> (Rowthorn, 2000, p. 159)

Government healthcare spending which has the objective of contributing to the mitigation of health disparities and inequalities has the effect of a regional policy, contributing to regional spending and investment. Thus public healthcare spending can decelerate long-term decline by lubricating structural adjustment and supporting higher levels of regional employment and investment than might otherwise be the case (cf. Kaldor, 1970).

The nature of budgetary policy will also have ramifications for the nature and extent of access to health services. For example it has been argued by the WHO (2002) that ill health and poverty induce a vicious circle of cumulative causation which simultaneously increases budget demands and reduces budget revenues, resulting in budget deficits that destabilise the macro-economy. From this perspective poverty and ill health are to be prevented so as to avoid the problems of deficit financing which only seek to destabilise social spending programmes in the long run.

In contrast, Post Keynesians, building on Keynes' revolutionary *General Theory*, would argue that adherence to balanced budgets is likely to exacerbate economic downturns and lead to unnecessary reductions in social welfare programmes, impacting on healthcare access. They argue that falling employment and falling tax revenues, when combined with a balanced budgetary policy, will lead to unnecessary reductions in funding for social welfare programmes, which will in turn impact on the eligibility and coverage (implicit or explicit) of publicly provided healthcare and impact on health. Instead, Post Keynesians advocate deficit financing combined with a range of automatic fiscal stabilisers to intervene and prevent vicious downward spirals of unemployment, reduced healthcare expenditure, poverty and ill health (cf. Davidson, 2002).

Second, Post Keynesians consider the impact on health on economic growth for the macroeconomic framework, i.e. how healthcare investment contributes to health, productivity, economic growth and macroeconomic stability. For example, Bloom *et al.* (2001b) have highlighted the fact that when health, in the form of life expectancy, is introduced into cross-country growth regressions it appears to have a significant positive effect on the rate of economic growth. They note that a one-year improvement in a population's life expectancy contributes to a 4 percent increase in output. Post Keynesians argue that there is a need to broaden the human capital conceptualisation of the nexus between health and growth. They highlight that although public expenditure on health may create 'human capital' for the individuals receiving healthcare resources, which may augment aggregate economic growth, there is also a variety of other macroeconomic benefits that flow from one individual to others, e.g. increased income multipliers and greater tax revenues to governments, that need to be recognised and studied.

Third, health, as it contributes to increases in life expectancy, is likely to impact on savings rates over time, further affecting the growth and level of effective demand. The impact of life expectancy on savings rates has been recognised by health economists and explored by rationally maximising lifecycle models developed to study this issue (see Bloom *et al.*, 2002). The macroeconomic implications of such effects are then considered in terms of a 'loanable funds' concept of savings whereby the direction of causality runs from saving to investment and economic growth. Post Keynesians reject the lifecycle hypothesis and the loanable funds model of savings and investment on both theoretical and empirical grounds.

Post Keynesians focus on the scarcity of demand and the attention that must be accorded to income effects, its distribution, its impact and links to effective demand and its associated impact on savings. This suggests an alternative macroeconomic conception of the links between health and saving. Post Keynesians reverse the direction of causality between investment and savings, arguing that in modern credit-money economies investment creates savings, rather than the other way around. The expansion of effective demand requires an extension of credit, and that generally involves the creation of money. Money is viewed as endogenously created within the private sector 'to meet the needs of trade'. (Post Keynesians argue that loans create deposits and reserves, rather than reserves and deposits creating loans, as in the traditional credit multiplier story.) Higher levels of saving induced by improved life expectancy would reduce spending, aggregate demand and employment.

A seminal study by Sheldon Danziger *et al.* (1982–3) of the Institute for Poverty of the University of Wisconsin, for example, using cross-sectional data of 9494 households, found that the average propensity to save actually rose for cohorts of age 65 and older. 70-year-olds saved more than 65-year-olds, and 75-year-olds saved more than 70-year-olds, and so on, at all levels of income. This result appeared robust for many different definitions of income. The authors concluded that many suppositions of the life-cycle hypothesis about the relationship between savings and age which underlies much theorising, many measures of economic well-being, and important policy judgements did not appear to accord with reality. There is a need to update and refine such studies; but the basic point is that there is a need to examine the actual relationship between the income, spending and saving of the elderly and evaluate its impact on the structure of aggregate demand and levels of investment, i.e. to assess the empirical adequacy of life-cycle explanations of consumption and savings decisions.

Fourth, modelling assumptions about the level of employment are relevant in considering the effects of a rising dependency rate and its implications for economic growth and medical expenditure (see Jackson, 1998). The standard neoclassical approach to modelling demographic change assumes that the economy exhibits full employment in the long run. The import of this assumption is that there is no demographic slack in the economy. Given that their working life is ostensibly over, the rising healthcare needs of the elderly adversely affect the rate of economic growth by inducing non-income-generating healthcare expenditures. An increasing dependency ratio thus results in employment substitution from other, more productive, areas of the economy to less productive and more labour-intensive care industries, i.e. a sort of elderly crowding-out hypothesis (cf. Bloom *et al.*, 2001a).

Post Keynesians reject such full employment assumptions, maintaining that *a posteriori* advanced monetary production economies typically operate with a degree of chronic unemployment and excess capacity. This means that at the aggregate level there is unlikely to be any shortage of workers. An increasing dependency effect need not directly impact on economic growth nor give rise to intergenerational conflicts. Fluctuations in the level of employment instead may insulate labour markets from demographic shifts in the labour market. (Economies that exhibit historically high levels of employment may find themselves dealing with the problems of lack of demographic slack. In the absence of global monetary institutions that permit the coordinated expansion of global aggregate demand and employment, such considerations are likely to be the exception and not the rule.)

Fifth, the nature of healthcare financing will have consequences at both the macroeconomic and microeconomic levels as well as in terms of the overall level of healthcare spending. Post Keynesians argue that the structure of taxation should reflect some egalitarian principles, not least because this underpins the level of aggregate demand:

> If fiscal policy is used as a deliberate instrument for the more equal distribution of incomes, its effect in increasing the propensity to consume is, of course, all the greater.
>
> (Keynes, 1936, p. 95)

Broadly speaking, healthcare spending that is financed through general taxation is more progressive and equitable. Financing of healthcare expenditure through the whole tax base typically reduces tax distortions in the economy and lowers administrative and transaction costs.

Systems of employer-related insurance are likely to distort labour markets, add to macroeconomic instability and undermine efforts to provide access to healthcare services. In the US, for example, employers, who are the principal source of health insurance, receive tax subsidies in order to promote greater health insurance coverage. As the macroeconomic environment worsens, those who lose jobs lose any health insurance provided by their employer. Such labour market fluctuations, affecting both participation rates and levels of unemployment, impacts on health insurance coverage.[4] The system of promoting health insurance coverage through tax subsidisation serves as a double whammy for those who are laid off. Those who lose their job face both lower incomes, through unemployment, and higher prices, by being denied access to subsidised employer programmes. It is for such reasons that Cawley and Simon (2003) have found empirical evidence that suggests that a 10% increase in local unemployment rate may be associated with a 3.1% increase in the probability that an adult lacks health insurance. Post Keynesians would argue that these microeconomic considerations need to be integrated into broader conceptions of the interdependence in the economy and the salience for the government's macroeconomic role understood.

CONCLUDING COMMENTS

It has been argued that a Post Keynesian approach to health economics can generate numerous insights that can inform the way in which economists and non-economists think about health and health care, informing and contributing to diverse areas such as methodology, microeconomics, industrial organisation and macroeconomics. Post Keynesian economics offers an interesting perspective on health economics and should be further developed in the spirit of encouraging a dynamic, more plural and relevant health economics. The next stage is to take these prefatorial remarks and furnish a more specific set of contributions that will contribute to the future evolution of both health economics and Post Keynesianism. Hopefully, Post Keynesians will no longer neglect the economics of health and healthcare. And those interested in health and healthcare will no longer neglect the economics of Post Keynesians.

NOTES

1 In developing countries the link between illness and disability and the reduction in incomes and hourly wages is especially strong. This reflects the fact that, typically, a higher percentage of the work force is engaged in manual labour than in industrial countries (see Strauss and Thomas, 1998).

2 In arguing for general tax financing of the universal provision of healthcare it should not be inferred that Post Keynesians would argue for healthcare provision to be exclusively controlled and provided by the state. Indeed, this is not what Keynes (1936, p. 378) had in mind in urging a 'comprehensive socialisation of investment' as a civilised response to managing aggregate demand to ameliorate the problems of unemployment. Many have interpreted this as an argument for nationalisation in the provision of basic state services to underpin the management of effective demand. This is wrong. Rather, Keynes was arguing that more rational institutions for allocating capital could, and should, be devised so as to reconcile public and private interest. But this need not entail public provision nor 'exclude all manner of compromises and of devices by which public authority will co-operate with private initiative … it is not the ownership of the instruments of production which it is important for the State to assume. If the State is able to determine the aggregate amount of resources devoted to augmenting the instruments and the basic rate of reward to those who own them, it will have accomplished all that is necessary' (Keynes, 1936, p. 378).

3 Moreover, Post Keynesians would reject the notion that such time-series estimates reflect permanent long-run behaviour. Instead, Post Keynesians argue that many of the discrepancies observed between time-series and cross-sectional estimates of the income elasticity of health are perhaps econometric and definitional. As Bunting (2004) has argued forcibly, time series elasticities reflect cross-sectional ones plus cross-sectional shifts, i.e. it is not true that cross-sectional parameters measure current or short-run behaviour while times-series parameters measure permanent or long-run behaviour. Indeed, Bunting (2004) demonstrates times-series data has no independent locus beyond cross-sectional behaviour. This is consistent with a historical approach which rejects the predominant ergodic, closed-system equilibrium approach to economic analysis whereby there is a long-period equilibrium around which the economy fluctuates or towards which the economy tends and which is unaffected by the short-period movements of the economy. As Kalecki (1968, p. 263) observed, the long run is 'a slowly changing component of a chain of short period situations; it has no independent entity'.

4 Such arrangements exacerbate the problems of maintaining an adequate level of effective demand and compound access problems. Research by Cawley and Simon (2003) suggests that 851,000 Americans, the majority of whom were men, lost health insurance through the 2001 recession.

Bibliography

Acheson, D. (1998) *Independent Inquiry into Inequalities in Health: Report* (Chairman: Sir Donald Acheson), London, TSO.

Adriaansen, W. and van der Linden, J. (1991) (eds) *Post-Keynesian Thought in Perspective*, Groningen, Wolters-Noordhof.

Anderson, S.J. and Dunn, S.P. (2006) 'Galbraith and the management of specific demand: Evidence from the tobacco industry', *Journal of Institutional Economics*, 2(3), 273–296.

Anderton, A., Hurd, S. and Coates, G. (1998) 'Economics and business studies trends in GCE A-Level', *Journal of the Economics and Business Education Association*, 2(3), 21–25.

Andrews, P.W.S. (1949a) 'A reconsideration of the theory of the individual business', *Oxford Economic Papers*, 1(1), 54–89.

Andrews, P.W.S. (1949b) *Manufacturing Business*, London, Macmillan.

Andrews, P.W.S. (1964) *On Competition in Economic Theory*, London, Macmillan.

Andrews, P.W.S. and Brunner, E. (1951) *Capital Development in Steel*, London, Macmillan.

Andrews, P.W.S. and Brunner, E. (1962) 'Business profits and the quiet life', *Journal of Industrial Economics*, 11(1), 72–78.

Andrews, P.W.S. and Brunner, E. (1975) *Studies in Pricing*, London, Macmillan.

Arestis, P. (1990) 'Post Keynesianism: A new approach to economics', *Review of Social Economy*, 48(3), 222–246.

Arestis, P. (1992) *The Post Keynesian Approach to Economics: An Alternative Analysis of Economic Theory and Policy*, Aldershot, Edward Elgar.

Arestis, P. (1996a) 'Post-Keynesian economics: Towards coherence, critical survey', *Cambridge Journal of Economics*, 20, 111–135.

Arestis, P. (1996b) 'Kalecki's role in Post Keynesian economics: an overview', in J. E. King (ed.) *An Alternative Macroeconomic Theory: The Kaleckian Model and Post Keynesian Economics*, London, Kluwer Academic Publishers.

Arestis, P. (1997) *Money, Pricing, Distribution and Economic Integration*, London, Macmillan.

Arestis, P. and Eichner, A.S. (1988) 'The post-Keynesian and Institutionalist theory of money and credit', *Journal of Economic Issues*, 22(4), 1003–1021.

Arestis, P. and Sawyer, M.C. (1993) 'Political economy: an editorial manifesto', *International Papers in Political Economy*, 1(1), 1–38.

Arestis, P. and Howells, P. (1996) 'Theoretical reflections on endogenous money: the problem with "convenience lending"', *Cambridge Journal of Economics*, 20(5), 539–552.

Arestis, P. and Sawyer, M. (1997a) *The Relevance of Keynesian Economic Policies Today*, London, Macmillan.

Arestis, P. and Sawyer, M. (1997b) 'Unemployment and the independent European system of central banks: prospects and some alternative arrangements', *American Journal of Economics and Sociology*, 56(3), 353–367.

Arestis, P. and Sawyer, M.C. (1998) 'Keynesian policies for the new millennium', *Economic Journal*, 108(1), 181–195.

Arestis, P. and Sawyer, M.C. (1999) 'The macroeconomics of New Labour', *Economic Issues*, 4(1), 39–58.

Arestis, P., Biefang-Frisancho Mariscal, I. and Howells, P. (1994) 'Realism in Post Keynesian Quantitative Analysis' in M. Glick (ed.) *Competition, Technology and Money: Classical and Post-Keynesian perspective*, Aldershot, Edward Elgar.

Arestis, P., Dunn, S.P. and Sawyer, M.C. (1999a) 'Post Keynesian economics and its critics', *Journal of Post Keynesian Economics*, Summer, 21(4), 527–550.

Arestis, P., Dunn, S.P. and Sawyer, M.C. (1999b) 'On the coherence of Post Keynesian economics: a comment upon Walters and Young', *Scottish Journal of Political Economy*, 46(3), 339–345.

Arrow, K.J. (1963) 'The welfare economics of medical care', *American Economic Review*, 53, 941–973.

Arrow, K.J. (1985) 'Informational structure of the firm', *American Economic Review: AEA Papers and Proceedings*, 75(2), 303–307.

Arrow, K.J. and Hahn, F.H. (1971) *General Competitive Analysis*, Edinburgh, Oliver and Boyd.

Asimakopulos, A. (1975) 'A Kaleckian theory of income distribution', *Canadian Journal of Economics*, 8(3), 313–333.

Backhouse, R.E. (1988) 'The value of Post Keynesian economics: a neoclassical response to Harcourt and Harmouda', *Bulletin of Economic Research*, 40(1), 35–41.

Backhouse, R.E. (1992) 'Should we ignore methodology?', *Royal Economic Society Newsletter*, 78, July, 4–5.

Backhouse, R.E. (1998) 'If mathematics is informal, then perhaps we should accept that economics is informal too', *Economic Journal*, 108, 1848–1858.

Baran, P.A. and Sweezy, P.M. (1966) *Monopoly Capital: An essay on the American economic and social order*, Harmondsworth, Penguin, 1968.

Basile, L. and Salvadori, N. (1994) 'On the existence of a solution to Kalecki's pricing equations', *Journal of Post Keynesian Economics*, 16(3), 435–438.

Bateman, B.W. (1987) 'Keynes's changing conception of probability', *Economics and Philosophy*, 3, 97–119.

Bateman, B.W. (1996) *Keynes's Uncertain Revolution*, Ann Arbor, University of Michigan Press.

Baumol, W.J. (1982) 'Contestable markets: an uprising in the theory of industry structure', *American Economic Review*, 72, 1–15.

Bell, D. and Kristol, I. (1981) (eds) *The Crisis in Economic Theory*, New York, Basic Books.

Bellante, D. (1992) 'The fork in the Keynesian road: Post Keynesians and Neo-Keynesians', in M.Skousen (ed.) *Dissent on Keynes: A Critical Appraisal of Keynesian Economics*, New York, Prager, 117–129.

Belman, D. (1992) 'Unions, the quality of labor relations and firm performance' in L. Mishel and P.B. Voos (eds) *Unions and Economic Competitiveness*, New York, M.E. Sharpe.

Bernstein, P.L. (1996) *Against the Gods: The Remarkable Story of Risk*, New York, John Wiley and Sons.

Bhaskar, R. (1978) *A Realist Theory of Science*, 2nd edition, London, Harvester Wheatsheaf.

Bigo, V. (2006) 'Open and closed systems and the Cambridge school', *Review of Social Economy*, 64(4), 493–514.

Birch, T.D. (1985) 'Marshall and Keynes revisited', *Journal of Economic Issues*, March, 194–200.

Blaug, M. (1992) *The Methodology of Economics*, Cambridge, UK, Cambridge University Press.

Block, W. (1988) 'On Yeager's "Why Subjectivism?"', *Review of Austrian Economics*, 2, 199–208.

Block, W. (1999) 'Austrian theorizing: recalling the foundations', *Quarterly Journal of Austrian Economics*, 2(4), 21–39.

Blomqvist, A.G. and Carter, R.A.L. (1997) 'Is health care really a luxury?', *Journal of Health Economics*, 16, 207–229.

Bloom, D.E., Canning, David and Sevilla, J. (2001a) *Economic Growth and the Demographic Transition*, Working Paper 8685, http://www.nber.org/papers/w8685, Cambridge, MA, National Bureau of Economic Research.

Bloom, D.E., Canning, David and Sevilla, J. (2001b) *The Effect of Health on Economic Growth: Theory and Evidence*, Working Paper 8587, http://www.nber.org/ papers/w8587, Cambridge, MA, National Bureau of Economic Research.

Bloom, D.E., Canning, David and Graham, B. (2002) *Longevity and Life Cycle Savings*, Working Paper 8808, http://www.nber.org/papers/w8808, Cambridge, MA, National Bureau of Economic Research.

Bodenheimer, T.S. and Grumbach, K. (2005), *Understanding Health Policy: A Clinical Approach*, 4th edition, New York, Lange Medical Books/McGraw-Hill.

Boulding, K. (1966) 'The concept of need for health services', *Milbank Memorial Fund Quarterly*, 44(4), 202–223.

Brandis, R. (1985) 'Marx and Keynes? Marx or Keynes? (review article)', *Journal of Economic Issues*, September, 643–659.

Braverman, H. (1974) *Labour and Monopoly Capital: The Organisation of Work in the Twentieth Century*, New York, Monthly Review Press.

Brazelton, R. (1981) 'Post Keynesian Economics: an institutional compatibility', *Journal of Economic Issues*, 15(2), 531–542.

Brindle, P., Emberson, J., Lampe, F., Walter, M., Whincup, P., Fahey, T. and Ebrahim, S. (2003) 'Predictive accuracy of Framingham coronary risk score in British men: prospective cohort study' *British Medical Journal*, 327, 1267–1271.

Buchanan, J.M. (1987) 'Constitutional Economics', in J. Eatwell, M. Milgate and P. Newman (eds) *The New Palgrave: A Dictionary of Economics*, London, Macmillan.

Buchanan, J.M., Burton, J. and Wagner, R.E. (1978) *The Consequences of Mr Keynes*, Hobart Paper 78, London, Institute for Economic Affairs.

Bunting, D. (2004) 'Expenditure symmetry in macroeconomics', paper presented at Eastern Economic Association Annual Conference, Washington, DC, 20–22 February 2004.

Caldwell, B.J. (1989) 'Post Keynesian methodology: an assessment', *Review of Political Economy*, 1(1), 43–64.

Cameron, J. and Ndhlovu, T.P. (1999) 'Keynes and the distribution of uncertainty: Lessons from the Lancashire spinning industry and the General Theory', *Review of Social Economy*, 57(1), 99–123.

Canterbery, E.R. (1984) 'Galbraith, Sraffa, Kalecki, and supra-surplus', *Journal of Post-Keynesian Economics*, 7(1), 77–90.

Caplan, B. (1999) 'The Austrian search for realistic foundations', *Southern Economic Journal*, 65(4), 823–838.

Carabelli, A. (1988) *On Keynes's Method*, New York, St Martin's Press.

Carson, J. (1994) 'Existence and uniqueness of solutions to Kalecki's pricing equations', *Journal of Post Keynesian Economics*, 16(3), 411–434.

Carvalho, F.J.C. (1983–4) 'On the concept of time in Shacklean and Sraffian economics', *Journal of Post Keynesian Economics*, 6(2), 265–280.

Carvalho, F.J.C. (1984–5) 'Alternative analyses of short and long run in Post Keynesian economics', *Journal of Post Keynesian Economics*, 7(2), 214–234.

Carvalho, F.J.C. (1988) 'Keynes on probability, uncertainty and decision-making', *Journal of Post Keynesian Economics*, 11(1), 66–81.

Carvalho, F.J.C. (1990) 'Keynes and the long period', *Cambridge Journal of Economics*, 14, 277–290.

Cassidy, J. (1996) 'The decline of economics', *New Yorker*, December 2, 50–64.

Cawley, J. and Simon, K.I. (2003) *Health Insurance Coverage and the Macroeconomy*, Working Paper 10092, http://www.nber.org/papers/w10092, National Bureau of Economic Research.

Chandler, A.D. (1962) *Strategy and Structure*, Cambridge, MA, MIT Press.

Chandler, A.D. (1977) *The Visible Hand: The Managerial Revolution in American Business*, Cambridge, MA, Harvard University Press.

Chandler, A.D. (1990) *Scale and Scope: The Dynamics of Industrial Capitalism*, Cambridge, MA and London, Harvard University Press.

Chandler, A.D. (1992) 'Organisational capabilities and the economic history of the industrial enterprise', *Journal of Economic Perspectives*, 6(3), 79–100.

Chase, R.X. (1992) 'Keynes's principle(s) of effective demand: redefining his revolution (review of E. Amadeo's book)', *Journal of Economic Issues*, 26, 865–890.

Chasse, J.D. (1991) 'John R. Commons and John Maynard Keynes: two philosophies of action', *Journal of Economic Issues*, June, 441–448.

Chick, V. (1983) *Macroeconomics after Keynes: A Reconsideration of the General Theory*, Oxford, Philip Allen.

Chick, V. (1992) 'The small firm under uncertainty: a puzzle of the general theory', in W.J. Gerrard and J. Hillard (eds) *The Philosophy and Economics of J.M. Keynes*, Aldershot, Edward Elgar.

Chick, V. (1995) 'Is there a case for Post Keynesian economics?', *Scottish Journal of Political Economy*, 42(1), 20–36.

Chick, V. (1998) 'Knowing one's place: the role of formalism in economics', *Economic Journal*, 108, 1859–1869.

Chick, V. and Dow, S. (2005) 'The meaning of open systems', *Journal of Economic Methodology*, 12(3), 363–381.

Clark, C.M.A (1987–8) 'Equilibrium, market process, and historical time', *Journal of Post Keynesian Economics*, 10(2), 270–281.

Clark, C.M.A. (1989) 'Equilibrium for what? Reflections on social order in economics', *Journal of Economic Issues*, 23, 597–606.

Clark, C.M.A. (1992) 'An Institutionalist critique of Sraffian economics', *Journal of Economic Issues*, 26, 457–468.

Clark, C.M.A. (1993) 'Spontaneous order versus instituted process: the market as cause and effect', *Journal of Economic Issues*, 27(2), 373–385.

Clark, J.M. (1940) 'Toward a concept of workable competition', *American Economic Review*, 30(2), 241–256.

Clifton, J.A. (1983) 'Administered prices in the context of capitalist development', *Contributions to Political Economy*, 2, 23–38.

Clower, R. (1969) 'Introduction' in R. Clower (ed.) *Monetary Theory*, Harmondsworth, UK, Penguin.

Coase, R.H. (1937) 'The nature of the firm'. Reprinted in G.J. Stigler and K.E. Boulding (eds) *Readings in Price Theory: Selected by a Committee of the American Economic Association*, London, George Allen and Unwin, 1953.

Coase, R.H. (1991) 'The nature of the firm: influence' in O.E. Williamson and S.G. Winter (eds) *The Nature of the Firm: Origins, Evolution and Development*, Oxford, Oxford University Press.

Coast, J. (1999) 'The appropriate uses of qualitative methods in health economics', *Health Economics*, 8, 345–353.

Coddington, A. (1976) 'Keynesian economics: the search for first principles', *Journal of Economic Literature*, 14(4), 1258–1273.

Coddington, A. (1983) *Keynesian Economics: The Search for First Principles*, London, Allen & Unwin.

Comim, F. (1999) 'Forms of life and "horses for courses": introductory remarks', *Economic Issues*, 4(1), 21–37.

Commons, J.R. (1934) *Institutional Economics – Its Place in Political Economy*, New York, Macmillan.

Conlisk, J. (1996) 'Why bounded rationality?', *Journal of Economic Literature*, 34, 669–700.

Cottrel, A. (1994) 'Post Keynesian monetary economics', *Cambridge Journal of Economics*, 18(4), 587–606.

Cowling, K. and Waterson, M. (1976) 'Price–cost margins and market structure', *Economica*, 43(171), 267–274.

Cowling, K. and Sugden, R. (1987) *Transnational Monopoly Capitalism*, Brighton, Wheatsheaf.

Cowling, K. and Sugden, R. (1993) 'Control, Markets and Firms' in C. Pitelis (ed.) *Transaction Costs, Markets and Hierarchies*, Oxford, Basil Blackwell.

Cowling, K. and Sugden, R. (1998) 'The essence of the modern corporation: markets, strategic decision-making and the theory of the firm', *The Manchester School*, 66(1), 59–86.

Crocco, M. (1997) 'Uncertainty, technological change and Keynes' probability', in S.P. Dunn, et al. (eds) *The Second Annual Post Graduate Economics Conference: Papers and Proceedings*, Leeds, UK, Leeds, University Press.

Culyer, A.J. (1995) 'Need: the idea won't do – but we still need it', *Social Science and Medicine*, 40(6), 727–730.

Culyer, A. and Newhouse, J. (2000) (eds) *A Handbook of Health Economics: Volume 1A*, London, Elsevier.

Cyert, R.M. and March, J. (1963) *A Behavioral Theory of the Firm*, Englewood Cliffs, NJ, Prentice-Hall.

Cyert, R.M. and Simon, H.A. (1983) 'The behavioural approach: with emphasis on economics', *Behavioural Science*, 28, 95–108. Reprinted in P.E. Earl (ed) *Behavioural Economics: Volume 1*, Aldershot, Edward Elgar, 1988.

Dahlman, C.J. (1979) 'The problem of externality', *Journal of Law and Economics*, 22(1), 141–162.

Danziger, S., Gaag, J. van der, Smolensky, E. and Taussig, M.K. (1982–3) 'The life-cycle hypothesis and the consumption behavior of the elderly', *Journal of Post Keynesian Economics*, 2, 208–227.

Dasgupta, P. (1998) *Modern Economics and its Critics – 1*, Cambridge University, Mimeo.

Davidson, P. (1972) *Money and the Real World*, 2nd edition, London, Macmillan, 1978.

Davidson, P. (1974) 'A Keynesian view of Friedman's theoretical framework for monetary analysis', in R.J. Gordon (ed.) *Milton Friedman's Monetary Framework: A Debate with his Critics*, London, University of Chicago Press.

Davidson, P. (1977) 'Money and general equilibrium'. Reprinted in *Money and Employment: The Collected Writings of Paul Davidson, Volume 1*, London, Macmillan, 1990.

Davidson, P. (1980) 'Causality in economics', Journal of Post Keynesian Economics, Vol. 2. Reprinted in *Inflation, Open Economics and Resources*: *The Collected Writings of Paul Davidson, Volume 2*, London, Macmillan, 1991.

Davidson, P. (1981) 'Post Keynesian economics', in D. Bell and I. Kristol (eds) *The Crisis in Economic Theory*, New York, Basic Books.

Davidson, P. (1982) *International Money and the Real World*, London, Macmillan.

Davidson, P. (1982–3) 'Rational expectations, a fallacious foundation for studying crucial decision-making processes', *Journal of Post Keynesian Economics*, 5, pp. 182–197. Reprinted in *Inflation, Open Economics and Resources*: The Collected Writings of Paul Davidson, Volume 2, London, Macmillan, 1991.

Davidson, P. (1985a) 'Incomes policy as a social institution', in S. Maitak and I. Lipnowski (eds) *Macroeconomic Conflict and Social Institutions*, Cambridge, MA, Ballinger. Reprinted in *Inflation, Open Economics and Resources: The Collected Writings of Paul Davidson, Volume 2*, London, Macmillan, 1991.

Davidson, P. (1985b) 'Liquidity and not increasing returns is the ultimate source of unemployment equilibrium', *Journal of Post Keynesian Economics*, 7, 373–384.

Davidson, P. (1988) 'A technical definition of uncertainty and the long-run non-neutrality of money', *Cambridge Journal of Economics*, Vol. 12, pp. 329–338. Reprinted in *Inflation, Open Economics and Resources: The Collected Writings of Paul Davidson, Volume 2*, London, Macmillan, 1991.

Davidson, P. (1989a) 'Markets and governments: the comparison of means and objectives under different economic-systems', *Challenge*, Vol. 32, No. 5. Reprinted in *Inflation, Open Economics and Resources: The Collected Writings of Paul Davidson, Volume 2*, London, Macmillan, 1991.

Davidson, P. (1989b) 'Shackle and Keynes vs rational expectations theory on the role of time, liquidity and financial markets' in S. Frowen (ed.) *Business, Time and Thought: Conference in Honour of G.L.S. Shackle*, London, Macmillan. Reprinted in *Inflation, Open Economics and Resources: The Collected Writings of Paul Davidson, Volume 2*, London, Macmillan, 1991.

Davidson, P. (1989c) 'The economics of ignorance or the ignorance of economics?', *Critical Review*, 3(3–4), 467–487.

Davidson, P. (1991a) 'Is probability theory relevant for uncertainty? A Post Keynesian perspective', *Journal of Economic Perspectives*, 5(1), 129–143.

Davidson, P. (1991b) 'Is probability theory relevant for uncertainty? A different perspective', an earlier draft of Davidson (1991a) in *Inflation, Open Economics and Resources: The Collected Writings of Paul Davidson, Volume 2*, London, Macmillan, 1991.

Davidson, P. (1991c) *Controversies in Post Keynesian Economics*, Aldershot, Edward Elgar.

Davidson, P. (1992) 'Eichner's approach to money and macroeconomics', in W. Milberg (ed.) *The Megacorp and Macrodynamics*, New York, M.E. Sharpe.

Davidson, P. (1992–3) 'Reforming the world's money', *Journal of Post Keynesian Economics*, 15(2), 153–179.

Davidson, P. (1993a) 'The elephant and the butterfly: or hysteresis and Post Keynesian economics', *Journal of Post Keynesian Economics*, 15(3), 309–322.

Davidson, P. (1993b) 'Austrians and Post Keynesians on economic reality: rejoinder to critics', *Critical Review*, 7(2–3), 423–444. Reprinted in L. Davidson (ed.) *Uncertainty, International Money, Employment and Theory: The Collected Writings of Paul Davidson, Volume 3*, London, Macmillan, 1999, pp. 38–55.

Davidson, P. (1993c) *Can the Free Market Pick Winners?*, New York, M.E. Sharpe.

Davidson, P. (1994) *Post Keynesian Macroeconomic Theory: A Foundation for Successful Economic policies for the Twenty First Century*, Aldershot, Edward Elgar.

Davidson, P. (1996) 'Reality and economic theory', *Journal of Post Keynesian Economics*, Vol. 18, pp. 479–508. Reprinted in L. Davidson (ed.) *Uncertainty, International Money, Employment and Theory: The Collected Writings of Paul Davidson, Volume 3*, London, Macmillan, 1999, pp. 3–29.

Davidson, P. (1998a) 'Twenty years old and growing stronger everyday', *Journal of Post Keynesian Economics*, 21(1), 3–10.

Davidson, P. (1998b) 'Volatile financial markets and the speculator', *Economic Issues*, 3(2), 1–18.

Davidson, P. (1999a) 'Keynes principle of effective demand versus the bedlam of the new Keynesians', *Journal of Post Keynesian Economics*, 21(Summer), 571–588.

Davidson, P. (1999b) 'Taxonomy, communication, and rhetorical strategy', *Journal of Post Keynesian Economics*, 22(1), 125–129.

Davidson, P. (1999c) 'Can money be neutral even in the long run? Chartalism vs monetarism', in L. Davidson (ed.) *Uncertainty, International Money, Employment and Theory: The Collected Writings of Paul Davidson, Volume 3*, London, Macmillan, 1999, pp. 196–210.

Davidson, P. (2002) *Financial Markets, Money and the Real World*, Cheltenham, Edward Elgar.

Davidson, P. and Weintraub, S. (1978) 'A statement of purposes', *Journal of Post Keynesian Economics*, 1(1), 3–8.

Davidson, P. and Davidson, G.S. (1984) 'Financial markets and Williamson's theory of governance: Efficiency versus concentration versus power', *Quarterly Review of Economics and Business*, Vol. 24 (Winter). Reprinted in *Money and Employment, The Collected Writings of Paul Davidson, Volume 1*, London, Macmillan, 1991.

Davidson, P. and Davidson, G. (1996) *Economics for a Civilised Society, 2nd edition*, London, Macmillan.

Davies, J.E., and Lee, F.S. (1988) 'A Post Keynesian appraisal of the contestability criterion', *Journal of Post Keynesian Economics*, 1, 3–24.

Davis, J.B. (1994) *Keynes's Philosophical Development*, Cambridge, UK, Cambridge University Press.

Davis, J.B. (2001) (ed.) *The Social Economics of Health Care*, London, Routledge.

Davis, J.B. (2003) *The Theory of the Individual in Economics: Identity and Value*, London, Routledge.

Day, R.D. (1967) 'Profits, learning and the convergence of satisficing to marginalism', *Quarterly Journal of Economics*, Vol. 81, pp. 302–311. Reprinted in P.E. Earl (ed.) *Behavioural Economics: Volume 1*, Aldershot, Edward Elgar, 1988.

Demsetz, H. (1997) 'Hermeneutics and the interpretative element in the analysis of the market process', *Center for Market Process Working Paper*, Fairfax, VA, George Mason University.

Dennison, H.S. and Galbraith, J.K. (1938) *Modern Competition and Business Policy*, New York, Oxford University Press.

Department of Health (2000) *The NHS Plan*, London, The Stationery Office.

Department of Health (2002) *Delivering the NHS Plan*, London, The Stationery Office.

Dequech, D. (1997a) ‘Different views on uncertainty and some policy implications’, in P. Davidson, and J.A. Kregel, (eds) *Improving the Global Economy: Keynesians and the Growth of Output and Employment*, Cheltenham, Edward Elgar.

Dequech, D. (1997b) ‘Uncertainty in a strong sense: meaning and sources’, *Economic Issues*, 2(2), 21–43.

Dequech, D. (1997c) ‘A brief note on Keynes, unknown probabilities and uncertainty in a strong sense’, *History of Economic Ideas*, 5(2), 101–110.

Dequech, D. (1999a) ‘Expectations and confidence under conditions of uncertainty’, *Journal of Post Keynesian Economics*, 21, 415–430.

Dequech, D. (1999b) ‘On some arguments for the rationality of conventional behaviour under uncertainty’, in C. Sardoni, and P. Kreisler, (eds) *Keynes, Post Keynesianism and Political Economy: Essays in Honour of Geoff Harcourt, Volume Three*, London, Routledge.

DiMasi, J.A., Hansen, R.W. and Grabowski, H.G. (2003) ‘The price of innovation: new estimates of drug development costs’, *Journal of Health Economics*, 22(2), 151–185.

Dixon, (1986) ‘Uncertainty, Unobstructedness and Power’, *Journal of Post Keynesian Economics*, 8(4), 585–90.

Donaldson, C. and Karen, G. (1993) *Economics of Health Care Financing: The Visible Hand*, London, Palgrave MacMillan.

Dosi, G. (1982) ‘Technological paradigms and technological trajectories’, *Research Policy*, 2, 147–162.

Dosi, G. (1988a) ‘Sources, procedures and microeconomic effects of innovation’, *Journal of Economic Literature*, 36, 1120–1171.

Dosi, G. (1988b) ‘The nature of the innovative process’, in G. Dosi, C. Freeman, G. Silverberg and L. Soete (eds) *Technical Change and Economic Theory*, London, Pinter.

Dosi, G. and Orsenigo, L. (1988) ‘Co-ordination and transformation: an overview of structures, behaviours and change in evolutionary environments’, in G. Dosi, C. Freeman, G. Silverberg and L. Soete (eds) *Technical Change and Economic Theory*, London, Pinter.

Dosi, G. and Egidi, M. (1991) ‘Substantive and procedural uncertainty’, *Journal of Evolutionary Economics*, 1, 145–168.

Dostaler, G. (1988) ‘La théorie post-Keynesienée, la “Théorie Generale” et Kalecki’, *Cahiers d’Economie Politique*, 123–142.

Dow, S.C. (1985) *Macroeconomic Thought: A Methodological Approach*, Oxford, Basil Blackwell.

Dow, S.C. (1990a) ‘Post Keynesianism as political economy: a methodological discussion’, *Review of Political Economy*, 2(3), 345–358.

Dow, S.C. (1990b) ‘Beyond dualism’, *Cambridge Journal of Economics*, 14(2), 143–158.

Dow, S.C. (1991) ‘The Post Keynesian school’, in D. Mair, and A.G. Miller (eds) *A Modern Guide to Economic Thought*, Aldershot, Edward Elgar.

Dow, S.C. (1995) ‘Conversation’, in J.E. King (ed.) *Conversations with Post Keynesians*, London, Macmillan.

Dow, S.C. (1996a) *The Methodology of Macroeconomic Thought: a Conceptual Analysis of Schools of Thought in Economics*, Aldershot, Edward Elgar.

Dow, S.C. (1996b) 'Horizontalism: a critique', *Cambridge Journal of Economics*, 20, 497–508.

Dow, S.C. (1997a) 'Methodological pluralism and pluralism of method', in A. Salanti and E. Screpanti (eds) *Pluralism in Economics: Theory, History and Methodology*, Aldershot, Edward Elgar, pp. 89–99.

Dow, S.C. (1997b) 'Mainstream Economic Methodology', *Cambridge Journal of Economics*, 21(1), 73–93.

Dow, S.C. (1997c) 'Tony Lawson: Economics and Reality', *New Political Economy*, 2(3), 527–531.

Dow, S.C. (1999) 'Post Keynesianism and critical realism: what is the connection?', *Journal of Post Keynesian Economics*, 22(1), 15–33.

Dow, S.C. (2001) 'Post Keynesian methodology', in R. Holt and S. Presman (eds) *The New Guide to Post Keynesian Economics*, London, Routledge.

Dow, S.C. and Earl, P.E. (1984) 'Methodology and Orthodox Monetary Policy', *Economie Appliqué*, 37, 143–163.

Dow, S.C. and Hillard, J. (eds) (1995) *Keynes, Knowledge and Uncertainty*, Aldershot, Edward Elgar.

Downie, J. (1958) *The Competitive Process*, London, Duckworth.

Downward, P.M. (1994) 'A reappraisal of case study evidence on business pricing: Neoclassical and Post Keynesian perspectives', *British Review of Economic Issues*, 16(39), 23–43.

Downward, P.M. (1995) 'A Post Keynesian perspective of U.K. manufacturing pricing', *Journal of Post Keynesian Economics*, 17(3), 403–426.

Downward, P.M. (1999) *Pricing in Post Keynesian Economics: A Realist Appraisal*, Aldershot, Edward Elgar.

Downward, P.M. (2000) 'A realist appraisal of Post Keynesian pricing theory', *Cambridge Journal of Economics*, 24, 211–224.

Downward, P.M. (2003) (ed.) *Applied Economics and the Critical Realist Critique*, London, Routledge.

Downward, P.M. (2004) 'On leisure demand: a Post Keynesian critique of neoclassical theory', *Journal of Post Keynesian Economics*, 26(3), 371–395.

Downward, P.M. and Reynolds, P. (1996) 'Alternative Perspectives on Post Keynesian Price Theory', *Review of Political Economy*, 8, 67–78.

Downward, P.M. and Mearman, A. (1999) 'Realism and econometrics: Alternative perspectives', Paper presented to the Conference of the Association of Heterodox Economists, 30 March, 1999, University of Nottingham.

Downward, P. and Mearman, A. (2006) 'Retroduction as mixed-methods triangulation in economic research: reorienting economics into social science', *Cambridge Journal of Economics*, Advance Access published on April 13, 2006 (http://cje.oxfordjournals.org/papbyrecent.dtl)

Downward, P.M., Reynolds, P. and Lavoie, M. (1996) 'Realism, simulations and Post Keynesian pricing: a response to Lee', *Review of Political Economy*, 8(4).

Downward, P., Finch, J.H. and Ramsay, J. (2002) 'Critical realism, empirical methods and inference: a critical discussion', *Cambridge Journal of Economics*, 26, 481–500.

Dugger, W.M. and Sherman, H.J. (1994) 'Comparison of Marxism and Institutionalism', *Journal of Economic Issues*, 28(1), 101–127.

Dulbecco, P. and Garrouste, P. (1999) 'Towards an Austrian theory of the firm', *Review of Austrian Economics*, 11, 43–64.

Dunlop, J.T. (1938) 'The movement of real and money wage rates', *Economic Journal*, 48, 413–434.

Dunn, S.P. (1996) 'A Post Keynesian contribution to the theory of the firm', *Leeds University Business School discussion paper series*, University of Leeds, E96/18.

Dunn, S.P. (1997) 'Bounded rationality, uncertainty and a Post Keynesian approach to transaction costs', *Leeds University Business School discussion paper series*, University of Leeds, E97/08.

Dunn, S.P. (1999) 'Bounded rationality, "fundamental" uncertainty and the firm in the long run', in S.C. Dow and P. Earl (eds) *Contingency, Complexity and the Theory of the Firm: Essays in Honour of Brian Loasby, Volume Two*, Cheltenham, Edward Elgar.

Dunn, S.P. (2000a) 'Wither Post Keynesianism?', *Journal of Post Keynesian Economics*, 22(3), 343–364.

Dunn, S.P. (2000b) 'Fundamental' uncertainty and the firm in the long run', *Review of Political Economy*, 12(4), 419–433.

Dunn, S.P. (2001a) 'Uncertainty, strategic decision-making and the essence of the modern corporation: extending Cowling and Sugden', *The Manchester School*, 69(1), 31–41.

Dunn, S.P. (2001b) 'A Post Keynesian approach to the theory of the firm', in S.C. Dow and J. Hillard (eds) *Post Keynesian Econometrics and the Theory of the Firm: Beyond Keynes, Volume One*, Cheltenham, Edward Elgar.

Dunn, S.P. (2001c) 'Galbraith, uncertainty and the modern corporation', in M. Keaney (ed.) *Economist with a Public Purpose: Essays in Honour of John Kenneth Galbraith*, London, Routledge.

Dunn, S.P. (2001d) 'Bounded rationality is not fundamental uncertainty: a Post Keynesian perspective', *Journal of Post Keynesian Economics*, 23(4), 567–588.

Dunn, S.P. (2001e) *An Investigation into a Post Keynesian contribution to the Theory of the Firm*, Unpublished PhD Manuscript, Leeds University Business School.

Dunn, S.P. (2002) "Towards a transmutable economics? A comment on Wynarczyk", *Economic Issues*, 7(1), 15–20.

Dunn, S.P. (2005) 'John Kenneth Galbraith and the multinational corporation', *Challenge*, 48(2), 90–112.

Dunn, S.P. (2006) 'Prolegomena to a Post Keynesian Health Economics', *Review of Social Economy*, 64(3), 273–292.

Dunn, S.P. and Anderson, S.J. (2007) 'J.K. Galbraith's challenge to the accepted sequence: the management of the consumer', *Econômica*, January, 337–351.

Dutt, A. (1992) 'Keynes, market forms and competition', in B. Gerrard and J. Hillard (eds) *The Philosophy and Economics of J.M. Keynes*, Cheltenham, Edward Elgar.

Earl, P.E. (1983) *The Economic Imagination: Towards a Behavioural Analysis of Choice*, with a foreword by G.L.S. Shackle, Brighton, Wheatsheaf Books.

Earl, P.E. (1984) *The Corporate Imagination: How Big Companies Make Mistakes*, Brighton, Wheatsheaf Books.

Earl, P.E. (1986) *Lifestyle Economics: Consumer Behaviour in a Turbulent World*, Brighton, Wheatsheaf Books.

Earl, P.E. (1988) *Behavioural Economics*, Aldershot, Edward Elgar.

Earl, P.E. (1989) 'Bounded rationality, psychology and financial evolution: some behavioural perspectives on Post Keynesian Analysis', in J. Pheby (eds) *New Directions in Post Keynesian Economics*, Aldershot, Edward Elgar.

Earl, P.E. (1990) 'Economics and psychology: a survey', *Economic Journal*, 100, 718–755.

Earl, P.E. (1991) 'Principal-agent problems and structural change in the advertising industry', *Prometheus*, 9, December, 274–295.

Earl, P.E. (1992a) 'Scientific research programmes and the prediction of corporate behaviour', *Cyprus Journal of Economics*, 5(2), 75–95.

Earl, P.E. (1992b) 'The evolution of co-operative strategies: three automotive industry case studies', *Human Systems Management*, 11(2), 89–100.

Earl, P.E. (1993) 'The economics of G.L.S. Shackle in retrospect and prospect', *Review of Political Economy*, 5(2), 245–261.

Earl, P.E. (1994) 'Herbert Alexander Simon', in G. Hodgson, et al. (eds) *The Elgar Companion to Institutional and Evolutionary Economics*, Vol. 2, Aldershot, Edward Elgar, pp. 284–287.

Earl, P.E. (1995) *Microeconomics for Business and Marketing*, Aldershot, Edward Elgar.

Earl, P.E. (1996a) *Management, Marketing and the Competitive Process*, Aldershot, Edward Elgar.

Earl, P.E. (1996b) 'Shackle, entrepreneurship and the theory of the firm', in S. Pressman and J. Smithin (eds) *Explorations in Political Economy: Malvern after Ten Years*, London, Routledge.

Earl, P.E. (1998) 'Consumer goals as journeys into the unknown', in M. Bianchi (ed.) *The Active Consumer: Novelty and Surprise in Consumer Choice*, London, Routledge, pp. 122–139.

Earl, P.E. (1999) 'Marketing as information economics', in S. Macdonald and J. Nightingale (eds) *Information and Organisation: A Tribute to the Work of Don Lamberton*, Amsterdam, Elsevier, pp. 243–261.

Earl, P.E. (2000) *The Legacy of Herbert A. Simon in Economic Analysis*, Cheltenham, Edward Elgar.

Earl, P.E. (2005) 'Economics and psychology in the twenty-first century', *Cambridge Journal of Economics*, 29, 909–926.

Earl, P.E. and Kay, N. (1985) 'How economists can accept Shackle's critique of economic doctrines without arguing themselves out of a job', *Journal of Economic Studies*, 12, 34–48.

Edward, R.T. (2001) 'Paradigms and research programmes: is it time to move from health care economics to health economics', *Health Economics*, 10, 635–649.

Eichner, A.S. (1969) *The Emergence of Oligopoly: Sugar Refining as a Case Study*, Baltimore, Johns Hopkins Press.

Eichner, A.S. (1973) 'A theory of the determination of the mark up under oligopoly', *Economic Journal*, 83(332), 1184–1200.

Eichner, A.S. (1976) *The Megacorp and Oligopoly*, Cambridge, UK, Cambridge University Press.

Eichner, A.S. (1985) *Towards a New Economic Theory: Essays in Post Keynesianism and Institutionalist Theory*, London, Macmillan.

Eichner, A.S. (1991) *The Macrodynamics of Advanced Market Economies*, New York, M.E. Sharpe.

Eichner, A.S. and Kregel, J. (1975) 'An essay on Post Keynesian theory: a new paradigm in economics', *Journal of Economic Literature*, 13, 1293–1314.

Evans, R.G. (1983) *Strained Mercy: The Economics of Canadian Health Care*, Butterworths, Toronto.

Finch, J.H. (1999) 'The methodological implications of Post Marshallian economics', in S.C. Dow and P. Earl (eds) *Economic Organisation and Economic Knowledge: Essays in Honour of Brian Loasby, Volume Two*, Cheltenham, Edward Elgar.

Finch, J.H. (2000) 'Is post-Marshallian economics an evolutionary research tradition?', *European Journal of History of Economic Thought*, 7(3), 377–406.

Fine, B. (2002) *The World of Consumption*, London, Routledge.

Fitzroy, F.R. and Mueller, D. (1984) 'The co-operation and conflict in contractual organisations'. Reprinted in D. Mueller (ed.) *The Modern Corporation: Profits, Power, Growth and Performance*, London, Harvester Wheatsheaf, 1986.

Fleetwood, S. (1999) (ed.) *Critical Realism in Economics: Development and Debate*, London, Routledge.

Fontana, G. (2005) 'A history of Post Keynesian economics since 1936: some hard (and not so hard) questions for the future', *Journal of Post Keynesian Economics*, 27(3), 409–422.

Ford, J.L. (1993) 'G.L.S. Shackle (1903–1992): A life with Uncertainty', *Economic Journal*, 103(418), 683–697.

Forstater, M. (2003) 'Public employment and environmental sustainability', *Journal of Post Keynesian Economics*, 25(3), 385–406.

Forstater, M. (2004) 'Green jobs: addressing the critical issues surrounding the environment, workplace and employment', *International Journal of Environment, Workplace and Employment*, 1(1), 53–61.

Forstater, M. (2006) 'Green jobs', *Challenge*, 49(4), 58–72.

Foss, N.J. (1993) 'The theory of the firm: contractual and competence perspectives', *Journal of Evolutionary Economics*, 3, 127–144.

Foss, N.J. (1994a) 'The theory of the firm: the Austrians as precursors and critics of modern theory', *Review of Austrian Economics*, 7, 127–144.

Foss, N.J. (1994b) 'The two Coasian traditions', *Review of Political Economy*, 6, 35–61.

Foss, N.J. (1996a) 'Whither the competence perspective?', in N.J. Foss and C. Knudsen, *Towards a Competence Theory of the Firm*, London, Routledge.

Foss, N.J. (1996b) 'Firms, incomplete contracts, and organizational learning', *Human Systems Management*, 15, 17–26.

Foss, N.J. (1997a) 'Research in strategy, economics, and Michael Porter', *Journal of Management Studies*, 33, 1–24.

Foss, N.J. (1997b) *Resources and Strategy: A Reader*, Oxford, Oxford University Press.

Foss, N.J. (1997c) 'Austrian insights and the theory of the firm', *Advances in Austrian Economics*, 4, 175–198.

Foss, N.J. (1997d) 'The resource-based perspective, an assessment and diagnosis of problems', *Danish Research Unit for Industrial Dynamics Working Paper No. 97–1*.

Fourie, F.C.v.N. (1993) 'In the beginning there were markets?' in C. Pitelis (ed.) *Transaction Costs, Markets and Hierarchies*, Oxford, Basil Blackwell.

Freeman, R. and Medoff, J.L. (1984) *What do Unions do?*, New York, Basic Books.

Friedman, M. (1953) *Essays in Positive Economics*, Chicago, University of Chicago Press.

Fusfeld, D.R. (1990) 'Economics and the determinate world view', *Journal of Economic Issues*, June, 355–359.

Galbraith, J.K. (1958) *The Affluent Society*, 2nd edition, Harmondsworth, Penguin.

Galbraith, J.K. (1967) *The New Industrial State*, 2nd edition, Harmondsworth, Penguin, 1974.

Galbraith, J.K. (1970) *Economics, Peace and Laughter*, Harmondsworth, Penguin.

Galbraith, J.K. (1973a) 'Power and the useful economist', *American Economic Review*, 63(1), 1–11.

Galbraith, J.K. (1973b) *Economics and the Public Purpose*, Harmondsworth, Penguin.

Galbraith, J.K. (1973c) 'Controls or competition – What's at issue? A comment (in notes)', *Review of Economics and Statistics*, 55(4), 524.

Galbraith, J.K. (1975) *Money: Whence it Came, Where it Went*, Harmondsworth, Penguin.

Galbraith, J.K. (1977) *The Age of Uncertainty*, London, BBC.

Galbraith, J.K. (1978) 'On Post Keynesian economics', *Journal of Post Keynesian Economics*, 1(1), 8–11.

Galbraith, J.K. (1979) *Annals of an Abiding Liberal*, London, Andre Deutsch.

Galbraith, J.K. (1981) *A Life in Our Times: Memoirs*, Houghton Mifflin, Boston, MA.

Galbraith, J.K. (1991) 'Economics in the century ahead', *Economic Journal*, 101(404), 41–46.

Galbraith, J.K. (1994) *A Tenured Professor*, London, Sinclair-Stevenson.

Galbraith, J.K. (1998) 'John Maynard Keynes: from retrospect to prospect', *Journal of Post Keynesian Economics*, 21(1), 11–14.

Galbraith, J.K. Jr. (1996) 'What is to be done (about economics)?', in S. Medema and W. Samuels (eds) *Foundations of Research in Economics: How Should Economists Do Economics?*, Aldershot, Edward Elgar.

Garegnani, P. (1978) 'Notes on consumption, investment and effective demand I', *Cambridge Journal of Economics*, 2(4), 335–353.

Garegnani, P. (1979) 'Notes on consumption, investment and effective demand II', *Cambridge Journal of Economics*, 3(1), 63–82.

Garner, A.C. (1982) 'Uncertainty, human judgement, and economic decisions', *Journal of Post Keynesian Economics*, 4(3), 413–424.

Garrison, R. (1999) 'Hayek made no contribution? It just ain't so!', *Freeman*, 49(5), 6–7.

Gerdtham, U.-G. and Jonsson, B. (2000) 'International comparisons of health expenditure', in A. Culyer, and J. Newhouse, (eds) *A Handbook of Health Economics: Volume 1A*, London, Elsevier.

Gerrard, W.J. (1989) *Theory of the Capitalist Economy: Towards a Post-Classical Synthesis*, Oxford, Basil Blackwell.

Gerrard, W.J. (1992a) 'From *A Treatise on Probability* to the *General Theory*: continuity or change in Keynes's thought?', in W.J. Gerrard, and J.V. Hillard (eds) *The Philosophy and Economics of J.M. Keynes*, Aldershot, Edward Elgar.

Gerrard, W.J. (1992b) 'Human logic in Keynes's thought: escape from the Cartesian vice', in P. Arestis and V. Chick (eds) *Recent Developments in Post Keynesian Economics*, Aldershot, Edward Elgar.

Giammanco, M.D. (1998) 'Scarcity of resources in a Sraffian framework of international trade', *Metroeconomica*, 49(3), 301–318.

Giddens, A. (2003) *Runaway World*, London, Routledge.

Glaister, K. (1996) 'Theoretical perspectives on strategic alliance formation' in Earl, P. (ed) *Management, marketing and the competitive process*, Aldershor, Edward Elgar.

Goode, R. (1994) 'Gardiner means on administered prices and administrative inflation', *Journal of Economic Issues*, March, 173–186.

Hahn, F. (1975) 'Revival of political economy: the wrong issues and the wrong argument', *Economic Record*, 51, 360–364.

Hahn, F. (1977) 'Keynesian economics and general equilibrium theory', in G.C. Harcourt (ed.) *The Microfoundations of Macroeconomics*, London, Macmillan.

Hahn, F. (1982) 'The Neo-Ricardians', *Cambridge Journal of Economics*, 6, 353–374.

Hahn, F. (1984) *Equilibrium and Macroeconomics*, Oxford, Basil Blackwell.

Hahn, F. (1985) 'In praise of economic theory', *The 1984 Jevons Memorial Fund Lecture*, London, University College.

Hahn, F. (1989) 'Robinson–Hahn love-hate relationship: an interview', in G.R. Feiwel (ed.) *Joan Robinson and Modern Economic Theory*, London, Macmillan.

Hahn, F. (1992a) 'Reflections', *Royal Economic Society Newsletter*, 77, April.
Hahn, F. (1992b) 'Answer to Backhouse: Yes', *Royal Economic Society Newsletter*, 78, July.
Hall, R.F. and Hitch, C.J. (1939) 'Price theory and business behaviour', *Oxford Economic Papers*, 2, 13–33.
Hamilton, D.B. (1987) 'Institutional economics and consumption', *Journal of Economic Issues*, 21(4), 1531–1554.
Hamouda, O. and Harcourt, G.C. (1988) 'Post Keynesianism: from criticism to coherence?', *Bulletin of Economic Research*, 40(1), 1–30. Reprinted in Claudio Sardoni (ed.) *On Political Economists and Modern Political Economy: Selected Essays of Geoff Harcourt*, London, Routledge.
Hansmann, H.B. (1996) *The Ownership of Enterprise*, Cambridge, MA, The Belknap Press of Harvard University Press.
Harcourt, G.C. (1972) *Some Cambridge Controversies in the Theory of Capital*, Cambridge, UK, Cambridge University Press.
Harcourt, G.C. (1980) 'Discussion: of Tarshis (1980)', *American Economic Review*, 70(2).
Harcourt, G.C. (1981) 'Notes on an economic querist: G.L.S. Shackle', *Journal of Post Keynesian Economics*, 4(1), 136–144.
Harcourt, G.C. (1985) 'Post-Keynesianism: quite wrong and/or nothing new?', in P. Arestis and T. Skouras (eds) *Post Keynesian Economic Theory: a Challenge to Neo Classical Economics*, Brighton, Wheatsheaf Books.
Harcourt, G.C. (1992a) 'Marshall, Sraffa, and Keynes: incompatible bedfellows?', in C. Sardoni (ed.) *On Political Economists and Modern Political Economy: Selected Essays of G.C. Harcourt*, London, Routledge.
Harcourt, G.C. (1992b) 'Reflections on the development of economics as a discipline', in C. Sardoni (ed.) *On Political Economists and Modern Political Economy: Selected Essays of G.C. Harcourt*, London, Routledge.
Harcourt, G.C. and Kenyon, P. (1976) 'Pricing and the investment decision', *Kyklos*, 29, 449–477. Reprinted in C.Sardoni (ed.) *On Political Economists and Modern Political Economy: Selected Essays of G.C. Harcourt*, London, Routledge.
Harcourt, G.C. and King, J.E. (1995) 'Talking about Joan Robinson: Geoff Harcourt in conversation with John King', *Review of Social Economy*, 53(1), 31–64.
Harcourt, G.C. and Spajic, L.D. (1997) *Post Keynesianism*, working Paper, University of Cambridge.
Hargreaves Heap, S.P. (1986–7) 'Risk and culture: a missing link in the Post Keynesian tradition', *Journal of Post Keynesian Economics*, 9(2), 267–278.
Harley, S. and Lee, F.S. (1997) 'Research selectivity, managerialism, and the academic labor process: the future of non-mainstream economics in U.K. universities', *Human Relations*, 50(11), 1427–1460.
Harrod, R.F. (1972) 'Imperfect competition, aggregate demand and inflation', *Economic Journal*, 82, 392–401.
Hauck, K., Shaw, R. and Smith, P. (2002) 'Reducing avoidable inequalities in health: a new criterion for setting health care capitation payments' *Health Economics*, 11, 667–677.
Hayek, F.A. (1937) 'Economics and knowledge', *Economica*, IV (N.S.), 33–54.
Hayek, F.A. (1967) 'The theory of complex phenomena', in F.A. Hayek, *Studies in Philosophy, Politics, and Economics*, London, Routledge & Kegan Paul, pp. 22–42.
Heilbroner, R. and Milberg, W. (1995) *The Crisis of Vision in Modern Economic Thought*, Cambridge, UK, Cambridge University Press.

Hendry, D.F. and Doornik, J.A. (1997) 'The implications for econometric modelling of forecast failure', *Scottish Journal of Political Economy*, 44, 437–471.

Henry, J.F. (1984–85) 'On equilibrium', *Journal of Post Keynesian Economics*, 6(2), 214–222.

Henry, J.F. and Wray, L.R. (1998) 'Economic time', *The Jerome Levy Economics Institute*, Working Paper No. 255.

Henry, S.G.B., Sawyer, M.C. and Smith, P. (1976) 'Models of inflation in the UK: an evaluation', *National Institute Economic Review*, 76.

Hey, J.D. (1995) 'Managing editors' Annual Report on the EJ", *Royal Economic Society Newsletter*, 88, January.

Hicks, J.R. (1977) *Economic Perspectives*, Oxford, Oxford University Press.

Hicks, J.R. (1979) *Causality in Economics*, Oxford, Basil Blackwell.

Hodgson, G.M. (1985) 'Persuasion, expectations and the limits to Keynes', in T. Lawson, and H. Pesaran, (eds) *Keynes' Economics: Methodological Issues*, London, Croom Helm.

Hodgson, G.M. (1986) 'Behind methodological individualism', *Cambridge Journal of Economics*, 10(3), 211–224.

Hodgson, G.M. (1988) *Economics and Institutions*, Oxford, Polity Press.

Hodgson, G.M. (1989) 'Post Keynesianism and Institutionalism: the missing link', in Pheby, J. (ed.) *New Directions in Post Keynesian Economics*, Aldershot, Edward Elgar.

Hodgson, G.M. (1993) *Economics and Evolution: Bringing Life Back into Economics*, Cambridge, Polity Press.

Hodgson, G.M. (1994) 'Optimisation and evolution: Winter's critique of Friedman revisited', *Cambridge Journal of Economics*, 18(4), 413–430.

Hodgson, G.M. (1996) 'Corporate culture and the nature of the firm', in J. Groenewegen (ed.) *Transaction Cost Economics and Beyond*, Boston, Kluwer, pp. 249–269.

Hodgson, G.M. (1997a) 'The fate of the Cambridge capital controversy', in P. Arestis and M.C. Sawyer (eds) *Capital Controversy, Post Keynesian Economics and the History of Economics: Essays in Honour of Geoff Harcourt*, London, Routledge, pp. 95–110.

Hodgson, G.M. (1997b) 'The ubiquity of habits and rules', *Cambridge Journal of Economics*, 21(6), 663–684.

Hodgson, G.M. (1998a) 'Competence and contract in the theory of the firm', *Journal of Economic Behaviour and Organisation*, 35, 179–201.

Hodgson, G.M. (1998b) 'Evolutionary and competence based theories of the firm', *Journal of Economic Studies*, 25(1), 25–56.

Hodgson, G.M. (1998c) 'The approach of institutional economics', *Journal of Economic Literature*, 36(1), 166–192.

Hodgson, G.M. (1999a) *Economics and Utopia: Why the Learning Economy is not the End of History*, London, Routledge.

Hodgson, G.M. (1999b) 'Transaction costs and the evolution of the firm', in *Evolution and Institutions: On Evolutionary Economics and the Evolution of Economics*, Cheltenham, Edward Elgar, pp. 199–219.

Hodgson, G.M. (1999c) 'Post Keynesianism and Institutionalism: another look at the link', in M. Setterfield (ed.) *Growth, Employment and Inflation: Essays in Honour of John Cornwall*, London, Macmillan, pp. 72–87.

Hodgson, G.M. (2000a) 'What is the essence of institutional economics?', *Journal of Economic Issues*, 34(2), 317–330.

Hodgson, G.M. (2000b) 'Shackle and institutional economics: some bridges and barriers', in P. Earl (ed.) *Essays in Honour of G.L.S. Shackle*, London, Routledge.

Hodgson, G.M. (2001a) *How Economics Forgot History: The Problem of Historical Specificity in Social Science*, London, Routledge.

Hodgson, G.M. (2001b) 'From Veblen to Galbraith: what is the essence of institutional economics?', in M. Keaney (ed.) *Economist with a Public Purpose: Essays in Honour of John Kenneth Galbraith*, London, Routledge.

Hodgson, G.M. (2001c) 'Frank Knight as an institutional economist', in J. Biddle, J.B. Davis, and S.G. Medema, (eds) *Econmics Broadly Considered: Essays in Honour of Warren J. Samuels*, London, Routledge.

Hodgson, G.M. (2004) *The Evolution of Institutional Economics*, London, Routledge.

Hodgson, G.M. (2006) *Economics in the Shadows of Darwin and Marx: Essays on Institutional Themes*, Cheltenham, Edward Elgar.

Hodgson, G.M. and Rothman, H. (1999) 'The editors and authors of economic journals: a case of institutional oligopoly?', *Economic Journal*, 109(453), F165–F186.

Holt, R.P.F. (1996) 'What is Post Keynesian Economics?' Paper presented at the 4th Post Keynesian Workshop, June-July, Knoxville, TN, USA.

Holt, R.P.F. and Pressman, S. (2001) (eds) *The New Guide to Post Keynesian Economics*, London, Routledge.

Holt, R.P.F., Rosser, J.B. and Wray, L.R. (1998) 'Paul Davidson: the truest Keynesian?', *Eastern Economic Journal*, 24(4), 495–506.

Hoover, K. (1995) 'Why does methodology matter for economics?', *Economic Journal*, 105(430), 715–734.

Horgan, J. (1997) *The End of Science: Facing the Limits of Knowledge in the Twilight of the Age of Science*, New York, Broadway Books.

IMS Health (2001) *US Leading Products by DTC Spend. January 2000–December 2000*. IMS Health Inc. [http://www.imshealth.com/public/structure/dispcontent/1,2779,1203–1203–143221,00.html].

Institute of Medicine (2001) *Crossing the Quality Chasm*, Washington, National Academy Press.

Ioannides, S. (1999) 'Towards an Austrian perspective on the firm', *Review of Austrian Economics*, 11, 77–97.

Jackson, W.A. (1998) *The Political Economy of Population Ageing*, Cheltenham, Edward Elgar.

Jenkins, S. (1993) *The Times*, 3 February.

Jensen, H.E. (1983) 'J.M. Keynes as a Marshallian', *Journal of Economic Issues*, March, 67–94.

Jensen, H.E. (1990) 'Are there Institutionalist signposts in the economics of Alfred Marshall?', *Journal of Economic Issues*, 24(2), 405–413.

Kaldor, N. (1934) 'The equilibrium of the firm', *Economic Journal*, 44(March), 60–76.

Kaldor, N. (1959) 'Economic growth and the problem of inflation: Part 2', *Economica*, 26(4), 287–298.

Kaldor, N. (1970) 'The case for regional policies', *Scottish Journal of Political Economy*, 17(3), 337–348.

Kaldor, N. (1972) 'The irrelevance of equilibrium economics', *Economic Journal*, 82, 1237–1255.

Kaldor, N. (1978) *Further Essays on Economic Theory*, London, Duckworth.

Kaldor, N. (1983) 'Keynesian economics after fifty years', in D. Worswick, and J. Tevithick, (eds) *Keynes and the Modern World*, Cambridge, Cambridge University Press.

Kaldor, N. (1985) *Economics without equilibrium*, Cardiff, University College Press.

Kaldor, N. and Robinson, J. (2000) 'Profit margins Inquiry. Note on alternative hypotheses as to the determination of profit margins', *Review of Political Economy*, 12(3), 267–271.

Kalecki, M. (1934) 'Trzy uklady', *Ekonomista, Vol. 3* (English version appears in Kalecki, 1990).

Kalecki, M. (1939) *Essays in the Theory of Economic Fluctuations*, London, Allen and Unwin.

Kalecki, M. (1940) 'The supply curve of an industry under imperfect competition', *Review of Economic Studies*, 7, 91–112.

Kalecki, M. (1954) *Theory of Economic Dynamics*, London, Allen and Unwin.

Kalecki, M. (1968) 'Trend and the business cycle', *Economic Journal*, 78, 263–276.

Kalecki, M. (1971) *Selected Essays on the Dynamics of the Capitalist Economy*, Cambridge, Cambridge University Press.

Kalecki, M. (1990) *Capitalism: Business Cycles and Full Employment, Collected Works*, Vol. 1, (ed.) J. Osiatynski, Oxford, Clarendon Press.

Kay, N. (1984) *The Emergent Firm: Knowledge, Ignorance and Surprise in Economic Organisation*, London, Macmillan.

Kay, N. (1989) 'Post Keynesian economics and new approaches to industrial economics', in J. Pheby, (ed.) *New Directions in Post Keynesian Economics*, Aldershot, Edward Elgar.

Kenyon, P. (1980) 'Discussion: of Tarshis (1980)', *American Economic Review*, 70(2), 26–28.

Keynes, J.M. (1921) *Treatise on Probability*. Reprinted in J.M. Keynes (1973) *The Collected Writings of J.M. Keynes*, Vol. VIII, London, Macmillan for the Royal Economic Society.

Keynes, J.M. (1926) *The End of Laissez Faire*, London, Hogarth Press. Reprinted in J.M. Keynes (1973) *The Collected Writings of J.M. Keynes*, Vol. IX, *Essays in Persuasion*, London, Macmillan for the Royal Economic Society.

Keynes, J.M. (1930a) *A Treatise on Money, 1: The Pure Theory of Money*. Reprinted in J.M. Keynes (1971) *The Collected Writings of J.M. Keynes*, Vol. V, London, Macmillan for the Royal Economic Society.

Keynes, J.M. (1930b) *A Treatise on Money, 2: The Applied Theory of Money* Reprinted in J.M. Keynes (1971) *The Collected Writings of J.M. Keynes*, Vol. VI, London, Macmillan for the Royal Economic Society.

Keynes, J.M. (1930c) 'Economic possibilities for our grandchildren', *The Nation and Athenaeum*, 11 and 18 October. Reprinted in *Essays in Persuasion*, London, Rupert Hart-Davis, 1951.

Keynes, J.M. (1931) *Essays in Persuasion*. Reprinted in J.M. Keynes (1972) *The Collected Writings of J.M. Keynes*, Vol. IX, London, Macmillan for the Royal Economic Society.

Keynes, J.M. (1933) *Essays in Biography*. Reprinted in J. M. Keynes (1973) *The Collected Writings of J.M. Keynes*, Vol. X, London, Macmillan for the Royal Economic Society.

Keynes, J.M. (1934) 'Poverty in the midst of plenty: is the economic system self adjusting?', *The Listener*. Reprinted in J.M. Keynes (1973b) *The Collected Writings of J.M. Keynes*, Vol. XIII, *The General Theory and After: Part I, Preparation*, London, Macmillan for the Royal Economic Society.

Keynes, J.M. (1936) *The General Theory of Employment, Interest and Money*, Macmillan, London. Reprinted in J.M. Keynes (1973) *The Collected Writings of J.M. Keynes*, Vol. VII, London, Macmillan for the Royal Economic Society.

Keynes, J.M. (1937) 'The General Theory of Employment', *Quarterly Journal of Economics*, February, Vol. 51, pp. 209–223. Reprinted in J.M. Keynes (1973c) *The Collected Writings of J.M. Keynes*, Vol. XIV, *The General Theory and After: Part II, Defence and Development*, London, Macmillan for the Royal Economic Society.

Keynes, J.M. (1939) 'Relative movements of real wages and money wages', *Economic Journal*, 49(1), 34–51.

Keynes, J.M. (1973a) *The Collected Writings of J.M. Keynes*, Vol. XII, *Economic Articles and Correspondence*, London, Macmillan for the Royal Economic Society.

Keynes, J.M. (1973b) *The Collected Writings of J.M. Keynes*, Vol. XIII, *The General Theory and After: Part I, Preparation*, London, Macmillan for the Royal Economic Society.

Keynes, J.M. (1973c) *The Collected Writings of J.M. Keynes*, Vol. XIV, *The General Theory and After: Part II, Defence and Development*, London, Macmillan for the Royal Economic Society.

Keynes, J.M. (1979) *The Collected Writings of J.M. Keynes*, Vol. XXIX, *The General Theory and After: A Supplement*, London, Macmillan for the Royal Economic Society.

Keynes, J.M. (1982) *The Collected Writings of J.M. Keynes*, Vol. XXVIII, *Social, Political and Literary Writings*, London, Macmillan for the Royal Economic Society.

King, J.E. (1995) *Conversations with Post Keynesians*, London, Macmillan.

King, J.E. (1996) *Post Keynesian Economics: an Annotated Bibliography*, Aldershot, Edward Elgar.

King, J.E. (2002) (ed.) *A History of Post Keynesian Economics since 1936*, Cheltenham, Edward Elgar.

King, J.E. (2003) (ed.) *The Elgar Companion to Post Keynesian Economics*, Cheltenham, Edward Elgar.

King, M. (1992) 'Fisher on methodology' (letter to the editor), *Royal Economic Society Newsletter*, 79, October.

Kirzner, I.M. (1973) *Competition and Entrepreneurship*, Chicago, University of Chicago Press.

Kirzner, I.M. (1985) 'Uncertainty, discovery, and human action', in I.M. Kirzner, *Discovery and the Capitalist Process*, Chicago, University of Chicago Press, 1985.

Kirzner, I.M. (1997) 'Entrepreneurial discovery and the competitive market process: an Austrian approach', *Journal of Economic Literature*, 35, 60–85.

Kirzner, I.M. (1999) 'Creativity and/or alertness: A reconsideration of the Schumpeterian Entrepreneur', *Review of Austrian Economics*, 11, 5–17.

Klamer, A. (1984) *The New Classical Macroeconomics: Conversations with New Classical Economists and their Opponents*, Brighton, Wheatsheaf.

Klein, P.A. (1988) 'Of paradigms and politics', *Journal of Economic Issues*, June, 435–441.

Klein, P.A. (1990) 'Institutionalism as a school – a reconsideration', *Journal of Economic Issues*, June, 381–388.

Klein, P.A. (1992) 'Institutionalists, radical economists, and class', *Journal of Economic Issues*, June, 535–544.

Klein, P.A. (1994) 'A reassessment of Institutionalist–mainstream relations', *Journal of Economic Issues*, March, 197–207.

Klein, P.G. (1999) 'Entrepreneurship and corporate governance', *Quarterly Journal of Austrian Economics*, 2(2), 19–42.

Knight, F.H. (1921) *Risk, Uncertainty and Profit*, London, LSE, reprinted 1946.

Koppl, R. (1991) 'Animal Spirits', *Journal of Economic Perspectives*, 5, 203–210.

Kregel, J.A. (1973) *The Reconstruction of Political Economy: an Introduction to Post-Keynesian Economics*, London, Macmillan.

Kregel, J.A. (1976) 'Economic methodology in the face of uncertainty: the modelling methods of Keynes and the Post Keynesians', *Economic Journal*, 86, 209–225.

Kregel, J.A. (1977) 'On the existence of expectations in English neoclassical economics', *Journal of Economic Literature*, 15(2), 495–500.

Kregel, J.A. (1980) 'The theoretical consequences of economic methodology: Samuelson's foundations', *Metroeconomica*, 32(1), 25–38.

Kregel, J.A. (1983) 'The microfoundations of the "Generalisation of the General Theory" and "Bastard Keynesianism": Keynes' theory of employment in the long and the short period', *Cambridge Journal of Economics*, 7, 343–361.

Kregel, J.A. (1986) 'Conceptions of equilibrium: the logic of choice and the logic of production', in I.M. Kirzner (ed.) *Subjectivism, Intelligibility and Economic Understanding: Essays in Honor of Ludwig M. Lachmann on his Eightieth Birthday*, New York, New York University Press, pp. 157–170.

Kregel, J.A. (1998a) 'Keynes and the new Keynesians on market competition', in R.J. Rotheim (ed.) *New Keynesian Economics/Post Keynesian Alternatives*, London, Routledge, pp. 39–50.

Kregel, J.A. (1998b) 'Aspects of a Post Keynesian theory of finance', *Journal of Post Keynesian Economics*, 21(1), 3–10.

Kriesler, P. (1987) *Kalecki's Microanalysis*, Cambridge, Cambridge University Press.

Krugman, P. (1998a) 'The hangover theory: Are recessions the inevitable payback for good times? More on the Dismal Science', *Slate Magazine*, December.

Krugman, P. (1998b) 'Two cheers for formalism', *Economic Journal*, 108(451), 1829–1836.

Langlois, R.N. (1984) 'Internal organisation in a dynamic context: some theoretical consideration', in M. Jussawalla and H. Ebenfield (eds) *Communication and Information Economics*. Amsterdam, North-Holland.

Langlois, R.N. (1988) 'Economic change and the boundaries of the firm', *Journal of Institutional and Theoretical Economics*, 144, 635–657.

Langlois, R.N. (1992) 'Orders and organizations: toward an Austrian theory of social institutions', in B. Caldwell and S. Boehm (eds) *Austrian Economics: Tensions and New Directions*, Boston, Kluwer.

Langlois, R.N. (1995a) 'Transaction costs, production costs and the passage of time', in S.G. Medema (ed.) *Coasean Economics*, Dordrecht, Kluwer. (Page references are to the mimeo.)

Langlois, R.N. (1995b) 'Do firms plan?', *Constitutional Political Economy*, 6, 247–261.

Langlois, R.N. and Everett, M. (1992) 'Complexity, genuine uncertainty, and the economics of organisation', *Human Systems Management*, 11, 67–76.

Langlois, R.N. and Foss, N. (1999) 'Capabilities and governance: the rebirth of production in the theory of economic organization,' *Kylos*, 52, 201–218.

Langlois, R.N. and Robertson, P. (1995) *Firms, Markets and Economic Change*, London, Routledge.

Langlois, R.N. and Foss, N.J. (1998) 'Capabilities and governance: the rebirth of production in the theory of economic organization,' *Kylos*, 52, 201–218.

Lanzillotti, R.F. (1958) 'Pricing objectives in large companies', *American Economic Review*, 48(5), 921–940.

Lanzillotti, R.F. (1964) *Pricing, Production and the Marketing Policies of Small Manufacturers*, Pullman, Washington State University Press.

Lavoie, M. (1992) *Foundations of Post-Keynesian Economic Analysis*, Aldershot, Edward Elgar.

Lavoie, M. (1994) 'A Post Keynesian approach to consumer choice', *Journal of Post Keynesian Economics*, 16(4), 539–562.

Lavoie, M. (1996a) 'Horizontalism, structuralism, liquidity preference and the principle of increasing risk', *Scottish Journal of Political Economy*, 43(3), 275–300.

Lavoie, M. (1996b) 'Mark-up pricing versus normal cost pricing in Post Keynesian models', *Review of Political Economy*, 8, 91–100.

Lawson, C. (1994) 'The transformational model of social activity and economic analysis: a reinterpretation of the work of J.R. Commons', *Review of Political Economy*, 6(2), 186–204.

Lawson, C., Peacock, M. and Pratten, S. (1996) 'Realism, underlabouring and institutions', *Cambridge Journal of Economics*, 20, 137–151.

Lawson, T. (1985) 'Uncertainty and economic analysis', *Economic Journal*, 95, 909–927.

Lawson, T. (1987) 'The relative/absolute nature of knowledge and economic analysis', *Economic Journal*, 97, 951–970.

Lawson, T. (1989a) 'Abstraction, tendencies and stylised facts: a realist approach to economic analysis', *Cambridge Journal of Economics*, 13, 59–78.

Lawson, T. (1989b) 'Realism and instrumentalism in the development of econometrics', *Oxford Economic Papers*, 41(1), 236–258.

Lawson, T. (1992) 'Methodology: non-optional and consequential' (letter to the editor), *Royal Economic Society Newsletter*, 79, October, 2–3.

Lawson, T. (1994a) 'The nature of Post Keynesianism and its links to other traditions: a realist perspective', *Journal of Post Keynesian Economics*, 16(4), 503–538. Reprinted in D.L. Prychitko (ed.) *Why Economists Disagree: An Introduction to the Contemporary Schools of Thought*, New York, State University of New York Press.

Lawson, T. (1994b) 'Realism and Hayek: A case of continuous transformation', in M. Colonna, H. Hagemann and O.F. Hamouda (eds) *Capitalism, Socialism and Information: The Economics of F.A. Hayek, Volume II*, Cheltenham, Edward Elgar.

Lawson, T. (1994c) 'Why are so many economists so oppposed to methodology?', *Journal of Economic Methodology*, 1(1), 105–134.

Lawson, T. (1995a) 'A Realist perspective on contemporary "economic theory"', *Journal of Economic Issues*, 29(1), 1–32.

Lawson, T. (1995b) 'The "Lucas critique": A generalisation', *Cambridge Journal of Economics*, 19(2), 257–276.

Lawson, T. (1996a) 'Developments in economics as Realist social theory', *Review of Social Economy*, 54(4), 405–422. Reprinted in S. Fleetwood (ed.) *Critical Realism in Economics: Development and Debate*, London, Routledge, 1999.

Lawson, T. (1996b) 'The predictive science of economics?', in S. Medema, and W. Samuels, (eds) *How Should Economists Do Economics?*, Cheltenham, Edward Elgar.

Lawson, T. (1996c) 'Keynes and Hayek: a commonality', *History of Economics Review*, 25(Winter–Summer), 96–114.

Lawson, T. (1997a) *Economics and Reality*, London, Routledge.

Lawson, T. (1997b) 'Horses for courses', in P. Arestis and M. Sawyer (eds) *Markets, Unemployment and Economic Policy: Essays in Honour of Geoff Harcourt*, Vol. II, London, Routledge.

Lawson, T. (1998a) 'Social relations, social reproduction and stylized facts', in P. Arestis (ed.) *Method Theory and Policy in Keynes: Essays in Honour of Paul Davidson, Vol. 3*, Cheltenham, Edward Elgar.

Lawson, T. (1998b) 'Clarifying and developing the economics and reality project: closed and open-system, deductivism, prediction and teaching', *Review of Social Economy* 56, 356–375.

Lawson, T. (1999a) 'Connections and distinctions: Post Keynesianism and critical realism', *Journal of Post Keynesian Economics*, 22(1), 3–14.

Lawson, T. (1999b) 'Economics and explanation', *Revue Internationale de Philosophie* (special issue on the philosophy of economics).

Lawson, T. (1999c) 'Feminism, realism and universalism', *Feminist Economics*, 5(2), 25–59.

Lawson, T. (2003) *Reorienting Economics*, London, Routledge.

Lawson, T. (2004a) 'Philosophical under-labouring in the context of modern economics: aiming at truth and usefulness in the meanest of ways', in John Davis, Alain Marciano and Jochen Runde (eds) *The Elgar Companion of Economics and Philosophy*, Aldershot, Edward Elgar.

Lawson, T. (2004b) 'Modern economics: the problem and a solution', in Edward Fullbrook (ed.) *The Student's Guide to What's Wrong with Economics*, London, Anthem Press (an imprint of Wimbledon Publishing Company).

Lawson, T. (2004c) 'Reorienting economics: on heterodox economics, themata and the uses of mathematics in economics', *Journal of Economic Methodology*, 11(3), 329–340.

Lawson, T. (2005a) 'Methodological issues in the study of gender', in Nobuko Hara (ed.) *Gender Study: Theory, History and Policy*, Tokyo, Hosei University Press.

Lawson, T. (2005b) 'A perspective on modern economics', in George Steinmetz (ed.) *The Politics of Method in the Human Sciences*, Durham, USA, Duke University Press, pp. 366–392.

Lawson, T. (2005c) 'The (confused) state of equilibrium analysis in modern economics: an (ontological) explanation', *Journal of Post Keynesian Economics*, 27(3), 423–444.

Lawson, T. (2006a) 'The nature of heterodox economics', *Cambridge Journal of Economics*, 30(2), 483–507.

Lawson, T. (2006b) 'The nature of institutionalist economics', *Evolutionary and Institutional Economics Review*, 2(1), 7–20.

Lawson, T. (2006c) 'Tensions in modern economics. The case of equilibrium analysis', in Valeria Mosini (ed.) *Equilibrium in Economics: Scope and Limits,* London, Routledge.

Lawson, T. (2007a) 'Gender and social change', in Jude Brown (ed.) *The Future of Gender*, Cambridge, Cambridge University Press, pp. 136–162.

Lawson, T. (2007b) 'An orientation for a green economics?', *International Journal of Green Economics*, 1(3/4), 250–267.

Lazonick, W. (1991) *Business Organisation and the Myth of the Market Economy*, Cambridge, Cambridge University Press.

Le Grand, J. (1997) 'Knights, knaves or pawns? Human behaviour and social policy', *Journal of Social Policy*, 26, 149–169.

Le Grand, J. (2000) 'From knight to knave? Public policy and market incentives', in P. Taylor-Gooby (ed.) *Risk, Trust and Welfare*, Houndmills, Macmillan.

Lee, F.S. (1981) 'The Oxford challenge to Marshallian supply and demand: the history of the Oxford Economists' Research Group", *Oxford Economic Papers*, 33(3), 340.

Lee, F.S. (1985) '"Full cost" prices, classical price theory, and long period method analysis: a critical evaluation', *Metroeconomica*, 37(2), 199–220.

Lee, F.S. (1986) 'Post Keynesian view of average direct costs: a critical evaluation of the theory and empirical evidence', *Journal of Post Keynesian Economics*, 8(3), 400–424.

Lee, F.S. (1988) 'A New Dealer in agriculture: G. C. Means and the writing of industrial prices', *Review of Social Economy*, 46, 180–202.

Lee, F.S. (1989) 'G. C. Means's doctrine of administered prices', *Thames Papers in Political Economy*, Summer. Reprinted in P. Arestis, and Y. Kitromilides, (eds) *Theory and Policy in Political Economy: Essays in Pricing Distribution and Growth*, Cheltenham, Edward Elgar, 1990.

Lee, F.S. (1990) 'The modern corporation and Gardiner Mean's critique of neoclassical economics', *Journal of Economic Issues*, 24(3), 673–693.

Lee, F.S. (1990–91) 'Marginalist controversy and Post Keynesian price theory', *Journal of Post Keynesian Economics*, 13.

Lee, F.S. (1991) 'The history of the Oxford challenge to Marginalism, 1934–1952', *Banca Nazionale del Lavoro Quarterly Review*, 179.

Lee, F.S. (1994) 'From post Keynesian to historical price theory, part 1: Facts, theory and empirically grounded pricing model', *Review of Political Economy*, 6(3), 303–336.

Lee, F.S. (1995a) 'From post Keynesian to historical price theory, part 2: Facts, theory and empirically grounded pricing model', *Review of Political Economy*, 7(1), 72–124.

Lee, F.S. (1995b) 'The death of Post Keynesianism', *Post Keynesian Economics Study Group Newsletter*, 4.

Lee, F.S. (1996) 'Pricing, the pricing model and post-Keynesian price theory', *Review of Political Economy*, 8(1), 87–99.

Lee, F.S. (1997) 'Philanthropic foundations and the rehabilitation of big business, 1934–1977: a case study of directed economic research', *Research in the History of Economic Thought and Methodology*, 15.

Lee, F.S. (1998) *Post Keynesian Price Theory*, Cambridge, Cambridge University Press.

Lee, F.S. (2000a) (ed.) 'On the genesis of Post Keynesian economics: Alfred S. Eichner, Joan Robinson and the founding of Post Keynesian economics', in *Research in the History of Economic Thought and Methodology*, Vol. 18-C, Twentieth-Century Economics, JAI, Elsevier, 2000.

Lee, F.S. (2000b) 'The social history of Post Keynesian economics in America, 1971–1995', *Journal of Post Keynesian Economics*, 23(1), 141–162.

Lee, F.S. (2002) 'Theory creation and the methodological foundation of Post Keynesian economics', *Cambridge Journal of Economics*, 26(6), 789–804.

Lee, F.S. (2007) 'The research assessment exercise, the state and the dominance of mainstream economics in British universities', *Cambridge Journal of Economics*, 31(2), 309–325.

Lee, F.S. and Samuels, W.J. (1992) *The Heterodox Economics of Gardiner C. Means: A Collection*, New York, M.E. Sharpe.

Lee, F.S. and Earl, P.E. (1993) *The Economics of P.W.S. Andrews: A Collection*, Aldershot, Edward Elgar, 1993.

Lee, F.S. and Young, W. (1993) *Oxford Economics and Oxford Economists*, London, Macmillan.

Lee, F.S. and Harley, S. (1998) 'Peer review, the research assessment exercise and the demise of nonmainstream economics', *Capital and Class*, 66, 22–51.

Lee, F.S., Irving-Lesman, J., Earl, P. and Davies, J. (1986) 'P.W.S. Andrews' theory of competitive oligopoly: a new interpretation, *British Review of Economic Issues*, 8(19), 13–40.

Leijonhufvud, A. (1993) 'Towards a not-too-rational macroeconomics', *Southern Economic Journal*, 60(1), 1–13.

Leontief, W.W. (1951) *The structure of the American Economy, 1919–1939*, 2nd edn (enlarged), White Plains, New York: International Arts and Sciences Press.

Leslie, T.E.C. (1888) *Essays in Political Economy*, 2nd edition. (1st edition 1879), London, Longmans, Green.

Lewin, P. and Phelan, S.E. (2000) 'An Austrian theory of the firm', *Review of Austrian Economics*, 13, 59–79.

Lewis, P. and Runde, J. (1999) 'A critical realist perspective on Paul Davidson's methodological writings on – and rhetorical strategy for – Post Keynesian economics', *Journal of Post Keynesian Economics*, 22(1), 35–56.

Littlechild, S.C. (1986) *The Fallacy of the Mixed Economy*, 2nd edition, Hobart Paper 80, London, Institute for Economic Affairs.

Loasby, B.J. (1967) 'Management economics and the theory of the firm', *Journal of Industrial Economics*, 15, 165–176. Reprinted in P.E. Earl (ed.) *Behavioural Economics: Volume 1*, Edward Elgar, Aldershot, 1988.

Loasby, B.J. (1976) *Choice, Complexity and Ignorance: An Enquiry into Economic theory and Practise of Decision Making*, Cambridge, Cambridge University Press.

Loasby, B.J. (1983) 'G.L.S. Shackle as historian of economic thought', in W.J. Samuels (ed.) *Research in the History of Economic Thought and Methodology*, Vol. 1, Greenwich, CT, JAI Press, pp. 209–221.

Loasby, B.J. (1989) *The Mind and Method of the Economist*, Aldershot, Edward Elgar.

Loasby, B.J. (1991) *Equilibrium and Evolution*, Manchester, Manchester University Press.

Lucas, R.E. and Rapping, L.A. (1969) 'Real wages, employment and inflation', *Journal of Political Economy*, 77, 721–754.

Lucas, R.E. and Rapping, L.A. (1970) 'Price expectations and the Phillips curve', *American Economic Review*, 59, 342–350.

McGuire, T.G. (2000) 'Physician agency', in A. Culyer and J. Newhouse (eds) *A Handbook of Health Economics: Volume 1A*, London, Elsevier.

Machin, S. and Oswald, A. (2000) 'UK economics and the future supply of academic economists', *Economic Journal*, 110, 334–349.

McKenna, E.J. and Zannoni, D.C. (1999) 'Post Keynesian economics and critical realism: a reply to Parsons', *Journal of Post Keynesian Economics*, 22(1), 57–70.

McMaster, R. (2001) 'The National Health Service, the "internal market" and trust', in J.B. Davis, (ed.) *The Social Economics of Health Care*, London, Routledge.

Malcolmson, D. (1984) 'Efficient labour organisations: incentives, power and the transaction cost approach' in F. Stephen (ed.) *Firm Organisations and Labour*, London, Macmillan.

Marchionatti, R. (1998) 'On Keynes's animal spirits', *Kyklos*, 52, 415–439.

Marglin, S. (1974) 'What do bosses do? The origins and functions of hierarchy in capitalist production', *Review of Radical Political Economics*, 6, 60–112.

Marris, R. (1964) *The Economic Theory of 'Managerial' Capitalism*, London, Macmillan.

Marris, R. and Mueller, D. (1980) 'The corporation, competition and the invisible hand'. (Originally published in *Journal of Economic Literature*) Reprinted in D. Mueller (ed.) *The Modern Corporation: Profits, Power, Growth and Performance*, London, Harvester Wheatsheaf, 1986.

Marshall, A. (1920) *Principles of Economics*, London, Macmillan.

Marshall, M.N., Shekelle, P.G., Davies, H.T.O. and Smith, P.C. (2003) 'Public reporting on quality in the United States and the United Kingdom', *Health Affairs*, 22(3), 134–148.

Marx, K. (1976) *Capital*, Vol. 1. (translated by B. Fowkes), Harmondsworth, Penguin.

Maynard, A. and Kanavos, P. (2000) 'Health economics: an evolving paradigm', *Health Economics*, 9, 183–190.

Means, G.C. (1933) 'The corporate revolution', in *G.C. Means Papers, Series 1*, cited in Lee, F.S. (1990).

Means, G.C. (1935) 'Industrial prices and their relative inflexibility', *U.S. Senate Document 13, 74th Congress, 1st Session*, Washington, DC.

Means, G.C. (1936) 'Notes on inflexible prices', *American Economic Review*, 26, Supplement.

Means, G.C. (1962) *Pricing power and the public interest*, New York, Harper and Brothers.

Means, G.C. (1972) 'The administered price thesis reconfirmed', *American Economic Review*, 62, 292–306.

Mearman, A. (2002a) *A Contribution to the Methodology of Post Keynesian Economics*, PhD, thesis, Leeds, University of Leeds.

Mearman, A. (2002b) 'To what extent is Veblen an open-systems theorist?', *Journal of Economic Issues*, 36(2), 573–580.

Mearman, A. (2006) 'Critical realism in economics and open-systems ontology: a critique', *Review of Social Economy*, 64(1), 47–75.

Meeks, J.G.T. (1991) 'Keynes on the rationality of decision procedures under uncertainty: the investment decision', in Meeks, J.G.T. (ed.) *Thoughtful Economic Man: Essays on Rationality, Moral Rules and Benevolence*, Cambridge, Cambridge University Press.

Minsky, H.P. (1975) *John Maynard Keynes*, New York, Columbia University Press.

Minsky, H.P. (1996) 'Uncertainty and the institutional structure of capitalist economies', *Journal of Economic Issues*, 30(2), 357–368.

Mongiovi, G. (1994) 'Capital, expectations, and economic equilibrium: some notes on Lachmann and the so-called "Cambridge School"', *Advances in Austrian Economics*, 1, 257–277.

Mongiovi, G. (2000) 'Shackle on equilibrium: a critique', *Review of Social Economy*, 58(1), 108–124.

Moore, B. (1988) *Horizontalists and Verticalists*, Cambridge, Cambridge University Press.

Moynihan, R. (2003a) 'The making of a disease: female sexual dysfunction', *British Medical Journal*, 326, 45–47.

Moynihan, R. (2003b) 'Who pays for the pizza? Redefining the relationships between doctors and drug companies. 2: Disentanglement', *British Medical Journal*, 326, 1193–1196.

Moynihan, R., Heath, I. and Henry, D. (2002) 'Selling sickness: the pharmaceutical industry and disease mongering', *British Medical Journal*, 324, 886–891.

Munford, K. (1999) 'What is happening to the UK graduate student in economics?', *Royal Economic Society Newsletter*, 104, January.

Mushkin, S.J. (1962) 'Health as investment', *Journal of Political Economy*, 70, 129–157.

Myrdal, G. (1957) *Economic Theory and Underdeveloped Regions*, London, Duckworth.

Nash, S.J. (2000) *Implicit Contracts, Uncertainty, and Moral Hazard: An Elaboration of the Knightian Theory of the Firm*, unpublished PhD, Dissertation, Cambridge, Cambridge University.

Nelson, R. and Winter, S. (1982) *An Evolutionary Theory of Economic Change*, Cambridge, MA, Harvard University Press.

Northover, P. (1999) 'Evolutionary growth theory and forms of realism', *Cambridge Journal of Economics*, 23, 33–63.

O'Donnell, R.M. (1989) *Keynes: Philosophy, Economics and Politics*, Macmillan, London.

O'Donnell, R.M. (1991) (ed.) *Keynes as Philosopher-Economist*, London, Macmillan, pp. 3–102.

O'Donnell, R.M. (1995) 'Keynes on aesthetics', in A.F. Cottrell and M.S. Lawlor (eds) *New Perspectives on Keynes: Annual Supplement to Volume 27, History of Political Economy*, Durham and London, Duke University Press.

O'Driscoll, G.P. and Rizzo, M.J. (1995) *The Eonomics of Time and Ignorance*, 2nd edition, London, Routledge.

Okun, A.M. (1981) *Prices and Quantities*, Washington, DC, Brookings Institute.

Ormerod, P. (1994) *The Death of Economics*, London, Faber and Faber.

Ormerod, P. (2000) 'The *Death of Economics* revisited', Keynote address to the Association of Heterodox Economics, London, June.

Ouchi, W. (1980) 'Markets, bureaucracies and clans', *Administrative Science Quarterly*, 25, 129–141.

Parker Foster, G. (1986) 'The endogeneity of money and Keynes's general theory', *Journal of Economic Issues*, December, 953–968.

Parker Foster, G. (1990) 'Keynes and Kalecki on saving and profit: some implications', *Journal of Economic Issues*, June, 415–422.

Parker Foster, G. (1991) 'The compatibility of Keynes's ideas with Institutionalist philosophy', *Journal of Economic Issues*, June, 561–568.

Parker, R. (1993) 'Can economists save economics?', *The American Prospect*, 13, Spring.

Parry, W. (1987) 'Ergodic theory', in J. Eatwell, M. Milgate and P. Newman (eds) *The New Palgrave*, London, Macmillan.

Pasinetti, L. (1974) *Growth and Income Distribution: Essays in Economic Theory*, Cambridge, Cambridge University Press.

Pasinetti, L. (1977) *Lectures in the Theory of Production*, New York, Columbia University Press.

Pasinetti, L.L. (1981) *Structural change and economic growth: a theoretical essay on the dynamics of the Wealth of Nations*, Cambridge: Cambridge University Press.

Penrose, E. (1955) 'Research on the business firm: limits to the growth and size of firms', *American Economic Review*, 45, 531–543.

Penrose, E. (1959) *The Theory of the Growth of the Firm*, London, Macmillan.

Petersen, K. (1983) *Ergodic Theory*, Cambridge, Cambridge University Press.

Phillips, R.J. (1985–6) 'Marx, the classical firm, and economic planning', *Journal of Post Keynesian Economics*, 8(2), 266–276.

Pitelis, C. (1991) *Market and Non-Market Hierarchies*, Oxford, Basil Blackwell.

Pitelis, C. and Sugden, R. (1986) 'The separation of ownership and control in the theory of the firm: a reappraisal', *International Journal of Industrial Organisation*, 4, 69–86.

Plsek, P.E. and Greenhalgh, T. (2001) 'The challenge of complexity in health care', *British Medical Journal*, 323, 625–628.

Plumptre, A.F.W. (1983) 'Keynes in Cambridge', *Canadian Journal of Economics*, August 1947, pp. 366–371. Reprinted in J.C. Wood (ed.) *John Maynard Keynes: Critical Assessments*, Vol. I, London, Croom Helm.

Pollin, R. (1991), 'Two theories of money supply endogeniety: some empirical evidence', *Journal of Post Keynesian Economics*, 13(3), 366–396.

Potts, J. (2000) *The New Evolutionary Microeconomics: Complexity, Competence and Adaptive Behaviour*, Cheltenham, Edward Elgar.

Pratten, S. (1996a) 'The "closure" assumption as a first step: neo-Ricardian economics and post-Keynesianism', *Review of Social Economy*, 54, 423–443. Reprinted in S. Fleetwood (ed.) *Critical Realism in Economics: Development and Debate*, London, Routledge, 1999.

Pratten, S. (1996b) 'Coherence in Post Keynesian economics', in P. Arestis, G. Palma, and M. Sawyer, (eds) *Capital Controversy, Post Keynesian Economics and the History of Economic Theory: Essays in Honour of Geoff Harcourt (Vol. 1)*, London, Routledge.

Pratten, S. (1997) 'The nature of transaction cost economics', *Journal of Economic Issues*, September, 781–803.

Pressman, S. and Summerfield, G. (2002) 'Sen and capabilities', *Review of Political Economy*, 14(4), 429–434.

Propper, C. and Dasgupta, P. (2000) 'Editorial introduction: the state of academic economics in the UK', *Economic Journal*, 110, 291.

Prychitko, D.L. (1993) 'After Davidson, who needs the Austrians: reply to Davidson', *Critical Review*, 7(2–3), 371–380.

Radner, R. (1968) 'Competitive equilibrium under uncertainty', *Econometrica*, 36(1), 31–58.

Radner, R. (1970) 'New ideas in pure theory: problems in the theory of markets under uncertainty', *American Economic Review*, 50, 454–460.

Rassuli, A. and Rassuli, K.M. (1988) 'The realism of Post Keynesian economics; a marketing perspective', *Journal of Post Keynesian Economics*, 10, 455–473.

Reinhardt, U.E. (2004) 'An information infrastructure for the pharmaceutical market', *Health Affairs*, 23(1), 107–112.

Reynolds, P. (1987) *Political Economy: A Synthesis of Kaleckian and Post Keynesian Economics*, London, Harvester Wheatsheaf.

Reynolds, P. (1990) 'Kaleckian and Post Keynesian theories of pricing: some extensions and implications', in P. Arestis and Y. Kitromilides (eds) *Theory and Policy in Political Economy: Essays in Pricing Distribution and Growth*, Cheltenham, Edward Elgar.

Rice, T. (2002) *The Economics of Health Reconsidered*, 2nd edition. AcademyHealth: Health Administration Press.

Richardson, G.B. (1959) 'Equilibrium, expectations and information', *Economic Journal*, 69, 223–227.

Richardson, G.B. (1960) *Information and Investment*, Oxford, Oxford University Press.

Robinson, J.V. (1942) *An Essay on Marxian Economics*, London, Macmillan.

Robinson, J.V. (1956) *The Accumulation of Capital*, 1st edition, London, Macmillan.

Robinson, J.V. (1962a) *Economic Philosophy*, Harmondsworth, Penguin.

Robinson, J.V. (1962b) *Essays in the Theory of Economic Growth*, London, Macmillan.

Robinson, J.V. (1972) 'The second crisis of economic theory', *American Economic Review*, Papers and Proceedings, May.

Robinson, J.V. (1977) 'What are the questions?', *Journal of Economic Literature*, 15(4), 1318–1339.

Robinson, J.V. (1978) 'History versus equilibrium', in Robinson, J.V. (ed.) *Contributions to Modern Economics*, Oxford, Blackwell.

Robinson, J.V. (1980) 'Time in economic theory', *Kylos*, 33, 219–229.

Robinson, J.V. (1985) 'Spring cleaning', published as 'The theory of normal prices and reconstruction of economic theory', in Feiwel, G. (ed.) *Issues in Contemporary Macroeconomics and Distribution*, London, Macmillan.

Robinson, J.V. and Eatwell, J. (1973) *An Introduction to Modern Economics*, London, McGraw Hill.

Roncaglia, A. (1995) 'On the compatibility between Keynes's and Sraffa's viewpoints on output levels', in G. Harcourt, A. Roncaglia and R. Rowley (eds) *Income and Employment in Theory and Practice*, New York, St Martin's Press.

Rosen, S. (1997) 'Austrian and neoclassical economics: any gains from trade?', *Journal of Economic Perspectives*, 11(4), 139–152.

Rosenberg, N. (1982) *Inside the Black Box: Technology, Economics and History*, Cambridge, Cambridge University Press.

Rosenberg, N. (1994) *Exploring the Black Box: Technology and Economics*, Cambridge, Cambridge University Press.

Rosser, J.B., Jr (1998) 'Complex dynamics in New Keynesian and Post Keynesian models', in Roy J. Rotheim (ed.) *New Keynesian Economics/Post Keynesian Alternatives*, London, Routledge, pp. 288–302.

Rosser, J.B., Jr (1999) 'On the complexities of complex economic dynamics', *Journal of Economic Perspectives*, 13(3), 169–192.

Rosser, J.B., Jr (2000) *From Castastrophe to Chaos: A General Theory of Economic Discontinuities, Vol. I: Mathematics, Microeconomics, Macroeconomics, and Finance*, 2nd edition, Boston/Dordrecht/London, Kluwer.

Rosser, J.B., Jr (2001) 'Alternative Keynesian and Post Keynesian perspectives on uncertainty and expectations', *Journal of Post Keynesian Economics*, 23(4), 545–566.

Rothbard, M.N. (1988) 'Timberlake on the Austrian theory of money: a comment', *Review of Austrian Economics*, 2, 179–187.

Rotheim, R. (1998) (ed.) *New Keynesian Economics/Post Keynesian Alternatives*, London, Routledge.

Rotheim, R. (1999) 'Post Keynesian economics and realist philosophy', *Journal of Post Keynesian Economics*, 22(1), 71–103.

Rothschild, K.W. (1947) 'Price theory and oligopoly', *Economic Journal*. Reprinted in G.J. Stigler and K.E. Boulding (eds) *Readings in Price Theory: Selected by a Committee of the American Economic Association*, London, Allen and Unwin, 1953.

Rowthorn, R. (2000) 'Kalecki Centenary Lecture: The political economy of full employment in modern Britain', *Oxford Bulletin of Economics and Statistics*, 62(2), 139–173.

Rumelt, R.P., Schendel, D. and Teece, D.J. (1991) 'Strategic management and economics', *Strategic Management Journal*, 12(special issue, Winter), 5–29.

Runde, J. (1990) 'Keynesian uncertainty and the weight of arguments', *Economics and Philosophy*, 6, 275–292.

Runde, J. (1993) 'Paul Davidson and the Austrians: reply to Davidson'. *Critical Review*, 7(2–3), 381–397.

Runde, J. (1994) 'Keynes after Ramsey: in defence of *A Treatise on Probability*', *Studies in History and Philosophy of Science*, 25, 97–121.

Runde, J. (1997a) 'Abstraction, idealisation and economic theory', in P. Arestis, G. Palma, and M.C. Sawyer, (eds) *Markets, Unemployment and Economic Theory: Essays in Honour of Geoff Harcourt (Volume 2)*, London, Routledge.

Runde, J. (1997b) 'Keynesian methodology', in G.C. Harcourt, and P. Riach, (eds) *General Theory, 2nd edition*, London, Routledge, pp. 222–243.

Runde, J. (1998) 'Assessing causal economic explanations', *Oxford Economic Papers*, 50, 151–172.

Rutherford, M. (1989) 'What is wrong with the new institutional economics (and what is still wrong with the old)?', *Review of Political Economy*, 1(3), 299–318.

Salerno, J.T. (1989) 'Comment on Tullock's 'Why Austrians are wrong about depressions', *Review of Austrian Economics*, 3, 141–145.

Samuels, W.J. (1989) 'Some fundamentals of the economic role of government', *Journal of Economic Issues*, June, 427–433.

Samuels, W.J. (1995) 'The present state of institutional economics', *Cambridge Journal of Economics*, 19, 569–590.

Samuels, W.J. and Lee, F.S. (1994) *A Monetary Theory of Employment by Gardiner C. Means*, New York, M.E. Sharpe.

Samuelson, P.A. (1969) 'Classical and neo-classical monetary theory', in R. Clower (ed.) *Monetary Theory*, Harmondsworth, Penguin.

Sardoni, C. (1987) *Marx and Keynes on Economic Recessions: The Theory of Unemployment and Effective Demand*, Brighton, Harvester-Wheatsheaf.

Sargent, T.J. (1993) *Bounded Rationality in Macroeconomics*, Oxford, Clarendon Press.

Sawyer, M.C. (1982) *Macroeconomics in Question: The Keynesian–Monetarist Orthodoxies and the Kaleckian Alternative*, Sussex, Wheatsheaf.

Sawyer, M.C. (1985a) *The Economics of Industries and Firms*, 2nd edition, London, Croom Helm.

Sawyer, M.C. (1985b) *The Economics of Michal Kalecki*, London, Macmillan.

Sawyer, M.C. (1988a) (ed.) *Post Keynesian Economics*, Aldershot, Edward Elgar.

Sawyer, M.C. (1988b) 'Comment', in J.A. Kregel, E. Matzner and A. Roncaglia (eds), *Barriers to Full Employment*, London, Macmillan.

Sawyer, M.C. (1989) *The Challenge of Radical Political Economy*, London, Harvester Wheatsheaf.

Sawyer, M.C. (1990) 'On the Post Keynesian tradition and industrial economics', *Review of Political Economy*, 2(1), 43–68. Reprinted in M.C. Sawyer, *Unemployment, Imperfect Competition and Macroeconomics: Essays in the Post-Keynesian Tradition*, Aldershot, Edward Elgar.

Sawyer, M.C. (1991) 'Post-Keynesian economics: the state of the art' in Willem Adriaansen and Joep van der Linden (eds) *Post-Keynesian Thought in Perspective*, Wolters-Noordhoff. Reprinted in M.C. Sawyer, *Unemployment, Imperfect Competition and Macroeconomics: Essays in the Post-Keynesian Tradition*, Aldershot, Edward Elgar.

Sawyer, M.C. (1992a) 'Keynes's macroeconomic analysis and imperfect competition', in W.J. Gerrard and J.V. Hillard (eds) *The Philosophy and Economics of J.M. Keynes*, Aldershot, Edward Elgar.

Sawyer, M.C. (1992b) 'On imperfect competition and macroeconomic analysis', in A. del Monte, (ed.) *Recent Advances in the Theory of Industrial Organization*, London, Macmillan. Reprinted in M.C. Sawyer, *Unemployment, Imperfect Competition and Macroeconomics: Essays in the Post-Keynesian Tradition*, Aldershot, Edward Elgar.

Sawyer, M.C. (1992c) 'On the origins of Post-Keynesian pricing theory and macroeconomics', in P. Arestis and V. Chick (eds) *Recent Developments in Post-Keynesian Economics*, Aldershot, Edward Elgar.

Sawyer, M.C. (1992d) 'Questions for Kaleckians: a response', *Review of Political Economy*, 4(2), 152–162.

Sawyer, M.C. (1993) 'The nature and role of the market', in C. Pitelis (ed.) *Transaction Costs, Markets and Hierarchies*, Oxford, Basil Blackwell.

Sawyer, M.C. (1994) 'Post-Keynesian and Marxian notions of competition, towards a synthesis', in M. Glick (ed.) *Competition, Technology and Money: Classical and Post-Keynesian Perspectives*, Aldershot, Edward Elgar.

Sawyer, M.C. (1995) *Unemployment, Imperfect Competition and Macroeconomics: Essays in the Post Keynesian Tradition*, Aldershot, Edward Elgar.

Sawyer, M.C. (1996) 'Money, finance and interest rates: some Post Keynesian reflections', in P. Arestis (ed.) *Keynes, Money and the Open Economy: Essays in Honour of Paul Davidson, Volume 1*, Aldershot, Edward Elgar.

Sawyer, M.C. (2000) (ed.) *The Intellectual Legacy of Michal Kalecki*, Aldershot, Edward Elgar.

Schefold, B. (1980) 'The general theory for a totalitarian state? A note on Keynes's preface to the German edition of 1936', *Cambridge Journal of Economics*, 4(2), 175–176.

Schlesinger, A. Jr (1984) 'The political Galbraith', *Journal of Post Keynesian Economics*, 7(1), 7–17.

Schumpeter, J.A. (1936) 'Review of *The General Theory of Employment, Interest and Money* by John Maynard Keynes', in *Journal of the American Statistical Association*, 31(196), 791–795.

Schumpeter, J.A. (1943) *Capitalism, Socialism and Democracy*, London, Allen and Unwin.

Schumpeter, J.A. (1954) *A History of Economic Analysis*, London, Routledge.

Selgin, G.A. (1988) 'Praxeology and understanding: an analysis of the controversy in Austrian economics', *Review of Austrian Economics*, 2, 19–56.

Sen, A. (2002) 'Why health equity?' *Health Economics*, 11(8), 659–666.

Sent, E.-M. (1997) 'Sargent versus Simon: bounded rationality unbound', *Cambridge Journal of Economics*, 21(3), 323–338.

Shackle, G.L.S. (1955) *Uncertainty in Economics: and Other Reflections*, Cambridge, Cambridge University Press.

Shackle, G.L.S. (1959) 'Review of H.A. Simon's *Models of Man*', *Economic Journal*, 69(September), 547–549.

Shackle, G.L.S. (1967) *The Years of High Theory: Invention and Tradition in Economic Thought 1926–1939*, Cambridge, Cambridge University Press.

Shackle, G.L.S. (1972) *Epistemics and Economics*, Cambridge, CUP.

Shackle, G.L.S. (1979a) 'On Hick's causality in economics: a review article', *Greek Economic Review*, 1(2), 43–55.

Shackle, G.L.S. (1979b) *Imagination and the Nature of Choice*, Edinburgh, Edinburgh University Press.

Shackle, G.L.S. (1980) 'Imagination, Unknowledge and Choice', *Greek Economic Review*, 2, 95–110.

Shackle, G.L.S. (1983–4) 'The romantic mountain and the classic lake: Alan Coddington's Keynesian economics', *Journal of Post Keynesian Economics*, 6(2), 241–251.

Shamasunder, B. and Bero, L. (2002) 'Financial ties and conflicts of interest between pharmaceutical and tobacco companies' *JAMA*, 288, 738–744.

Shapiro, N. (1983) 'An economic theory of business strategy: a review article', *Journal of Post Keynesian Economics*, 5(3), 483–488.

Shapiro, N. (1988) 'The firm and its profits', *Jerome Levy Working Paper*, No. 2, March.

Shapiro, N. (1991) 'Firms, markets and innovation', *Journal of Post Keynesian Economics*, 14, 49–60.

Shapiro, N. (1994) 'Ownership and management', in P. Davidson and J.A. Kregel (eds) *Employment, Growth and Finance: Economic Reality and Economic Growth*, Cheltenham, Edward Elgar.

Shapiro, N. (1995) 'Markets and mark-ups: Keynesian views', in S.C. Dow and J. Hillard (eds) *Keynes, Knowledge and Uncertainty*, Cheltenham, Edward Elgar.

Shapiro, N. (1997) 'Imperfect competition and Keynes', in G.C. Harcourt and P. Riach (eds) *General Theory* 2nd edition, London, Routledge, pp. 83–92.

Shapiro, N. and Mott, T. (1995) 'Firm determined prices: the Post Keynesian conception', in P. Wells (ed.) *Post Keynesian Economic Theory*, London, Kluwer.

Siakantaris, N. (2000) 'Experimental economics under the microscope', *Cambridge Journal of Economics*, 24, 267–281.

Silk, L. (1989) 'Yes, Virginia, Institutionalists do exist', *Journal of Post Keynesian Economics*, 12(1), 3–9.

Simon, H.A. (1957) *Models of Man: Social and Rational*, New York, Wiley.

Simon, H.A. (1959) 'Theories of decision-making in economics', *American Economic Review*, 49, 253–283. Reprinted in P.E. Earl (ed.) *Behavioural Economics: Volume 1*, Aldershot, Edward Elgar, 1988.
Simon, H.A. (1961) *Administrative Behaviour*, 2nd edition, New York, The Free Press.
Simon, H.A. (1972) 'Theories of bounded rationality', in C.B. McGuire and R. Radner (eds) *Decision and Organisation*, London, North-Holland.
Simon, H.A. (1976) 'From substantive to procedural rationality', in S. Latis (ed.) *Method and Appraisal in Economics*, Cambridge, Cambridge University Press.
Simon, H.A. (1979) 'Rational decision making in business organisation', *American Economic Review*, 69(September), 493–513.
Simon, H.A. (1987a) 'Behavioural economics', in J. Eatwell, M. Milgate and P. Newman, (eds) *The New Palgrave*, London, Macmillan.
Simon, H.A. (1987b) 'Bounded rationality', in J. Eatwell, M. Milgate and P. Newman, (eds) *The New Palgrave*, London, Macmillan.
Simon, H.A. (1991) 'Organisations and markets', *Journal of Economic Perspectives*, 5(2), 25–44.
Skidelsky, R. (1992) *John Maynard Keynes: Volume II, The Economist as Saviour, 1920–1937*, London, Macmillan.
Skidelsky, R. (2000) *John Maynard Keynes, Volume III: Fighting for Britain, 1937–1946*, London, Macmillan.
Sraffa, P. (1960) *Production of Commodities by means of Commodities: Prelude to a Critique of Economic Theory*, Cambridge, Cambridge University Press.
Steedman, I. (1977) *Marx after Sraffa*, London, New Left Books.
Steedman, I. (1992) 'Questions for Kaleckians', *Review of Political Economy*, 4(2), 125–151.
Steedman, I. (1999) '*Production of Commodities by Means of Commodities* and the open economy', *Metroeconomica*, 50(3), 260–277.
Steedman, I. and Metcalfe, J.S. (1981) 'On duality and basic commodities in an open economy', *Australian Economic Papers*, 20, 133–141.
Steindl, J. (1954) *Maturity and Stagnation in American Capitalism*, Oxford, Basil Blackwell.
Steindl, J. (1993) 'Steedman versus Kalecki', *Review of Political Economy*, 5(1), 119–123.
Stigler, G.J. (1961) 'The economics of information', *Journal of Political Economy*. 69, 213–225.
Strauss, J. and Thomas, D. (1998) 'Health, nutrition and economic development', *Journal of Economic Literature*, 36, 766–817.
Sugden, R. (1983) 'Why transnational corporations?', University of Warwick Economics Research Paper No. 22.
Sweezy, P. (1939) 'Conditions of Demand under oligopoly', *Journal of Political Economy*, 47, 568–573.
Tarshis, L. (1939) 'Changes in real and money wages', *Economic Journal*, 49, 150–154.
Tarshis, L. (1980) 'Post Keynesian economics: a promise that bounced?', *American Economic Review*, 70(2), 10–14.
The Economist (1998) 'Economists: doctored', 9–15 May, p. 35.
Thompson, G., Levacic, F. and Mitchell, J. (1991) (eds) *Markets, Hierarchies, and Networks: the Co-ordination of Social Life*, London, Sage.
Timberlake, R.H., Jr (1987) 'A critique of Monetarist and Austrian doctrines on the utility and value of money', *Review of Austrian Economics*, 1, 81–96.
Timberlake, R.H., Jr (1988) 'Reply to Comment by Murray N. Rothbard', *Review of Austrian Economics*, 2, 189–197.

Tirole, J. (1988) *The Theory of Industrial Organisation*, Cambridge, MA, MIT Press.

Tool, M. (1988a) (ed.) *Evolutionary Economics, Volume I: Foundations of Institutionalist Thought*, New York, M.E. Sharpe.

Tool, M. (1988b) (ed.) *Evolutionary Economics, Volume II: Institutionalist Theory and Policy*, New York, M.E. Sharpe.

Toporowski, J. (1996) 'Kalecki, Marx and the economics of socialism', in J.E. King (eds) *An Alternative Macroeconomic Theory: The Kaleckian Model and Post Keynesian Economics*, Boston, Kluwer, pp. 189–186.

Torr, C. (1993) 'What can Austrian economists learn from post Keynesians?: reply to Davidson', *Critical Review*, 7(2–3), 399–406.

Trigg, A.B. (1994) 'On the relationship between Kalecki and the Kaleckians', *Journal of Post Keynesian Economics*, 17(1), 91–109.

Tufts Center for the Study of Drug Development (2002) *Impact Report: Analysis and Insight into Critical Drug Development Issues*, 4(5), September/October.

Tullock, G. (1988) 'Why the Austrians are wrong about depressions', *Review of Austrian Economics*, 2, 73–78.

Tullock, G. (1989) 'Reply to Comment by Joseph T. Salerno', *Review of Austrian Economics*, 3, 147–149.

Vaughn, K. (1994) *Austrian Economics in America: the Migration of a Tradition*, Cambridge, Cambridge University Press.

Veblen, Thorstein B. (1898) 'Why is economics not an evolutionary science?', *Quarterly Journal of Economics*, 12(3), 373–397.

Veblen, T. (1899) *The theory of the Leisure Class*, London, Unwin Books, reprinted 1970.

Vihanto, M. (1999) 'Austrian school of economics', in P.A. O'Hara (ed.) *Encyclopaedia of Political Economy, Volume 1*, London, Routledge, pp. 23–27.

Walters, B. and Young, D. (1997) 'On the coherence of Post-Keynesian economics', *Scottish Journal of Political Economy*, 44(3), 329–349.

Walters, B. and Young, D. (1999a) 'Post-Keynesianism and coherence: a reply to Arestis, Dunn and Sawyer', *Scottish Journal of Political Economy*, 46(3), 346–348.

Walters, B. and Young, D. (1999b) 'Is critical realism the appropriate basis for Post-Keynesianism?', *Journal of Post Keynesian Economics*, 22(1), 105–123.

Weber, M. (1930) *The Protestant Ethic and the Spirit of Capitalism* (1st edition 1904–5), London, Allen and Unwin.

Weitzman, M.L. (1982) 'Increasing returns and the foundation of unemployment theory', *Economic Journal*, 92(December), 781–809.

WHO (2001) *Macroeconomics and Health: Investing in Health for Economic Development* (Jeff Sachs, principal author), Report of the Commission on Macroeconomics and Health, December, World Health Organization.

Williams, A. (1987) 'Health economics: the cheerful face of the dismal science?', in A. Williams (ed.), *Health and Economics*, Houndmills, Macmillan.

Williamson, O.E. (1975) *Markets and Hierarchies: Analysis and Anti-Trust Implications: A Study in the Economics of Internal Organisation*, New York, Free Press.

Williamson, O.E. (1979) 'Transaction-cost economics: the governance of contractual relations', *Journal of Law and Economics*, 22, 233–261.

Williamson, O.E. (1981) 'The modern corporation: origins, evolution, attributes', *Journal of Economic Literature*, 19, 1537–1568.

Williamson, O.E. (1983) 'The economics of governance: framework and implications', Yale University Discussion Paper No. 153, July.

Williamson, O.E. (1985) *The Economic Institutions of Capitalism: Firms, Markets, Relational Contracting*, London, Macmillan.

Williamson, O.E. (1987) *Antitrust Economics*, Oxford, Basil Blackwell.

Williamson, O.E. (1996) *The Mechanisms of Governance*, Oxford, Oxford University Press.

Winslow, E.G. (1986a) '"Human Logic" and Keynes's economics', *Eastern Economic Journal*, 12, 413–430.

Winslow, E.G. (1986b) 'Keynes and Freud: psychoanalysis and Keynes's account of the "Animal Spirits" of capitalism', *Social Research*, 53, 549–578.

Winslow, E.G. (1989) 'Organic interdependence, uncertainty and economic analysis', *Economic Journal*, 99, 1173–1182.

Winslow, E.G. (1990) 'Bloomsbury, Freud, and the vulgar passions', *Social Research*, 57, 785–819.

Winslow, E.G. (1992) 'Psychoanalysis and Keynes's account of the psychology of the trade cycle', in W.J. Gerrard, and J.V. Hillard, (eds) *The Philosophy and Economics of J.M. Keynes*, Cheltenham, Edward Elgar.

Winslow, E.G. (1993) 'Keynes on rationality', in W.J. Gerrard (ed.) *The Economics of Rationality*, London, Routledge.

Witt, U. (1999) 'Do entrepreneurs need firms? A contribution to a missing chapter in Austrian economics', *Review of Austrian Economics*, 11, 99–109.

Wray, L.R. (1998) *Understanding Modern Money: the Key to Full Employment and Price Stability*, Cheltenham, Edward Elgar.

Wynarczyk, P. (1992) 'Comparing alleged incommensurables: institutional and Austrian economics as rivals and possible complements?', *Review of Political Economy*, 4(1), 18–36.

Wynarczyk, P. (1999) 'On Austrian – Post Keynesian overlap: just how far is New York from Knoxville, Tennessee?', *Economic Issues*, 4(2), 31–48.

Yeager, L. (1987) 'Why subjectivism?', *Review of Austrian Economics*, 1, 5–31.

Yeager, L. (1988) 'Reply to Comment by Walter Block', *Review of Austrian Economics*, 2, 209–210.

Yeager, L. (1997) 'Austrian economics, Neoclassicism, and the market test', *Journal of Economic Perspectives*, 11(4), 153–165.

Yu, T.F. (1999) 'Toward a praxeological theory of the firm', *Review of Austrian Economics*, 11, 77–97.

Index

Figures are given in italics, n denotes notes.

For Product Safety Concerns and Information please contact our EU representative GPSR@taylorandfrancis.com Taylor & Francis Verlag GmbH, Kaufingerstraße 24, 80331 München, Germany

T - #0103 - 160425 - C0 - 234/156/14 - PB - 9780415588799 - Gloss Lamination